MAN
and the
Environment

This book is printed on paper containing a substantial amount of recycled fiber. The paper has been supplied by the Wausau Paper Company of Wausau, Wisconsin.

In addition to making considerable use of recycled fiber, Wausau is one of the first major paper mills to develop the high temperature recovery process of paper making chemicals. Their recovery process has contributed greatly to pollution abatement of the Wisconsin river—a problem of grave concern to environmentalists.

MAN
and the
Environment

Wes Jackson

California State University,
Sacramento

Foreword by Paul Ehrlich

Second Edition

WM. C. BROWN COMPANY PUBLISHERS
Dubuque, Iowa

BIOLOGY SERIES

Consulting Editor
E. Peter Volpe
Tulane University

Copyright © 1971, 1973 by Wm. C. Brown Company Publishers

Library of Congress Catalog Card Number: 72-86732

ISBN 0—697—04698—2

Second Printing, 1974

Printed in the United States of America

Credits

1. Reprinted with permission of The Macmillan Co. from *Collected Poems* by William Butler Yeats. Copyright 1934 by The Macmillan Co., renewed by 1962 by Bertha Georgia Yeats.
2. Copyright 1966 by George Gaylord Simpson. Reprinted from his volume, *Biology and Man,* by permission of Harcourt, Brace Jovanovich, Inc.
3. "Primitive Man's Relationship to Nature" by Daniel A. Guthrie. *BioScience* 21:721-723. 1 July 1971. Copyright 1971 by the American Institute of Biological Sciences.
4. Bible, Genesis 1:26. From the advertisement "Now Is the Time for All Good Men to Come to the Aid of Their Planet" by Leo Burnett Co., Inc. Copyright 1969 by Leo Burnett Co., Inc.
5. "The Historical Roots of Our Ecological Crisis" by Lynn White, Jr. *Science* 155:1203-1207. 10 March 1967. Copyright 1967 by the American Association for the Advancement of Science.
6. From "The Attitude Lag," an editorial by Eugene P. Odum. *BioScience* 19:403. May 1969. Copyright 1969 by the American Institute of Biological Sciences.
7. "Man and the Air" by LaMont C. Cole. *Population Bulletin* 24:103-113. December 1968. Copyright 1968 by the Population Reference Bureau, Inc.
8. From "Evolution of the Earth's Atmosphere" by S. I. Rasool. *Science* 157:1466-1467. 22 September 1967. Copyright 1967 by the American Association for the Advancement of Science.
9. From "The Atmospheres of Mars and Venus" by Von R. Eshleman. Copyright 1969 by Scientific American, Inc. All rights reserved.
10. "Perhaps Pollution Ruined Venus" by Jeffrey D. Alderman, Associated Press Writer. Copyright by the Associated Press.
11. From "Winds, Pollution, and the Wilderness" by Lester Machta. *The Living Wilderness* 33:3-8. Summer 1969. Copyright 1969 by The Wilderness Society.
12. From "Automobile Engines: Pollution and Power" by Israel Katz. *Science* 162:1221-1222. 13 December 1968. Copyright 1968 by the American Association for the Advancement of Science.
13. "The Car: An Electric Challenge," *Time* 94:55. 14 November 1969. Copyright 1969 by Time, Inc.
14. From "Steam Automobiles: Advocates Seek Government Support for Research" by Andrew Jamison. *Science* 161:27-29. 5 July 1968. Copyright 1968 by the American Association for the Advancement of Science.
15. From "Methanol: A New Fuel?" by Ronald G. Minet. *Science* 157:1373-1374. 22 September 1967. Copyright 1967 by the American Association for the Advancement of Science.
16. From "Diminishing the Role of Sulfur Oxides in Air Pollution," an editorial by Philip H. Abelson. *Science* 157:1265. 15 September 1967. Copyright 1967 by the American Association for the Advancement of Science.
17. Senate Report on the Air Quality Act of 1967.
18. From "Pollution: The Wake of the 'Torrey Canyon' " by John Walsh. *Science* 160:167-169. 12 April 1968. Copyright 1968 by the American Association for the Advancement of Science.
19. "Oil in the Ecosystem" by Robert W. Holcomb. *Science* 166:204-206; 10 October 1969. Copyright 1969 by the American Association for the Advancement of Science.
20. From "Oil Spills—An Old Story" by S. W. A. Gunn, a letter to *Science* 165:967. 5 September 1969. Copyright 1969 by the American Association for the Advancement of Science.
21. "Questions About the Alaskan Pipeline" by George Marshall. Taken from *Alaska Wilderness* by Robert Marshall. Pp. xviii-xix. University of California Press, 1970.
22. "Thermal Pollution" by LaMont C. Cole. *BioScience* 19:989-992. November 1969. Copyright 1969 by the American Institute of Biological Sciences.
23. From "Thermal Addition: One Step from Thermal Pollution" by Sharon Friedman. *BioScience* 19:60-61. January 1969. Copyright 1969 by the American Institute of Biological Science.
24. Executive Order 11288, Section 7.
25. "The Effects of Pesticides" by William A. Niering. *BioScience* 18:869-875. September 1968. Copyright 1968 by the American Institute of Biological Sciences.
26. "Monitoring Pesticide Pollution" by Philip A. Butler. *BioScience* 19:889-891. October 1969. Copyright 1969 by the American Institute of Biological Sciences.
27. From a letter by Robert Van den Bosch in *Science* 164:497. 2 May 1969. Copyright 1969 by the American Association for the Advancement of Science.
28. "Mercury in Man" by Neville Grant. *Environmental* 13 (May) 1971. Published by the Committee for Environmental Information. Reprinted with permission.
29. From a letter by David E. Elrick in *Science* 154:1275. 6 December 1966. Copyright 1966 by the American Association for the Advancement of Science.
30. A letter by Edward S. Deevey, Jr. in *Science* 154:68. 7 October 1966. Copyright 1966 by the American Association for the Advancement of Science.
31. Reprinted by permission from *The Christian Science Monitor.* Copyright 1969 by The Christian Science Publishing Society. All rights reserved.
32. "Shock at Sea." *Time* 94:40. 15 August 1969. Copyright 1969 by Time, Inc.
33. From "Radioiodine Fallout Over the Midwest in May" by Lester Machta. *Science* 160:64-66. 5 April 1968. Copyright 1968 by the American Association for the Advancement of Science.
34. From "Nerve Gas: Dugway Accident Linked to Utah Sheep Kill" by Philip M. Boffey. *Science* 162: 1460-1464. 27 December 1968. Copyright 1968 by the American Association for the Advancement of Science.
35. "Academy Changes Army Gas Dump Plan," an editorial by Philip M. Boffey. *Science* 165:45. 4 July 1969. Copyright 1969 by the American Association for the Advancement of Science.
36. "Energy: How Much Can We Use?" by Charles A. Washburn. Written at the request of the editor for incorporation in second edition.
37. From *October the First is too Late* by Fred Hoyle. Pp. 180-183. Copyright © 1966 by Fred Hoyle. Reprinted by permission of Harper & Row, Publishers, Inc.

38. From *Environment, Power & Society* by Howard T. Odum. Copyright 1971 by John Wiley & Sons, Inc.

* From *The Sound of Mountain Water* by Wallace Stegner. Copyright 1969 by Wallace Stegner. Reprinted by permission of Doubleday & Co., Inc.

39. Lee Merriman Talbot from *Wildlands in Our Civilization*, ed. David Brower. Copyright 1964 by the Sierra Club.

40. From "California's Natural Land and Water Reserve System" by Kenneth S. Norris. *BioScience* 18:415-417. May 1968. Copyright 1968 by the American Institute of Biological Sciences.

41. From *Deserts on the March*, by Paul B. Sears. Copyright 1935, 1947 by the University of Oklahoma Press.

42. "A Letter from the Arctic" by Samuel Wright. *The Living Wilderness* 33:5-6. Spring 1969. Copyright 1969 by The Wilderness Society.

43. From "National Parks: Traffic Jams Turn Attention to Roads" by Luther J. Carter. *Science* 161:770-772. 23 August 1968. Copyright 1968 by the American Association for the Advancement of Science.

44. "We Must Earn Again for Ourselves What We Have Inherited: A Lesson in Wilderness Economics" by Garrett Hardin, from *Wilderness: The Edge of Knowledge*. Copyright 1970 by the Sierra Club.

45. From "Animals from the Amazon Basin" a letter by Paul Gregory Heltne. *Science* 157:134. 14 July 1967. Copyright 1967 by the American Association for the Advancement of Science.

46. From "California's Natural Land and Water Reserve System" by Kenneth S. Norris. *BioScience* 18:415-417. May 1968. Copyright 1968 by the American Institute of Biological Sciences.

47. From "Among Wild Whales" by Roger Payne. From *The New York Zoological Society Newsletter* November (1968):1-6.

48. A letter by Edward C. Stone and Richard B. Vasey in *Science* 160:836-837, and a letter by Bestor Robinson in *Science* 160:833-836. 24 May 1968. Copyright 1968 by the American Association for the Advancement of Science.

49. From "Forest Fires: Suppression Policy Has Its Ecological Drawbacks" by Mark Oberle. *Science* 165:568-571. 8 August 1969. Copyright 1969 by the American Association for the Advancement of Science.

50. From a letter by Amédeé A. Peugnet in *Science* 158:205, 13 October 1967. Copyright 1967 by the American Association for the Advancement of Science.

51. "Eco-catastrophe!" by Paul Ehrlich. *Ramparts* 8:24-28. September 1969. Copyright 1969 by Ramparts Magazine, Inc. By permission of the editors.

52. From "The Resolution of Conflicts in Conservation through Adult Education" by Charles A. Dambach. *BioScience* 18:864-868. September 1968. Copyright 1968 by the American Institute of Biological Sciences.

53. From "Action by State Departments of Conservation" by Charles H. W. Foster. *BioScience* 18:418-420. May 1968. Copyright 1968 by the American Institute of Biological Sciences.

54. "International Environmental Problems—A Taxonomy" by Clifford S. Russell and Hans H. Landsberg. *Science* 172:1307-1314. June 25, 1971. Copyright 1971 by The American Association for the Advancement of Science.

55. "The Population Crisis Is Here *Now*" by Walter E. Howard. *BioScience* 19:779-784. September 1969. Copyright 1969 by the American Institute of Biological Sciences.

56. "Nobody Ever Dies of Overpopulation" by Garrett Hardin. *Science,* 171:527. February 12, 1971. Copyright 1971 by The American Association for the Advancement of Science.

57. "The Social Consequences of Population Growth" by Benjamin Viel. *PRB Selection,* No. 30. October 1969. Copyright 1969 by The Population Reference Bureau, Inc.

58. "Living With Overpopulation" by Angus Wright. Written at the request of the editor for incorporation in second edition.

59. "Birth Control and Economic Development" by Stephen Enke. *Science* 164: 798-802. 16 May 1969. Copyright 1969 by the American Association for the Advancement of Science.

60. "Population Policy: Will Current Programs Succeed?" by Kingsley Davis. *Science* 158:730-739. 10 November 1967. Copyright 1967 by the American Association for the Advancement of Science.

61. "Parenthood: Right or Privilege?" by Garrett Hardin. *Science.* 169:427. 31 July 1970. Copyright 1970 by The American Association for the Advancement of Science.

62. "Do Roman Catholic Countries Have the Highest Birth Rates?" *Population Profile,* July 1968. Copyright 1968 by the Population Reference Bureau, Inc.

63. "Population Control, Sterilization, and Ignorance" an editorial by Thomas Eisner, Ari van Tienhoven, and Frank Rosenblatt. *Science* 167:337. 23 January 1970. Copyright 1970 by the American Association for the Advancement of Science.

64. From "From Magic to Science: A History of Contraception," *The Case for Population Control.* Copyright 1971, Medcom, Inc.

65. "Coping with Contraceptive Failure" by Garrett Hardin, *Perspectives in Biology and Medicine,* August 1966. Copyright 1966 by the University of Chicago Press.

66. "The Tragedy of the Commons" by Garrett Hardin. *Science* 162:1243-1248. 13 December 1968. Copyright 1968 by the American Association for the Advancement of Science.

67. "The Tragedy of the Commons Revisited" by Beryl L. Crowe. *Science* 166:1103-1107. 28 November 1969. Copyright 1969 by the American Association for the Advancement of Science.

68. From the *Journals of Lewis and Clark* by Meriwether Lewis. Used with the permission of the American Philosphical Society.

69. From "Food Production in Prehistoric Europe" by H. T. Waterbolk. *Science* 162: 1903-1101. 6 December 1968. Copyright 1968 by the American Association for the Advancement of Science.

70. From "Digging Up Prehistoric America" by Robert Claiborne. *Harper's Magazine* 232:69-74. April 1966. Copyright 1966 by Harper's Magazine, Inc. Permission granted by the Julian Bach, Jr., Literary Agency.

71. "Japan: A Crowded Nation Wants to Boost Its Birthrate" by Philip M. Boffey. *Science* 167:960-962. 13 February 1970. Copyright 1970 by the American Association for the Advancement of Science.

72. Bible, Revelation 6:5, 6.

73. From *Famine—1975!* by William and Paul Paddock. Copyright 1971 by Little, Brown and Co.

74. State of the Union Message, 10 January 1967.

75. By James Bonner from *The Next Ninety Years.* Copyright 1967 by California Institute of Technology.

76. "Agricultural Production in the Developing Countries" by G. F. Sprague. *Science* 157:774-778. 18 August 1967. Copyright 1967 by the American Association for the Advancement of Science.

77. From "Can We Prepare for Famine? A Social Scientist's View" by E. James Archer. *BioScience* 18:685-690. July 1968. Copyright 1968 by the American Institute of Biological Sciences.

78. From "Paying the Piper" by Paul R. Ehrlich. *New Scientist* 36:652-655. 14 December 1967. Copyright 1967 by Cromwell House.

79. From pp. 6-7 in *Ecology and Field Biology* by Robert Leo Smith. Copyright © by Robert Leo Smith. Reprinted by permission of Harper & Row, Publishers, Inc.

80. From a letter by Jean Mayer in *Science* 152:291. 15 April 1966. Copyright by the American Association for the Advancement of Science.

81. From "Malnutrition, Learning, and Behavior," an editorial by Philip H. Abelson. *Science* 164:17. 4 April 1969. Copyright 1969 by the American Association for the Advancement of Science.

82. From a book review of *Famine—1975!* (William and Paul Paddock) by James Bonner in *Science* 157:914-915. 25 August 1967. Copyright 1967 by the American Association for the Advancement of Science.

83. Concurrent Resolution of the Senate, 22 January 1969.

84. "Dry Lands and Desalted Water" by Gale Young. *Science* 167:339-343. 23 January 1970. Copyright 1970 by the American Association for the Advancement of Science.

85. From "Water Importation into Arid Lands" by Jay M. Bagley. *Science* 162:478. 25 October 1968. Copyright 1968 by the American Association for the Advancement of Science.

86. From "The Use of Arid Lands," an editorial by Dael Wolfle in *Science* 164: 1345. 20 July 1969. Copyright 1969 by the American Association for the Advancement of Science.

87. "Dam Building and the Four Criteria" by Wes Jackson.

88. From "Think Big (An Open Letter to the Secretary of the Interior)" by Bruce Stewart. *Harper's Magazine* 231:62-63. August 1965. Copyright 1965 by Harper's Magazine, Inc. Reprinted by permission of the author.

89. "The Myth of Fertility Dooms Development Plans" by Darryl G. Cole. *The National Observer* 7:10. 22 April 1968. Copyright 1968 by Dow Jones and Co., Inc.

90. From "Brazil: A Prodigy of Growth" by William E. Moran, Jr. *Population Bulletin* 25:89-90. September 1969. Copyright 1969 by the Population Reference Bureau, Inc.

91. From "Human Food from Ocean and Land" by K. O. Emery and C. O'D. Iselin. *Science* 157:1279-1281. 15 September 1967. Copyright 1967 by the American Association for the Advancement of Science.

92. By Howard T. Odum from *The World Food Problem*. Vol. III by the President's Science Advisory Committee. U. S. Government Printing Office, 1967.

93. From *Population Environment and People* edited by Noel Hinrichs. Copyright © 1971 by McGraw-Hill, Inc. Used by permission of McGraw-Hill Book Company.

to LAURA, SCOTT and SARA

Contents

Contents

Contents

Contents

Foreword

In the almost two years that have passed since I first wrote a foreword to *Man and the Environment* a lot has transpired. On the bright side, more and more scientists have been rallying to the defense of our planet. Perhaps the most dramatic events have been the publication of *Limits of Growth* by the Meadows group at MIT, and the "Blueprint for Survival" by *The Ecologist* magazine. And, in the United States, the excellent report of the President's Commission on Population Growth and the American Future has demonstrated that a governmental body can come to grips with many of the tough questions inherent in the population-environment crisis.

But there has been a dark side also. An environmental "backlash" has developed as private citizens, politicians, industries, and technologists began to see that the environmental movement threatened both their cherished life-styles and their bank accounts. A vast array of ecological quacks has appeared, foisting simplistic solutions on a public already overloaded with misinformation. Some say that everything can be solved by population control. Others say that almost all our troubles come from post-Second-World-War technological mistakes, and that neither population growth nor increased affluence have been substantial factors. Others claim that the fault lies entirely with the capitalist system. Still others claim that ecology is a Communist plot.

As this backlash grows, so does the mortal threat to our civilization. While a counterproductive debate continues over whether population growth, affluence, or technological error is "more important" in the crisis, nothing is done about limiting any one of these three. They continue to interact multiplicatively to produce an environmental impact which the MIT *Study of Critical Environmental Problems* (SCEP) estimated was increasing at 5% per year. If SCEP is right, the impact is doubling every 14 years. Therefore, when the earth's ecosystems are absorbing only *one-half* of the punishment they can take without collapse, the ultimate eco-catastrophe will be but *14 years in the future.*

One of the great hopes for mankind is that increasing numbers of people will inform themselves about their extreme jeopardy, overwhelm the backlash, and move society quickly onto the road toward survival. The readings in this book should help with that educational process.

Paul R. Ehrlich

Preface

This second edition represents a later stage in the evolution of concern over the old problem of man and his relationship to the environment. In the preface of the first edition, I mentioned that the majority of topics revealed two central but intertwined threads: population-food and environmental destruction. At that time it was not clear to me that resource depletion was likely a greater problem to the people of the planet than pollution. The selection of readings revealed this. Caught up in the swirl of the immediate, the future was nebulous. Consequently, instead of attention only to Human Behavior, The Environment (Pollution) and Population-Food, this edition also includes sections on Resources and The Future.

There are some new introductions, introductions rewritten to make them more inclusive or more timely, and some editorial-type statements over major subjects instead of the usual selected readings. The newly selected readings, of course, represent the most important changes for this edition. They include a selection concerning primitive man and his relationship to nature, a topic beginning to be of importance to more than anthropologists. One reading consists of questions asked by George Marshall (brother of Alaskan explorer, Robert) about the Alaskan pipeline. Most of them remain unanswered, even though the pipeline now seems inevitable. An article on mercury discusses the broad dimensions of that element as a natural and "unnatural" pollutant in the environment. Three readings on energy represent three qualitatively different perspectives. The paper by Washburn acquaints the student with the broad dimensions of the energy picture. The other two selections on energy were chosen because few have considered the consequences of "unlimited" energy or an energy ethic as Hoyle and Odum have. The fate of whales as a consequence of greed is demonstrated by a series of graphs. A classification of international environmental problems should help bring into focus the problems we face in getting international agreement on solutions to environmental problems. Three new readings on population, two by Garrett Hardin present aspects of that problem not at all widely discussed.

Finally, in the Future section is an essay on "The Human Enterprise" by George Wald.

All in all these changes make the edition less dated than the first. This is not to say that the contributions of the people who cooperated on the first edition are now unimportant. The contributions of Martha Bieri, Rachel Stucky and Robert Hill are especially lasting, and for them I am forever grateful.

Charles Washburn and Angus Wright, Environmental Studies faculty at California State University, Sacramento, not only have influenced the choices for this edition, but their articles written at my insistence for inclusion, I think, are outstanding. I am grateful also to Jerry Langham, biologist at CSU, Sacramento for reviewing parts of the book, and to Roberta Cole for her careful reading of the manuscript.

The thoughtful study and comments of my wife, Dana, have once again been most significant.

The problems of the planet seem to worsen by the week. The campaigns to make this the environmental decade seem to be sputtering. If our hope had to rest on men in power to save the planet, we would all despair. But some members of each new class in environmental studies think, "We can do it!" To them I am especially grateful.

HUMAN BEHAVIOR

The major problems facing the planet are the products of human behavior. Contemporary man stands inside a "triangle of crisis," with the world population-food problem moving toward him on one side, the global depletion of his sustaining resources advancing toward him on another side, and pollution driving on the third side. The three sides are so interrelated that movement of any one of them toward the middle decreases the length of the other two sides while the inner area is decreased.

Pressure from these three man-induced forces has suddenly become a dangerous reality. We are now beginning to ask where we as a species went wrong in creating such a crisis for our planet. An examination of man's written history is inadequate because history is only five to six thousand years old. The population was increasing, and erosion of the land was well under way by the time history was first written. In a push further back in time, some 9,000 to 10,000 years ago, we see the advent of agriculture, in the foothills of the Zagros Mountains at first, but soon spreading into widely separated areas. Neolithic hunters, essentially all at once, domesticated the major cereals, legumes, root crops, and animals currently used. Civilizations came later.

An agricultural environment was not responsible for shaping man's endocrine and nervous system, because 100 centuries, or indeed 400 generations, is not long enough for any fundamental change. Man's biological nature, then, including the basis of his behavior, was shaped not in an environment that recorded history on templates, not in an agricultural setting, but in self-maintaining ecosystems which supported him as a hunter.

If the fall of man was the partaking of the forbidden fruit of agriculture, what aspects of man's biological nature promoted his own fall? Selections 2 and 3 will not completely answer this question or others we have about humanity. But Simpson's focus on pre-agricultural times brings us closer to the roots of our problems than does attention to recent events. However, we must be careful not to romanticize the hunter as being wiser than his

1

technological descendent.[1] *Environmental limitations, primarily energy limitations, were responsible for his ecological stability. As reading 3 will show, man's attitudes probably have not changed.*

Once man made a break from his hunting past, from the mature ecosystem of which he was an intimate part, new problems were introduced. Agriculture localized and inflated the energy budget, increased the concentrations of people and altered the instrumentalities for getting food. New systems of ethics likely emerged. Though the highest level of ecological stability is the hunting environment, within an agricultural context, certain practices and eventually ethics are more ecologically sound than others. The controversial paper by Lynn White, Jr., reading 5, addresses itself to a post-hunting ethic, the Judaeo-Christian ethic, or we might say an "inflated energy ethic."

[1] See reading 68 "Indian Method of Hunting Buffalo."

The Four Ages of Man

WILLIAM BUTLER YEATS

He with body waged a fight,
But body won; it walks upright.

Then he struggled with the heart;
Innocence and peace depart.

Then he struggled with the mind;
His proud heart he left behind.

Now his wars on God begin;
At stroke of midnight God shall win.

The Biological Nature of Man

The answer to the ancient question "What is man?"
must be based first on man's biological character.

GEORGE GAYLORD SIMPSON

It has often and confidently been asserted, that man's origin can never be
known: but ignorance more frequently begets confidence than does knowledge:
it is those who know little, and not those who know much, who so positively
assert that this or that problem will never be solved by science. (1)

Those words were written by Charles Darwin nearly 100 years ago and were
published in 1871 in the introduction to his book on *The Descent of Man.* In his
even better known work on *The Origin of Species* (2), which had appeared 12
years earlier, he had been content to say (somewhat coyly) that by that work
"light would be thrown on the origin of man and his history." Others soon
indicated the nature of that light. Thomas Henry Huxley's classic *Man's Place
in Nature (3)* was published in 1863, and by 1871 numerous other naturalists of
the first rank had already accepted the evolutionary origin of the human species.
Darwin's own contribution to the problem of man's origin firmly established two
points: first, *Homo sapiens,* like all other organisms, has evolved from prior,

extremely different species by natural means and under the directive influence of natural selection; and second, man is the descendant of apes or monkeys of the Old World.

Darwin's first point, that man is the product of evolution involving natural selection, has been attacked on emotional grounds, but it was not and is not now honestly questionable on strictly scientific grounds and by anyone really familiar with the facts. The second point, of man's descent from an Old World ape or monkey, was for some time more open to scientific dispute. However, here, too, the debate was often more emotional than objective. In some pedagogic circles it became usual to maintain that man is not descended from an ape but from a common ancestor neither man nor ape nor, if one cared to go still further afield, monkey. Some went so far as to attempt to enlist Darwin posthumously in their own pussyfooting ranks by saying that he never maintained that man arose from an ape but only from a common ancestor . . . and so forth. In fact, although Darwin was slow to enter the dispute, when he did so he was more honest than those supposed defenders. He flatly said, "We must conclude, however much the conclusion may revolt our pride, that our early progenitors would have been properly . . . designated (as apes or monkeys)." The unscientific and really un-called-for remark on pride does little to modify the forthrightness of the conclusion.

Darwin's conclusions in 1871 already covered what is most vital for consideration of man's biological status. Subsequent discovery and study have fully corroborated Darwin and have added an enormous amount of detail. That is interesting and important, and most of what I have to say here concerns it. At this point, however, the essential thing is that Darwin put the whole subject of the nature of man on a new and sound footing. To be sure, in the introduction of *The Descent of Man,* from which I have already quoted, Darwin went on to say that, "The conclusion that man is the codescendant with other species of some ancient, lower, and extinct form, is not in any degree new." He then cited Lamarck, Wallace, Huxley, Lyell, Vogt, Lubbock, Büchner, Rolle, Haeckel, Canestrini, and Barrago as "having taken the same side of the question." In fact, as regards this particular point, Darwin was doing too much honor to those worthies, some still famous and some now forgotten. It is true that they had all discussed the descent of man before Darwin himself did so in an explicit way, but with the sole exception of Lamarck they had done so after publication of *The Origin of Species* and on the basis of that work by Darwin. As for the few who really had postulated an evolutionary origin for man before *The Origin of Species,* their views were largely philosophical speculations inadequately or not at all supported by objective evidence and sometimes, as in the case of Lamarck, reaching a conclusion only approximately correct on grounds that were flatly wrong (4).

What Is Man?

The question "What is man?" is probably the most profound that can be asked by man. It has always been central to any system of philosophy or of theology. We know that it was being asked by the most learned humans 2000 years ago, and it is just possible that it was being asked by the most brilliant australopithecines 2 million years ago. The point I want to make now is that all attempts to answer that question before 1859 are worthless and that we will be better off if we ignore them completely. The reason is that no answer had a solid, objective base until it was recognized that man is the product of evolution from primeval apes and before that through billions of years of gradual but protean change from some spontaneously, that is, naturally, generated primordial monad.

It is the biological nature of man, both in his evolutionary history and in his present condition, that presents us with our only fixed point of departure. These are the facts we can find out for ourselves, in great, ever-increasing detail and soundness, open to all of us in irrefutable observations. Their interpretation is in some respects ambiguous and disputable, but interpretation at a given point becomes increasingly clear and undisputed as time goes on. Doubtfulness moves outward with the expanding frontier of knowledge.

I do not mean to say that the biological study of man or even that the scientific study of man in terms broader than biological can here and now—if ever —provide a satisfactorily complete answer to the question "What is man?" The other, older approaches through metaphysics, theology, art, and other nonbiological, nonscientific fields can still contribute, or can now contribute anew. But unless they accept, by specification or by implication, the nature of man as a biological organism, they are merely fictional fancies or falsities, however interesting they may be in those nonfactual categories. I am here concerned with man's biological nature in a rather broad sense, on the grounds that this is a necessary, even though it is not a completely sufficient, approach to comprehension of man's nature.

Already in Darwin's day it was clearly established that among living animals the great apes are anatomically most similar to man. Some anatomists, reluctant to acknowledge their poor relatives, stressed differences between man and any apes: the larger human brain, obviously; the longer and less divergent first toe of man; the absence or, more commonly, the only-sporadic presence in us of certain apish muscles and other structures. Such discussions completely missed the point. Of course men and apes differ. In itself, that means only that we belong to different species. The point at issue is not whether we differ, but in what way and how closely the different species are related.

All later study has corroborated the special relationship between men and apes and has made knowledge of it more precise. The evidence has lately been greatly increased in extent, in detail, and in its basic character. It now includes such fundamental points as the numbers and shapes of chromosomes, the exact molecular structure of hemoglobins, the resemblances and differences of serum proteins, and many others (5). All the evidence agrees and the conclusion is unequivocal. Man is not identical with apes in these or other respects. However, he is clearly related to the apes, and among the apes he is most particularly related to chimpanzees and gorillas, which are closely related between themselves. A necessary inference from this evidence is that the common ancestor of apes and men was itself a member of the ape family. Not only that; we had a common ancestor with gorilla and chimpanzee after their ancestry had become distinct from that of the other living apes (orangutan and gibbons). Our relationships to gorilla and to chimpanzee are about equal, although gorillas may have become somewhat more specialized with respect to the common ancestry.

Evidence from Fossils

More precise evidence as to relationships and as to the course of anatomical change in the human ancestry must come from fossils. There are special reasons why pertinent fossils are comparatively uncommon: Crucial stages apparently occurred in the tropics, where preservation and discovery of fossils are difficult and where exploration has generally lagged; populations of apes and of pre-humans were always small, not at all comparable with the great herds of grazing animals, for example, common as fossils; and the habits and abilities of apes and pre-humans were such as to reduce chances of natural burial and preservation as fossils.

Nevertheless, a great many fossils have been recovered and discovery is active at present. We are far from having the whole story, but parts of it are increasingly clear.

In Darwin's time only one really distinctive kind of fossil ape *(Dryopithecus)* and only one really distinctive kind of fossil man (Neanderthal) were known. From the former, Darwin correctly inferred that by late Miocene, at least, the lineages of apes and monkeys had separated. He was not clear as to the possible implications for separation of the strictly human lineage, which he thought might have occurred much earlier. As regards Neanderthal man Darwin could only express surprise that in spite of their antiquity the Neanderthals had brain capacities probably greater than the average for modern man.

Now it is known that apes more or less similar to *Dryopithecus* were widespread and, as apes go, numerous through the Miocene and Pliocene of Europe, Asia, and Africa (6). Present estimates place the beginning of the Miocene at approximately 25 million years ago (7). The divergence of apes and Old World monkeys is thus at least that old. There is, in fact, some evidence that this divergence occurred in the Oligocene, which preceded the Miocene and began some 10 million years earlier. Divergence of apes and monkeys was identical with divergence of the human ancestry and monkeys, because the earliest apes were also ancestral to man. The time of the final split of the specifically prehuman lineage from that leading to gorilla and chimpanzee has not yet been closely determined. On present evidence it seems most likely to have occurred during the Miocene, that is, quite roughly between 10 and 25 million years ago. The earliest known forms that may be definitely on a prehuman line as distinct from a pre-gorilla-chimpanzee line are *Ramapithecus* from India and the closely similar, indeed probably identical supposed genus *Kenyapithecus* from Africa (8). Unfortunately those animals are known only from teeth and fragments of jaws, so that their affinities are somewhat uncertain and the anatomy of their skulls and skeletons is entirely unknown. The known specimens are approximately 10 million years old, give or take a few million.

The next significant group of fossils is that of the australopithecines, literally "southern monkeys" although they almost certainly were not exclusively southern and with complete certainty were not monkeys. They are surely and comparatively well known from East and South Africa, doubtfully and, at best, poorly known from elsewhere in Africa and from Eurasia. In Africa they are clearly divisible into two distinct groups. There is dispute as to whether those groups should not be subdivided still further and whether they should be called species or genera. Although the specialists can become enraged over those questions, they have no real importance for others, the important fact being simply that the two separate groups did exist, a point on which even the specialists now agree. Both groups resemble apes much more than we do now, but both are more nearly related to us than to the apes—another point on which the specialists have finally agreed after years of wrangling. They definitely belong to the human family, Hominidae.

One group, typified by *Australopithecus robustus* or, as it is also often called, *Paranthropus robustus,* retained some particularly primitive (more or less ape-like) features and yet became somewhat aberrantly specialized. It cannot have been directly ancestral to modern man. The other group, typified by *Australopithecus africanus,* although also primitive within the human family, more closely resembles our own genus, *Homo.* Both groups are now believed to have appeared at least 2 million years ago. For a long time, perhaps 1-1/2 million years, there were at least two distinct lineages of the human family living in Africa and probably throughout the warmer parts of the Old World. One, more primitive and aberrant, showed little progress and finally became extinct. The other, more progressive, evolved into *Homo.* A matter still under sharp dispute is whether the latter lineage included *Australopithecus africanus* as our direct ancestor, or whether for a time there were not actually three distinct lines: the two kinds of australopithecines and still another more directly related to *Homo.* The latter suggestion arises from Leakey's discovery of what he calls *Homo habilis* (9). However, some authorities believe that supposed species not to be on a distinct lineage but to belong to the line leading from *Australopithecus africanus* eventually to *Homo sapiens.*

That dispute is interesting and we hope it may soon be settled, but it is far less important than the fact that our ancestry passed through a stage closely similar to *Australopithecus africanus* if it was not that group itself. Our ancestors were then fully bipedal, ground-living animals, using their hands for manipulation as we do but perhaps not quite so skillfully. Their teeth were so like ours as to be hard to distinguish, but their brains were little larger than those of apes, and if we could see them alive their physiognomy, while distinctive, would probably strike us as more apelike than manlike.

By a time probably not later than 500,000 years ago and perhaps earlier, gradual evolution from australopithecines had reached a stage that was human in a more restricted sense, belonging not only to the human family, Hominidae, but also to the same genus as ourselves, *Homo.* Doting and ambitious discoverers have given many different names to such early fossil men, including *Pithecanthropus* and *Sinanthropus,* but most of them are now usually placed in a single species, *Homo erectus.* Bodily anatomy and even physiognomy were now almost fully human, but to our eyes there was still a coarse or brutish cast of countenance because of heavy brow ridges over the eyes and a low, small brain case. The brain size was neatly intermediate between australopithecines (or modern apes) and modern man.

Finally, and still gradually, our own species, *Homo sapiens,* emerged. Although not entirely certain, it is now the usual opinion that the quite varied fossils known collectively as Neanderthal men belonged to *Homo sapiens* and only represent ancient races that were at first primitive (not so far removed from *Homo erectus*) and later somewhat aberrant. The more aberrant late Neanderthals became extinct as such, although it is probable that some of their genes survive.

So much for more or less direct knowledge of man's physical, anatomical origin. The main points are these:

1. Man evolved from apes also ancestral to chimpanzees and gorillas, but less specialized than the latter.

2. The divergence of man's ancestry from the apes was early marked by bipedalism and upright posture, with extensive correlations and implications in anatomy, habits, and capabilities.

3. Also early was divergent dental evolution, again with other implications, for example as to diet and means of defense. It is not known whether posture and dentition diverged from the apes simultaneously or in which order.

4. Only after evolution of human posture and dentition was essentially complete did man's brain begin to enlarge beyond that of the apes. (Intelligence depends not only on size of the brain but also on its internal anatomy, and we do not know the internal anatomy of our fossil ancestors' brains. However, it is fairly certain that a species with average brain size as in apes could not be as intellegent as *Homo sapiens.*)

Systematics of Modern Man

Now let us briefly consider the taxonomic, biological systematic nature of mankind as it exists today. First and most important is the fact that mankind *is* a kind, a definite and single species. A biological species is an evolutionary unit composed of continuing populations that regularly interchange genes by interbreeding and that do not or cannot have such regular interchange with other species (10). The definition clearly applies to mankind: all human populations can and, as opportunity occurs, do interbreed, producing fertile offspring and thus continuing the species and keeping it bound together as a unit. It is unlikely that, for example, a Greenland Eskimo has ever interbred with a South African Bushman, but since all intervening populations can and do interbreed they are nevertheless members of the same species. That species, *Homo sapiens,* is not connected with any other species by interbreeding.

Comparison of Eskimo and Bushman brings up the obvious (although occasionally denied) fact that the human species includes quite diverse races. A race is simply a population (or group of populations) that is genetically distinguished from others. The distinction is not absolute. It is unlikely that Negroes, for example, have any genes that do not occur in some white populations, or that whites have any genes absent in all Negro populations. The usual situation is that a race has certain genes and gene combinations that are more frequent in it than elsewhere, and therefore typical in that sense, but not confined to the race. Races always grade into each other without definite boundaries. There is not now and never has been such a thing as a pure race, biologically speaking. Any two human populations, no matter how small or how large, differ in some respects, so that there is no fixed number of races. One could count thousands or two, and no matter how many are counted, there will be some populations and many individuals that do not clearly fit into one or another. Moreover, races are evanescent in the course of evolution. A given race may change, disappear by fusion with others, or die out altogether while the species as a whole simply continues its evolutionary course (11).

Races of man have, or perhaps one should say "had," exactly the same biological significance as the subspecies of other species of mammals. Widespread animals have local populations that live under diverse conditions and that may become temporarily and in part isolated from each other. They may then more or less accidentally have different proportions of genes (in stricter technical language, of alleles) from other such populations, and if the situation continues long enough, they will almost inevitably evolve somewhat different adaptations to local conditions. Primitive men were relatively few in number and relatively immobile, but they spread over enormous areas—the whole land area of the earth except for Antarctica and a few small islands. They evolved into races or, in better biological terms, into subspecies exactly as any other animal would have under those circumstances. Racial differentiation in man was originally geographic and, for the most part, adaptive.

That was the original biological significance of race. One must say that Negroes were biologically superior to whites, if reference is to prehistoric times, when the races were originating, and to African conditions, to which Negroes were biologically adapted and whites were not. At the present time race has virtually no strictly biological significance because of two crucial changes. First, human adaptation to different environments is now mostly cultural and is directly biological only in lesser part, so that the prehistoric biological adaptations have lost much of their importance. Second, tremendous increases in population size, in mobility, and in environmental changes brought about by man himself have the result that extremely few men are now living under the conditions to which their ancestors were racially adapted.

Evolution does not necessarily proceed at the same rate in different populations, so that among many groups of animals it is possible to find some species that have evolved more slowly, hence are now more primitive, as regards some particular trait or even over-all. It is natural to ask—as many have asked—whether among human races there may not similarly be some that are more primitive in one way or another or in general. It is indeed possible to find single characteristics that are probably more advanced or more primitive in one race than in another. For example, the full lips and kinky hair of some Negroes are almost certainly progressive traits in comparison with the more primitive, decidedly apelike thin lips and straight hair of most whites. However, that does not mean that whites in general are more primitive than Negroes or otherwise inferior to them. Overall primitiveness and progressiveness in comparison of different groups of animals is practically confined to cases in which the groups are of different species, so that genes of the more rapidly evolving species cannot be transferred to the lagging species. Human races all belong to the same species and have generally had enough interbreeding so that genetic progress, as distinct from local adaptation, could and evidently did spread through the entire species. Only if some race entirely ceased to interbreed with any other would it be likely for it to fall behind and become definitely inferior. Let us hope that will not happen.

Resemblances, Anatomical and Psychological

Regardless of the diversity of races, it is obvious that all men resemble one another much more than any of them differ from each other. They all share the basic qualities, anatomical, physiological and psychological, that make us human, *Homo sapiens,* and no other species that is or ever was. Something has already been said of anatomical peculiarities of *Homo sapiens* with respect to living apes and human ancestors. Here are some of the most striking human anatomical traits:

Normal posture is upright.

Legs are longer than arms.

Toes are short, the first toe frequently longest and not divergent.

The vertebral column has an *S* curve.

The hands are prehensile, with a large and strongly opposable thumb.

Most of the body is bare or has only short, sparse, inconspicuous hair.

The joint for the neck is in the middle of the base of the skull.

The brain is uniquely large in proportion to the body and has a particularly large and complex cerebrum.

The face is short, almost vertical under the front of the brain.

The jaws are short, with a rounded dental arch.

The canine teeth are usually no larger than the premolars, and there are normally no gaps in front of or behind the canines.

The first lower premolar is like the second, and the structure of the teeth in general is somewhat distinctive.

Given those characteristics, a museum curator could readily identify any specimen of *Homo sapiens* that was added to the collections, or that happened to walk into his office. However, we who are pondering the question "What is man?" must feel that these anatomical features, fully diagnostic as they are, yet do not amount to an answer adequate for our purposes. Even if we were defining, say, a species of mouse, the anatomical definition would not take us far toward understanding "What is mouse?" or, better, "What is mouseness?" unless we related the bodily mouse to the behaving mouse and the thinking mouse. Even thus, human anatomy reflects truly essential man-ness or human nature only to the extent that it is related to human activities and psychology. Already in *The Descent of Man* (1) Darwin discussed such traits in which man appears to be most distinctive. His points, here greatly abbreviated and paraphrased, were as follows:

In proportion with his higher intelligence, man's behavior is more flexible, less reflex or instinctive.

Man shares such complex factors as curiosity, imitation, attention, memory, and imagination with other relatively advanced animals, but has them in higher degree and applies them in more intricate ways.

More, at least, than other animals, man reasons and improves the adaptive nature of his behavior in rational ways.

Man regularly both uses and makes tools in great variety.

Man is self-conscious; he reflects on his past, future, life, death, and so forth.

Man makes mental abstractions and develops a related symbolism; the most essential and complexly developed outcome of these capacities is language.

Some men have a sense of beauty.

Most men have a religious sense, taking that term broadly to include awe, superstition, belief in the animistic, supernatural, or spiritual.

Normal men have a moral sense; in later terms, man ethicizes.

Man is a cultural and social animal and has developed cultures and societies unique in kind and in complexity.

The last point, which some students now consider the most important of all, was least emphasized by Darwin, who was here mainly concerned with the relationship of social evolution to the origin of the moral sense. Darwin's general purpose was not to characterize *Homo sapiens* as the unique species that he is. The purpose was to show that the characteristics that make him unique are nevertheless foreshadowed in other animals, and that the evolution of man from other, earlier, quite distinct species is therefore plausible. We are no longer concerned with *whether* man evolved, because we know that he did. We are still very much concerned with *how* he evolved, with what is most characteristically human about him and how those characteristics arose. The list of traits discussed by Darwin is still valid from this somewhat different point of view.

That list should not be taken as involving so many separate and distinct things. These are aspects of the behavior, capacities, and accomplishments of a species that is characterized by all of them together and not by each or any one separately. They interact and interlock not only with each other but also with the previously mentioned physical or anatomical characteristics of man. For example, complex human societies, especially the modern industrial civilization rapidly spreading to the whole world, require specialization of activities by different members of society further involving manipulation of complex machines. Such specialization, which is nongenetic, requires individual flexibility and could not occur in a mainly instinctive animal. The machines are tools and could only have been devised by a reasoning, toolmaking animal. Invention also required manual deftness, which was provided by (and which also gave selective value to) the structure of the human hand, which required upright posture and could not have been acquired by a quadruped. Further evolution of the early cultural adaptations that led eventually to modern industry also had increased intelligence as a necessary concomitant, and that eventually required larger brains, which in turn involved change in skull structure and in stance—and so on. Even the changing pattern of the teeth can be related to this unitary complex.

The Major Evolutionary Changes

Because all the specifically human traits are integrated within the whole that is human, and because each of the traits as well as their integration must have arisen gradually, it is somewhat questionable to speak of definite milestones or even of particular critical phases in the evolution of man. Yet there are three among these slow and coordinated changes that seem particularly basic for the concept of human-ness. The most crucial single anatomical point is acquisition of upright posture and strictly bipedal locomotion. Most of the other main peculiarities of human anatomy either follow from that or are coadapted with it. The other two major factors are cultural, but are no less biological since both represent attainment and maintenance of biological adaptation by cultural means. They are tool making and language.

Extremely crude but unmistakable stone tools are found in the oldest rock strata containing indisputable members of the human family, nearly, if not quite, 2 million years old. It will be difficult to authenticate still older and more primitive stone tools, because they must have consisted of natural pebbles or rock fragments picked up and used with little or no modification. It has long been maintained that deliberate manufacture of a tool is the distinctive human trait, since many other animals, even including some insects, use natural objects as tools but do not make tools. Now it has been found that chimpanzees may trim and shorten twigs or straws for use as tools (12), and although that simple behavior is almost too primitive to be called tool making, it sufficiently demonstrates that the capacity for tool making is biologically ancient and prehuman. If one wants a more diagnostic statement, it probably is true that man is the only living animal that uses tools to make tools. However, that trait would follow soon and inevitably once tool making really got under way. A stone used to knock flakes off an incipient stone ax is already a machine tool.

Ancient tools more perishable than stone are rarely preserved. Nevertheless, the course of increasing diversity and complication of tools can be followed well enough to demonstrate the gradual and inconstant but generally continual progress through prehistory. The tremendously accelerated progress in historic times is very well documented and is familiar to all of us in general outline, at least. The whole sweep from stone axes to electronic computers is a natural and comprehensible extension of the biological capacities of an unusual species. It is uniquely wonderful, and yet, lest we stand too much in awe of our own products, let us remember that a digital computer is merely a rapid and automated tool for what amounts to counting on fingers.

As posture is focal for consideration of man's anatomical nature and tools are for consideration of his material culture, so is language focal for his mental nature and his non-material culture (13). Language is also the most diagnostic single trait of man: all normal men have language; no other now-living organisms do. That real, incomparably important, and absolute distinction has been blurred by imprecise use of the word "language" not only in popular speech but also by some scientists who should know better, speaking, for example, of the "language of the bees" (14).

In any animal societies, and indeed in still simpler forms of aggregation among animals, there must be some kind of communication in the very broadest sense. One animal must receive some kind of information about another animal. That information may be conveyed by specific signals, which may be of extremely diverse kinds both as to form and as to modality, that is, the sensory mode by which it is received. The odor of an ant, the movements of a bee, the color pattern of a bird, the howl of a wolf, and many thousands of others are all signals that convey information to other animals and that, in these and many other examples, are essential adaptations for behavioral integration in the species involved.

Human language is also a system of interpersonal communication and a behavioral adaptation essential for the human form of socialization. Yet human language is absolutely distinct from any system of communication in other animals. That is made most clear by comparison with other animal utterances, which most nearly resemble human speech and are most often called "speech." Nonhuman vocables are, in effect, interjections. They reflect the individual's physical or, more frequently, emotional state. They do not, as true language does, name, discuss, abstract, or symbolize. They are what the psychologists call affective; such purely affective so-called languages are systems of emotional signals and not discourse. The difference between animal interjection and human language is the difference between saying "Ouch!" and saying "Fire is hot."

That example shows that the nonlanguage of animal interjection is still present in man. In us it is in effect not a part of language, but the negative of language, something we use in place of speech. In part we even use the same signals as do the apes, a fact already explored to some depth by Darwin in another of his basic works, *The Expression of the Emotions in Man and Animals* (15). Much more is now known about such expressions in animals, and particularly in our closer relatives the apes and monkeys, and it is not surprising to find that the non-linguistic, affective system is particularly complicated in them and has not progressed but may even have retrogressed in man. Still we do retain that older system along with our wholly new and wholly distinct system of true language. It is amusing that the human affective interjectional reaction to a bad smell is practically the same as in all other primates, down even to the most primitive.

Attempts To Trace Language

Darwin's study and many later studies sought to trace the evolutionary origin of language from a prehuman source. They have not been successful. As a recent expert in the field (16) has said, "The more that is known about it (that is, communication in monkeys and apes), the less these systems seem to help in the understanding of human language."

Many other attempts have been made to determine the evolutionary origin of language, and all have failed. Because language is so important for any concept of man and because this is an interesting example of methodology and limitations, it is worthwhile to consider some of these futile attempts. One, fairly obvious once the idea of linguistic evolution had arisen, was by comparison of living languages. One result was a supposed genetic sequence: (i) isolating languages, like Chinese, which string together invariable word roots; (ii) agglutinating languages, like Mongolian, which modify roots by tacking on prefixes and suffixes; and (iii) flexional languages, like Latin, which modify by (partly) internal changes in words. The trouble is that these categories are not really distinct and, especially, that they did not historically occur in this sequence. For example, Chinese was probably flexional at one time and is now becoming agglutinating with a possibility of becoming flexional again. English was flexional until quite recently and is now mostly isolating with a strong dash of agglutination. Moreover at the present time no languages are primitive in the sense of being significantly close to the origin of language. Even the peoples with least complex cultures have highly sophisticated languages, with complex grammar and large vocabularies, capable of naming and discussing anything that occurs in the sphere occupied by their speakers. Tales of tribal natives who cannot count beyond 4 and who have vocabularies of only two or three hundred words betray the shortcomings of gullible travelers, not of the natives (17).

Another approach is to follow back directly historical records, which cover several thousand years for some European, Asiatic, and north African languages. It is then possible to project still further and to reconstruct, for example, a proto-Indo-European anterior to Sanskrit. But this still leaves us tens or hundreds of thousands of years—perhaps even more—from the origin of language. The oldest language that can reasonably be reconstructed is already modern, sophisticated, complete from an evolutionary point of view.

Still another attempt, which now seems very naive, is through the ontogeny of language, that is, the acquisition of language by children. This relies on the famous but, as it happens, quite erroneous saying that ontogeny repeats phylogeny. In fact the child is not evolving or inventing primitive language but is learning a particular modern language, already complete and unrecognizably different from any possible primitive language. Moreover, the child is doing this with a modern brain already genetically constructed (through the long, long action of natural selection) for the use of complete, wholly nonprimitive language.

It is a tempting hypothesis that the time, at least, of the origin of language might be determined by structural characteristics in fossils. One rather elaborate attempt departed from the fact that all linguistic phonetic systems, varied as they are, depend in part on the shape of the lower jaw and the hard palate, anatomically quite different in typical members of the human and the ape families. It was postulated that speech began when these anatomical parts reached human form, which was in the australopithecines or somewhat earlier. But the postulate is clearly wrong. Audible signals capable of expressing language do not require any particular phonetic apparatus, but only the ability to produce sound, any sound at all. Almost all mammals and a great number of other animals can do that. Moreover, a number of animals, not only birds but also some mammals, can produce sounds recognizably similar to those of human language, and yet their jaws and palates are radically nonhuman. A parrot is capable of articulating a human word but is completely incapable of understanding what the word means.

Given any method of sound production, the capacity for language depends not on characteristics of the sound apparatus but on the central nervous system. Speech is particularly connected with the left temporal lobe of the human brain, as shown, for example, by the fact that ability to speak is generally lost if that lobe is severely damaged. The gross development of the lobe can be seen in plaster casts of the insides of fossil skulls, and that, too, has been proposed as a means of determining whether or not a given fossil individual could speak. But all mammals have left temporal lobes, some smaller and some larger. Those with smaller lobes do not speak just a little and those with larger lobes more. There is no graded sequence: normal men speak completely; other animals, whatever the relative size of their temporal lobes, do not speak at all.

The essential anatomical and physiological basis of speech is nevertheless in the structure and function of the brain (18). That basis is not fully known, but it evidently involves not just a language center, such as might be localized in the temporal lobe, but an intricate and widespread system of associative connections throughout much of the brain. (The nature or presence of these connections cannot be determined in fossils.) Thus sensations of any kind derived from an external object or event can be generalized according to similarities with others. Each kind can then be associated with a distinctive symbol, which does not resemble the object or event at all but which arbitrarily stands for it. That symbol, a supreme element in the nature of man, is the word, and it is not surprising that words meaning "word," abstraction and symbolization on still another level, have acquired such mystical and philosophical overtones. *(Λόγος!)*

It is still possible but it is unlikely that we will ever know just when and how our ancestors began to speak. Yet it is certain that this ability depends on physical, structural, and chemical characteristics of the nervous system which evolved from our nonspeaking ancestors under the force of natural selection. The capacity for this unique kind of symbolization is quite general. It does not determine what symbol will be used for a given concept, but that any symbol can be associated with any concept. Thus we are all using exactly the same genetic capacity and symbolizing the same concept when various of us say "woman," "Weib," "femme," "mujer," "zhenshchina," or "imra," depending on whether we happen to have been raised in England, Germany, France, Spain, Russia, or Egypt. The words do not resemble each other and even less resemble the concept they stand for. Moreover, they can be written in different ways, as in Latin, Arabic, or Chinese characters, that do not resemble each other and that have no physical resemblance to the spoken words. They can even be associated with some symbol that is not verbal at all, as in this example with the simplified representation of Venus's mirror that biologists use to designate females: ♀.

Conclusion

Language has become far more than a means of communication in man. It is also one of the principal (although far from the only) means of thought, memory, introspection, problem-solving, and all other mental activities. The uniqueness and generality of human symbolization have given our mental activities not only a scope but also a quality far outside the range of other animals. It keeps us aware, to greater extent than can otherwise be, of past and future, of the continuity of existence and its extension beyond what is immediately sensed. Along with other peculiarly human capacities, it is involved in what I consider the most important human characteristic from an ethical point of view: foresight. It is the capacity to predict the outcome of our own actions that makes us responsible for them and that therefore makes ethical judgement of them both possible and necessary (19).

Above the individual level, language and related powers of symbolization make possible the acquisition, sharing, and preserving of knowledge far beyond what would be possible for any single individual. That is an indispensable element in all forms of human social organization and cultural accomplishment, even the most primitive.

It is obvious that I have by no means touched on all aspects of the biological nature of man. That would be impossible in one essay by one author. Those familiar with recent developments in biology may particularly miss reference to molecular biology and especially to the compound called DNA, now known to be largely involved in heredity and also in control of biochemical activities in cells. Those subjects are extremely fascinating at present and may be portentous for the future. However, in my opinion nothing that has so far been learned about DNA has helped significantly to understand the nature of man or of any other whole organism. It certainly is necessary for such understanding to examine what is inherited, how it is expressed in the developing individual, how it evolves in populations, and so on. Up to now the triumphs of DNA research have had virtually no effect on our understanding of those subjects. In due course molecular biology will undoubtedly become more firmly connected with the biology of whole organisms and with evolution, and then it will become of greater concern for those more interested in the nature of man than in the nature of molecules.

Finally, it should be pointed out that although man is a unique animal and although we properly consider his nature in the light of his peculiarities, he also has many non-peculiarities. Man is not *merely* an animal, that is, his essence is not simply in his shared animality. Nevertheless he *is* an animal and the nature of man includes and has arisen from the nature of all animals. Indeed if all the material characteristics of man could be enumerated, it would surely be found that the vast majority of them also occur in other animals. In fact at the level of molecular structure and interaction, information storage and transfer, energy transactions, and other defining characteristics of life, man is hardly significantly different from a bacterium—another illustration of the fact that that level of study is not particularly useful in considering the nature of man.

Like other animals, man develops, is born, grows, reproduces, and dies. Like other animals, he eats, digests, eliminates, respires, locomotes. He bends the qualities of nature to his own ends, but he is as fully subject to nature's laws as is any other animal and is no more capable of changing them. He lives in biological communities and has a niche and an ecology, just as do robins and earthworms. Let us not forget those aspects of man's nature. But let us also remember that man stands upright, builds and makes as never was built or wrought before, speaks and may speak truth or a lie, worships and may worship honestly or falsely, looks to the stars and into the mud, remembers his past and predicts his future, and writes (perhaps at too great length) about his own nature.

REFERENCES AND NOTES

1. C. Darwin, *The Descent of Man, and Selection in Relation to Sex* (Murray, London, 1871).
2. ——, *On the Origin of Species by Means of Natural Selection, or The Preservation of Favoured Races in the Struggle for Life* (Murray, London, 1859).
3. T. H. Huxley, *Evidence as to Man's Place in Nature* (Williams and Norgate, London, 1863).
4. Lamarck's view (unknown to most Neo-Lamarckians) was that *all* organisms are evolving toward and will eventually become human, after which they will degenerate through the inorganic world and eventually be spontaneously generated as lowly organisms and start again on the path to man. Today's amoeba is tomorrow's man, day after tomorrow's mineral, and still another day's amoeba once more. In the state of knowledge and philosophy of Lamarck's day it would perhaps be too strong to label his views as absurd, but they were certainly less sensible and less progressive than has often been claimed.
5. These new data are well exemplified in S. L. Washburn, Ed., *Classification and Human Evolution* (Aldine, Chicago, 1963).
6. E. L. Simons and D. R. Pilbeam, *Folia Primatol.* No. 46 (1965).
7. On this and other absolute (year) dates see D. E. Savage, J. F. Evernden. G. H. Curtis, G. T. James, *Am. J. Sci.* 262, 145 (1964).
8. E. L. Simons, *Postilla* (Yale Peabody Museum) No. 57 (1961); *Proc. Nat. Acad. Sci. U.S.* 51, 528 (1964).
9. L. S. B. Leakey, P. V. Tobias, M. D. Leakey, J. R. Napier, *Nature* 202, 3 (1964); P. V. Tobias, *Science* 149, 22 (1965). For discussion and dissent see P. L. DeVore, Ed., *The Origin of Man* (transcript of a symposium, Wenner-Gren Foundation, New York, 1965).
10. Age-long argument on the definition of species is perhaps sufficiently summarized in G. G. Simpson, *Principles of Animal Taxonomy* (Columbia Univ. Press, New York, 1961) and E. Mayr, *Animal Species and Evolution* (Harvard Univ. Press, Cambridge, 1963).
11. On animal races see especially Mayr (10). On the perennial, knotty problem of human races, a sensible general statement with many references is in Th. Dobzhansky, *Mankind Evolving* (Yale Univ. Press, New Haven, 1962).

12. J. Goodall, in *Primate Behavior,* I. DeVore, Ed. (Holt, Rinehart and Winston, New York, 1965). p. 425.
13. The literature on human culture and linguistics is as voluminous as that of any field of science. Some recent studies especially pertinent to my text are: A. L. Bryan, *Current Anthropol.* 4, 297 (1965); M. Critchley, in *Evolution after Darwin,* S. Tax, Ed. (Univ. of Chicago Press, Chicago, 1960), vol. 2, p. 289; A. S. Diamond, *The History and Origin of Language* (Philosophical Library, New York, 1959); E. L. DuBrul, *Evolution of the Speech Apparatus* (Thomas, Springfield, Ill., 1958); B. R. Fink, *Perspectives Biol. Med.* 7, 85 (1963); C. F. Hockett, in *The Evolution of Man's Capacity for Culture,* J. N. Spuhler, Ed. (Wayne State Univ. Press, Detroit, 1959), p. 32; C. F. Hockett and R. Ascher, *Current Anthropol.* 5, 135 (1964); A. Kortlandt, *ibid.* 6, 320 (1965). See also works cited in 16.
14. Misuses of the term "language" are too widely exemplified to need citation. The distinction is discussed by several of the authors cited in *13,* also (among other places) in J. B. S. Haldane and H. Spurway, *Insectes Sociaux* 1, 247 (1954) and J. B. S. Haldane, *Sci. Progr.* No. 171, 385 (1955).
15. C. Darwin, *The Expression of the Emotions in Man and Animals* (Murray, London, 1872).
16. J. B. Lancaster, in *The Origin of Man,* P. L. DeVore, Ed. (transcript of a symposium, Wenner-Gren Foundation, New York, 1965). See also discussions by A. R. Diebold, Jr., T. A. Sebeok, D. Slobin in the same volume, and bibliography on pp. 149-150.
17. I first began to appreciate the richness and complexity of "primitive" languages when I visited the Kamarakotos of Venezuela in 1939, and I commented on it in G. G. Simpson, *Los Indios Kamarakotos* (Ministerio de Fomento, Caracas, 1940).
18. N. Geschwind, *Brain* 88, 237 (1965).
19. G. G. Simpson, *Am. Psychologist* 21, 27 (1966).
20. During 1965 varying versions of this essay were presented as lectures at Randolph Macon College, the University of Paris, and the University of Washington. I have profited by discussions on those occasions.

3

Primitive Man's Relationship to Nature

DANIEL A. GUTHRIE

In discussing the causes of our environmental crisis, many authors seem to consider modern man's relationship to his environment as somehow unnatural. This attitude is due, in part, to a belief that primitive man lived in harmony with nature, a harmony that has been lost by modern society. Both Christianity (White, 1967) and Christianity coupled with technology (Roszak, 1969) have been blamed for this loss of harmony with nature. Yi-Fu Tuan (1970) and Richard Wright (1970) have disputed this belief by showing that Christians are not alone in their exploitation of the environment but share this trait with other cultures. Still, the attitude persists that primitive man, especially the American Indian, was somehow attuned to nature. This belief appears in Stewart Udall's book *The Quiet Crisis* (1964) in which he speaks of the land wisdom of the Indians, and in Theodore Roszak's *The Making of a Counter Culture* (1969) in which the kinship of primitive man to nature, as reflected through his belief in spirits and magic, is taken as an indication of a primitive ability to live in harmony with the environment. More recently Fertig (1970) has attempted to show that "Indians were part of a natural order between whose people and other animal and plant life there was a well-nigh perfect symbiosis" and concluded that "the Indians' nearly forgotten land wisdom, his ecological sense, is indispensable to our survival." It is my contention that primitive man was no better in his attitude toward his environment than we are today and that the concept of primitive man living in harmony with nature is a serious distortion of the facts.

For the purposes of this discussion, primitive cultures can be viewed as differing from modern society in three significant ways. The first two of these are in population size and in the level of technological sophistication. The populations of primitive peoples were small and the waste products of their cultures were for the most part biodegradable and did not occur in such concentrations as to overwhelm the ability of natural systems to deal with them. The situation is far different today. Not only is our population density such that our wastes cannot be accommodated easily by natural processes, but we turn the resources of our environment into new synthetic forms that cannot be degraded by natural processes and that may actually poison them. Furthermore, our technological sophistication allows a much greater level of consumption than was possible for primitive man. This very real difference in ability to affect the environment between primitive people and modern society must not be confused with a difference in attitude toward the environment.

The other significant difference between modern society and primitive cultures is in the way that primitive people view nature. The flavor of this relationship is expressed by Simpson (1964) in the following story.

Years ago I lived for a time with a group of uncivilized Indians in South America. Their world is very different from ours: in space, a saucer a few miles across; in time, from a few years to a few generations back into a misty past; in essence, lawless, unpredictable, and haunted. Anything might happen. The Kamarakoto Indians quite believe that animals become men and men become stones; for them there is neither limitation nor reason in the flux of nature. There is also a brooding evil in their world, a sense of wrongness and fatality that they call *kanaima* and see manifested in every unusual event and object.

The level of invalid perceptions might be called the lower superstition. It is nevertheless superior in some respects to the higher superstitions celebrated weekly in every hamlet of the United States. The legendary metamorphoses of my Indian friends are grossly naive, but they do postulate a kinship through all of nature. Above all, they are not guilty of teleology. It would never occur to the Indians that the universe, so largely hostile, might have been created for their benefit.

The religions of primitive peoples, full of spirits and myths, often express a kinship with nature or what Cassirer (1944) calls a sympathetic view of nature. This view is often expressed by American Indians when speaking of nature. Roszak quotes a Wintu (California) Indian as saying:

The white people never cared for land or deer or bear. When we Indians kill meat, we eat it all up. When we dig roots, we make little holes. . . . We shake down acorns and pinenuts. We don't chop down the trees. We only use dead wood. But the white people plow up the ground, pull up the trees, kill everything. The tree says "Don't. I am sore. Don't hurt me." But they chop it down and cut it up. The spirit of the land hates them. . . . The Indians never hurt anything, but the white people destroy all.

Similarly, Udall (1964) refers to many Indian sayings such as "the land is our mother" and "Our fathers received the land from God" to show the reverence that the Indians had for their environment.

While primitive man thus may view his relationship with nature quite differently from modern man (see also Kluckhohn and Murray, 1956), his actions toward nature are another matter. Tuan (1970) has pointed out that a wide gap may exist between a culture's ideals and their expression in the real world. This is not to deny that many Indian actions were and are ecologically sound. In order for primitive man to survive he, of necessity, had to develop a certain harmony with nature. To put it bluntly, those tribes that did not develop some "ecological consciousness" soon became extinct. However, I believe that this ecological consciousness was not arrived at through careful analysis of the environment, but rather through a trial and error approach. Harmony with nature, thus arrived at, did not prevent the existence of polluting habits, when these habits did not immediately threaten the survival of the society, nor did this harmony with nature prevent the acceptance of new inventions or ways of life that were ecologically disastrous.

Thus, the Sioux Indian, who would not drive stakes in his mother, the earth, or cut her with a plow, showed no qualms about driving a herd of buffalo over a cliff or about starting a range fire to drive the buffalo. The Indian, like the wolves, often ate only the choicest parts of the buffalo, the tongues, when game was plentiful, or left some of his kill unused (Wheat, 1967). Indeed, primitive man's hunting abilities are believed by Martin and Wright (1967) to have been the cause of widespread extinction of large mammals during the Pleistocene. Early man was nomadic in part because prolonged habitation in any one area depleted game and firewood and accumulated wastes to the extent that the region was no longer habitable. One wonders, looking at Mesa Verde cliff dwellings, how it was to live over a garbage dump. Was their custom of throwing all garbage over the edge of the cliff in front of their homes any different from our current civilized attitudes?

Finally, it has been shown that the American Indian was quite willing to take advantage of advances in technology to further exploit his environment. Farb (1968) has documented the effect of the horse on the lives of the Plains Indians. Long accustomed to hunting and traveling on foot, the horse caused a revolution in hunting ability. Buffalo robes were a sign of wealth to the Plains Indians and with the advent of the horse, the hunter could kill more buffalo than one woman could clean. The result was the spread of polygyny and even the acceptance of "squaw men," men who did women's work as wives, not for any sexual purpose but so that more hides could be processed. There is some feeling that even if the white man had not overhunted buffalo with firearms, the buffalo would soon have been exterminated by overhunting on the part of the Indians. Other examples of acceptance of new technologies without regard to their effect upon the environment are to be seen in the Navaho acceptance of sheep, and the subsequent overgrazing in the Southwest, and in the litter of bottles and junked cars to be found on Indian reservations today.

Perhaps there are some primitive peoples living in limited areas such as islands who have a clear view of the limitations of their resources and of the need to conserve them. Lyle's story (1967) of the Tikopian Islanders gives some indication of this. The American Indian, however, shared with the early white settlers of our continent a feeling that there were limitless horizons toward which he could expand. Despite his expression of a kinship with nature and his possession of a few ecologically sound practices, his actions show him to be no better than the early white settlers in his understanding of his basic dependence upon his environment.

A return to the "ecological intuitions and memories of the Red Man," as called for by some authors (Fertig, 1970), is not a solution to our current ecological problems. The Indian's actions toward nature were, and are, identical to those of modern man. What concern for the environment there was existed for the express purpose of guaranteeing human survival. A true reverence for nature, where nonhuman organisms are given a right to survival equal to that of man, has never been part of man's emotional makeup. Man shares with all other animals a basic lack of concern about his effect upon his surroundings. Grizzly bears tear up hillsides in search of ground squirrels and marmots and destroy trees and shrubbery in fits of anger. Herd animals cause erosion on the plains by wearing paths in the topsoil. Many animals, such as bears and wolves, are known to kill more than is necessary for their survival when game is plentiful. We tend to view these actions of animals as part of nature's plan and so they are, but these actions are on a limited scale destructive of the environment. Furthermore, they are no different in kind from the actions of primitive or modern man. Man's attitude toward the environment has not changed in the millennia since his evolution from lower animals. Only his population size and the sophistication of his technology are different.

I personally doubt that large numbers of people can ever develop a new emotion of concern for their environment in which animal life is considered equally as valuable as human life. However, there are signs that this may not be necessary. Unlike many undeveloped countries, most U.S. citizens are not primarily concerned with the basic survival issues of food and shelter. Our great wealth allows us to concern ourselves with the "quality" of our lives. Furthermore, as we become increasingly withdrawn from the land, our interest in its preservation increases. Meier (1966) has pointed out that the cities, repeatedly castigated for their pollution, are the sources of most of our concern about resources. The rancher in Wyoming, living at a population density similar to that of primitive man, is not worried about air pollution nor does he show concern about leaving rusting farm equipment lying about his land. Further, he, like primitive man, views coyotes and eagles as direct threats to his livestock, and prairie dogs and rabbits as threats to his crops. This frontier attitude toward nature is not seen in the reaction of Alaskans to conservationist's efforts to prevent the development of the North Slope oil fields. One wonders, too, if those who abandon the cities for rural communes in order to avoid pollution and to return to a life style in harmony with nature will develop this frontier attitude toward the environment when their crops and livestock are threatened? It is the city dweller, divorced from a direct dependence upon the land, who has taken the lead in conserving our wildlife and natural areas. Urban citizens can afford to view the eagle and coyote as beautiful creatures, not economic liabilities, and to view land they do not own or have an economic interest in as worthy of preservation in a natural state. Further, it is the urban resident who is most affected by overcrowding and pollution.

To be sure, this attitude of concern stems more from self-interest in recreational use of the environment and in the quality of the air and water that we use than from any true respect for the rights of nonhuman organisms. As such, we are likely to save "scenic wonders" and ignore swamps, or to favor oil production and boat marinas over natural areas. Still, much can be done through informing the public as to what is truly in their interest. Many swamps have been saved, not out of a public interest in swamps, but because they were necessary wintering places for migratory game birds or spawning grounds for commercial shellfish.

Our population is becoming increasingly urban, and it will be the urban majority that will determine the nation's conservation policies and have a major voice in pollution and population control. As our population becomes increasingly divorced from the land, it is the duty of every scientist, working through every educational device available, to keep the urban American aware of the natural condition of his country and of his interest in its preservation.

REFERENCES

Cassirer, Ernst. 1944. *An Essay on Man.* Yale University Press, New Haven, Conn. 237 p.
Farb, Peter. 1968. Rise and fall of the Indian of the wild West. *Natur. Hist.,* 77: 32-41.
Fertig, Fred. 1970. Child of nature, the American Indian as an ecologist. *Sierra Club Bull.,* 55: 4-7.
Kluckhohn, Clyde, and Henry A. Murray. 1956. *Personality in Nature, Society and Culture.* Alfred A. Knopf, New York. 701 p.
Lyle, David. 1967. The Human race has, maybe, thirty-five years left. *Esquire,* 68: 116-118.
Martin, Paul S., and H. E. Wright, Jr. (eds.). 1967. Pleistocene extinctions. *Proc. 7th Cong. Int. Assoc. for Quaternary Res.,* Vol. 6. Yale University Press, New Haven, Conn.
Meier, Richard L. 1966. Technology, resources and urbanism—the long view. In: *Future Environments of North America,* F. Frazer Darling and John P. Milton (eds.), Natural History Press, Garden City. P. 277-288.
Roszak, Theodore, 1969. *The Making of a Counter Culture.* Doubleday & Co., Garden City, N.Y. 303 p.
Simpson, George G. 1964. *This View of Life, the World of an Evolutionist.* Harcourt, Brace & World, Inc., New York, 308 p.
Tuan, Yi-Fu. 1970. Our treatment of the environment in ideal and actuality. *Amer. Sci.,* 58: 244-249.
Udall, Stewart L. 1964. *The Quiet Crisis.* Avon Books, New York. 244 p.
Wheat, Joe Ben. 1967. A Paleo-Indian Bison kill. *Sci. Amer.,* 216: 44-52.
White, Jr., Lynn. 1967. The historical roots of our ecologic crisis. *Science,* 155: 1203-1207.
Wright, Richard T. 1970. Responsibility for the ecological crisis. *Bio Science,* 20: 851-853.

MAN'S PERSPECTIVE

The Ainu on Hokkaido, the large north island of Japan, practice a religion which centers around Nature. The high point of their ritual is the sacrifice of the bear. Past generations of Ainu, heavily dependent upon the bear for food and warmth, placated his spirit before taking his life. It is doubtful if there was ever wanton destruction of bears among the Ainu. Judaeo-Christian groups, on the other hand, were not so respectful of Nature.

There is a view that much of the ecologic crisis may be attributed to the Judaeo-Christian influence (reading 5). Although it is dangerous to pull from context passages which support a particular point of view— especially from the Bible, where so many conflicting passages exist— Genesis 1:26 (reading 4) may provide a clue to—and cue for Western man's behavior.

Before new ways can be implemented, attitudes—which are notoriously recalcitrant (reading 6)—must change. A willingness to survey objectively the earth's resources and systems, past and present, can give us some hint of what we must do to secure a viable future.

4   Genesis 1:26

Let us make man in our image, after our likeness: and let them have dominion over the fish of the sea, and over the fowl of the air, and over the cattle, and over every creeping thing that creepeth upon the earth.

5   The Historical Roots Of Our Ecologic Crisis

Lynn White, Jr.

A conversation with Aldous Huxley not infrequently put one at the receiving end of an unforgettable monologue. About a year before his lamented death he was discoursing on a favorite topic: man's unnatural treatment of nature and its sad results. To illustrate his point he told how, during the previous summer, he had returned to a little valley in England where he had spent many happy months as a child. Once it had been composed of delightful grassy glades; now it was becoming overgrown with unsightly brush because the rabbits that formerly kept such growth under control had largely succumbed to a disease, myxamatosis, that was deliberately introduced by the local farmers to reduce the rabbits' destruction of crops. Being something of a Philistine, I could be silent no longer, even in the interests of great rhetoric. I interrupted to point out that the rabbit itself had been brought as a domestic animal to England in 1176, presumably to improve the protein diet of the peasantry.

All forms of life modify their contexts. The most spectacular and benign instance is doubtless the coral polyp. By serving its own ends, it had created a vast undersea world favorable to thousands of other kinds of animals and plants. Ever since man became a numerous species he has affected his environment notably. The hypothesis that his fire-drive method of hunting created the world's great grasslands and helped to exterminate the monster mammals of the Pleistocene from much of the globe is plausible, if not proved. For 6 millennia at least, the banks of the lower Nile have been a human artifact rather than the swampy African jungle which nature, apart from man, would have made it. The Aswan Dam, flooding 5000 square miles, is only the latest stage in a long process. In many regions terracing or irrigation, overgrazing, the cutting of forests by Romans to build ships to fight Carthaginians or by Crusaders to solve the logistics problems of their expeditions, have profoundly changed some ecologies. Observation that the French landscape falls into two basic types, the open fields of the north and the *bocage* of the south and west, inspired Marc Bloch to undertake his classic study of medieval agricultural methods. Quite unintentionally, changes in human ways often affect nonhuman nature. It has been noted, for example, that the advent of the automobile eliminated huge flocks of sparrows that once fed on the horse manure littering every street.

The history of ecologic change is still so rudimentary that we know little about what really happened, or what the results were. The extinction of the European aurochs as late as 1627 would seem to have been a simple case of overenthusiastic hunting. On more intricate matters it often is impossible to find solid information. For a thousand years or more the Frisians and Hollanders have been pushing back the North Sea, and the process is culminating in our own time in the reclamation of the Zuider Zee. What, if any, species of animals, birds, fish, shore life, or plants have died out in the process? In their epic combat with Neptune have the Netherlanders overlooked ecological values in such a way that the quality of human life in the Netherlands has suffered? I cannot discover that the questions have ever been asked, much less answered.

People, then, have often been a dynamic element in their own environment, but in the present state of historical scholarship we usually do not know exactly when, where, or with what effects man-induced changes came. As we enter the last third of the 20th century, however, concern for the problem of ecologic backlash is mounting feverishly. Natural science, conceived as the effort to understand the nature of things, had flourished in several eras and among several peoples. Similarly there had been an age-old accumulation of technological skills, sometimes growing rapidly, sometimes slowly. But it was not until about four generations ago that Western Europe and North America arranged a marriage between science and technology, a union of the theoretical and the empirical approaches to our natural environment. The emergence in widespread practice of the Baconian creed that scientific knowledge means technological power over nature can scarcely be dated before about 1850, save in the chemical industries, where it is anticipated in the 18th century. Its acceptance as a normal pattern of action may mark the greatest event in human history since the invention of agriculture, and perhaps in nonhuman terrestrial history as well.

Almost at once the new situation forced the crystallization of the novel concept of ecology; indeed, the word *ecology* first appeared in the English language in 1873. Today, less than a century later, the impact of our race upon the environment has so increased in force that it has changed in essence. When the first cannons were fired, in the early 14th century, they affected ecology by sending workers scrambling to the forests and mountains for more potash, sulfur, iron ore, and charcoal, with some resulting erosion and deforestation. Hydrogen bombs are of a different order: a war fought with them might alter the genetics of all life on this planet. By 1285 London had a smog problem arising from the burning of soft coal, but our present combustion of fossil fuels threatens to change the chemistry of the globe's atmosphere as a whole, with consequences which we are only beginning to guess. With the population explosion, the carcinoma of planless urbanism, the now geological deposits of sewage and garbage; surely no creature other than man has ever managed to foul its nest in such a short order.

There are many calls to action, but specific proposals, however worthy as individual items, seem too partial, palliative, negative: ban the bomb, tear down the billboards, give the Hindus contraceptives and tell them to eat their sacred cows. The simplest solution to any suspect change is, of course, to stop it, or, better yet, to revert to a romanticized past: make those ugly gasoline stations look like Anne Hathaway's cottage or (in the Far West) like ghost-town saloons. The "wilderness area" mentality invariably advocates deep-freezing an ecology, whether San Gimignano or the High Sierra, as it was before the first Kleenex was dropped. But neither atavism nor prettification will cope with the ecologic crisis of our time.

What shall we do? No one yet knows. Unless we think about fundamentals, our specific measures may produce new backlashes more serious than those they are designed to remedy.

As a beginning we should try to clarify our thinking by looking, in some historical depth, at the presuppositions that underlie modern technology and science. Science was traditionally aristocratic, speculative, intellectual in intent; technology was lower-class, empirical, action-oriented. The quite sudden fusion of these two, towards the middle of the 19th century, is surely related to the slightly prior and contemporary democratic revolutions which, by reducing social barriers, tended to assert a functional unity of brain and hand. Our ecologic crisis is the product of an emerging, entirely novel, democratic culture. The issue is whether a democratized world can survive its own implications. Presumably we cannot unless we rethink our axioms.

The Western Traditions of Technology and Science

One thing is so certain that it seems stupid to verbalize it: both modern technology and modern science are distinctly *Occidental*. Our technology has absorbed elements from all over the world, notably from China; yet everywhere today, whether in Japan or in Nigeria, successful technology is Western. Our science is the heir to all the sciences of the past, especially perhaps to the work of the great Islamic scientists of the Middle Ages, who so often outdid the ancient Greeks in skill and perspicacity: al-Razi in medicine, for example; or Ibn al-Haytham in optics; or Omar Khayyam in mathematics. Indeed, not a few works of such geniuses seem to have vanished in the original Arabic and to survive only in medieval Latin translations that helped to lay the foundations for later Western developments. Today, around the globe, all significant science is Western in style and method, whatever the pigmentation or language of the scientists.

A second pair of facts is less well recognized because they result from quite recent historical scholarship. The leadership of the West, both in technology and in science, is far older than the so-called Scientific Revolution of the 17th century or the so-called Industrial Revolution of the 18th century. These terms are in fact outmoded and obscure the true nature of what they try to describe—significant stages in two long and separate developments. By A.D. 1000 at the latest—and perhaps, feebly, as much as 200 years earlier—the West began to apply water power to industrial processes other than milling grain. This was followed in the late 12th century by the harnessing of wind power. From simple beginnings, but with remarkable consistency of style, the West rapidly expanded its skills in the development of power machinery, labor-saving devices, and automation. Those who doubt should contemplate that most monumental achievement in the history of automation: the weight-driven mechanical clock, which appeared in two forms in the early 14th century. Not in craftsmanship but in basic technological capacity, the Latin West of the later Middle Ages far outstripped its elaborate, sophisticated, and esthetically magnificent sister cultures, Byzantium and Islam. In 1444 a great Greek ecclesiastic, Bessarion, who had gone to Italy, wrote a letter to a prince in Greece. He is amazed by the superiority of Western ships, arms, textiles, glass. But above all he is astonished by the spectacle of waterwheels sawing timbers and pumping the bellows of blast furnaces. Clearly, he had seen nothing of the sort in the Near East.

By the end of the 15th century the technological superiority of Europe was such that its small, mutually hostile nations could spill out over all the rest of the world, conquering, looting, and colonizing. The symbol of this technological superiority is the fact that Portugal, one of the weakest states of the Occident, was able to become, and to remain for a century, mistress of the East Indies. And we must remember that the technology of Vasco da Gama and Albuquerque was built by pure empiricism, drawing remarkably little support or inspiration from science.

In the present-day vernacular understanding, modern science is supposed to have begun in 1543, when both Copernicus and Vesalius published their great works. It is no derogation of their accomplishments, however, to point out that such structures as the *Fabrica* and the *De revolutionibus* do not appear overnight. The distinctive Western tradition of science, in fact, began in the late 11th century with a massive movement of translation of Arabic and Greek scientific works into Latin. A few notable books—Theophrastus, for example—escaped the West's avid new appetite for science, but within less than 200 years effectively the entire corpus of Greek and Muslim science was available in Latin, and was being eagerly read and criticized in the new European universities. Out of criticism arose new observation, speculation, and increasing distrust of ancient authorities. By the late 13th century Europe had seized global scientific leadership from the faltering hands of Islam. It would be as absurd to deny the profound originality of Newton, Galileo, or Copernicus as to deny that of the 14th century scholastic scientists like Buridan or Oresme on whose work they built. Before the 11th century, science scarcely existed in the Latin West, even in Roman times. From the 11th century onward, the scientific sector of Occidental culture has increased in a steady crescendo.

Since both our technological and our scientific movements got their start, acquired their character, and achieved world dominance in the Middle Ages, it would seem that we cannot understand their nature or their present impact upon ecology without examining fundamental medieval assumptions and developments.

Medieval View of Man and Nature

Until recently, agriculture has been the chief occupation even in "advanced" societies; hence, any change in methods of tillage has much importance. Early plows, drawn by two oxen, did not normally turn the sod but merely scratched it. Thus, cross-plowing was needed and fields tended to be squarish. In the fairly light soils and semiarid climates of the Near East and Mediterranean, this worked well. But such a plow was inappropriate to the wet climate and often sticky soils of northern Europe. By the latter part of the 7th century after Christ, however, following obscure beginnings, certain northern peasants were using an entirely new kind of plow, equipped with a vertical knife to cut the line of the furrow, a horizontal share to slice under the sod, and a moldboard to turn it over. The friction of this plow with the soil was so great that it normally required not two but eight oxen. It attacked the land with such violence that cross-plowing was not needed, and fields tended to be shaped in long strips.

In the days of the scratch-plow, fields were distributed generally in units capable of supporting a single family. Subsistence farming was the presupposition. But no peasant owned eight oxen: to use the new and more efficient plow, peasants pooled their oxen to form large plow-teams, originally receiving (it would appear) plowed strips in proportion to their contribution. Thus, distribution of land was based no longer on the needs of a family but, rather, on the capacity of a power machine to till the earth. Man's relation to the soil was profoundly changed. Formerly man had been part of nature; now he was the exploiter of nature. Nowhere else in the world did farmers develop any analogous agricultural implement. Is it coincidence that modern technology, with its ruthlessness toward nature, has so largely been produced by descendants of these peasants of northern Europe?

This same exploitive attitude appears slightly before A.D. 830 in Western illustrated calendars. In older calendars the months were shown as passive personifications. The new Frankish calendars, which set the style for the Middle Ages, are very different: they show men coercing the world around them—plowing, harvesting, chopping trees, butchering pigs. Man and nature are two things, and man is master.

These novelties seem to be in harmony with larger intellectual patterns. What people do about their ecology depends on what they think about themselves in relation to things around them. Human ecology is deeply conditioned by beliefs about our nature and destiny—that is, by religion. To Western eyes this is very evident in, say, India or Ceylon. It is equally true of ourselves and of our medieval ancestors.

The victory of Christianity over paganism was the greatest psychic revolution in the history of our culture. It has become fashionable today to say that, for better or worse, we live in "the post-Christian age." Certainly the forms of our thinking and language have largely ceased to be Christian, but to my eye the substance often remains amazingly akin to that of the past. Our daily habits of action, for example, are dominated by an implicit faith in perpetual progress which was unknown either to Greco-Roman antiquity or to the Orient. It is rooted in, and is indefensible apart from, Judeo-Christian teleology. The fact that Communists share it merely helps to show what can be demonstrated on many other grounds: that Marxism, like Islam, is a Judeo-Christian heresy. We continue today to live, as we have lived for about 1700 years, very largely in a context of Christian axioms.

What did Christianity tell people about their relations with the environment?

While many of the world's mythologies provide stories of creation, Greco-Roman mythology was singularly incoherent in this respect. Like Aristotle, the intellectuals of the ancient West denied that the visible world had had a beginning. Indeed, the idea of a beginning was impossible in the framework of their cyclical notion of time. In sharp contrast, Christianity inherited from Judaism not only a concept of time as nonrepetitive and linear but also a striking story of creation. By gradual stages a loving and all-powerful God had created light and darkness, the heavenly bodies, the earth and all its plants, animals, birds, and fishes. Finally, God had created Adam and, as an afterthought, Eve to keep man from being lonely. Man named all the animals, thus establishing his dominance over them. God planned all of this explicitly for man's benefit and rule: no item in the physical creation had any purpose save to serve man's purposes. And, although man's body is made of clay, he is not simply part of nature: he is made in God's image.

Especially in its Western form, Christianity is the most anthropocentric religion the world has seen. As early as the second century both Tertullian and Saint Irenaeus of Lyons were insisting that when God shaped Adam he was foreshadowing the image of the incarnate Christ, the Second Adam. Man shares, in great measure, God's transcendence of nature. Christianity, in absolute contrast to ancient paganism and Asia's religions (except, perhaps, Zoroastrianism), not only established a dualism of man and nature but also insisted that it is God's will that man exploit nature for his proper ends.

At the level of the common people this worked out in an interesting way. In antiquity every tree, every spring, every stream, every hill had its own *genius loci,* its guardian spirit. These spirits were accessible to men, but were very unlike men; centaurs, fauns, and mermaids show their ambivalence. Before one cut a tree, mined a mountain, or dammed a brook, it was important to placate the spirit in charge of that particular institution, and to keep it placated. By destroying

pagan animism, Christianity made it possible to exploit nature in a mood of
indifference to the feelings of natural objects.

It is often said that for animism the Church substituted the cult of saints.
True; but the cult of saints is functionally quite different from animism. The saint
is not *in* natural objects; he may have special shrines, but his citizenship is in
heaven. Moreover, a saint is entirely a man; he can be approached in human
terms. In addition to saints, Christianity of course also had angels and demons
inherited from Judaism and perhaps, at one remove, from Zoroastrianism. But
these were all as mobile as the saints themselves. The spirits *in* natural objects,
which formerly had protected nature from man, evaporated. Man's effective
monopoly on spirit in this world was confirmed, and the old inhibitions to the
exploitation of nature crumbled.

When one speaks in such sweeping terms, a note of caution is in order.
Christianity is a complex faith, and its consequences differ in differing contexts.
What I have said may well apply to the medieval West, where in fact technology
made spectacular advances. But the Greek East, a highly civilized realm of equal
Christian devotion, seems to have produced no marked technological innovation
after the late 7th century, when Greek fire was invented. The key to the contrast
may perhaps be found in a difference in the tonality of piety and thought which
students of comparative theology find between the Greek and the Latin Churches.
The Greeks believed that sin was intellectual blindness, and that salvation was
found in illumination, orthodoxy—that is, clear thinking. The Latins, on the
other hand, felt that sin was moral evil, and that salvation was to be found in right
conduct. Eastern theology has been intellectualist. Western theology has been
voluntarist. The Greek saint contemplates; the Western saint acts. The implications of Christianity for the conquest of nature would emerge more easily in the
Western atmosphere.

The Christian dogma of creation, which is found in the first clause of all the
Creeds, has another meaning for our comprehension of today's ecologic crisis. By
revelation, God had given man the Bible, the Book of Scripture. But since God
had made nature, nature also must reveal the divine mentality. The religious
study of nature for the better understanding of God was known as natural
theology. In the early Church, and always in the Greek East, nature was conceived primarily as a symbolic system through which God speaks to men: the ant
is a sermon to sluggards; rising flames are the symbol of the soul's aspiration. This
view of nature was essentially artistic rather than scientific. While Byzantium
preserved and copied great numbers of ancient Greek scientific texts, science as
we conceive it could scarcely flourish in such an ambience.

However, in the Latin West by the early 13th century natural theology was
following a very different bent. It was ceasing to be the decoding of the physical
symbols of God's communication with man and was becoming the effort to
understand God's mind by discovering how his creation operates. The rainbow
was no longer simply a symbol of hope first sent to Noah after the Deluge: Robert
Grosseteste, Friar Roger Bacon, and Theodoric of Freiberg produced startlingly
sophisticated work on the optics of the rainbow, but they did it as a venture in
religious understanding. From the 13th century onward, up to and including
Leibnitz and Newton, every major scientist, in effect, explained his motivations
in religious terms. Indeed, if Galileo had not been so expert an amateur theologian

he would have got into far less trouble: the professionals resented his intrusion. And Newton seems to have regarded himself more as a theologian than as a scientist. It was not until the late 18th century that the hypothesis of God became unnecessary to many scientists.

It is often hard for the historian to judge, when men explain why they are doing what they want to do, whether they are offering real reasons or merely culturally acceptable reasons. The consistency with which scientists during the long formative centuries of Western science said that the task and the reward of the scientist was "to think God's thoughts after him" leads one to believe that this was their real motivation. If so, then modern Western science was cast in a matrix of Christian theology. The dynamism of religious devotion, shaped by the Judeo-Christian dogma of creation, gave it impetus.

An Alternative Christian View

We would seem to be headed toward conclusions unpalatable to many Christians. Since both *science* and *technology* are blessed words in our contemporary vocabulary, some may be happy at the notions, first, that, viewed historically, modern science is an extrapolation of natural theology and, second, that modern technology is at least partly to be explained as an Occidental, voluntarist realization of the Christian dogma of man's transcendence of, and rightful mastery over, nature. But, as we now recognize, somewhat over a century ago science and technology—hitherto quite separate activities—joined to give mankind powers which, to judge by many of the ecologic effects, are out of control. If so, Christianity bears a huge burden of guilt.

I personally doubt that disastrous ecologic backlash can be avoided simply by applying to our problems more science and more technology. Our science and technology have grown out of Christian attitudes toward man's relation to nature which are almost universally held not only by Christians and neo-Christians but also by those who fondly regard themselves as post-Christians. Despite Copernicus, all the cosmos rotates around our little globe. Despite Darwin, we are *not,* in our hearts, part of the natural process. We are superior to nature, contemptuous of it, willing to use it for our slightest whim. The newly elected Governor of California, like myself a churchman but less troubled than I, spoke for the Christian tradition when he said (as is alleged), "when you've seen one redwood tree, you've seen them all." To a Christian a tree can be no more than a physical fact. The whole concept of the sacred grove is alien to Christianity and to the ethos of the West. For nearly two millennia Christian missionaries have been chopping down sacred groves, which are idolatrous because they assume spirit in nature.

What we do about ecology depends on our ideas of the man-nature relationship. More science and more technology are not going to get us out of the present ecologic crisis until we find a new religion, or re-think our old one. The beatniks, who are the basic revolutionaries of our time, show a sound instinct in their affinity for Zen Buddhism, which conceives of the man-nature relationship as very nearly the mirror image of the Christian view. Zen, however, is as deeply conditioned by Asian history as Christianity is by the experience of the West, and I am dubious of its viability among us.

Possibly we should ponder the greatest radical in Christian history since Christ: Saint Francis of Assisi. The prime miracle of Saint Francis is the fact that he did not end at the stake, as many of his left-wing followers did. He was so clearly heretical that a General of the Franciscan Order, Saint Bonaventure, a great and perceptive Christian, tried to suppress the early accounts of Franciscanism. The key to an understanding of Francis is his belief in the virtue of humility —not merely for the individual but for man as a species. Francis tried to depose man from his monarchy over creation and set up a democracy of all God's creatures. With him the ant is no longer simply a homily for the lazy, flame a sign of the thrust of the soul toward union with God; now they are Brother Ant and Sister Fire, praising the Creator in their own ways as Brother Man does in his.

Later commentators have said that Francis preached to the birds as a rebuke to men who would not listen. The records do not read so: he urged the little birds to praise God, and in spiritual ecstasy they flapped their wings and chirped rejoicing. Legends of saints, especially the Irish saints, had long told of their dealings with animals but always, I believe, to show their human dominance over creatures. With Francis it is different. The land around Gubbio in the Apennines was being ravaged by a fierce wolf. Saint Francis, says the legend, talked to the wolf and persuaded him of the error of his ways. The wolf repented, died in the odor of sanctity, and was buried in consecrated ground.

What Sir Steven Ruciman calls "the Franciscan doctrine of the animal soul" was quickly stamped out. Quite possibly it was in part inspired, consciously or unconsciously, by the belief in reincarnation held by the Cathar heretics who at that time teemed in Italy and southern France, and who presumably had got it originally from India. It is significant that at just the same moment, about 1200, traces of metempsychosis are found also in western Judaism, in the Provencal *Cabbala*. But Francis held neither to transmigration of souls nor to pantheism. His view of nature and of man rested on a unique sort of pan-psychism of all things animate and inanimate, designed for the glorification of their transcendent Creator, who, in the ultimate gesture of cosmic humility, assumed flesh, lay helpless in a manger, and hung dying on a scaffold.

I am not suggesting that many contemporary Americans who are concerned about our ecologic crisis will be either able or willing to counsel with wolves or exhort birds. However, the present increasing disruption of the global environment is the product of a dynamic technology and science which were originating in the Western medieval world against which Saint Francis was rebelling in so original a way. Their growth cannot be understood historically apart from distinctive attitudes toward nature which are deeply grounded in Christian dogma. The fact that most people do not think of these attitudes as Christian is irrelevant. No new set of basic values has been accepted in our society to displace those of Christianity. Hence we shall continue to have a worsening ecologic crisis until we reject the Christian axiom that nature has no reason for existence save to serve man.

The greatest spiritual revolutionary in Western history, Saint Francis, proposed what he thought was an alternative Christian view of nature and man's relation to it: he tried to substitute the idea of the equality of all creatures, including man, for the idea of man's limitless rule of creation. He failed. Both our present science and our present technology are so tinctured with orthodox Christian arrogance toward nature that no solution for our ecologic crisis can be expected from them alone. Since the roots of our trouble are so largely religious, whether we call it that or not, we must rethink and refeel our nature and destiny. The profoundly religious, but heretical, sense of the primitive Franciscans for the spiritual autonomy of all parts of nature may point a direction. I propose Francis as a patron saint for ecologists.

The Attitude Lag   6

EUGENE P. ODUM

In the 1920's sociologist William F. Ogburn introduced the concept of "cultural lag" to indicate that man's social customs and attitudes change more slowly than his technical culture. My father, the late Howard W. Odum, also a sociologist, preferred to think of this tendency in the more positive sense of an "achievement lag." Certainly, cultural or achievement lags often contribute to malfunctions in society. Furthermore, as an ecologist I am convinced that what might be termed an "attitude lag" is at the root of much of the current maladjustment between man and his environment.

As man begins to tax the limits of the biosphere his basic attitude and strategy toward the environment must undergo an about-face, or at least a basic reorientation of goals becomes necessary, if high quality rather than mere quantity of human existence is to be the primary motivation for human society. In cybernetic language we are faced with the problem of going from the positive transient state, when everything is growing and expanding at a great rate, to the steady state when growth rates approach zero and enough is enough, so to speak. We are also talking about avoiding a negative transient state of declining numbers and resources! Sooner or later transition from youth to maturity must be faced by all kinds of life, and by life at all levels of organization whether it be cell, teenager, or ecosystem. What is good, desirable, or adaptive—howsoever one wishes to express it—in the youthful stage is oftentimes bad, undesirable, or unadaptive in the mature system. Thus, in the pioneer society as in the early successional ecosystem high birth rates, rapid growth, and exploitation of accessible and unused resources are advantageous. As human beings we can be justly proud of the fact that we have succeeded in modifying and controlling our natural environment to our very great collective advantage. An aggressive or war-like approach to nature is a perfectly natural and desirable drive during the establishment and growth phases of societal systems. However, as the saturation level is approached this drive becomes increasingly unadaptive, and must be shifted to the opposite pole as, for example, to considerations of birth control, recycling of resources, territoriality (i.e., regulation of land use) and symbiosis (i.e., peaceful co-existence of man and nature). The danger is not so much that man may not adapt to the equilibrium state, but he may not apply the brakes fast enough to avoid the serious overshoots and severe, perhaps disastrous, oscillations that befall any system capable of rapid change but which lacks adequate feedback control.

POLLUTION

What we don't know—or refuse to recognize—is that modern man has been altering his total environment so swiftly that the whole "great chain of life" on this planet is endangered.

All of us live on a tiny spaceship which is hurtling through the universe at a speed 600 times faster than the fastest jet plane— carrying with it its own limited resources for sustaining life.

What we have now is all that we will ever have to keep us alive. Having already set foot on the lifeless moon, we shall presumably find that we are the only creatures in our solar system. As lonely astronauts on our own ceaseless journey through space, what do we have as our basic equipment for survival?

Above us, a narrow band of usable atmosphere, no more than seven miles high, with no "new" air available to us.

Beneath us, a thin crust of land with only one-eighth of the surface hospitable to human life.

And around us, a finite supply of "usable" water that we must perpetually cleanse and re-use.

These are the elements of man's physical environment. This is the "envelope" in which our planet is eternally sealed.

Together, and left alone, land, air, and water work well as an "ecosystem" to maintain the great chain of life, and the delicate balance of nature, from ocean depth to mountain top.

But man, since he first rose up on two legs, has been tampering with this system. He cannot help it. Everything we do alters our environment: the ways we grow food and build shelter and create what we call "culture" and "civilization."

Now, entering the last three decades of the 20th century, we face the shocking realization that we have gone too far too fast and too heedlessly—and now we are forced to cope with some of the consequences of our "progress" as a species.

For, increasingly, all over the world scientists and statesmen and specialists in many fields are coming to agree on the pressing paradoxes of our modern age:

33

As societies grow richer, their environments grow poorer.
As the array of objects expands, the vigor of life declines.
As we acquire more leisure to enjoy our surroundings, we
find less around us to enjoy.

Most of life could not exist on Earth without the atmosphere as it is now constituted. This atmosphere is in intimate contact with nearly every living cell on the surface of our planet. What is the composition of the atmosphere and how did it get that way (reading 8)? How much stress can the atmosphere sustain before it will no longer support life? How does the Earth's atmosphere compare with that of other planets in our solar system (reading 9)? Is there a chance the atmosphere of the Earth will some day resemble that of Mars or Venus (readings 9 and 10)?

Man And The Air   7

Atmospheric elements and living organisms are linked together in cycles which may be highly vulnerable to the impact of technology.

LAMONT C. COLE

Man is changing the world environment. He has been doing this almost from the time of his appearance as a new species a million or so years ago, but now he has become so numerous and technologically adept that there is a real danger he may destroy the ability of the earth to support life.

Early man subsisted by gathering wild foods and by hunting and fishing. At some point he discovered that he could use fire to drive game animals, and this was the start of man-made air pollution and soil erosion. However, early man was incredibly lucky. In many places the forests he burned were replaced by grasslands which supported increasing populations of grazing mammals, and these grasslands—including our North American prairies—developed soils that would eventually place them among the world's most valuable lands for agriculture. Although the evidence is lost in the past, man's first use of grasslands was probably for the grazing of domestic animals, and this grazing probably helped to inhibit the regeneration of forests.

Early agricultural man would have found it virtually impossible to cope with the heavy sod of grasslands, and so he confined his efforts to the flood plains of rivers where the soil was fertile, well watered and easy to cultivate with simple tools. He learned to store food so that the produce of the growing season could support him and his domestic animals throughout the year. Then he started to build towns and cities and to expand his numbers, and he felt the need for more agricultural land and year-round agriculture. These needs were satisfied by building dams and canals for irrigation. Great civilizations grew up in the valleys of rivers such as the Tigris, Euphrates, Nile, and Indus, and their human populations multiplied.

There were, however, side effects. The very crowding of people into towns and cities exposed them to frequent epidemics, and these, together with wars and famines, took a frightful toll of human life. The smoke from man-made fires polluted the atmosphere, and the erosion of soil from burned-over and overgrazed slopes polluted bodies of water and sometimes blocked streams to create swamps and marshes with attendant health hazards such as malaria. At this stage man could not anticipate the disasters that his own activities were bound to create. Without adequate drainage, for instance, his irrigation works would cause water to move upward through the soil, where it would evaporate and deposit a fertility-destroying layer of salts on the surface.

The Ravaging of Resources

As soils were rendered lifeless by salts and as irrigation systems filled with silt, great civilizations vanished. Pliny tells of the farmers of the great Babylonian Empire, dating from before 2000 B.C., who harvested two annual crops of grain and grazed sheep on the land between crops. But by the twelfth century Otto of Freising could write in his *Chronicon:* "But what now is Babylon . . . ? A shrine of sirens, a home of lizards and ostriches, a den of serpents." Today less than 20 percent of the land in modern Iraq is cultivated and more than half of the national income is from oil. The landscape is dotted with mounds representing forgotten towns, the old irrigation works are filled with silt (the end product of soil erosion), and the ancient seaport of Ur is now 150 miles from the sea with its buildings buried under silt as deep as 35 feet.

We hear a great deal today about the "underdeveloped" and "developing" nations but, as in the case of Iraq, many of them could more accurately be described as *overdeveloped* nations. Modern Iran was once the seat of the great Persian Empire where Darius I was the "King of Kings" 2400 years ago. Ancient Greece had forested hills, ample water and productive soils, and it is clear from Plato's *Critias* (or *Atlanticus)* that he knew that deforestation and overgrazing could cause soil erosion and the drying up of springs. Apparently nobody listened to his warnings.

The glories of ancient Mali and Ghana in west Africa were legends in medieval Europe. In the land that once exported the cedars of Lebanon to Egypt, the erosion-proof Roman roads and the soil beneath them now stand several feet above the rock desert. But about 1940, Dr. Walter Loudermilk of the U. S. Soil Erosion Service found the cedars to be flourishing as of old in a churchyard where the soil had remained and where the grazing of goats had been prevented for 300 years. In China and India, ancient irrigation systems stand abandoned and filled with silt. When the British assumed the rule of India two centuries ago, the population was about 60 million. Today it is over 500 million and most of its land problems have been created in the past century through deforestation and plowing and the resulting erosion and siltation, all stemming from efforts to support such fantastic population growth.

Everyone knows about the wonders of ancient Egypt. The annual spring flood of the Nile watered and fertilized the soil, and crops could be grown for seven months each year. Extensive irrigation systems were established before 2000 B.C. The country was the granary of the Roman Empire, and agriculture flourished for 4000 years or more. But in 1902 a dam was built at Aswan to prevent the spring flood and permit year-round irrigation. Now the soils are deteriorating from salinization, and a higher Aswan Dam is being built to bring more land under cultivation. Meanwhile, population growth has virtually destroyed any possibility that the new agricultural land can significantly raise the per capita level of nutrition.

In various parts of South America and Africa, modern aerial reconnaissance has revealed ancient ridged fields on flood plains. These are the remnants, according to J. J. Parsons and W. M. Denevan, of "a specialized system of agriculture that physically reshaped large parts of the South American continent." In many parts of Mexico towns that were originally located to take advantage of superior springs now must carry in water from distant sites. And in Guatemala and Yucatan the ruins of the Mayan civilization stand as stark evidence of what the land was once capable of supporting.

In our own young country thousands of acres of agricultural land have been lost to erosion and gullying, and thousands more to strip mining. The inherent fertility of our best agricultural land is declining so that yields can only be maintained or increased by massive programs of fertilization. In our irrigated lands of the West there is the constant danger of salinization, while from Long Island to southern California we have lowered water tables so greatly that in coastal regions salt water is seeping into the aquifers. Meanwhile, an estimated 2000 irrigation dams in the United States are now useless impoundments of silt, sand, and gravel, and a conservatively estimated million acres of land per year are being sacrificed to paving, building, and other manifestations of "progress."

This is what man has done to the land. In the last 300 years, moreover, he has been able to *accelerate* his destructive processes by obtaining energy from the fossil fuels—coal, peat, natural gas, and petroleum. Several recent surveys have found that modern "progressive" farmers expend more calories running their machinery than they remove from the land in crops. Now, quite suddenly, man has come to realize that these fuels will soon be exhausted—various estimates of the timetable give us anywhere from 20 years to a half-dozen generations. By then, present thinking holds, we shall have converted to nuclear energy. But uranium and thorium are also exhaustible resources, and modern reactors convert less than one percent of the energy in their fuel into electricity—as compared with some 40 percent for conventional plants burning fossil fuels. Indeed, the nuclear age threatens us with a wholly new magnitude of global contamination.

To fully appreciate modern man's impact on his environment, we must consider how the earth's atmosphere and hydrosphere (the surface waters) have reached their present state. They are made up of an exquisite "mix" of elements and are related to one another through biochemical mechanisms which are dangerously vulnerable to the influence of man.

How the Atmosphere Evolved

Modern geological experts are pretty well agreed that the primitive earth did not have an atmosphere of the gases now present. Degassing of rocks in the earth's interior, by volcanic activity and other processes, produced both a gaseous atmosphere and the water vapor that eventually gave rise to the hydrosphere. Whatever the composition of this original atmosphere, it was very different from the present one, which is of biological origin.

Neglecting contaminants, our atmosphere at sea level now consists by volume of about 78 percent nitrogen, 21 percent oxygen, 0.03 percent carbon dioxide, and minor amounts of other gases. This is a very curious composition in view of the fact that nitrogen is a scarce element on earth and is not among the 18 chemical elements that account for 99.9 percent of the mass of all known terrestrial matter. Also curious is the fact that oxygen, although abundant, is highly reactive chemically and almost never occurs in an uncombined state outside of the atmosphere. Both of these gases occur in the atmosphere only because living organisms keep putting them there.

The earth's atmosphere could not have contained more than traces of free oxygen before the origin of photosyntheis—the process by which green plants take in water and carbon dioxide and, with the aid of energy from sunlight, combine them to produce organic matter and liberate oxygen as a by-product. Gradually, through perhaps two billion years since the origin of photosynthesis, some of the organic matter in the bodies of living things has become buried— mostly in marine sediments—and so has been prevented from recombining with oxygen. It is this process which has produced the large reservoir of oxygen in the atmosphere as well as the stores of fossil fuels that we are now extracting and burning to keep our economy going. The amount of oxygen in the atmosphere probably has not undergone significant change since the end of the Carboniferous period some 300 million years ago, and we should not expect it to change so long as photosynthesis can keep up with oxidation.

The oxygen cycle which I have just sketched is linked to the equally delicate biochemical cycles of other elements such as carbon, sulfur and nitrogen. Let us briefly consider the third of these elements.

All living things require nitrogen because the main structural components of their bodies are nitrogen compounds called proteins. Since animals and most microorganisms make their proteins directly or indirectly from the constituents of plant proteins, we must again focus on green plants to understand how the composition of the atmosphere is maintained. Higher plants cannot build proteins directly from the atmosphere's molecular nitrogen. Certain types of bacteria and blue-green algae must first convert the molecular nitrogen to ammonia and nitrate, in which forms it can be used by higher plants and passed on as proteins to animals, including man. When plants and animals die, other bacteria known as "decomposers" break down their proteins and inert nitrogen compounds, and additional bacteria called "dentrifiers" release a fresh supply of molecular nitrogen into the air. It is only because of these bacteria that plants and animals have not long ago extracted all of the nitrogen from the atmosphere—thereby making further plant plant and animal life impossible on most of the earth. I am terrified to recall that I have twice heard prominent chemists say, and have once read in a textbook, that it would be desirable to find a way to *block* dentrification because ammonia and nitrate are so important to agriculture!

These and other complex interconnections equally essential for life have thus far assured the constancy of our atmosphere, and they have done so despite the fact that photosynthesis stops in darkness, at low temperatures, and when other requirements of living things are not met. The crucial point in all of this is that neither man nor other familiar living things could survive without the photosynthesis of plants—most of which are in the oceans—or without a host of microorganisms whose very existence is unknown to most persons. Today, through our various forms of pollution, we are thoughtlessly putting these very organisms in jeopardy!

The Growth of Pollution

Like soil erosion and deforestation, man-made pollution has an ancient history. Neolithic man started polluting the environment with his fires, though the major resulting pollutants—smoke, soot, silt—also existed without man. But many new pollutants appeared as civilization advanced. The Romans mined lead in Britain and smelted it there, and it is said that the sites of these old smelting operations can still be recognized by the improverished vegetation growing on the poisoned soil. In Rome the lead went into paints, water pipes, and the lining of vessels in which wine was stored. Recent studies of Roman bones have shown concentrations of lead which indicate that many members of the upper classes must have suffered from lead poisoning; it has even been suggested that this may have contributed to the decline of the Empire.

As cities grew they began to concentrate materials produced over a wide area into a small space, and these materials gave rise to wastes, pollution problems arose. Otto's *Chronicon* tells us that when Frederick Barbarossa's army arrived in Rome in the summer of 1167 ". . . the ponds, caverns, and ruinous places around the city were exhaling poisonous vapors, and the air in the entire vicinity had become densely laden with pestilence and death." Waters were also polluted. The name "Rhine" was supposedly derived from the German word for "pure," but by the 13th century St. Hildegard wrote that the Rhine's waters, if drunk unboiled, would "produce noxious blue fluids in the body."

Man added a whole new dimension to environmental pollution when he started burning fossil fuels for energy. In the year 1306 a citizen of London was tried and executed for burning coal in the city, but three centuries later coal combustion was a way of life and London had a smog problem. This new source of energy made it possible for many more people simultaneously to inhabit the earth than ever before, and the resulting colonization and exploitation of new lands further aggravated environmental deterioration. With the start of the 20th century, petroleum assumed a growing role as a source of energy. The internal combustion engine and a huge, diverse chemical industry have released into the environment countless new materials to which the world's living things have never before had to adapt. Miraculously, man's run of dumb luck has continued —and the biogeochemical cycle on which his life depends have kept on functioning. But since World War II man-made stresses on the environment have so intensified that it would be incredible if such luck long continued.

The pollution problem, of course, is not limited to the by-products of our commercial activities. Waste matter is also a major culprit. We have continued to dispose of our wastes as of old—largely by dumping them into the atmosphere and hydrosphere—and human populations are now so dense that it is difficult to see how we can ever reclaim a clean environment. As Dean Charles Bradley of Montana State College wrote in 1962: "If river-disposal of waste were suddenly denied the city of St. Louis, the city fathers would have to decide what else to do with the daily discharge of 200,000 gallons of urine and 400 tons of solid body-wastes, to say nothing of all the industrial wastes."

Because of these biological wastes and other pollutants, it has been estimated by the U. S. Food and Drug Administration that we are now exposing ourselves and our environment to over a half-million man-made substances, and that this number is growing by 400-500 new chemicals per year. Just in the period since World War II we have asked the environment to cope with such unprecedented classes of materials as synthetic pesticides, plastics, antibiotics, radioisotopes and detergents. The end of our production of novel chemicals is not in sight. No more than a minute fraction of these substances, singly or in combination, has been tested for toxicity to the marine diatoms that produce some 70 percent of the earth's annual supply of oxygen. Nor have they been tested for toxicity to the equally vital forms involved in the cycles of nitrogen and other essential elements.

For the 48 coterminous United States I have attempted some calculations of the oxygen balance. I took the figures for production and imports of fossil fuels for the year 1966, corrected these for exports and non-combustible residues, and calculated the amount of oxygen that would be required for their combustion. Then I made what I believe to be a good estimate of the amount of oxygen produced by photosynthesis within our borders that year. The amount of oxygen produced turned out to be not quite 60 percent of the amount consumed.

The implication is clear: we are absolutely dependent on oxygen which is produced outside our borders—mostly in the Pacific Ocean and brought in by atmospheric circulation. If we should inadvertently kill enough marine diatoms or the organisms they depend on for fixed nitrogen, we would start running out of oxygen to breathe. Yet these organisms are now being exposed to our half-million chemicals. There is evidence that the insecticide DDT can suppress photosynthesis in bodies of water, and this chemical has not become world-wide in distribution. More frightening yet to me are the herbicides or "weed killers" —chemicals specifically designed to be poisonous to plants. At present the military is taking most of our production of these chemicals and shipping it to Vietnam to kill rice and defoliate jungle vegetation. What will happen if a few tankers loaded with concentrated herbicides are sunk in the Pacific? The fate of Lake Erie and many lesser bodies of water has shown that man is indeed capable of blocking the oxygen cycle through sheer carelessness.

Our Contaminated Air

Earlier I described the atmosphere as it would exist if it were free of contaminants. In our actual atmosphere, however, more than 3,000 foreign chemicals have been identified. The air of our cities is rich in solid matter such as soot, fly ash, particles of rubber from tires and asbestos from brake linings—all of which have implications for public health. Our smoke stacks and exhaust pipes pour forth carbon monoxide, sulfur dioxide and various oxides of nitrogen; these chemicals can affect health and, in the case of the sulfur and nitrogen oxides, they are capable of corroding metal and concrete. Ethyl gasoline causes our automobiles to release so much lead to the atmosphere that snow near the North Pole contains 300 percent more lead than it did in 1940. And, to increase agricultural output, we have processed phosphate rock into fertilizer, releasing as a by-product poisonous fluorine which ironically sometimes kills vegetation and live-stock in the vicinity of the fertilizer plants. Ironically also, our biodegradable detergents are compounds of phosphorus, and we are discarding this precious element so recklessly that it has become one of our most significant water pollutants.

What about our ever-increasing use of fossil fuels? We are burning them at a rate which is putting carbon dioxide into the atmosphere more rapidly than the oceans can assimilate it. Carbon dioxide is quite transparent to solar radiation but quite opaque to the longwave heat radiation from earth to space. In other words it acts as a heat trap which has the potential for altering the earth's climates. The precise form that such changes might take are still very controversial and uncertain, but the combustion of fossil fuels is one more example of the way we are playing Russian roulette with our environment. Nevertheless, our leaders are determined in the name of progress to see industry expand to build more, larger, and higher-flying airplanes that will pollute the upper atmosphere, and to take more land out of photosynthetic production for housing and other "good things."

People are grasping at straws for ways to keep our economy growing. We are told that bacteria, fungi and yeasts will convert fossil fuels directly into food for man. Not only are the fossil fuels exhaustible, but, unfortunately, this proposed new type of food production will not generate any oxygen. We are told that nuclear energy will provide the answer to air pollution.

This may be the cruelest hoax of all. Before the controlled release of atomic energy, the total amount of radioactivity under human control consisted of about 10 curies, in the form of about 10 grams of radium divided among the world's hospitals and laboratories. Great concern and publicity arose whenever a few millicuries were lost or misplaced. Those who can recall this concern will not take lightly the news that a nuclear power plant now being constructed on the shores of Lake Ontario near Oswego, New York, will, by the company's own estimate, release 130 curies per day into the atmosphere. This plant is actually to be a small one in terms of present dreams. It represents only about 2 percent of the generating capacity for which nuclear plant permits were sought from the Atomic Energy Commission in 1967.

Present-day reactors produce prodigious quantities of extremely hazardous and long-lived radioisotopes such as Strontium^{90} and Cesium^{137} which, everyone agrees, should be stored for at least 600 years before being released into the environment. Yet one Atomic Energy Commission found that about 5 percent of the underground storage tanks were leaking after only about 20 years.

In all of the foregoing instances of pollution, the fundamental problem as I see it, is our fetish for equating growth with progress. Economists state that companies must grow to survive. We take pride in a gross national product growing at between 4 and 5 percent per year, and we try to ignore the fact that our per capita production of trash is growing at about the same rate. We are told that our electrical generating capacity must increase by 10 percent per year, but we forget that all of that energy must eventually be imposed on the environment as heat; I don't believe that there is any way short of repealing the laws of thermodynamics to sustain such growth without bringing disaster to our environment.

In a related field, growing populations are viewed by many planners simply as expanding markets—and here we come to a fundamental problem. There must be *some* level of human population that the earth could support indefinitely without undergoing deterioration, but we don't know what that level is. Through the first million or so years of man's existence, his population probably doubled no more often than once in every 50,000 years. During the summer of 1968 the human population passed the 3.5 billion mark, and, if present trends should continue, this population would double again every 35 years! There is no possibility that the earth's environment can long sustain such pressure; in fact I consider it very improbable that the earth could continually support, on a nondestructive basis, a population as large as the *present* one. We shall have to decide, and soon, what quality of life we want for ourselves and what steps in pollution and population control are necessary to get it.

Unfortunately, our big decisions are made on economic grounds. Factories burning fossil fuels don't *have* to release particulates and sulfur and nitrogen oxides into the atmosphere; nor do nuclear plants, barring accidents, *have* to release radioisotopes into the environment. They do these things because it would cost money not to. Pollution by automobiles could surely be controlled at some expense and perhaps with some loss of performance. There are valuable raw materials in wornout automobile bodies; if economics made the mining of fresh ore as expensive as reclaiming used metals, our auto graveyards would vanish. No-return glass bottles are the thing today, and Federal law even prohibits the re-use of liquor bottles—thereby adding to the burden of trash. Even tin cans could have salvage value, as they did for a while during the tin shortage of World War II. The organic matter in garbage and sewage could be converted to fertilizers, but not at present competitive costs. Other wastes could be burned in smokeless incinerators and the heat could be made to do useful work, as is being done on a small scale in Europe.

Who Should Pay for Pollution?

Influencing all the foregoing choices we might make is the question: *Who should pay for pollution?* Our system now allows the public utility, the manufacturer, the chemical company and the incinerating firm to dump pollutants into the air at little or no cost. Other people pay the bill: the city government which must repair its roads and bridges and replace its trees far too often, and the emphysema sufferer who must frequent a doctor's office. If the bills for pollution were handed back to the *sources* of pollution, we might see some surprising improvements in the quality of our air. But such a system of social accounting, I hasten to point out, involves political and ethical decisions rather than purely technological ones.

Meanwhile, we are on a collision course with disaster. It is encouraging to know that we already have, or can develop, the technology to reverse our course. But it is disturbing to realize that we have not yet applied this technology in an effective way. We know how to regulate population size and how to do it economically. We could control pollution and even do a great deal to clean up our filthy and deteriorating environment—provided, of course, that we have not already made disaster inevitable by dooming some species on which the continuation of life depends or by burdening ourselves with a load of defective genes that will make future human generations inviable. Surely, man faces no more urgent problem than the need to save his environment. What will be required is intense collaboration by the best minds among biologists, physical scientists, sociologists, economists, political scientists, and policy makers!

Origin and Evolution of the Air

Evolution of the Earth's Atmosphere   8

S. I. RASOOL

We living things are a late outgrowth of the metabolism of our Galaxy. The carbon that enters so importantly into our composition was cooked in the remote past in a dying star. From it at lower temperatures nitrogen and oxygen were formed. These, our indispensable elements, were spewed out into space in the exhalations of red giants and such stellar catastrophes as super-novae, there to be mixed with hydrogen, to form eventually the substance of the sun and the planets, and ourselves. The waters of ancient seas set the pattern of ions in our blood. The ancient atmospheres molded our metabolism.

George Wald

The present composition of the earth's atmosphere is 78 percent nitrogen, 21 percent oxygen, and 1 percent argon, with traces of carbon dioxide, water vapor, and ozone. The atmospheres of Mars and Venus, on the other hand, are predominately composed of carbon dioxide, while those of Jupiter and Saturn contain mainly hydrogen, helium, methane, and ammonia. Such a wide variety in the composition of the atmospheres of the planets appears most intriguing when one considers that all nine planets were probably formed at the same time and out of the same chemically homogeneous mixture of gas and dust; that is, the primitive solar nebula.

The most likely explanation for this diversity in composition seems to be that the planetary atmospheres have undergone important evolutionary changes during their long history of about 4.5 billion years. On the earth, the evidence for such changes is manifold. Ever since Louis Pasteur demonstrated that spontaneous generation of life does not take place at the present time, it has become obvious that if life originated on the earth, as it probably did, the atmospheric conditions in the early history of the planet must have been quite different in order for the chemical evolution to have taken place. Also, it appears that relative to the sun, the earth is deficient by several orders of magnitude, not only in hydrogen and helium, which being the lightest can be assumed to have escaped from the gravitational field of the earth, but also in carbon, nitrogen, and the cosmically abundant rare gases (neon, argon-36, krypton, and xenon). A comparison of the deficiency factors of these elements with those of nonvolatiles such as sodium, magnesium, aluminum, and silicon, strongly suggests that the earth lost all elements which could have been gaseous at temperatures of a few hundred degrees during the very early history of the planet. The relatively small amounts of carbon, hydrogen, nitrogen, and oxygen now present in the crust, hydrosphere, and atmosphere were probably outgassed from the interior and accumulated slowly during the lifetime of the earth.

Both biochemical arguments and geological evidence, therefore, strongly suggest that the atmosphere of the earth has undergone major evolutionary changes during its long history. Whether the atmospheres of Mars and Venus have also gone through similar stages of evolution is a question which cannot be answered without more knowledge about their composition. Future *in situ* exploration of these planets and a search for the rare gases, especially neon which is deficient on earth by a factor of 10^{10}, will provide important clues to the origin of these atmospheres.

For the earth there is convincing evidence that the present atmosphere and hydrosphere arose largely from the interior by volcanic emanations. But the sequence of events which led to present-day composition of N_2 and O_2 has yet to be established. What is the history of volatiles now present at the surface of the earth? Has the carbon, nitrogen, oxygen, and hydrogen always been in the form of CO_2, N_2, H_2O, and H_2, or did carbon and nitrogen combine with hydrogen early in the earth's history to form CH_4 and NH_3? Under what atmospheric conditions did life originate on earth and how did the appearance of life change the atmosphere? These are some of the basic questions which must be answered in order to paint a coherent picture of the evolution of the earth's atmosphere. Opinions on these questions are many and varied. Sometimes they are almost diametrically opposed. The Oparin-Urey theory of the origin of life on the earth, supported by the laboratory experiments of Miller and, more recently, of Ponnamperuma, suggest a primitive atmosphere composed mainly of CH_4 with small amounts of NH_3, H_2, and H_2O vapor. On the other hand, the school of thought led by Abelson, and supported also by laboratory experiments on the synthesis of amino acids, holds that the early atmosphere of the earth was made up of CO_2, CO, H_2, N_2, and H_2O vapor.

Geologists are also divided on the subject. Holland has presented a model for the evolution of the atmosphere in which, during the very early stage after the formation of the earth and at the commencement of outgassing, the dominant gases could have been CH_4 and H_2, provided free hydrogen did not "escape" as rapidly as it does today. Rubey, on the other hand, believes that the early atmosphere was probably made of CO_2 and N_2 because not enough hydrogen was available to keep CH_4 from converting into CO_2. Holland's model is supported by the calculations of Rasool and McGovern, who have investigated the thermal properties of model primitive atmospheres of the earth. They find that in an atmosphere with a ratio percent of 99 CH_4 to 1 percent H_2 the average exospheric temperature may be as low as $650^\circ K$ (compared with the present-day value of $1500^\circ K$), thus making the escape of hydrogen a relatively slow phenomenon. However, Abelson has argued that if methane were abundant in the primitive atmosphere, the earliest rocks should contain unusual amounts of organic matter, which apparently is not the case.

Despite the disagreement over the composition of the primitive atmosphere, it is almost certain that it was devoid of free oxygen. How and when did free oxygen then become a major constituent of the atmosphere? The late Lloyd V. Berkner and L. C. Marshall have presented detailed calculations of the photochemistry of H_2O, indicating that free oxygen was limited to about 0.1 percent of the present atmospheric level during the entire prebiological history and accumulated slowly to the present amount since the start of photosynthesis about 800 million years ago. This theory is probably the most widely accepted explanation for the growth of oxygen in the earth's atmosphere. However, difficulties arise when one attempts to construct an evolutionary model of the atmosphere which would be consistent from the prebiological period to the present. For example, it is not well understood whether the small amount of O_2 suggested to be present in the primitive atmosphere would not be sufficient to rapidly oxidize CH_4 and NH_3 into CO_2 and N_2. It may be that the production of even this small amount of free oxygen in the upper atmosphere by the photodissociation of water vapor was inhibited by the presence of NH_3 itself.

The Atmospheres of Mars and Venus   9

VON R. ESHLEMAN

The atmosphere of Venus is hot and dense and the atmosphere of Mars is cold and thin.

Venus, the earth and Mars are within a factor or two of being the same distance from the sun and the same size. All three planets were doubtless formed from the same primordial source of matter at the same time. The atmospheres of all three appear to have been created after the initial supplies of light gases (hydrogen and helium) were largely lost to space. It is generally thought that these secondary atmospheres represent gases "exhaled" from the main body of the planet, with atmospheric evolution proceeeding for aeons to produce the markedly different conditions we find on the three planets today.

It has recently been suggested that if all life on the earth were destroyed, the atmosphere would slowly begin to change and eventually would resemble the atmosphere of either Venus or Mars.

The space probes to Mars and Venus have emphasized, I think, that biological processes themselves may play a more central role in the characteristics of planetary atmospheres than we have thought.

It would seem that our relative ignorance of the possible global effects of small changes in the composition and temperature of the earth's atmosphere should give us serious and immediate concern about man's use of the atmosphere as a garbage dump. In the past 100 years the percentage of atmospheric carbon dioxide has increased 15 percent, primarily owing to man's burning of fossil fuels. This same activity now uses 15 percent of the biological production of oxygen and in the future could become the major sink. Smog, jet contrails, deforestation and pollution of the earth's waters may affect the constituents and temperature of the atmosphere by only minute amounts, yet they may nonetheless have far-reaching consequences. Let us hope that continuing studies of the earth and its planetary neighbors will lead rapidly to a fuller understanding of planetary atmospheres in general. At the same time it behooves us to take strong steps to eliminate the known harmful effects of man's activities and to minimize those effects that are not yet fully understood. Whatever else we may wish to know, we hardly wish to test whether a lifeless earth would become like Mars or like Venus.

10   Perhaps Pollution Ruined Venus

JEFFREY D. ALDERMAN

When Apollo 132 lands on Venus in the year, say, 2,000, what will man find?

The duller members of the scientific community say he will find a lifeless planet shrouded in lethal gases such as carbon monoxide.

Carbon monoxide? Yep, the very same stuff that billows from every automobile exhaust pipe here on earth.

And this coincidence has not gone unnoticed by some of the more imaginative scientists. These men theorize that Venus may once have had life but that it was done in by a gigantic case of air polution.

Could it be, as these learned men suggest, that the noxious fumes weren't always there? Was the air there once as fresh as it is here on earth?

Perhaps when man sets foot on Venus he will find the remains of a society that perished in an atmosphere that strangled life.

Perhaps he'll see Venusian streets littered with skeletons, their bony hands either clutching at their throats or reaching hopelessly toward gasmasks they carried with them.

He may see a 400-mile traffic jam that never unjammed, with dead drivers behind each steering wheel and air conditioners switched to "on" position.

An inspection of the Venusian congress may reveal a bill which died in committee, to outlaw gas-powered vehicles in favor of electric ones. Another bill passed over might be one for control of water pollution, industrial wastes and sewage. Still another might have preserved the planet's only forest—at the end, only two scrub pines and a weeping willow.

The Venusian monetary system undoubtedly would have been based on the most precious element on the planet, oxygen. Venusian alchemists would have spent all their time trying to turn soot into either oxygen or the planet's second most precious element, water. Only the rich could have afforded the ultimate Venusian vacation—two weeks in an oxygen tent.

Perhaps an old political campaign banner saying "A chicken in every pot and a gasmask on every face," would be found.

The planet would have one garbage dump, stretching over half the Venusian surface. The other half would be a large, crowded city.

The weather forecast in the final edition of the Venus Times would read: "Temperature inversion will raise thermometer to record 515 degrees. Four-foot soot-fall expected overnight."

And will man, as he surveys the wreck that was Venus, feel contempt for the Venusians much as he does now for the departed dinosaur?

Probably.

And perhaps another writer at another time, looking down on earth from a planet circling a distant star, will wonder about the noxious fumes obscuring earth and speculate whether there was once life here.

Effects on Wilderness

A classic example of the effect of polluted air on wilderness is the 1,300,000 ponderosa pine trees dead or dying from Los Angeles smog. Before that time the public had considered air pollution a city problem and something that you escape from when you enter the wilderness. Dr. Machta (reading 11) dispels that myth.

Winds, Pollution, and the Wilderness   11

LESTER MACHTA

Wilderness stands as a splendid sanctuary from human encroachment on the ground, but no barriers can exclude wind-borne pollution. Man can clean up the atmosphere if he is willing to pay the price, but we foresee no way of modifying the winds to spare a favored region.

The concentrations of air pollutants are almost always smaller far from a city, as in a wilderness, than nearby. But this absolute level of contamination is only one measure of comparison of urban to wilderness harm. Society accepts urban pollution and the use of pesticides because these grew slowly and seem inextricably bound to a higher standard of living. Some of the modern technology, such as pesticides, have been used in the wilderness. But, in contrast to the city dweller, man-made air-borne pollutants from afar yield very few benefits to balance their cost to those enjoying a wilderness.

It is often not appreciated that gaseous and fine particulate matter injected into the atmosphere remains there until scavenging processes or chemical reactions remove it. Proof of the pervasiveness of air-borne pollution as a global problem was dramatically illustrated by radioactive fallout over every part of the earth, land and sea, pole to pole, from nuclear tests exploded at very few locations. Most commonly, pollutants are washed out of the air in rain and snow, but this contaminates soil, lakes, and rivers, usually remote from the source of pollution. The reason some imagine that the atmosphere can be used as a boundless sewer is its tremendous volume, which swallows the pollutants and usually dilutes them to acceptable levels. The atmosphere is indeed enormous, containing about five million trillion tons of air. But as we have discovered in the past few decades, even this vast envelope of air is insufficient to cope with man's ability to produce ever larger amounts of pollutants.

Our early atmosphere contained virtually no oxygen, but much more carbon dioxide than now exists. Green life converted carbon dioxide to its "waste," oxygen, producing the present 20 per cent oxygen. But man, particularly during the past 80 years of industrialization, has now reversed the process. His burning of fossil fuels—coal and oil—stored from the past has now raised the present carbon dioxide content of the air over 10 percent since the end of the last century. Each year the clean atmosphere increases its carbon dioxide content by about one-quarter of a percent, according to records at Mauna Loa, Hawaii, and at Antarctica. This growth rate is only half the estimated release rate from burning of fuels; the remaining half of the output is absorbed mainly by the oceans. More carbon dioxide in the air is not necessarily detrimental; trees and other plants can grow faster in the presence of higher concentrations.

There is special concern about the growth of carbon dioxide in the air because of its vital importance in establishing the heat balance of the atmosphere. As the carbon dioxide increases so should the temperature in the lower atmosphere, by blanketing outgoing radiation from the earth—the "greenhouse" effect. Fortunately, recent calculations suggest that the warming from increased carbon dioxide should be very small. During the first half of the twentieth century, there has been, in fact, a gradual small warming, but this trend has been replaced over the past twenty years by a slight cooling. It is speculated that this latter effect may also be attributed to pollution in the form of increased dustiness which, by reflecting and scattering sunlight back to space, cools the lower atmosphere. The greater dustiness may have counteracted the warming due to increased carbon dioxide. Some observations in non-urban environments show increases with time in atmospheric turbidity or dustiness; similar measurements in urban regions reveal higher turbidity than nearby rural areas. One must be cautious in necessarily blaming climatic trends on human activities; there have also been climatic fluctuations before 1900 when human intervention was less likely.

The more important aspect of air pollution to a wilderness comes from sources immediately upwind, rather than undergoing global dilution. Certain topographic and weather features might provide some protection for the wilderness, but in general, there is little to impede the air-borne plume from a factory chimney or a DDT aerial spray blowing to an otherwise inaccessible region. The wind speeds in the lower atmosphere typically blow 5 to 25 miles per hour. Thus wilderness areas many tens of miles from a city or farm can be affected by wind-borne pollution within a few hours. During this travel time, the pollutants are diluted and often depleted. Dilution is accompanied by both horizontal and vertical mixing. Horizontal mixing reduces concentrations near a plume center, but a wider area contains low concentrations. Vertical mixing of contaminants from low altitude sources carries pollution aloft and is always beneficial in reducing ground level concentrations. The wind direction is variable. Thus, pollution from a single source may reach a wilderness only infrequently. But as industrialization grows, pesticide usage increases, and new roads ring the wilderness, the frequency of successively higher levels of pollution can be expected, since winds from many directions will bring pollution to the wilderness.

Topographic barriers such as mountains and special weather patterns frequently impede atmospheric mixing. It is clear that the air within a valley cannot mix horizontally beyond the valley walls. This is evident to aircraft passengers observing smoke from chimneys meander within the natural terrain channels, like river beds. Some of the more infamous air pollution episodes have occurred within or downwind of industrialized valleys: The Donora, Pennsylvania, and the Trail, British Columbia cases, for example.

But of greater significance, because it changes, is the lid that nature can impose to impede vertical mixing. Normally, the temperature decreases with altitude; the greater the decrease the more vigorous the up-and-down mixing. But under certain weather situations one finds a temperature increase with height (called an inversion), sometimes at the ground but more often aloft, lasting for many days. This inversion inhibits upward mixing through it. When the mixing lid lies below about 5,000 feet, the pollution from many of the current massive sources cannot be diluted adequately to maintain acceptable air quality levels at the ground. This latter circumstance is common to the California coastal area and is one of the prime reasons why Los Angeles smog is so notorious.

There is a world-wide "lid" to up-down mixing called the tropopause, located at about 35,000 feet over the United States. About 75 per cent of the mass of the atmosphere lies below 35,000 feet. Pollutants released to the air take a few days to a few weeks to mix up to the tropopause, and in that time the horizontal winds keep the air in roughly the same band of latitudes as it started in. This is unfortunate because both the maximum industrialization and population lie in the temperate latitudes, say between 25° and 60°N. Air pollutants may stay in the same latitudinal band blowing around the world from west to east, mixing with three-quarters of the depth of air for up to a few months. For these meteorological reasons, not all of the atmospheric volume is available to dilute wastes released during the preceding few months.

The combination of channelling within valleys and imperfect vertical mixing produces particularly undesirable air pollution conditions. It has been found that some of the oxidants, components of smog created photochemically in the Los Angeles basin and contained below the mixing lid, channel through the Rim Forest of the San Bernardino Pass. Here one finds ponderosa pine with burned tips identical to those produced from controlled exposure to observed oxidant levels. The Rim Forest lies 4,400 feet above and four miles north of the city of San Bernardino, and over fifty miles from downtown Los Angeles. As another example, scientists at La Jolla, California, note a marked increase in carbon dioxide as a murky pall approaches from the north, capped below the mixing lid and sliding along the coastal mountain range. The source of the pollution again is the Los Angeles Basin, eighty miles to the north.

While the weather and the temperature inversions along the California coast are somewhat unique, other meteorological patterns can create persistent inversions over almost any part of the United States. The slow moving, light wind, high pressure weather system has been recognized as an air pollution culprit over both the eastern and western United States. In the east it is most common in the southern Appalachian Mountains, over the Great Smoky Mountains, in fact, and in the west over the Great Basin. The Smoky Mountains were named in colonial times because of the blue haze produced by atmospheric reactions involving turpenes from the trees. Nowadays, man's wastes add to those of nature. The prevalence of reduced visibility due to either source is a consequence of weather conditions in the southern Appalachian Mountains. The eastern high pressure systems or anticyclones are most frequent in October. Before the advent of pollution, man would eagerly look forward to their onset in October as beautiful Indian summers. Today, the sluggish anticyclones can be recognized by the air traveler by a layer of dirty air with a sharp top covering many thousands of square miles for several days. Since there are usually few clouds associated with an anticyclone, the abundant sunshine may produce photochemical smog of the Los Angeles variety to add to other pollutants. The light winds drift about aimlessly rather than follow the prevailing flow. A wilderness may be covered by air with attendant pollution from many diverse sources tens to hundreds of miles away.

The downwind decrease of pollutant concentration results from chemical reactions as well as from dilution. These atmospheric reactions which transform a given pollutant to another substance are complex and, by and large, imperfectly understood. Lest one imagine that such reactions are necessarily beneficial, one ought quickly to note at least two which are not. The photochemical oxidants of the Los Angeles smog start out as oxides of nitrogen, hydrocarbons, and other compounds, none of which are necessarily as toxic as the ozone, and other oxidants which they and sunlight produce. Sulfur dioxide oxidizes and its products react with water to form sulfuric acid. In many ways, the acid is more deleterious than the original gaseous sulfur dioxide and water.

The prime means by which the atmosphere cleanses itself is through precipitation scavenging—the removal of impurities by rain and snow. The deposition of pollutants in rainwater can cause damage far from the source. For example, in southern Sweden, during the past ten years, the rainwater and the lakes and rivers which it feeds have exhibited a dramatic increase of acidity. The once prosperous salmon industry is now almost extinct and there is concern over ancient stone monuments. The cause is thought to be sulfuric acid in rainwater from sulfur dioxide coming from heavily industrialized northwest Europe, probably over 100 miles away. Certain contaminants, like sulfates and artificial radioactivity, are observed in rainwater all over the world. They and others have been changed from an air to a soil or water contaminant and can enter humans and animals via food rather than inhalation. A second and largely unexplored mode of removal of dust from the atmosphere is filtration of air passing through forests. Conifers with their sticky needles are especially effective filters.

The details of the mechanism of washout of contaminants have been, and continue to be, a lively subject of research.

It may be surprising that some gases are also removed by falling water droplets. After pollutants have mixed vertically through many thousands of feet, it is found that, on the average, the lifetime of a typical pollutant particle is about two to four weeks. Within this time, if you will recall, the pollution from the industrialized temperate latitudes can remain in the same geographical band. Thus, the wastes from man's activities both contaminate the air and fall back to earth in the same general band of latitude in which they started.

The transport of pollution to a living wilderness is not purely theoretical; living things will respond, most often unfavorably, to such intrusion. The varied response of flora and fauna to pollution could occupy many pages in this journal; for our purposes, a few examples may be cited.

Michael Treshow in the August 1968 volume of *Phytopathology* states:

The historical record, as well as our own studies, have demonstrated how air pollution can entirely destroy vast acreages of sensitive vegetation. One classic illustration of devastation wrought by air pollutants is in the Copper Basin area of Tennessee, where about 7,000 acres of once rich deciduous forest were completely denuded and another 17,000 acres replaced with grassland species following the destruction of the native forest species. Gully erosion stripped away the soil, and even the climate was altered. The mean monthly maximum air temperature was up to 3.5 F higher, and rainfall nearly 10 per cent less, in the bare area. Timber and watersheds were similarly decimated in areas surrounding the town of Trail, B.C.; in Ontario, Canada; and in Anaconda, Mont., where sulfur oxides again were present in concentrations lethal to dominant conifers. In another incident, fluorides were reported to have been responsible for the needle burning and death of ponderosa pine over a 50-square-mile area near Spokane, Wash. Pine was eliminated as a dominant species in the immediate vicinity of the operations.

Sometimes the identification of pollution as the subtle damaging agent requires detective work. Dochinger reports that a white pine disease called chlorotic dwarf in the Northeast, Central, and Lake States has puzzled pathologists for the past 60 years. Certain trees in a stand appear to be congenital runts; the disease has been attributed to fungi, unfavorable soil, and a virus. Only recently has he demonstrated the damage to be due to air pollution.

Examples of the damage to fauna are equally numerous. In this case, it is not only the effluents from urbanization and industrialization but the pesticides and herbicides which are equally if not more at fault. Many animals and birds are capable of concentrating certain pollutants found in low concentrations in the environment. The widespread grazing habits of reindeer have introduced far more cesium-137, a product of nuclear testing, into their muscle tissue than was expected. Dead and dying robins had between three and twenty times more DDT in the residues of their brains as in the leaves that formed the source of food for the earthworms that, in turn, were eaten by the robins.

A Government report, "Restoring the Quality of Our Environment," states: "Such herbicides, though providing beneficial effects in agricultural regions, may produce serious adverse effects in natural communities, in state and national parks, and other areas dedicated to recreational purposes."

The tale of destruction from air pollution can continue almost endlessly. But it must be recognized that in the foreseeable future the solution lies in pollution control, not weather control. One cannot erect fences around the wilderness to restrain the winds. The cure for air pollution in the wilderness is the same as elsewhere: limit the emissions at the sources.

Smog and the Automobile

Although the word "smog" was coined in London to describe the clammy mixture of fog and smoke from the burning of soft coal, it is now also used to describe the photochemical effects on automobile exhaust in Los Angeles, Mexico City, Tokyo and all large cities. To make predictions about the control of polluted air in cities we could look at Los Angeles as the model of a city which happens to be "running hard and standing still," in spite of the Clean Air Act of 1970 and California's high air quality standards.

In our search for solutions to air pollution we must choose to have fewer petroleum-powered automobiles, stricter emmission standards, or both. Among approaches currently under consideration are: (1) control the conventional engine (reading 12); (2) permit only electric cars (reading 13) and control pollution where the electricity is generated; (3) introduce a steam-mobile (reading 14); or (4) employ other fuels such as natural gas, or methanol (reading 15). Each of these solutions has its own inherent problems.

12   Automobile Engines
Pollution and Power

ISRAEL KATZ

Almost everything that was done over the past 40 years to improve engine performance, such as increasing the power-volume ratio, raising the compression ratio, extending the valve overlap, increasing the crankshaft speed, and improving the resistance of engine parts to high combustion temperatures, has also contributed to contamination. Yet, I believe that we would be unwilling to compromise the present performance, reliability, and speed flexibility of the automotive engine to reduce the atmospheric pollutants issuing from the engine's exhaust. Despite the numerous gadgets proposed to cope with the problem, about the only thing that would really do the trick without penalizing performance is to go back to much larger engines with lower compression ratios and deliberately design them to run at about one-half present peak mean effective pressures and crankshaft speeds. Of course, this solution would currently be as unacceptable on economic grounds as the automotive diesel refined to eliminate its characteristic noise and roughness during acceleration.

About 20 years ago some of the then latest turbosupercharged aircraft piston engines utilizing internal cooling, direct injection, and dual valve timing (such as in the Lycoming 7755) as a function of load had the sophistication required to offset the degrading effects of high compression ratios and high piston speeds on incomplete combustion, but the amounts of tetraethyl lead to suppress knock and sodium di-bromide useful in the fuel to get rid of the metallic lead deposits in the combustion space made the exhaust efflux lethal. The problem in those days was to build an engine that would operate reliably in the Berlin airlift rather than keep the atmosphere clean. In the late 40's I ran some large turbo-compound engines of this kind at Cornell as well as at Pratt & Whitney Aircraft and found surprisingly low level of carbon monoxide in the exhaust during operation below 80 percent of full load at all speeds. In the early 50's, I witnessed the "Texaco Combustion Process" engine, which seemed unusually indifferent to octane rating. The engine ran on almost anything. My recollection is that I wasn't particularly impressed with the combustion chamber design and privately predicted nothing would come of it. Nevertheless, I recall that the design permitted a form of air-fuel mixing that promoted detonation resistance and might be worth another look from the standpoint of lowering atmospheric contamination from fuel additives, but I doubt whether the CO level would be reduced. Virtually every method for reducing pollution would introduce serious performance penalties.

I do not think that the automotive steam engine (even if somehow run condensing) would be especially attractive either in terms of economy or the instant response required of characteristic stop-and-go driving as well as of sudden accelerations as in high speed passing. Therefore, I doubt whether there is a truly practical solution to the pollution problem without inordinate costs to the car operator.

The Car   13
An Electric Challenge

TIME MAGAZINE

Silent, exhaust-free and otherwise kind to the environment. Powered by an simple motor that is 90% efficient. Easy to handle. Inexpensive to maintain.

Does this description fit some future vehicle that is still beyond man's technological grasp? It does not. [In 1969,] twelve shiny versions of this ideal car were lined up for public inspection at the first International Electric Vehicle Symposium in Phoenix, Ariz. Some of the models were familiar Volkswagens and Renaults, converted to run on battery power. Others were brand new and strange looking. General Electric unveiled its squat, three-door "Delta," which looks like a stylized descendant of the Jeep. Not to be outdone, Westinghouse showed off a sleek "Lotus Europa" sports car. Ford had a streamlined "Lead Wedge" that has whirred across Utah's salt flats at 138 m.p.h. Two Japanese electric cars were on display along with a British minicar costing about $1,000 and already in production.

The new era in transporation that such vehicles promise will be somewhat delayed. The one obstacle that keeps the electric car little more than a conversation piece and unable to compete with conventional automobiles is not the motor but the battery. As many as 16 expensive, low-energy-density batteries are needed to make an electric car go. Together they weigh the car down and completely fill what is now trunk space. More serious, no electric car can cruise much farther than 80 miles or longer than a few hours without having to stop to be recharged.

To create a new battery that would enable the electrics to match the performance of conventional cars, says Dr. J.H.B. George of Arthur D. Little, Inc., would take "hundreds of millions of dollars in a crash research program, or 50 to 100 years." As an alternate solution, G.E.'s Bruce Laumeister reckons, it is now possible to recharge today's batteries in a few minutes—but only with heavy-duty circuits and chargers that cost far more than the car itself.

Such glum speculation about electric cars is brightly optimistic compared with the realistic analysis of Economist Bruce C. Netschert, director of National Economic Research Associates. He bluntly points out that the U.S. economy is geared directly to the mighty internal-combustion engine. Conversion of the nation's 101 million vehicles to electricity, even if possible, would cause nothing less than an economic trauma.

The automobile industry could probably adapt to electric cars, but it would be a painful and costly process. For one thing, since electric cars tend to be extremely durable, "planned obsolescence" would itself become obsolete. For another, the new cars, to minimize the drain on their batteries, would have to be light, small and free of many of today's high-profit accessories. As for the oil industry, Netschert figures that it would lose fully half its market.

Does the combination of technical and economic problems mean that the electric passenger car will never come to be? Manufacturers do not seem to be discouraged. They are trying to develop better batteries while producing more and more electric golf carts, lift trucks, minibuses, industrial sweepers and postal delivery vans.

Meanwhile, the advantages of electric vehicles are being gradually recognized. Even better, the oil and automobile industries, aware of the rising tide of anti-pollution sentiment, and hearing the gentle sound of electric motors (and possibly steam engines) in the future, have already started projects to stay ahead of the competition. Ironically, by the time the electric car becomes competitive, the conventional car will probably be silent, fumeless, durable, small and less harmful to the environment.

14   Steam Automobiles
Advocates Seek Government Support for Research

ANDREW JAMISON

In May, [1968,] the Senate Committee on Commerce and the Public Works Committee's Subcommittee on Air and Water Pollution held joint hearings on the steam car. The hearings generally concentrated on one point: should the government subsidize research and development in an industry that traditionally has financed its own activities. Representatives from the automobile companies said such action would be undesirable and unnecessary. Proponents of steam cars said that in the interests of cleaner air, government support was essential.

So far the government has shown an unwillingness to subsidize research and development of steam cars, electric cars, or any other low-pollutant vehicles. Its position, as expressed by a Department of Transportation spokesman, has been to "leave it all to private enterprise." And private enterprise's position, as expressed by Henry Ford II and others, has been all but to ignore steam-powered vehicles because, as auto company spokesmen have candidly stated, they have a huge investment in the internal combustion engine. Ford and General Motors are conducting research on steam cars, but, as attested to at the Senate hearings, they feel that their most advantageous approach to pollution problems is the development of better emission controls for internal combustion engines.

The steam proponents testified, however, that internal combustion engines could never reach the low emission levels of steam engines without impractical and cumbersome controls. Charles and Calvin Williams, two steam engine manufacturers who have spent over 20 years developing steam vehicles, took Senator Edmund S. Muskie (D—Me.) and Senator Howard H. Baker (R—Tenn.) for a ride in their steam car. They said that their car had been tested for emissions of pollutants after 25,000 miles. It had produced a hydrocarbon level of 20 parts per million, a carbon monoxide level of 0.3 percent, and a nitrogen oxides level of 35 ppm. By comparison, the standards recently set for 1970 vehicles by the Department of Health, Education, and Welfare are 275 ppm for hydrocarbons, 1.5 percent for carbon monoxide, and 1500 ppm for nitrogen oxides. Even the Ford representative said that he found it difficult to envision a way to reduce the internal combustion engine emissions to the level already reached by steam cars. "Low emission is not an option with steam power," Charles Williams told the senators, "it is built in, requiring no 'clean air packages,' expensive catalytic mufflers, or other devices whose complexity requires tuning and maintenance."

This testimony led Muskie, chairman of the Subcommittee for Air and Water Pollution, to take a fairly critical view of the pleas the auto manufacturers made in behalf of the internal combustion engine. Muskie contended that the commitment to the standard engine was based on investment, consumer acceptance, and consumer familiarity, rather than on any actual superiority. "Doesn't all this," Muskie concluded, "add to the momentum of the status quo in a way that may run counter to the public interest?"

By their own admission the automotive companies have not expended the same time, energy, and commitment to steam car research that the "other side" —the steam car advocates—have. The companies' research has been minimal, and it has been heavily biased against steam cars. Ford and GM representatives contend that boiler explosions occur frequently in steam cars. They told the Senate Committee that steam vehicles would also be more cumbersome, expensive, and less efficient than the internal combustion vehicles. The proponents of steam presented an opposite picture. They said that their cars would be cheaper, less complicated mechanically, and safer. Not only were boiler explosions a thing of the past, they said, but the steam car's need for less fuel and less flammable fuels at that, make it safer than an internal combustion vehicle. In addition, they argued, the steam car would produce practically no pollutants, and would be relatively silent. The Williams brothers said that, with some financial support, their cars could compete favorably in terms of performance with the present internal combustion vehicles.

Steam cars have come a long way since the days of the old Stanley Steamer. The Williams car, for example, can reach speeds of up to 100 miles per hour, and takes less than 30 seconds to start up in any weather. It does away with many of the parts of the internal combustion vehicles, having no need for a carburetor, muffler, distributor, or air-pollution control equipment. It also employs a much simpler transmission and starter. However, steam cars have components that the internal combustion engine does not need, such as a boiler and combustion controls. Many of the basic components are the same for both, however—such as the pistons, cylinders, crankcase, and valves—so that, on a mass scale, there should not be a great deal of difference in price between the two; steam proponents actually claim that theirs would be significantly cheaper to produce. The Williams car can use any distillate fuel to heat the water, although kerosene has been standard. It averages about 30 miles per gallon of kerosene, and can go about 500 miles on 10 gallons of water; seepage causes the need for refilling. Although the Williams brothers claim that they use regular tap water and have had success with it, they admit that distilled water is, in the long run, better for the engine.

However, without government support, steam cars face difficulty. Lloyd D. Orr, professor of economics at Indiana University, told the senators that economic factors, such as resistance to change and so-called barriers to entry, including the high capital commitment necessary to establish a new automotive corporation, all play a part in keeping the steam producers from successfully competing with the internal combustion manufacturers. Theodore Johnson, executive vice president of Thermo Electron Corporation, a company that has tried to work with the motor companies in producing steam engines possibly for boats and golf carts, raised another point. He said that "consumers today do not perceive freedom from pollution in the exhaust of a vehicle as a desirable feature for which they are willing to pay very much."

In the past, Congress has generously provided money for projects considered necessary to the defense of the country. This is why the government took such an active role in the development of the aircraft industry. Congress has been much more wary of supporting projects that are not defense oriented. There have been exceptions, prominent among them being agriculture and health-related activities. But, in most nondefense cases, the government has not been in direct competition with corporations conducting research along similar lines, as it would be if it supported steam car research and development.

15   Methanol
A New Fuel?

RONALD G. MINET

The chemical process used to convert fuel gas, petroleum fractions, or even coal to methanol is essentially the same as the process used for production of ammonia. In both, the original raw material is converted to a mixture of carbon monoxide and hydrogen which is then further processed to produce the desired final product. The efficiency of conversion is approximately the same in both cases, and a substantial fraction of the carbon originally present in the fossil fuel disappears from the system as carbon dioxide. In the case of ammonia, all of the carbon is separated in this manner; with methanol, about two-thirds is removed.

The cost of erected facilities for the production of ammonia or methanol are roughly comparable. Once very large plants are designed for producing methanol, the relative simplicity possible in handling the product as compared with the requirements for liquifying and pressurizing the ammonia product will probably result in an advantage in the overall investment cost. Methanol can be stored at atmospheric pressure under all normal conditions and can be readily shipped by pipeline, by normal tank car, or tank truck. Because of its very low freezing point and low viscosity, it can be used easily for all conventional fuel requirements.

It is interesting to note that, with some adjustment to the carburetor, methanol can be used as a fuel in ordinary internal combustion engines. It is a completely clean fuel requiring no additives, lead, or other constituents which tend to aggravate atmospheric pollution problems. Of course, it would be essential that the internal combustion engine be adjusted properly to avoid formation of oxygenated hydrocarbon compounds in the exhaust gases.

Of even more interest is the possibility of utilizing methanol directly as a fuel for a direct conversion fuel cell. Substantial work in this direction has been carried out at Institute Francais du Petrole where demonstration cells have already been built and operated for many thousands of hours. Use of methanol in this manner would permit a ready transition from hydrocarbon fuels inside of city areas with a gradual replacement of internal combustion engines by electric motors powered by fuel cells.

Production of methanol could be taken over completely by large energy companies currently refining petroleum and distributing hydrocarbon fuels. The investment required to produce enough methanol to replace all existing fuels would certainly be extremely high, but may not be out of proportion to that required for producing low-sulfur conventional fuels such as is being required by legislation currently being enacted throughout the country.

Sulfur Pollution

Diminishing the Role of Sulfur Oxides in Air Pollution

16

PHILIP H. ABELSON

Each year, in the United States, more than 20 million tons of sulfur are discharged into the atmosphere, most of it in the form of SO_2. This gas is slowly converted into sulfuric acid, which is corrosive to many materials, including metals, building stones, and clothing. The toxicity of SO_2 and H_2SO_4 to plants and animals is controversial, as is the effect of these compounds when they are inhaled along with other components of smog. Because of the complexities of long-term and synergistic effects, many years must elapse before precise conclusions can be reached concerning the role of the sulfur compounds. In the meantime, the public is becoming impatient with slow progress made in overcoming air pollution. Already, in various cities restrictions are being placed on the amount of sulfur fuel may contain.

Principal targets for such restrictions are electric power generating plants. These are a major source of air pollutants when they use coal or residual oil as fuel. Coal, the principal fuel, contains various quantities of sulfur; a typical amount is 3 percent. Concern about air pollution has been a factor in the sudden acceptance of nuclear energy. Unless the pollution problems attending the use of coal are solved, the coal industry will face a gloomy future, caused in part by regulation, in part by competition from other energy sources.

Five means of meeting the sulfur pollution problem seem feasible. One is to use fuel containing only small amounts of sulfur. A second is to discharge the fumes from tall smokestacks (more than 200 meters high). If stacks are tall enough to pierce the inversion layer, the pollutants are thoroughly diluted before reaching the ground. A third method is to add a material such as powdered limestone to the flue-gas stream, following combustion, to convert the gaseous sulfur oxides into a solid form. A fourth is to convert the coal to gas and to remove the sulfur from the gas prior to combustion. A fifth method, which seems very interesting, is to pass the flue gases through a chemical processing plant, the sulfur being recovered in elemental form or as H_2SO_4. A number of variants of this method are under investigation.

Both sulfur and the H_2SO_4 are consumed on a large scale. The price of sulfur has advanced sharply during the last year and is currently quoted at close to $50 a ton. With present technology the value of the sulfur recovered from coal-fired power plants would about offset the cost of investment and operation of the processing plants. A combination of better technology with a higher price for sulfur may eventually convert a nuisance into a valued asset.

Legislation

Has our air improved in quality since the much-ballyhooed legislation of 1967? Worsened in quality? "Held its own"? How many major industries have been or are now involved in lawsuits arising out of their refusal to stop vandalizing the atmosphere? What are some of the fines being paid? Are they substantial enough to convince potential offenders that pollution is a bad investment? Can we expect a marked improvement in our air? When? Ever? How?

17   # Air Quality Act of 1967

SENATE REPORT

"The Air Quality Act of 1967 . . . serves notice that no one has the right to use the atmosphere as a garbage dump, and that there will be no haven for polluters anywhere in the country."

OIL IN THE ECOSYSTEM

The running aground of the tanker "Torrey Canyon" and the Santa Barbara blowout demonstrate—and through their notoriety have come to symbolize—the two major ways oil enters an ecosystem and some of the cruel consequences which follow. Tankers are getting larger and tanker traffic is increasing. The Oil Spill Panel has pointed out that if drilling continues at the present rate, by 1980 there will be 3,000 to 5,000 new offshore wells each year and a major pollution incident will occur annually. The blowout in the Santa Barbara channel alone spilled from one to three million gallons of oil into the ecosystem.

Plans to exploit the oil supplies recently discovered in Alaska has led to the threat of a third major way oil could enter the ecosystem, pipeline leaks or breaks. The consortium of seven oil companies, Alyeska Co., planning to build the 800 mile, 48 inch diameter pipeline from Prudhoe Bay on the Arctic Coast to Valdez on Prince William Sound, has been stopped. Even after three years of study, the Company does not yet know how to prevent major disasters.

Environmentalists asked for a five-year moratorium on construction, noting that earthquake fault zones were not well known in the area, the effect of the pipeline on permafrost needed more study, and a better system for the detection of oil leaks was necessary.

Reporting in *Science,* October, 1969, Luther J. Carter warned:

During 1968 nearly 500 oil pipeline leaks, each involving a loss of 50 barrels or more, occurred in the United States, and about a fifth of those were spills between 1,000 and 12,000 barrels. The pipes involved in these spills were mostly in the 8 to 12-inch range, and none was larger than 20 inches. The 48-inch trans-Alaska pipeline will be the largest ever built, and, at capacity, will carry 500,000 gallons of oil per mile.

Questions concerning the effects of the pipeline and the road projects necessary to maintain it were not seriously considered by the government. Some of these questions have been raised by George Marshall, brother of Robert Marshall, author and explorer of the central Brooks Range.

(Reading 21)

18   # Pollution
The Wake of the "Torrey Canyon"

JOHN WALSH

London. When the tanker *Torrey Canyon* ran aground near the southwest tip of England, it gave its name to a new kind of maritime disaster, the cost of which is counted not in human life but in widespread economic and ecological damage. This in part accounts for the special efforts subsequently made to assess the implications of the accident.

The government was criticized, for example, for waiting a full 10 days before ordering an attempt by aerial bombing to burn oil still left in the tanker. First the government hoped the ship might be refloated or the oil might be transferred. Then there were doubts that the oil could be effectively released by bombing, ignited, and kept alight. And Britain, as a major maritime nation, was reluctant to take a step such as bombing while the salvagers held out hopes and so many questions about responsibility were unanswered.

Pollution of the English coast by oil is a perennial problem. What was unprecedented was the scale of pollution threatened by the *Torrey Canyon,* loaded with 117,000 tons of Kuwait crude oil. Exposed to the threat were the beaches of the southern coasts of England, Britain's principal holiday area. Very heavy pressure was immediately exerted to "save the beaches."

With first priority given to safeguarding coastal amenities, the reflex action was to employ measures developed by the Navy in dealing with oil spills in harbors. This meant using detergents to emulsify and disperse the oil. Some 10,000 tons (2 million gallons) of detergents were used to treat 13,000 tons of oil on Cornish beaches, and another half million gallons were sprayed at sea.

In its effects on marine life this detergent "cure" proved much more damaging than the oil itself. The chief conclusion of the Plymouth Laboratory study is that, except for serious effects on some species of sea birds, the oil was not lethal to flora and fauna. Detergents used to disperse the oil, on the other hand, were highly toxic to marine life, most conspicuously to intertidal life such as limpets and barnacles. In the open sea, detergents in quantities as small as one part detergent per million parts of seawater proved lethal to planktonic growth.

Toxic Effects

Detergents used in spraying operations are mixtures of several compounds —a surfactant (or surface-active agent), an organic solvent, and a stabilizer. A stable emulsion of oil and water was necessary if the oil was to be dispersed. Solvents which enable the surfactants to mix with oil to form an emulsion contain a high proportion of aromatic hydrocarbons. Research indicated that the detergents with the highest proportion of aromatics are the best emulsifiers, and also the most toxic to flora and fauna.

Spraying of a half-million gallons of such detergent could be expected to have a devastating effect on plankton living near the surface of the water. Biologists reported surprisingly little damage to planktonic organisms in the spraying area.

The explanation, they suggest, is that toxic aromatics evaporate very rapidly from the surface of seawater. Otherwise, as the report puts it, "the biological consequences in the English Channel would have been vastly worse than they were."

The worst sufferers from the oil were sea birds; the heaviest casualties were suffered by diving birds—guillemots, razorbills, cormorants, and shags. Gulls seem to have learned to avoid oil, and very few were affected. Ornithologists have reported a decline in the number of auks and other diving birds breeding on southern British coasts in the last 30 years and have attributed it to oil pollution. Total casualties of the *Torrey Canyon* oil were estimated at 20,000 guillemots and 5000 razorbills. A sad aspect of the oil fouling of sea birds was the failure of rescue operations. The British are unrivaled bird lovers, and a big effort at cleaning birds was made by the government and by voluntary agencies and individuals. But of nearly 8000 birds recorded as treated, only 450 were alive by mid-April and only about 1 percent of the birds treated were expected to be returned to the sea.

Little Effect on Seals

Contrary to some predictions, effects on offshore fisheries seem to have been negligible. The seal population does not appear to be seriously affected, although some breeding caves were badly polluted by oil and scientists suggest that ill effects may become apparent later. No commercial shellfish ground was affected by oil, as such grounds were in France, and care was taken not to spray detergent near such beds.

France's battle with *Torrey Canyon* oil was different from Britain's, in part because the French had more time and perhaps because they profited from the British experience. The main difference was that the French shunned detergents. Oil came ashore on the coast of Brittany in higher concentrations than in most parts of Cornwall, but the French relied on mechanical means of removal and such natural effects as waves, tides, and bacterial degradation. Oil did do considerable damage to Breton shellfish beds, but these are expected to recover. At sea, a big patch of oil in the Bay of Biscay was successfully treated with powdered chalk. The chalk binds the oil into particles which sink to the bottom. The French estimate that 3000 tons of chalk will sink 20,000 tons of oil.

The two British reports give the impression that, after the accident, luck was with the defenders. A northerly wind blew for nearly 2 months afterward, at a time of year when the wind normally blows from the southwest. Under normal conditions much more oil would have come ashore, instead of being blown out to sea. It even appears that if the bombing and the burning of oil aboard the *Torrey Canyon* had been done earlier, a lot of unburned residue would have ended up on the beaches. The immediate costs of the wreck to Britain (estimated at £3 million), the setback to the tourist industry, and the damage to coastal ecology all could have been devastatingly increased if even half the oil in the *Torrey Canyon's* tanks had come ashore.

Research Needed

The Zuckerman committee asks that better means be developed for transferring cargo from disabled tankers and for destroying or dispersing oil at sea.

Detergents should be used judiciously, and less toxic detergents should be developed, both reports agree. And more research needs to be done on the neglected questions of the effects of pollution on marine life and ways of minimizing these effects.

And the odds are that there will be other *Torrey Canyon*s. Some 10 percent of the world's shipping accidents occur in Britain's heavily trafficked coastal waters. And tankers are getting bigger. The 210,000-ton Japanese supertanker *Idemitsu Maru,* for example, dwarfs the *Torrey Canyon.* And within a few years tankers of a half-million tons deadweight may be plying the seas.

The Plymouth Laboratories scientists say in summing up, "We are progressively making a slum of nature and may eventually find that we are enjoying the benefit of science and industry under conditions which no civilized society should tolerate."

19   Oil in the Ecosystem

ROBERT W. HOLCOMB

Oil pollution has been a human problem for most of this century, but it took the grounding of the tanker *Torrey Canyon* and the blowout of the well off the coast of Santa Barbara to draw public attention to the major problems that can arise in the production and shipping of petroleum. A five-fold increase in oil production is expected by 1980, and the potential for large-scale pollution can increase even faster because of changes in drilling location and shipping practice. Knowledge of how oil affects the environment is fragmentary and gives only dim clues about what to expect in the future.

The problems involved in oil studies are complex. Crude oil is not a single chemical but a collection of hundreds of substances of widely different properties and toxicities. Paul Galtsoff of the Bureau of Commercial Fisheries at Woods Hole, Massachusetts, stated recently that "oil in sea water should be regarded not as an ordinary pollutant but as a dynamic system actively reacting with the environment."

Viewing the problem of oil this way, one finds that biologists present an essentially unified account of how oil came to be an important part of the environment and that they can give a rough outline of the way oil interacts with the rest of the ecological system. However, it is still impossible to predict the behavior of specific oil spills, and little is known about the long-term effects of oil in the marine environment.

Most current research is directed toward the immediate problem of handling oil spills. There is little prospect that detailed ecological studies will increase dramatically in the near future, but plans are being considered for the establishment of broad-based environmental-monitoring programs.

Oil at Sea

In 1966, 700 million tons of oil—about half the world's total ocean tonnage —were shipped in 3281 tankers. In the best of worlds, this oil would remain in that part of the "ecological" system of interest only to humans—wells, tankers, refineries, and, finally, furnaces and machines. It is difficult to estimate just how far short we are of living in the best of worlds, but Max Blumer of Woods Hole Oceanographic Institute estimates that somewhere between 1 million and 100 million tons of oil are added to our oceans each year.

The major sources of this oil are handling errors, leaks from natural deposits, tanker and barge accidents, and illegal tanker bilge washings. Normal techniques of transferring oil to small coastal tankers, barges, and shore facilities result in a chronic source of coastal oil. The total amount of oil from this source is unknown, but the Massachusetts Division of Natural Resources says that, in Boston Harbor alone, a spill involving several tons of oil can be expected every third week. Less frequent, but more spectacular, are leaks from offshore deposits. These can occur naturally, but they have been associated with drilling operations since the 1930's, when fields in the Gulf of Mexico were opened. The biggest loss associated with the more than 9000 offshore wells was the million-gallon blowout early this year off the California coast near Santa Barbara. Tanker accidents are similar to well blowouts in that an occasional major catastrophe highlights a constant source of contamination. The grounding of the *Torrey Canyon* off the southwest coast of England in March 1967 was simply the most dramatic example of a type of accident that, on a worldwide basis, occurs more than once a week. Finally, deliberate dumping of bilge washings adds a considerable, but unknown, amount of oil to the oceanic environment. In 1962 Shell Oil Company developed a method to separate oil from such washings, and there is a tacit international agreement to use the method; however, shipmasters find the procedure inconvenient, and the dumping practice continues.

Although our oil resources are not unlimited, a quick look to the future indicates that pumping and shipping operations will continue to expand for the next few decades. The continental shelves of North and South America, Africa, and Australia all have oil. Seismic profiling has indicated the probable presence of oil in the North Sea, Persian Gulf, and Indonesia, and large deposits have been discovered in Alaska and Canada.

Oil from these new sources will be transported through pipelines and by gigantic tankers. Construction has already begun on a road that will be used to build the 800-mile, 48-inch, 900-million dollar pipeline from Alaska's North Slope to Valdez Bay, an ice-free port on the Gulf of Alaska. The large United States merchant vessel S.S. *Manhattan* was specially strengthened for travel in ice and fought her way through the Canadian Arctic in September. If such trial runs are judged successful, a fleet of six, quarter-million-ton vessels will be built for year-round service. (The *Torrey Canyon,* considered a large ship at the time of her grounding, had a displacement of 127,000 tons.)

The proposed drilling activities will involve greater risks of major losses because work must be done at sea or in inhospitable northern latitudes. The use of large tankers will reduce the probability of collisions and groundings, but there are few port facilities for these giants, so the possibility of spills during transfers to smaller tankers or barges will be increased. Major accidents, of course, will be of colossal proportions.

Behavior in Water

After coming in contact with water, crude oil rapidly spreads into a thin layer and the lighter fractions evaporate. In protected areas the oil often becomes adsorbed on particulate matter and sinks, but in open sea it tends to remain on the surface where wind and wave action aid in further evaporation. Some oil dissolves in seawater and some is oxidized but the hundreds of species of bacteria, yeasts, and molds that attack different fractions of hydrocarbons under a variety of physical conditions are primarily responsible for oil degradation.

Bacteria found in open seas tend to degrade only straight-chain hydrocarbons of moderate molecular weight, so branched-chain hydrocarbons of high molecular weight in the form of tarry chunks may persist for a long time. In still waters, a series of complex events results in almost complete degradation. In 1950, Soviet microbiologists showed that, after the lighter fractions of oil spilled on the Moskva River evaporated, the remaining oil was adsorbed by particles and sank. Bottom-dwelling microorganisms produced a new mixture of organic substances that were carried to the surface with bubbles of methane and other light gases. The new compounds again were adsorbed, sank, and the cycle was repeated. A number of cycles, repeated over several months, were necessary to degrade most of the oil.

Studies on the thoroughness of degradation have produced conflicting results. Research at Terrebonne Bay, Louisiana, in 1966 showed that essentially complete degradation occurs within a period of several months. Oil has been a consistent pollutant in the Bay since the 1930's, but analysis of bottom mud showed that significant concentrations of petrochemicals could be found only in areas that had received oil relatively recently. However, studies in the French Mediterranean, which will be discussed later, indicate that important chemicals are persistent in bottom sediments.

There is now a considerable body of literature on the interactions of microorganisms and petroleum products, most of it based on laboratory studies and much of it dating back to Soviet work in the 1930's and American work in the 1940's. However, these studies are scarcely past the descriptive stage, and, even when combined with field studies, they are not adequate for predicting the course of degradation of an oil spill.

Oil and Marine Life

The most visible victims of ocean oil are sea birds. It is impossible to even guess how many are killed each year, and about the only thing known for sure is that, once oiled, very few birds survive. After the *Torrey Canyon* disaster, 5711 oiled birds were cleaned off; apparently 150 of them returned to health and were released, but banding counts of these indicate that at least 37 died within the first month after release. Similar figures were obtained from French efforts at bird rehabilitation after the same disaster, and few of the 1500 diving birds cleaned after the Santa Barbara blowout survived.

It is believed that most deaths are the result of diseases, such as pneumonia, which attack the birds after they are weakened by the physical effects of the oil (feather matting, loss of buoyancy, flying difficulty, and others). However, the high death rate of cleaned birds is unexplained, so long-term toxicity of the oil cannot be ruled out.

The major studies of the effects of oil spills on species other than birds have produced a wide variety of results. Dr. Robert Holmes, the first director of a major study after the Santa Barbara blowout, has stated that plankton populations were unaffected, and, although his remark was challenged at the Massachusetts Institute of Technology symposium where it was made, it is generally agreed that visible damage to organisms other than birds has been relatively light.

On the other hand, in what is probably the best "before and after" study of a major spill, it was conclusively shown that almost the entire population of a small cove was killed by dark diesel oil from the tanker *Tampico Mara*. In March 1957, the tanker grounded at the mouth of a small, previously unpolluted cove on the Pacific coast of Baja California, Mexico, and, until destroyed by the sea, it blocked most of the cove's entrance. All signs of oil disappeared sometime between November 1957 and May 1958, but the ecology of the cove was radically changed. A few species returned within 2 months, but 2 years had elapsed before significant improvements were noted. Four years after the accident, sea urchin and abalone populations were still greatly reduced; and, at the last observations in 1967, several species present 10 years earlier had not returned.

Although toxicity studies in the ocean have been limited to a few large spills, considerable laboratory work has been done to determine the lethal concentrations of a number of chemicals on various species. Most toxic are the aromatic hydrocarbons (for example, benzene, toluene, and the xylenes), and investigators have recently shown that the low-boiling, saturated hydrocarbons are more toxic than formerly believed. The destructiveness of the *Tampico Mara* grounding was probably due to the saturated hydrocarbons, and it has been shown that aromatic hydrocarbons used to dissolve detergents in the effort to disperse oil from *Torrey Canyon* caused much of the damage. When a spill occurs at sea, a large portion of both these classes of compounds evaporates before reaching shore. This is probably the main reason that the Santa Barbara blowout was not more disastrous to shore life other than birds.

Biochemical Studies

Just enough is known about the higher-boiling, saturated hydrocarbons and the high-boiling, aromatic hydrocarbons to indicate that more study is needed. Saturated, higher-boiling compounds occur naturally in both crude oil and marine organisms, so they are probably not toxic; but work reported this year indicated that these compounds may affect the behavior of sea animals.

Blumer points out that very small amounts of certain chemicals are used by many species of sea animals as behavior signals in the vital activities of food finding, escaping from predators, homing, and reproduction. He has shown, for example, that starfish are attracted to their oyster prey by chemicals in concentrations of a few parts per billion. The responsible chemicals have not been identified, but Blumer believes that in many cases they may resemble the high-boiling, saturated hydrocarbons found in petroleum products. Because of the extreme sensitivity of the response and the similarity of the animal and petroleum chemicals, he thinks it is possible that pollution interferes with chemically stimulated behavior "by blocking the taste receptors and by mimicking natural stimuli."

Studies on chemically stimulated behavior of marine animals are in such an early stage that ideas about the role of sea oil in the process can only be considered speculative. However, the speculation indicated that the consequences—altered behavior of entire populations of commercially valuable species—are so serious that the matter deserves early attention.

Another matter still in the speculative stage, but with potentially hazardous consequences, is the significance of high-boiling, aromatic hydrocarbons. Crude oil and crude oil residues contain alkylated 4- and 5-ring aromatic hydrocarbons similar to those found in tobacco tars, but little is known about their role in the marine environment.

In 1964 Lucien Mallet, a French marine chemist, reported the presence of 3,4-benzopyrene, a known carcinogen, in sediments of the French Mediterranean. Concentrations ranged from 5.0 parts per million at a depth of 8 to 13 cm to 0.016 part per million at 200 cm. Similar concentrations have been found in other waters that had been polluted for a long time. Near the port of Villefranche, 3,4-benzopyrene in concentrations from 0.025 to 0.04 part per million have been found in plankton.

Benzopyrenes can be formed by algae, and they occur naturally in many soils in concentrations ranging from parts per million to parts per billion; thus their presence in marine sediments may not be cause for concern. However, the detection in sea cucumbers of concentrations that were slightly greater than those in the bottom sediments where these animals feed indicated that benzopyrenes in the marine environment may find their way into the food chain.

Pollutants tend to enter the food chain more easily and to pass through it with fewer changes in aquatic environments than they do in terrestrial environments. They can be introduced in solution through bottom sediments and even in dispersed droplets that are ingested by the numerous filter feeders that constitute an important part of aquatic food.

The presence of DDT in Lake Michigan's coho salmon drew public attention to the fact that some hydrocarbons pass through the aquatic food chain relatively unchanged. Work at Woods Hole has demonstrated that the ratios of olefinic hydrocarbons in zooplankton to those in livers of basking sharks and herring that feed on the plankton are so constant that they can be used to determine the feeding grounds of these species.

Obviously, studies should be conducted to see what concentrations of 3,4-benzopyrene and other potentially dangerous hydrocarbons must be in seawater or sediments before they are introduced into the food chain and whether the chemicals persist as they pass through the chain.

Priorities

Although the possible ill effects of long-term oil pollution point to the need for more studies on the complex chemical-biological relationships of oil and the environment, there is still work to be done on the immediate effects of oil spills.

Dale Straugh, who now directs the large Santa Barbara study, said in a telephone interview that oil spills will undoubtedly continue and that much of the research effort should concentrate on methods of handling them.

Present alternatives are (i) to "corral" the oil and hold it at sea, (ii) to pick it up mechanically, or (iii) to treat it chemically so it will emulsify, dissolve, or sink. None of these methods is particularly successful, and research on all of them is continuing. The major requirement for further development is engineering and chemical knowledge, but biological expertise is necessary in some areas.

It is primarily biological studies, especially those after the *Torrey Canyon* incident, that precipitated the government decision not to use chemical treatment when the shore area is used as a source of fresh water or as a beach, or when it is necessary for commercially valuable species. Toxicity tests of chemicals developed to treat oil are now routinely conducted, and the Federal Water Pollution Control Administration is developing a standard procedure for such tests. This action was prompted in part by reports that a dispersal agent, Corexit, used at Santa Barbara was more toxic than earlier tests indicated.

The step beyond toxicity tests is a giant one of determining subtle and long-term effects of sunken, dissolved, or dispersed oil. Biological knowledge has advanced far enough to rule them out or to provide unquestionably safe alternatives. This task would require difficult, long-term studies on the complex interactions of oil, seawater, and marine life, and there is nothing on the horizon to indicate that these studies will progress rapidly enough to play a large role in decisions about methods of handling oil spills.

Another area in which biological knowledge could be helpful is in simply monitoring the oil that enters the oceans and determining, at least by sampling, its effects. On this horizon there seems to be some light. Several studies designed to determine the feasibility of establishing broad-based centers for enviromental study are now in progress.

The systematic monitoring of the oceans, including their oil content, is a necessary step toward development of the capability of determining the world-wide consequences of effects that at present can be measured only in the laboratory or in relatively small field studies.

Oil Spills—An Old Story   20

S. W. A. GUNN

After charting the coastline of what is now Alaska, British Columbia, and Washington, the great English seaman, Captain George Vancouver, visited California in the *Discovery* in 1793, and made this entry in his log for Sunday, 10 November (1):

The surface of the sea, which was perfectly smooth and tranquil, was covered with a thick slimy substance, which, when separated, or disturbed by any little agitation, became very luminous, whilst the light breeze that came principally from the shore, brought with it a very strong smell of burning tar, or of some such resinous substance. The next morning the sea had the appearance of dissolved tar floating upon its surface, which covered the ocean in all directions within the limits of our view; and indicated that in this neighbourhood it was not subject to much agitation.

By coincidence, this was in the very area of Santa Barbara where the undersea oil well blew up recently, and following which the Department of the Interior stated that "there is a lack of sufficient knowledge of this particular geological area"!

REFERENCE

1. J. S. Marshall, *Vancouver's Voyage* (Mitchell Press, Vancouver, 1967), p. 112.

21   Questions About the Alaskan Pipeline

GEORGE MARSHALL

1. What will be the influence of the oil pipeline and road via the Dietrich River on the overall environment of the North Slope, the Brooks Range, and the regions south to Valdez?
2. Can ecological studies be made with a reasonable degree of reliability in a few months or even a year in relation to the proposed pipeline?
3. What will be the effect of the pipeline and road and activities related to them on the wilderness through which they pass?
4. What will be their effect on the rare, vast, and magnificent wilderness to the west of the Dietrich Valley in the Gates of the Arctic areas, and on the wilderness to the east?
5. What will be their effect on local and migrating wildlife?
6. Will any rare species of plants be eliminated?
7. If the pipeline and road are built via the Dietrich River route, will proposals for other trans-Brooks Range transportation routes, including the reopening of the Anaktuvuk Pass route and constructing a railroad or road along the North Fork of the Koyukuk, be abandoned?
8. If the pipeline and road are built via the Dietrich, will an overall plan be put into effect for the entire Brooks Range designating the greater part of it, and, in particular, the greater part of the Central Brooks Range, as wilderness?
9. Why is there so great a rush to bring oil from the North Slope before many essential questions can be answered in regard to environmental effects and public policy?
10. Why are oil companies accelerating their production programs both on the North Slope and at Santa Barbara, elsewhere on the West Coast, along the

Canadian Coast, in Cook Inlet, as soon as possible at Bristol Bay, and at various mainland fields?

11. Why have the dangers of oil spills from the trans-Brooks Range pipeline been played down by companies and officials in view of the *Torrey Canyon* and Santa Barbara disasters?

12. Why has very little attention been given to the fact that oil spills from the pipeline in the Brooks Range would pollute upper water-sheds of from one to three major river systems and could spread many miles downstream?

13. Why is there a rush to pump oil in vast quantities from the North Slope and elsewhere at a time when petroleum products may become obsolete for transportation and industrial power because of the necessity to stop air pollution from making our cities from New York, to Los Angeles, to Fairbanks uninhabitable?

14. Should the oil industry receive the kind consideration of the United States and Alaskan governments in view of its major responsibility, along with the automobile industry, in befouling the atmosphere over much of the Nation?

15. If the pollution of the biosphere, unless stopped or reduced severely, may shorten the time mankind can continue to live on the Earth, as a growing number of scientists warn, would not the acceleration of oil production and the opening of new fields in the Arctic and elsewhere best be reconsidered?

THERMAL POLLUTION

Thermal pollution has been of major concern only to a minority of pollution opponents. This is a bit amazing when one considers that the 120 degree temperature range which supports most of life on earth is such a tiny slit in the 20 million degree galactic range from absolute zero to the unimaginable heat of the younger stars.

While some predict the return of an ice age in the wake of widespread pollution, others suggest that the ice caps will melt and flood coastal areas. Less dramatic but perhaps as important is the ecological change which could result from only an annual average two-degree-centigrade increase in the temperature of a major river.

Most power plants in the United States convert the chemical energy of fossil fuel into electrical energy. But the supply of fossil fuel is finite—and rapidly diminishing. In addition, the decrease in oxygen, increase in carbon dioxide and considerable pollution which result from the operation of conventional power plants make them unacceptable for use in the future. With this in mind, the public often turn for a remedy to advocating the use of nuclear powered generators. This solution, however, leaves us with two main problems: (1) disposal of radioactive wastes and (2) cooling of the plant. Warm water irrigation of crops may serve as a beneficial solution to the disposal of that by-product of electric power, heat. More research is urgently needed.

22   Thermal Pollution

LaMont C. Cole

Introduction

There are etymological objections to the expression "thermal pollution," but it is gaining adoption and I shall here accept it without comment as a descriptive term for unwanted heat energy accumulating in any phase of the environment.

Any isolated body drifting in space as the earth is must either increase continuously in temperature or it must dispose of all energy received from external sources or generated internally by one of two processes. The energy may either be stored in some potential form or it must be reradiated to space.

In the past the earth has stored some of the energy coming to it from outside. This was accomplished by living plants using solar energy to drive endothermic chemical reactions, thereby creating organic compounds some of which were ultimately deposited in sediments. This process had two very important effects; in protecting the organic compounds from oxidation it created a reservoir of oxygen in the atmosphere; and it also eliminated the necessity for reradiating to space the heat energy that would have been released by the oxidation of those compounds. Part of the stored organic matter gave rise to the fossil fuels, coal, oil, and natural gas, which we are so avidly burning today—and now the earth must at last radiate that heat energy back to space, or its temperature will increase.

Many of the most important problems currently facing man are ecological problems arising from the unrestrained growth of the human population and the resultant increasing strains being placed on the earth's life support system. Our seemingly insatiable demand for energy is one important source of strains on the earth's capacity to support life, and I propose here to examine it in very elementary terms.

Well over 99.999% of the earth's annual energy income is from solar radiation and this must all be returned to space in the form of radiant heat. This has gone on forever, so to speak, and conditions on earth, since before the advent of man, have reflected the necessity of maintaining this balance of incoming and outgoing radiation. A ridiculously small proportion of the sunlight reaching us is used in photosynthesis by green plants. This energy powers all of the earth's microorganisms and animals and is converted to heat by their metabolism. In addition, man can obtain useful heat energy by burning organic matter in such forms as wood, straw, cattle dung, and garbage and other refuse. This is "free" energy in the sense that the earth would have reradiated it as heat even if man had not obtained useful work from it in the meantime. Physical labor performed by man and the work done by domestic animals are also means of utilizing this solar energy.

In addition, it is solar radiation that keeps the atmosphere and hydrosphere in motion. To the extent that man can utilize the energy of the winds, of falling water and of ocean currents, or can make direct use of sunlight, he can do so without imposing increased thermal stress on the total earth environment.

The earth has some other minor sources of energy that contribute to its natural radiation balance. The tides can be used to obtain useful energy and a plant in France is now producing electricity from this source. Also, tidal friction is very gradually slowing the rotation of the earth, thereby converting kinetic energy to heat which plays a small role in maintaining the earth's surface temperature before it is radiated to space. Heat is also emerging from the interior of the earth and current concepts attribute this heat to natural radioactivity. In some local areas this heat flux is concentrated, and in a few countries man utilizes it for such purposes as heating buildings and generating electricity. Italy generates more than 400,000 kw of electricity from geothermal heat and in the United States about 85,000 kw are derived from a geyser field north of San Francisco.

This then is the inventory of energy sources available to man without affecting the surface temperature of the earth or the quantity of heat energy that it must dispose of by radiation. It is important to note this because, at least in the "developed" nations, we actually seem to be regressing from the use of these natural energy sources. Certainly windmills, animal power, and manual labor are much less in evidence today than they were during my childhood, and useful work done by sailboats seems to be a thing of the past in our culture. When we burn fossil fuels or generate electricity by nuclear or thermonuclear reactions, we must inevitably impose an increased thermal stress on the earth environment and, to the extent that this heat is undesirable, it constitutes thermal pollution.

The Earth's Radiation Balance

I assume the mean temperature of the earth's surface to be 15 C or 288 K; this may be a degree too low or too high. In order to keep the discussion sufficiently simple-minded, I shall introduce three simplifications.

First, I shall treat the earth as though its entire surface was at a uniform temperature equal to its average value, thus ignoring temperature differences due to latitude, altitude, season, and time of day. The effect of this simplification is less drastic than one might expect. It is true if one measures radiation from several bodies at different temperatures and infers the mean temperature of the surfaces from the radiation, he will obtain values that are slightly too high. For example, if we have two otherwise identical areas, one at 0 C and the other at 50 C, the average of their combined radiation will equal that which would be given off by such an area at 28 C rather than at the true mean temperature of 25 C. For the earth as a whole, the error from this source is not likely to amount to even one degree, and the other two simplifications I shall make tend to cause small errors in the opposite direction.

Second, I assume that the earth radiates as a blackbody or perfect radiator. This is probably nearly correct; and, in any case, the assumption is conservative for our purposes here. If the earth is actually a gray body rather than a black one, it will have to reach a somewhat higher temperature to dispose of the same amount of heat energy.

Finally, I assume that the earth radiates its energy to outer space which is at a temperature of O K. This is not quite correct because the portions of the sky occupied by the sun, moon, stars, and clouds of interstellar matter are at temperatures above absolute zero, and the earth's surface must therefore be very slightly warmer than it would otherwise be.

Accepting these simplifications, we can now turn to the Stefan-Boltzmann law of elementary physics which states that radiation is proportional to the fourth power of the absolute temperature, and easily calculate the amount of energy radiated from the earth to space.[1] At a temperature of 15 C (288 K) the total radiation from the earth turns out to be 2 X 10^{24} ergs/sec.

Or, looked at the other way around, if we know the quantity of heat that the earth's surface must get rid of by radiation, we can calculate what its surface temperature must be for it to do so. For example, various students of the subject have concluded that the mean temperature difference between glacial and icefree periods is quite small, probably no more than 5 C (e.g., see Brooks, 1949). If we can assume that we are now about midway between these climatic types, then a rise of 3 C might be expected to melt the icecaps from Antarctica and Greenland thereby raising sea-level by some 100 m. This would drastically alter the world's

---

1. take the surface area of the earth as 5.1 x 10^{18} cm^2 and the value of the Stefan constant as 5.67 x 10^{-5} erg cm^{-2} deg^{-4} sec^{-1}.

coastlines as, for example, by putting all of Florida under water, and drowning most of the world's major cities. To do this would require a 4.2% increase in the earth's heat budget (an increase of 8.44 x 10^{22} ergs/sec). By the same reasoning, a 4.1% decrease in the energy budget could be expected to bring on a new ice age. As we shall see presently, however, these things are not really quite so simple and predictable.

Man's Effect on the Heat Budget

The amount of energy now being produced by man, I take to be 5 x 10^{19} ergs/sec or 25/1000 of 1% of the total radiated by the earth. Strangely enough, I am quite happy with this perhaps brash attempt to estimate a difficult quantity. Putnam (1953) estimated the fuel burned by man 16 years ago at 3.3 x 10^{19} ergs/sec. If he was correct then, and if energy demand then had been growing at the rate it is now growing, man would now be using twice what I have estimated. Kardashev (1964) estimates the energy now produced by civilization at "over 4 x 10^{19} ergs per second" which is consistent with my estimate.

There is another way of getting at the figure. The rate of combustion of fossil fuels in the United States is accurately known, as is our rate of generating electricity. Our electrical production as of 1966 corresponds to one-fifth of our fossil fuel consumption. If we assume the same ratio for the entire earth, for which we do have credible figures on electrical generation, the world energy production turns out to be 4.4 x 10^{19} ergs/sec. With this many independent estimates converging, I am happy with the figure of 5 x 10^{19} ergs/sec.

This is such a tiny part of the earth's output of energy that it is evident that the heat released by man now has an absolutely insignificant direct effect on the average temperature of the earth's surface. Will this be true if we go on increasing our demands for power? I have been hearing utility company officials assert that we must keep electrical generating capacity growing by 10% per year, but a more common projection is about 7%, at which rate the capacity would double every 10 years. I am confident that nonelectrical uses of fuel for such purposes as heating, industry, and transportation are growing at least as rapidly, and I am told that the "developing" countries are going to continue to develop. Let us examine the consequences of an energy economy that continues to grow at 7% per year.

Waggoner (1966) considers it at least possible that a warming of 1 C would cause real changes in the boundaries between plant communities. For this to occur, the earth's energy budget would have to increase by about 3 x 10^{22} ergs/sec. How long would it take man to cause this at an increased energy production of 7% per year? The answer is 91 years.

As already mentioned, a rise of 3 C could, in the opinion of competent authorities, melt the ice caps and produce an earth geography such as has never been seen by man, and on which there would be much less dry land for man. This would take about 108 years to achieve by present trends.

The highest mean annual temperature of any spot on earth is believed to be 29.9 C (302.9 K) at Massawa on the Red Sea in Ethiopia. I think it is safe to assume that if the average temperature of the whole earth was raised to 30 C, it would become uninhabitable. This would take 130 years under our postulated conditions—the time from the Victorian era to the present.

These calculations, rough as they are, make it clear that man is on a collision course with disaster if he tries to keep energy production growing by means that will impose an increased thermal stress on the earth. I have here ignored the fact that the fossil fuels, and probably uranium and thorium reserves also, would be exhausted before these drastic effects could be attained. The possibility exists, however, that a controlled fusion reaction will be achieved and bring these disastrous effects within the realm of possibility.

How can we avoid the consequences of the trends we are following? My answer would be to determine what level of human population the earth can support at a desirable standard of living without undergoing deterioration and then to move to achieve this steady state condition. I would like to see increased energy needs met by the direct utilization of solar energy. There are, however, vissionary scientists, and policy makers who will listen to them, who will grasp at any straw to keep man's exploitation of the earth forever growing. In my mind I can hear them planning to air condition part of the earth for man and for whatever then will supply his food, while the rest of the earth is allowed to radiate the excess heat by attaining a very high temperature. They will consider putting generating plants and factories on the moon and other planets and reducing the heat stress on earth by reflecting solar radiation back to space. This latter possibility brings us to consideration of some secondary effects of our expanding energy budget.

Side Effects of Energy Use

The combustion of fuel releases not only heat but also frequently smoke and various chemicals, the most important of which are water and carbon dioxide, into the environment.

Smoke and other particulate matter in the atmosphere scatters and absorbs incoming solar radiation, thus reducing the amount of energy absorbed by the surface. It has little effect on the outgoing longwave radiation, so the net effect is a tendency to cool the earth's surface. Several large volcanic eruptions within historic times have caused a year or so of abnormally low temperatures all over the earth. Perhaps the most striking case was the mighty eruption of Mt. Tomboro in the Lesser Sunda Islands in 1815. The following year, 1816, was the famous "year without a summer," during which snow fell in Boston every month. Actual measurements following the 1912 eruption of Mt. Katmai in the Aleutians showed a reduction of about 20% in the solar radiation reaching the earth.

Water vapor and carbon dioxide have an effect opposite to that of smoke; they are transparent to sunlight but absorb the longwave radiation from the earth and, by reradiating some of it back to earth, tend to raise the surface temperature. Man's combustion of fossil fuels has caused a measurable increase in the CO_2 content of the atmosphere, and now increasing numbers of jet airplanes are releasing great quantities of both water vapor and CO_2 at high altitudes. This would tend to raise the earth's temperature. However, a phenomenon of increasing frequency is the coalescence of the contrails of jet airplanes into banks of cirrus clouds which will reflect some of the incoming solar radiation back to space. Obviously, we cannot now be certain of the ultimate effects of the materials we are releasing to the atmosphere, but they certainly have the potential for changing climates.

On a more local scale, we are using prodigious quantities of water for cooling industrial plants, especially electrical generating plants, and this use is expected to increase at least as rapidly as our energy use grows[2] —perhaps more rapidly because nuclear plants waste more heat per kilowatt than plants burning fossil fuels. When heated water is discharged at a temperature above that of the air, we must expect an increase in the frequencies of mist and fog and, in winter, icing conditions.

Biological Effects of Thermal Pollution

The first and most obvious biological effect one thinks of is that bodies of water may become so hot that nothing can live in them. It is true that there are a few bacteria and blue-green algae that can grow in hot springs but even these are very unusual in water above 60 C. I know of only one case of a green alga living above 50 C—a species of *Protococcus* from Yellowstone Park. A few rotifers, nematodes, and protozoa have been found at above 50 C, and some, in a dried and encysted state, will survive much higher temperatures. In general, no higher organisms are to be expected actively living in water above about 35 C. I find it difficult to reconcile the data with the conclusion of Wurtz (1968, p. 139): "Water temperature would have to be increased to about 130 F (54.4 C) to destroy the microorganisms that are responsible for the self-purification capacity of a lake or stream." This statement is certainly incompatible with the recommendation of the National Technical Advisory Committee (1968) that: "All surface waters should be capable of supporting life forms of aesthetic value."

Another factor to be considered is the effect of temperature on the types of organisms present. Fish of any type are rare above 30 C. Diatoms, which are important members of aquatic food chains, decrease as temperature rises above 20 C, and they are gradually replaced by blue-green algae which are not important as food for animals, are often toxic, and are often the source of water blooms which kill the biota and make the water unfit for domestic use. Typically at about 30 C, diatoms and blue-greens are about equally represented and green algae exceed both. At 35 C, the diatoms are nearly gone, the greens are decreasing rapidly, and the blue-greens are assuming full dominance.

So far as animals are concerned, a body of water at a temperature of 30-35 C is essentially a biological desert. The green algae, which are well above their optimum temperature, can support a few types of cladoceran, amphiphod, and isopod crustaceans; bacteria and blue-green algae may abound; and mosquito larvae may do very well; rooted plants may grow in shallow regions; and a few crayfish, carp, goldfish, and catfish may endure. Largemouth bass can survive and grow at 32 C but they do not reproduce above about 24 C. A few other forms such as aquatic insects may inhabit the water as adults but may or may not be able to complete their life cycles there. Desirable game fishes such as Atlantic salmon, lake trout, northern pike, and walleyes require water below 10 C for reproduction.

Another effect of raising the temperature of water is to reduce the solubility of gases. The amount of oxygen dissolved in water in equilibrium with the atmosphere decreases by over 17% between 20 C and 30 C. At the same time,

2. Thermally more efficient electrical generating plants are considered possible: e.g., the "magnetohydrodynamic" generator (see Rosa and Hals. 1968).

the need of organisms for oxygen increases. As a rule of thumb, metabolic rate approximately doubles for a 10 C increase in body temperature, although the effect is sometimes greater. Krogh (1914) found that the rate of development of frog eggs is about six times as great at 20 C as at 10 C. Similar effects have been noted in the rate of development of mosquitos.

Dissolved oxygen is often in critically short supply for aquatic organisms and increased temperature aggravates the situation. This may be partially compensated by more rapid diffusion of oxygen from the air and, during daylight hours, by photosynthesis. On the other hand, decay of organic matter and other oxidative processes such as the rusting of iron are more rapid at high temperatures. In polluted water the effect of biochemical oxygen demand (BOD) is more severe at high temperatures. The addition of heat to estuaries may be more critical than in bodies of freshwater because saltwater has a slightly lower specific heat and because oxygen is less soluble in saltwater.

In contrast to the situation with gases, salts become more soluble in water as the temperature increases. Chemical reactions become more rapid and increased evaporation may further increase the concentration of dissolved salts. At the same time the rate of exchange of substances between aquatic organisms and the medium increases. Toxins are likely to have greater effects, and parasites and diseases are more likely to break out and spread. In general, water at a temperature above the optimum places a strain on metabolic processes that may make adaptation to other environmental factors more difficult. For example, the Japanese oyster can tolerate a wider range of salinity in winter than in summer (Reid, 1961, p. 267).

In addition, if the water contains plant nutrients, objectionable growths of aquatic plants may be promoted by increased temperature—extreme cases leading to heavy mortality of fishes and other animals. It has been reported that polluted water from Lake Superior which does not support algal blooms there will do so if warmed to the temperature of Lake Erie.

Still other factors come into play when a body of water is thermally stratified. In a deep cold lake such as Cayuga where we are currently threatened with a huge nuclear generating plant, the lake water mixes, usually in May, so the entire lake is well oxygenated. As the surface warms, the lake stratifies with a level of light, warm water (the epilimnion) floating with no appreciable mixing on a mass of dense cold water (the hypolimnion) in which the lake trout, their food organisms, and other things are living and consuming oxygen. This continues until the lake mixes again, usually in November, by which time the oxygen supply in the hypolimnion is seriously depleted. The power company plans to pump 750 million gallons per day from the hypolimnion at a temperature averaging perhaps 6 C and to discharge it at the surface at a temperature of about 21 C. They plan this despite a recommendation of the National Technical Advisory Committee (1968, p. 33) that: " . . . water for cooling should not be pumped from the hypolimnion to be discharged to the same body of water." The effect of this addition of heat on the average temperature of the lake will be trivially small, but the biological consequences can be out of all proportion to the amount of heating.

The heat will delay fall cooling of the epilimnion and hasten spring warming, so that the length of time the lake is stratified each year will be increased. The water from the hypolimnion is rich in available plant nutrients, and by warming it and discharging it in the lighted zone, the amount of plant growth will be increased. This means more organic matter sinking into the hypolimnion and using up oxygen when it decays. The threat to the welfare of the lake is very real.

Finally, we should comment on fluctuating temperatures. Many organisms can adapt to somewhat higher or lower temperatures if they have time. The water in reservoirs behind hydroelectric dams often becomes thermally stratified, and when it is released at the base of the dam, a stretch of cold stream is produced which can support a cold water fauna even in warm regions. But when water is only discharged during peak electrical generating hours, the stream becomes subject to severe temperature fluctuations that will exclude many sensitive organisms. Similarly, if fishes or other organisms acclimate to the warm discharge from a factory or power plant and congregate near it, they will be subjected to temperature shocks when the plant is shut down for maintenance or refueling.

Conclusion

Man cannot go on increasing his use of thermal energy without causing degradation of his environment, and if he is persistent enough, he will destroy himself. There are other energy sources that could be used, but no source can support an indefinitely growing population. As with so many other things, it is man's irresponsible proliferation in numbers that is the real heart of the problem. There is some population size that the earth could support indefinitely without undergoing deterioration, but people do not even want to consider what that number might be. I suspect that it is substantially below the present world population. One would think that any rational creature riding a space ship would take care not to damage or destroy the ship, but perhaps the word "rational" does not describe man.

REFERENCES

Brooks, C. E. P. 1949. *Climate Through the Ages.* Rev. ed. McGraw-Hill Book Co., New York.
Kardashev, N. S. 1964. Transmission of information by extraterrestrial civilizations. In: *Extraterrestrial Civilizations,* G. M. Tovmasyan (ed.). Trans. by National Aeronautics and Space Administration, Washington, D.C.
Krogh, A. 1914. On the influence of temperature on the rate of embryonic development. *Z. Allg. Physiol.,* 16: 163-177.
National Technical Advisory Committee. 1968. Water quality criteria. Report of the National Technical Advisory Committee to the Secretary of the Interior. Federal Water Pollution Control Administration, Washington, D.C.
Putnam, P. C. 1953. *Energy in the Future.* D. Van Nostrand Co., New York.
Reid, G. K. 1961. *Ecology of Inland Waters and Estuaries.* Reinhold Publishing Co., New York.
Rosa, R. J., and F. A. Hals. 1968. In defense of MHD, *Ind. Res.,* June 1968: 68-72.
Waggoner, P. E. 1966. Weather modification and the living environment. In: *Future Environments of North America,* F. F. Darling and J. F. Milton (eds.). Natural History Press, Garden City, N.Y.
Wurtz, C. B. 1968. Thermal pollution: The effect of the problem. In: *Environmental Problems,* B. R. Wilson (ed.). J. B. Lippincott Co., Philadelphia.

23   Thermal Addition
One Step From Thermal Pollution

SHARON FRIEDMAN

Many forms of aquatic and plant life are being threatened by the tons of heated water being spewed forth from electric and thermonuclear generating plants into the nation's rivers, lakes, and coastal waters.

Actually, the threat is more potential than real at present but it could become a serious hazard as the power needs of the nation increase and more and more generating plants are built on America's waterways. As one scientist put it at a meeting on this problem, "Today we can still talk about thermal addition, but tomorrow we may be talking about thermal pollution."

In 1958, the electricity demand was expected to quadruple by the year 2010. In 1965, estimates for the same time period indicated that the electricity demand would increase 32 times. Now these estimates have soared to as high as 256 times the present need by 2010. This would mean that even by 1980, electricity production may amount to 2 million megawatts. If engineering designs remain the same, this production would require 200 billion gallons of cooling water per day—the equivalent of one-sixth of the total volume of fresh-water runoff per day in the United States. During dryer seasons of the year, half would be needed for cooling purposes.

The advent of thermonuclear generating plants will increase the thermal addition problem since these plants have large generating capacities ranging from 1000 to 4000 megawatts. Nuclear power plants are less efficient than traditional ones and produce about 50% more waste heat per unit of electricity. These plants may each require up to 7 billion gallons of water a day for cooling. In 1968, the Atomic Energy Commission reported that 15 nuclear power plants were in operation in this country and that 87 more were either under construction or planned for the immediate future. Not included in these figures were the many proposed plants that are not far enough along to have applied for building permits.

Heated water is not the only problem for aquatic life brought on by the power plants. There are also metallurgical effects caused by loss of metals from power plant condenser tubes and biocidal problems caused by detergents, acids, and chlorine used to keep condenser tubes clean of fouling from biological growths and deposits. The nuclear plants may present another factor—radioactive materials.

Different environments and water temperatures mediate the effects of thermal addition. In the cooler waters of California and also those around England and Scotland, there is not much of a problem. But this does not mean there is no concern, since a buildup of power plants could radically change the situation.

Many species of aquatic life have different levels of temperature tolerance. For the primary producers, the grasses of the sea, a few degrees of higher temperature could make a difference, both in type and quantity, in the productivity of these organisms, which provide food and fuel for the entire ecological system. Invertebrates, which include many economically important shellfish, also react to thermal addition. But whether the reaction is beneficial or harmful depends on the latitude of their habitats and their exposure to sun during low tides among other factors.

While all fishes face some danger from thermal addition, the migratory fishes are particularly susceptible in the mixing zones where the heated water flows into cooler natural waters. Although no large fish kills can yet be blamed on thermal addition, there is some question as to whether certain fish could carry out their life cycle in slightly elevated temperatures, and what these higher temperatures would do to their food requirements and behavioral characteristics.

Thermal addition can be avoided by the use of cooling towers where water used in cooling is cooled, in turn, by either the atmosphere alone or with the aid of giant fans. This method is commonly used in England. This is the only way it is possible to have so many generating plants located in such a small area without doing severe damage to the environment.

Cooling towers have not found favor in the United States because of their added building and maintenance expense—sometimes amounting to millions of dollars. These towers also have other drawbacks: they are huge and unsightly, and one type—an open-circuit variety—loses a significant amount of water through evaporation to the atmosphere, sometimes causing fog and ice to develop as side effects.

With more knowledge of its effects, thermal addition may be put to good use in the future. Experimenters from Scotland have reported using the heated waters from a power plant to encourage production of flounder, sole and some shellfish.

Executive Order on Thermal Pollution 24

LYNDON B. JOHNSON

If discharge of cooling water is expected to create problems by significantly increasing the temperature of the receiving waters, facilities shall be installed, or operating procedures shall be established, to maintain water temperatures within acceptable limits.

PESTICIDES

Charles F. Wurster, Jr., writing in *Science* in 1968, reported, "Concentrations of DDT as low as a few parts per billion in water reduced photosynthesis in laboratory cultures of four species of coastal and oceanic phytoplankton representing four major classes of algae, and in a natural phytoplankton community from Woods Hole, Massachusetts. Toxicity to diatoms increased as cell concentration decreased." This stunning report forced us to totally reconceive the role of pesticides in our environment. Not only are organisms being killed, but the very machinery for harnessing sunlight is being disrupted.

The public must reexamine its answer to the question, "What is a pest?" Such taxonomic terms as "germ," "weed," and "bug," become, under careful scrutiny, vague categories of ignorance and misinformation. Yet, the onslaught against these culturally-frowned-on organisms is carried forward with the greatest confidence that the "right thing" is being done. We are essentially completely ignorant of the mutogenic danger of these chemicals. But, as an accused person is supposedly innocent until proven guilty, so are the pesticides. Arrogance, combined with ignorance, has hatched a serious threat to the life-process itself. American agriculture is so deeply involved in this warfare on pests that immediate "pull out" would be economically disastrous. To de-escalate will mean a depreciation in the superficial quality of agricultural products and a downturn in the efficiency of food production.

From 1959 to 1968, 3.79 million metric tons of synthetic organic pesticides (insecticides, fungicides, and herbicides) were produced by the U.S. alone. Until now, the developing nations have not been heavy users of pesticides, but they will likely employ these so-called "miracle producers" also. Dr. Norman E. Borlaug, 1970 Nobel Peace Prize winner for his plant breeding efforts which produced the "miracle wheat" in Mexico, has said that chemical fertilizers and pesticides are "absolutely necessary to cope with world hunger."

Can we ever return to a pre-pesticide agriculture? Do we want to? How many "bridges were burned" as we escalated our dependence on a pesticide-employing agriculture? If there are bridges that must be rebuilt, how much time will be required to rebuild them? How many species will become extinct during the "pull-out"? Or, as the demand for food increases, will we employ even more pesticides to satisfy the urgency of immediate production?

The Effects of Pesticides   **25**

WILLIAM A. NIERING

The dramatic appearance of Rachel Carson's *Silent Spring* (1962) awakened a nation to the deleterious effects of pesticides. Our technology had surged ahead of us. We had lost our perspective on just how ruthlessly man can treat his environment and still survive. He was killing pesty insects by the trillions, but he was also poisoning natural ecosystems all around him. It was Miss Carson's mission to arrest this detrimental use of our technological achievements. As one might have expected, she was criticized by special vested industrial interests and, to some degree, by certain agricultural specialists concerned with only one aspect of our total environment. However, there was no criticism, only praise, from the nation's ecosystematically oriented biologists. For those who found *Silent Spring* too dramatic an approach to the problem, the gap was filled two years later by *Pesticides and the Living Landscape* (1964) in which Rudd further documented Miss Carson's thesis but in more academic style.

The aim of this chapter is to summarize some of the effects of two pesticides —insecticides and herbicides—on our total environment, and to point up research and other educational opportunities for students of environmental science. The insecticide review will be based on representative studies from the literature, whereas the herbicide review will represent primarily the results of the author's research and experience in the Connecticut Arboretum at Connecticut College. Although some consider this subject controversial, there is really no controversy in the mind of the author—the issue merely involves the sound ecological use of pesticides only where necessary and without drastically contaminating or upsetting the dynamic equilibrium of our natural ecosystems. I shall not consider the specific physiological effects of pesticides, but rather their effects on the total environment—plants, animals, soil, climate, man—the biotic and abiotic aspects.

Environmental science or ecosystematic thinking should attempt to coordinate and integrate all aspects of the environment. Although ecosystems may be managed, they must also remain in a relative balance or dynamic equilibrium, analogous to a spider's web, where each strand is intimately interrelated and interdependent upon every other strand.

The Impact of Insecticides

Ecologists have long been aware that simplifying the environment to only a few species can precipitate a catastrophe. Our highly mechanized agricultural operations, dominated by extensive acreages of one crop, encourage large numbers of insect pests. As insurance against insect damage, vast quantities of insecticides are applied with little regard for what happens to the chemical once it is on the land. Prior to World War II, most of our insecticides were nonpersistent organics found in the natural environment. For example, the pyrethrins were derived from dried chrysanthemum flowers, nicotine sulphate from tobacco, and rotenone from the tropical derris plants. However, research during World War II and thereafter resulted in a number of potent persistent chlorinated hydrocarbons (DDT, dieldrin, endrin, lindane, chlordane, heptachor and others) to fight the ever-increasing hordes of insects, now some 3000 species plaguing man in North America.

In 1964, industries in the United States produced 783 million lb. of pesticides, half insecticides and the other half herbicides, fungicides, and rodenticides. The application of these chemicals on the nation's landscape[1] has now reached the point where one out of every ten acres is being sprayed with an average of 4 lb. per acre (Anonymous, 1966).

Positive Effects of Target Organisms

That market yields and quality are increased by agricultural spraying appears to have been well documented. Data from the National Agricultural Chemical Association show net increased yields resulting in from $5.00 to $100.00 net gains per acre on such crops as barley, tomatoes, sugar beets, pea seed, and cotton seed. However, Rudd (1964) questions the validity of these figures, since there is no explanation just how they were derived. His personal observations on the rice crop affected by the rice leaf miner outbreak in California are especially pertinent. The insect damage was reported as ruining 10% to 20% of the crop. He found this to be correct for some fields, but most of the fields were not damaged at all. In this situation, the facts were incorrect concerning the pest damage. It appears that not infrequently repeated spraying applications are merely insurance sprays and in many cases actually unnecessary. Unfortunately, the farmer is being forced to this procedure in part by those demanding from agriculture completely insect-free produce. This has now reached ridiculous proportions. Influenced by advertising, the housewife now demands perfect specimens with no thought of a regard for how much environmental contamination has resulted to attain such perfection. If we could relax our standards to a moderate degree, pesticide contamination could be greatly reduced. Although it may be difficult to question that spraying increases yields and quality of the marketable products, there are few valid data available on how much spraying is actually necessary, how much it is adding to consumer costs, what further pests are aggravated by spraying, and what degree of resistance eventually develops.

Negative Effects on Nontarget Organisms

Although yields may be increased with greater margins of profit, according to available data, one must recognize that these chemicals may adversely affect a whole spectrum of nontarget organisms not only where applied but possibly thousands of miles from the site of application. To the ecologist concerned with the total environment, these persistent pesticides pose some serious threats to our many natural ecosystems. Certain of these are pertinent to review.

1. *Killing of nontarget organisms.* In practically every spray operation, thousands of nontarget insects are killed, many of which may be predators on the

---

1. Dr. George Woodwell estimates that there are 1 billion lbs. of DDT now circulating in the biosphere.

very organisms one is attempting to control. But such losses extend far beyond the beneficial insects. In Florida, an estimated 1,117,000 fishes of at least 30 species (20 to 30 tons), were killed with dieldrin, when sand flies were really the target organism. Crustaceans were virtually exterminated—the fiddler crabs survived only in areas missed by the treatment (Harrington and Bidlingmayer, 1958).

In 1963, there was a "silent spring" in Hanover, New Hampshire. Seventy per cent of the robin population—350 to 400 robins—was eliminated in spraying for Dutch elm disease with 1.9 lb. per acre DDT (Wurster et al., 1965). Wallace (1960) and Hickey and Hunt (1960) have reported similar instances on the Michigan State University and University of Wisconsin campuses. Last summer, at Wesleyan University, my students observed dead and trembling birds following summer applications of DDT on the elms. At the University of Wisconsin campus (61 acres), the substitution of methoxychlor has resulted in a decreased bird mortality. The robin population has jumped from three to twenty-nine pairs following the change from DDT to methoxychlor. Chemical control of this disease is often overemphasized, with too little attention directed against the sources of elm bark beetle. Sanitation is really the most important measure in any sound Dutch elm disease control program (Matthysse, 1959).

One of the classic examples involving the widespread destruction of nontarget organisms was the fire ant eradication program in our southern states. In 1957, dieldrin and heptochlor were aerially spread over two and one-half million acres. Wide elimination of vertebrate populations resulted; and recovery of some populations is still uncertain (Rudd, 1964). In the interest of science, the Georgia Academy of Science appointed an ad hoc committee to evaluate this control-eradication program (Bellinger et al., 1965). It found that reported damage to crops, wildlife, fish, and humans had not been verified, and concluded, furthermore, that the ant is not really a significant economic pest but a mere nuisance. Here was an example where the facts did not justify the federal expenditure of $2.4 million in indiscriminate sprays. Fortunately, this approach has been abandoned, and local treatments are now employed with Mirex, a compound with fewer side effects. Had only a small percentage of this spray expenditure been directed toward basic research, we might be far ahead today in control of the fire ant.

2. *Accumulation in the food chain.* The persistent nature of certain of these insecticides permits the chemical to be carried from one organism to another in the food chain. As this occurs, there is a gradual increase in the biocide at each higher trophic level. Many such examples have been reported in the literature. One of the most striking comes from Clear Lake, California, where a 46,000-acre warm lake, north of San Francisco, was sprayed for pesty gnats in 1949, 1954, and 1957, with DDD, a chemical presumably less toxic than DDT. Analyses of the plankton revealed 250 times more of the chemical than originally applied, the frogs 2000 times more, sunfish 12,000, and the grebes up to an 80,000-fold increase (Cottam, 1965; Rudd, 1964). In 1954 death among the grebes was widespread. Prior to the spraying, a thousand of these birds nested on the lake. Then for 10 years no grebes hatched. Finally, in 1962, one nestling was observed, and the following year three. Clear Lake is popular for sports fishing, and the flesh of edible fish now caught reaches 7 ppm. which is above the maximum tolerance level set by the Food and Drug Administration.

In an estuarine ecosystem, a similar trend has been reported on the Long

Island tidal marshes, where mosquito control spraying with DDT has been practiced for some 20 years (Woodwell et al., 1967). Here the food chain accumulation shows plankton 0.04 ppm, shrimp 0.16 ppm, minnows 1 to 2 ppm, and ring-billed gull 75.5 ppm. In general, the DDT concentrations in carnivorous birds were 10 to 100 times those in the fish they fed upon. Birds near the top of the food chain have DDT residues about a million times greater than concentration in the water. Pesticide levels are now so high that certain populations are being subtly eliminated by food chain accumulations reaching toxic levels.

3. *Lowered reproductive potential.* Considerable evidence is available to suggest a lowered reproductive potential, especially among birds, where the pesticide occurs in the eggs in suffcient quantities either to prevent hatching or to decrease vigor among the young birds hatched. Birds of prey, such as the bald eagle, osprey, hawks, and others, are in serious danger. Along the northeast Atlantic coast, ospreys normally average about 2.5 young per year. However, in Maryland and Connecticut, reproduction is far below this level. In Maryland, ospreys produce 1.1 young per year and their eggs contain 3 ppm DDT, while in Connecticut, 0.5 young ospreys hatch and their eggs contain up to 5.1 ppm DDT. These data indicate a direct correlation between the amount of DDT and the hatchability of eggs—the more DDT present in the eggs, the fewer young hatched (Ames, 1966). In Wisconsin, Keith (1964) reports 38% hatching failure in herring gulls. Early in the incubation period, gull eggs collected contained over 200 ppm DDT and its cogeners. Pheasant eggs from DDT-treated rice fields compared to those from unsprayed lands result in fewer healthy month-old chicks from eggs taken near sprayed fields. Although more conclusive data may still be needed to prove that pesticides such as DDT are the key factor, use of such compounds should be curtailed until it is proved that they are not the causal agents responsible for lowering reproductive potential.

4. *Resistance to sprays.* Insects have a remarkable ability to develop a resistance to insecticides. The third spray at Clear Lake was the least effective on the gnats, and here increased resistance was believed to be a factor involved. As early as 1951, resistance among agricultural insects appeared. Some of these include the codling moth on apples, and certain cotton, cabbage, and potato insects. Over 100 important insect pests now show a definite resistance to chemicals (Carson, 1962).

5. *Synergistic effects.* The interaction of two compounds may result in a third much more toxic than either one alone. For example, Malathion is relatively "safe" because detoxifying enzymes in the liver greatly reduce its toxic properties. However, if some compound destroys or interrupts this enzyme system, as certain organic phosphates may do, the toxicity of the new combination may be increased greatly. Pesticides represent one of many pollutants we are presently adding to our environment. These subtle synergistic effects have opened a whole new field of investigation. Here students of environmental science will find many challenging problems for future research.

6. *Chemical migration.* After two decades of intensive use, pesticides are now found throughout the world, even in places far from any actual spraying. Penguins and crab-eating seals in the Antarctic are contaminated, and fish far off the coasts of four continents now contain insecticides ranging from 1 to 300 ppm in their fatty tissues (Anonymous, 1966).

The major rivers of our nation are contaminated by DDT, endrin, and dieldrin, mostly in the parts per trillion range. Surveys since 1957 reveal that dieldrin has been the main pesticide present since 1958. Endrin reached its maximum, especially in the lower Mississippi River, in the fall of 1963 when an extensive fish kill occurred and has since that time decreased. DDT and its cogeners, consistently present since 1958, have been increasing slightly (Breidenbach et al., 1967).

7. *Accumulation in the ecosystem.* Since chlorinated hydrocarbons like DDT are not readily broken down by biological agents such as bacteria, they may not only be present but also accumulate within a given ecosystem. On Long Island, up to 32 lb. of DDT have been reported in the marsh mud, with an average of 13 lb. presumed to be correlated with the 20 years of mosquito control spraying (Woodwell et al., 1967). Present in these quantities, burrowing marine organisms and the detritis feeders can keep the residues in continuous circulation in the ecosystem. Many marine forms are extremely sensitive to minute amounts of insecticides. Fifty per cent of a shrimp population was killed with endrin 0.6 parts per billion (ppb). Even 1 ppb will kill blue crabs within a week. Oysters, typical filter feeders, have been reported to accumulate up to 70,000 ppb. (Loosanoff, 1965). In Green Bay along Lake Michigan, Hickey and Keith (1964) report up to 0.005 ppm wet weight of DDT, DDE, and DDD in the lake sediments. Here the accumulation has presumably been from leaching or run-off from surrounding agricultural lands in Door County, where it is reported that 70,000 pounds of DDT are used annually. Biological concentration in Green Bay is also occurring in food chain organisms, as reported at Clear Lake, California. Accumulation of biocides, especially in the food chain, and their availability for recycling pose a most serious ecological problem.

8. *Delayed response.* Because of the persistent nature and tendency of certain insecticides to accumulate at toxic levels in the food chain, there is often a delayed response in certain ecosystems subjected either directly or indirectly to pesticide treatment. This was the case at Clear Lake, where the mortality of nontarget organisms occurred several years after the last application. This is a particularly disturbing aspect, since man is often the consumer organisms accumulating pesticide residues. In the general population, human tissues contain about 12 ppm DDT-derived materials. Those with meatless diets, and the Eskimos, store less; however, agricultural applicators and formulators of pesticides may store up to 600 ppm DDT or 1000 ppm DDT-derived components. Recent studies indicate that dieldrin and lindane are also stored in humans without occupational exposure (Durham, 1965). The possibility of synergistic effects involving DDT, dieldrin, lindane, and other pollutants to which man is being exposed may result in unpredictable hazards. In fact, it is now believed that pesticides may pose a genetic hazard. At the recent conference of the New York Academy of Science, Dr. Onsy G. Fahmy warned that certain chlorinated hydrocarbons, organophosphates and carbamates were capable of disrupting the DNA molecule. It was further noted that such mutations may not appear until as many as 40 generations later. Another scientist, Dr. M. Jacqueline Verrett, pointed out that certain fungicides (folpet and captan) thought to be nontoxic have chemical structures similar to thalidomide.

We are obviously dealing with many biological unknowns in our widespread use of presumably "safe" insecticides. We have no assurance that 12 ppm DDT in our human tissue, now above the permissible in marketable products for consumption, may not be resulting in deleterious effects in future generations. As Rudd warns (1964): " . . . it would be somewhat more than embarrassing for our 'experts' to learn that significant effects do occur in the long term. One hundred and eight million human guinea pigs would have paid a high price for their trust."

Of unpredicted delayed responses, we have an example in radiation contamination. In the Bravo tests on Bikini in 1954, the natives on Rongelap Atoll were exposed to radiation assumed to be safe. Now more than a decade later, tumors of the thyroid gland have been discovered in the children exposed to these presumably safe doses (Woodwell et al., 1966). Pesticides per se or synergisms resulting from their interaction could well plague man in now unforeseen or unpredictable ways in the future.

The Sound Use of Herbicides

In contrast to insecticides, herbicides are chemical weed-killers used to control or kill unwanted plants. Following World War II, the chlorinated herbicide 2, 4-D began to be used widely on broadleaf weeds. Later, 2, 4, 5-T was added, which proved especially effective on woody species. Today, over 40 weed-killers are available. Although used extensively in agriculture, considerable quantities are used also in aquatic weed control and in forestry, wildlife, and right-of-way vegetation management. Currently, large quantities are being used as defoliators in Vietnam.

Although herbicides in general are much safer than insecticides in regard to killing nontarget organisms and in their residual effects, considerable caution must be exercised in their proper use. One of the greatest dangers in right-of-way vegetation management is their indiscriminate use, which results in habitat destruction. Drift of spray particles and volatility may also cause adverse effects on nontarget organisms, especially following indiscriminate applications. In the Connecticut Arboretum, shade trees have been seriously affected as a result of indiscriminate roadside sprays (Niering, 1959). During the spring of 1957, the town sprayed the marginal trees and shrubs along a roadside running through the Arboretum with 2, 4-D and 2, 4, 5-T (1 part chemical: 100 parts water). White oaks overarching the road up to 2 feet in diameter were most seriously affected. Most of the leaves turned brown. Foliage of scarlet and black oaks of similar size exhibited pronounced leaf curling. Trees were affected up to 300 feet back from the point of application within the natural area of the Arboretum. White oak twigs near the sprayed belt also developed a striking weeping habit as twig elongation occurred—a growth abnormality still conspicuous after 10 years.

The effectiveness of the spray operation in controlling undesirable woody growth indicated a high survival of unwanted tree sprouts. Black birch and certain desirable shrubs were particularly sensitive. Shrubs affected were highly ornamental forms often planted in roadside beautification programs. The resulting ineffectiveness of the spray operation was indicated by the need for cutting undesirable growth along the roadside the following year.

In the agricultural use of herbicides, drift effects have been reported over much greater distances. In California, drift from aerial sprays has been reported up to 30 miles from the point of application (Freed, 1965).

Although toxicity of herbicides to nontarget organisms is not generally a problem, it has been reported in aquatic environments. For example, the dimethylamine salt of 2, 4-D is relatively safe for bluegill at 150 ppm, but the butyl, ethly, and isopropyl esters are toxic to fish at around 1 ppm (R. E. Johnson, personal communication). Studies of 16 aquatic herbicides on *Daphnia magna*, a microcrustacean, revealed that 2, 4-D (specific derivation not given) seemed completely innocuous but that several others (Dichlone, a quinone; Molinate, a thiolcarbamate; Propanil, an anilide; sodium arsenite and Dichlopenil, a nitrile) could present a real hazard to this lower food chain organism (Crosby and Tucker, 1966).

Effects of rights-of-way. The rights-of-way across our nation comprise an estimated 70,000,000 acres of land, much of which is now subjected to herbicide treatment (Niering, 1967). During the past few decades, indiscriminate foliar applications have been widespread in the control of undesirable vegetation, erroneously referred to as brush (Goodwin and Niering, 1962). Indiscriminate applications often fail to root-kill undesirable species, therefore necessitating repeated retreatment, which results in the destruction of many desirable forms. Indiscriminate sprays are also used for the control of certain broadleaf weeds along roadsides. In New Jersey, 19 treatments were applied during a period of 6 years in an attempt to control ragweed. This, of course, was ecologically unsound, when one considers that ragweed is an annual plant typical of bare soil and that repeated sprayings also eliminate the competing broadleaved perennial species that, under natural successional conditions, could tend to occupy the site and naturally eliminate the ragweed. Broadcast or indiscriminate spraying can also result in destruction of valuable wildlife habitat in addition to the needless destruction of our native flora—wildflowers and shrubs of high landscape value.

Nonselective spraying, especially along roadsides, also tends to produce a monotonous grassy cover free of colorful wildflowers and interesting shrubs. It is economically and aesthetically unsound to remove these valuable species naturally occurring on such sites. Where they do not occur, highway beautification programs plant many of these same shrubs and low-growing trees.

Recognizing this nation-wide problem in the improper use of herbicides, the Connecticut Arboretum established, over a decade ago, several right-of-way demonstration areas to serve as models in the sound use of herbicides (Niering, 1955; 1957; 1961). Along two utility rights-of-way and a roadside crossing the Arboretum, the vegetation has been managed following sound ecological principles, (Egler, 1954; Goodwin and Niering, 1959; Niering 1958). Basic techniques include basal and stump treatments. The former involves soaking the base of the stem for 12 inches; the stump technique involves soaking the stump immediately after cutting. Effective formulations include 2, 4, 5-T in a fuel oil carrier (1 part chemical: 20 parts oil). Locally, stem-foliage sprays may be necessary, but the previous two techniques form the basic approach in the selective use of weed-killers. They result in good root-kill and simultaneously preserve valuable wildlife habitat and aesthetically attractive native species, all at a minimum of cost to the agency involved when figured on a long-range basis. In addition to these gains, the presence of good shrub cover tends to impede tree invasion and to reduce future maintenance costs (Pound and Egler, 1953; Niering and Elger, 1955).

Another intriguing use of herbicides is in naturalistic landscaping. Dr. Frank Egler conceived this concept of creating picturesque natural settings in shrubby fields by selectively eliminating the less attractive species and accentuating the ornamental forms (Kenfield, 1966). At the Connecticut Arboretum we have landscaped several such areas (Niering and Goodwin, 1963). This approach has unlimited application in arresting vegetation development and preserving landscapes that might disappear under normal successional or vegetational development processes.

Future Outlook

Innumerable critical moves have recently occurred that may alter the continued deterioration of our environment. Secretary Udall has banned the use of DDT, chlordane, dieldrin, and endrin on Department of the Interior lands. The use of DDT has been banned on state lands in New Hampshire and lake trout watersheds in New York State; in Connecticut, commercial applications are limited to dormant sprays. On Long Island, a temporary court injuction has been granted against the Suffolk Couty Mosquito Control Board's use of DDT in spraying tidal marshes. The Forest Service has terminated the use of DDT, and in the spring of 1966 the United States Department of Agriculture banned the use of endrin and dieldrin. Currently, the Forest Service has engaged a top-level research team in the Pacific Southwest to find chemicals highly selective to individual forest insect pests and that will break down quickly into harmless components. The Ribicoff hearing, which has placed Congressional focus on the problem of environmental pollution and Gaylord Nelson's bill to ban the sale of DDT in the United States are all enlightened endeavors at the national level.

The United States Forest Service has a selective program for herbicides in the National Forests. The Wisconsin Natural Resources Committee has instituted a selective roadside right-of-way maintenance program for the State. In Connecticut, a selective approach is in practice in most roadside and utility spraying.

Although we have considerable knowledge of the effects of biocides on the total environment, we must continue the emphasis on the holistic approach in studying the problem and interpreting the data. Continued observations of those occupationally exposed and of residents living near pesticide areas should reveal invaluable toxicological data. The study of migrant workers, of whom hundreds have been reported killed by pesticides, needs exacting investigation.

The development of more biological controls as well as chemical formulations that are specific to the target organism with a minimum of side effects needs continuous financial support by state and federal agencies and industry. Graduate opportunities are unlimited in this field.

As we look to the future, one of our major problems is the communication of sound ecological knowledge already available rather than pseudoscientific knowledge to increase the assets of special interest groups (Egler, 1964; 1965; 1966). The fire ant fiasco may be cited as a case in point. And as Egler (1966) has pointed out in his fourth most recent review of the pesticide problem: " . . . 95% of the problem is not in scientific knowledge of pesticides but in scientific knowledge of human behavior. . . . There are power plays . . . the eminent experts who deal with parts not ecological wholes."

One might ask, is it really good business to reduce the use of pesticides? Will biological control make as much money? Here the problem integrates political science, economics, sociology, and psychology. Anyone seriously interested in promoting the sound use of biocides must be fully cognizant of these counter forces in our society. They need serious study, analysis, and forthright reporting in the public interest. With all we know about the deleterious effects of biocides on our environments, the problem really challenging man is to get this scientific knowledge translated into action through the sociopolitical pathways available to us in a free society. If we fail to communicate a rational approach, we may find that technology has become an invisible monster as Egler has succinctly stated (1966).

Pesticides are the greatest single tool for simplifying the habitat ever conceived by the simple mind of man, who may yet prove too simple to grasp the fact that he is but a blind strand of an ecosystem web, dependent not upon himself, but upon the total web, which nevertheless he has the power to destroy.

Here environmental science can involve the social scientist in communicating sound science to society and involve the political scientist in seeing that sound scientific knowledge is translated into reality. Our survival on this planet may well depend on how well we can make this translation.

REFERENCES

Ames, P. L. 1966. DDT residues in the eggs of the osprey in the northeastern United States and their relation to nesting success. *J. Applied Ecol.,* 3 (suppl.): 87-97.

Anonymous. 1966. Fish, wildlife and pesticides. U.S. Dept. of Interior, Supt. of Doc. 12 p.

Bellinger, F., R. E. Dyer, R. King, and R. B. Platt. 1965. A review of the problem of the imported fire ant. *Bull. Georgia Acad. Sci.,* Vol. 23, No. 1.

Breidenbach, A. W., C. G. Gunnerson, F. K. Kawahara, J. J. Lichtenberg, and R. S. Green. 1967. Chlorinated hydrocarbon pesticides in major basins, 1957-1965. *Public Health Rept.* 82: 139-156.

Carson, Rachel. 1962. *Silent Spring.* Houghton Mifflin, Boston, 368 p.

Cottam, C. 1965. The ecologists' role in problems of pesticide pollution. *Bio-Science,* 15: 457-463.

Crosby, D. G., and R. K. Tucker. 1966. Toxicity of aquatic herbicides to *Daphnia magna. Science,* 154: 289-290.

Dill, N. H. 1962-63. Vegetation management. *New Jersey Nature News,* 17: 123-130; 18: 151-157.

Durham, W. F. 1965. Effects of pesticides on man. *In* C. O. Chichester, ed., *Research in Pesticides.* Academic Press, Inc., New York.

Egler, F. E. 1954. Vegetation management for rights-of-way and roadsides. *Smithsonian Inst. Rept. for 1953:* 299-322.

————. 1964a. Pesticides in our ecosystem. *Am. Scientist,* 52: 110-136.

————. 1964b. Pesticides in our ecosystem: communication II: *BioScience,* 14: 29-36.

————.1965. Pesticides in our ecosystem: communication III. *Assoc. Southeastern Biologist Bull.,* 12: 9-91.

————. 1966. Pointed perspectives. Pesticides in our ecosystem. *Ecology,* 47: 1077-1084.

Freed, V. H. 1965. Chemicals and the control of plants. *In* C. O. Chichester, ed., *Research in Pesticides.* Academic Press, Inc., New York.

Goodwin, R. H., and W. A. Niering. 1959. The management of roadside vegetation by selective herbicide techniques. *Conn. Arboretum Bull.,* 11: 4-10.

————. 1962. What is happening along Connecticut's roadsides. *Conn. Arboretum Bull.,* 13: 13-24.

Harrington, R. W., Jr., and W. L. Bidlingmayer. 1958. Effects of dieldrin on fishes and invertebrates of a salt marsh. *J. Wildlife Management,* 22: 76-82.

Hickey, J. J., and L. Barrie Hunt. 1960. Initial songbird mortality following a Dutch elm disease control program. *J. Wildlife Management,* 24: 259-265.

Hickey, J. J., and J. A. Keith. 1964. Pesticides in the Lake Michigan ecosystem. *In* The Effects of Pesticides on Fish and Wildlife. U.S. Dept Interior Fish and Wildlife Service.

Keith, J. A. 1964. Reproductive success in a DDT-contaminated population of herring gulls, p. 11-12. *In* The Effects of Pesticides on Fish and Wildlife. U.S. Dept. Interior Fish and Wildlife Service.

Kenfield, W. G. 1966. *The Wild Gardner in the Wild Landscape.* Hafner, New York. 232 p.

Loosanoff, V. L. 1965. Pesticides in sea water. *In* C. O. Chichester, ed., *Research in Pesticides.* Academic Press, Inc., New York.

Matthysse, J. G. 1959. An evaluation of mist blowing and sanitation in Dutch elm disease control programs. N.Y.

Monitoring and Control

26   Monitoring Pesticide Pollution

PHILIP A. BUTLER

The widespread use of synthetic organochloride pesticides, reports of their persistence in the environment, and the repeated demonstrations of their toxicity to nontarget fauna alerted marine biologists to their potentially disastrous effects in the estuarine environment. Soon after World War II, detailed studies of DDT applications to salt marshes for mosquito control showed increased mortality of fish and shellfish. Such acute effects were readily identified, and measures could be initiated to prevent or at least restrict such applications.

But biologists became even more concerned with the probability that continued terrestrial applications of persistent pesticides would result in their being carried in surface water, adsorbed on silt and debris, through river basins and eventually into estuaries. Here, their chronic presence at subacute levels might cause irreversible changes before their presence was apparent.

The estuary is an extraordinarily important environment to a wide array of fish, shellfish, and other elements of the biota that are important for commercial or esthetic reasons.

Permanent residents of estuaries, such as the oyster, are accustomed to widely fluctuating levels of various environmental properties and are relatively tolerant to unusual changes. Oysters can close their valves and "withdraw" from the environment, when, for example, unacceptable amounts of fresh water or silt are temporarily present. Some animals, however, including many kinds of crabs, shrimp, and fish, use the estuary only as a nursery area or as a part of their migration pathway, and are physiologically adjusted to the estuary for only a particular segment of their life span. As a consequence, they are especially susceptible to drastic environmental changes. Low levels of pollutants might interfere with olfaction, for example, and prevent salmon from finding their "home" stream; and chemicals that changed the osmoregulating ability of crustaceans could prevent shrimp and crabs from migrating to their brackish-water growing areas.

The many possibilities for subtle harmful changes resulting from the accidental or intentional transport of pesticides into estuaries prompted the Bureau of Commercial Fisheries to initiate a program in 1958 to assess the extent of the problem.

The program had two major objectives: to determine the acute and chronic toxicity of the commonly used pesticides to representative estuarine animals under controlled test conditions; and to monitor the seasonal levels of polychlorinated pesticide pollution in the nation's estuaries where production of living marine resources is commercially important. This report describes the development of the monitoring segment of the program and summarizes regional trends in pesticide pollution levels as revealed by 3 years of data collection.

Development of Program

It seemed likely that pesticide pollution in estuaries would be not only intermittent but also at such low concentrations in the water mass that automated sensing devices would be generally unsatisfactory. Consequently, the first requirement for successful monitoring was the selection of a suitable bioassay technique.

The Bureau of Commercial Fisheries Biological Laboratory at Gulf Breeze, Florida, had been engaged for more than 20 years in studies on the ecology and management of the eastern oyster, *Crassostrea virginica.* Much was known about its physiology, and it appeared to be a desirable animal for preliminary tests.

Typically, a mature oyster is feeding 90% of the time and transports about 16 liters of water an hour through its gill system to extract the planktonic food. Its ability and tendency to pick up and store metal ions, present in only trace amounts in the surrounding water, are well known. The oyster is physiologically active the entire year throughout much of its extensive geographical range. Most important, it is sedentary and easily handled.

Exploratory experiment with oysters consisted in recording on a kymograph their shell movements and rates of water transport ("pumping") before and during exposure to controlled amounts of pesticides in aquariums with flowing seawater (Butler et al., 1960). Under normal conditions, the oyster closes its valves briefly up to 10 times an hour to expel accumulated pseudofeces. These experimental oysters showed intense physiological irritation after 10 hours exposure to 1 ppm of dieldrin. The valves were almost continually opening and closing. It was obvious that the feeding process could not be normal. The oysters pumped water and fed, however, when the concentration of dieldrin was lowered to 0.1 ppm.

After 2 weeks of continuous exposure to 0.1 ppm of dieldrin, however, the experimental oysters were only half as active as controls. The oysters quickly returned to their normal level of activity when the addition of dieldrin was stopped. This inhibition of the pumping rate in oysters exposed to environmental pollutants can be measured objectively but the technique is tedious and time-consuming.

The interference with normal activity suggested that oyster growth, or rate of shell disposition, would decrease in polluted water. To test this hypothesis, shell deposition in young oysters was measured before and after exposure to known concentrations of pesticides. Linear growth of the oyster does not proceed uniformly. An initial increase in the peripheral deposition of new shell is followed by a period during which this thin shell is strengthened by internal deposits. During this second stage, there may be no measurable increase in length. To encourage the immediate deposition of new shell, the edges of the valves are ground until all new and thin shell is removed. The oyster then occupies all of the shell cavity and has no alternative, in growing, except to deposit new shell on the periphery (Butler, 1965). Linear shell deposition amounts to about 0.5 mm per day for at least 5 days under average conditions in the laboratory, when the oyster has a continuous supply of unfiltered seawater.

In the presence of a toxicant, the oyster deposits smaller and smaller amounts of new shell as the concentration of the toxicant is increased. Thus, it is possible to determine the concentrations of a particular pesticide that causes a 50% decrease in shell growth as compared to control oysters under otherwise similar conditions and to relate the toxicity of one pesticide to that of any other pesticide tested under similar conditions.

In parallel experiments, we found that oysters remove and store chlorinated hydrocarbon pesticides present in the surrounding water at concentrations as low as 0.1 part per billion. Oysters continue to build up such residues in their tissues at uniform rates as long as the toxicant is present. This biological magnification may produce DDT residues, for example, 70,000 times as high as the DDT concentration in the test water supply. An important consideration in a monitor program is the fact that the oyster flushes these residues out of its tissues at a uniform rate when the water supply is no longer contaminated. By sampling an oyster population regularly, it is possible to determine when the water supply becomes contaminated and when the contamination stops. It is possible to get some idea of the magnitude of the pollution load in the estuary by extrapolation from laboratory experiments.

Since oysters are not universally present in estuaries of interest to commercial fisheries, tests were undertaken to determine the relative efficiency of other common mollusks in storing pesticide residues. In general, the eastern oyster, the Pacific oyster (*Crassostrea gigas*), the soft clam (*Mya arenaria*), and any of several mussels are equally suitable. The hard clam (*Mercenaria mercenaria*) is the least efficient at storing pesticides of any mollusks evaluated (Butler, 1966).

With the problem of a suitable bioassay animal solved, we were able to consider the other prerequisites of a successful monitor program. The sampling had to have continuity and be done at least monthly. The assistance and cooperation of many people were required because of the length of the coastlines to be covered. To accomplish analytical uniformity, which was essential, it seemed desirable to have all analyses made by the same laboratory, although this arrangement greatly increased the difficulties in handling the samples.

The program that finally evolved was made possible by entering into formal and informal research contracts with state conservation agencies and university and federal marine laboratories in 15 coastal states. We developed a technique for homogenizing the samples with a desiccant consisting of sodium sulfate plus 10% by weight of Quso, a micro-fine, precipitated silica. This desiccant prevents spoilage of the sample and degradation of pesticide residues for at least 30 days without refrigeration. As a result, samples could be sent by ordinary mail to the Gulf Breeze laboratory for analysis. We analyze samples by gas liquid chromatography with electron capture using two different columns, so that 10 of the most commonly used organochloride pesticides can be quantified at levels above 10 ppb.

In the nearly 4 years the program has been in effect, about 170 permanent stations have been established on the Atlantic, Gulf, and Pacific coasts, and more than 5000 samples have been analyzed.

Summary of Findings

Data collected during the first 3 years of this project do not indicate any consistent upward or downward trends in estuarine pesticide pollution. Distinct seasonal and geographic differences in pollution levels are apparent, however, as well as regional differences in sources and kinds of pesticide pollution. Although each sample is screened for 10 or more pesticides, DDT (including its metabolities) is the only one commonly present. Dieldrin is next in frequency of occurrence, followed by endrin, toxaphene, and mirex.

In the estuaries of Washington, less than 3% of the samples have been contaminated and the DDT residues have always been less than 0.05 ppm. On the Atlantic Coast, oysters from Maine estuaries are the least contaminated; about 10% of the samples had residues of DDT, all at levels below 0.05 ppm. Oyster samples from the other states monitored[1] contained DDT residues more often than not. In some areas that are intensively farmed, oyster samples always contain DDT residues, but the amounts of DDT plus metabolites are usually less than 0.5 ppm. Only rarely has the residue exceeded 1.0 ppm. The highest residue of DDT observed in oysters, 5.4 ppm, was the result of a single incident of gross pollution.

It should be pointed out that these DDT residues are not of sufficient magnitude to constitute a human health problem. Their presence indicates, however, the ubiquity of DDT in the estuarine food web.

Analyses of residue data from individual river basins that drain predominantly agricultural lands show characteristic seasonal trends. Typically, there is a pronounced peak in the late spring and a lesser increase in the fall. The height of these peaks may vary tenfold from one basin to another, depending on the farming practices. In one basin on the Texas coast, three seasonal peaks in DDT residue levels reflect the intensive truck farming in an area where the mild climate permits three harvests each year.

In the river basins receiving significant amounts of municipal wastes as well as agricultural runoff, the seasonal residue pattern is similar but the magnitude of the residues is proportionately higher. By contrast, in estuaries that receive industrial wastes containing pesticides, seasonal residue patterns are erratic and occasionally indicate single, massive injections of a pollutant into the drainage system such as would happen when waste-control systems are breached. In two areas, the monitor data demonstrated the industrial discharge of pesticide wastes whose presence had been unsuspected by the state agencies responsible for clean water programs.

Several times it has been possible to identify specific sources of pesticide pollution by placing trays of oysters at intervals in the drainage system when natural beds of oysters did not occur. Near and above the river mouth, where the water becomes too fresh for oysters, we have substituted the brackish water clam (*Rangia cuneata*) and the freshwater Asiatic clam (*Corbicula fluminea*) as bioassay animals.

In one locality where a specific pollution source was suspected, trays of oysters were located at about 2-mile intervals upstream toward an industrial complex. Pesticide residues in oysters analyzed during the succeeding 10 months at the several stations, listed in order of their nearness to the pollution source, averaged as follows: 25.0, 17.0, 5.0, 3.0, 0.05, and 0.02 ppm. Analysis of the residue data at any one of these stations demonstrated the intermittency and variation in the amount of waste discharged.

1. Alabama, California, Delaware, Florida, Georgia, Maryland, Mississippi, New Jersey, New York, North Carolina, South Carolina, Texas, Virginia.

Programs for control of noxious insects involving direct application of insecticides to a salt marsh, constitute still another important source of estuarine pollution. Although the use of the persistent pesticides for this purpose is declining with the increased knowledge of the harmful side effects, DDT is still popular because it is cheap and effective. The 1-pound-per-acre, or less, application rates seem disarmingly small, yet the persistence of this chemical is such that the accumulation of residues in the fauna may reach disastrous levels.

In one bay in New York, for example, DDT residues in soft clam populations are higher by an order of magnitude than at any of 15 other stations routinely sampled on Long Island. This unusually high residue is not caused by the use of more insecticide there for the control of mosquitos, but is a result of the bay being isolated from the sea for much of the year. Since bay water is not diluted by tidal action, the residues accumulate in the environment where they are adsorbed on silt and plankton that the clams ingest as they feed.

A different situation exists in an estuary of northwest Florida, where the stable fly (*Stomoxys calcitrans*) is an obnoxious pest during the summer tourist period. This fly lays its eggs in windrows of seaweed along the beaches, where the larvae then develop. Present control methods consist of spraying the windrows with a DDT formulation three or four times during the early part of the summer. The total amount of DDT used in spraying the approximately 100 miles of beach is relatively small. We calculated that if all of this DDT were evenly dispersed in the estuary at a single time the concentration would be less than 0.001 ppm. Chemical analyses of DDT residues in the plankton following the spray program, however, showed average accumulations of about 0.07 ppm. The DDT is washed into the estuary by tidal action in a relatively short time and, since there is only one tide a day in this area, the flushing rate is relatively slow. As a result, the DDT may persist adsorbed on silt or plankton for a matter of weeks. Plankton makes up the food supply of various small fish including the pinfish (*Lagodon rhomboides*). Analysis of random samples of this fish showed pesticide residues in the range of 0.1 to 0.5 ppm. The level of these residues increased the longer the fish were in the estuary, i.e., the older they were. In turn, pinfish are fed upon by various water birds, including the loon (*Gavia immen*). One analysis made of the liver of a loon shot in the vicinity showed that it contained about 180 ppm of DDT. Mullet (*Mugil cephalus*) are herbivorous fish that feed largely on plankton and consequently build up relatively large residues of DDT. In one series of analyses, for example, mullet gonads contained 3 to 10 ppm of DDT. At the top of this food chain is the bottlenose dolphin (*Tursiops truncatus*) which feeds extensively on mullet. Blubber samples from a small series of porpoise found dead in this area contained DDT residues ranging up to 800 ppm.

Evidence is substantial in the freshwater habitat that the accumulation of about 4 ppm of DDT in fish eggs may cause complete mortality of the brood. Apparently a similar situation exists in one estuary on the Texas coast. Levels of DDT residues in the ovary of the speckled seatrout (*Cynoscion nebulosus*) were as high as 8 ppm in the prespawning period in 1968, and there was no evidence of successful spawning later in the year. In a second estuary 100 miles away, ovarian DDT residues in seatrout were about 0.2 ppm and a normal number of young of the year were observed.

These data demonstrate the importance of trophic magnification of persistent pesticides in the food web and indicate that even relatively small applications of pesticides in pest control programs can be magnified astoundingly at higher trophic levels. Pesticides are, of course, not all bad. Many are essential to the production and protection of foodstuffs and other agricultural products, in the management of our natural resources, and for the amelioration of our daily existence.

Our difficulties arise from the use of broad spectrum toxicants that may contaminate the environment for months and years. These persistent pesticide chemicals, resistant to decay, may be carried by surface drainage waters to areas far from the point of application. Through the process of co-distillation, they pass into the atmosphere or are airborne on dust particles and carried by winds to every part of the globe, to contaminate even the polar regions and the mid-ocean environment. The use of such pesticides must be limited to those purposes for which there is no substitute. They must not be used on the basis of economy and expediency. Theoretically, all pesticides are used on a cost-benefit ratio. It appears, however, that even after a quarter century of use and research on DDT, we still do not know the true extent of the damage it has inflicted on the environment. It is essential that laboratory and field tests to evaluate synthetic pesticides be so thorough that we can be assured they will have no irreversible effect on the environment.

REFERENCES

Butler, Philip A. 1965. Reaction of some estuarine mollusks to environmental factors. In: Biological problems in water pollution, third seminar 1962, p. 92-104. U.S.P.H.S. Publication No. 999-WP-25.
———. 1966. Pesticides in the marine environment. *J. App. Ecol.,* 3 (Suppl): 253-259.
Butler, Philip A., Alfred J. Wilson, Jr., and Alan J. Rick. 1960. Effect of pesticides on oysters. *Proc. Nat. Shellfish Assoc.* 51: 23-32.

Fewer Pesticides—More Control 27

ROBERT VAN DEN BOSCH

Recently, as a member of a research team concerned with cotton pest control, I strongly advocated the use of DDT over alternative materials, because of its less severe impact on the agroecosystem. The advocacy of DDT earned me a somewhat heretical reputation among my colleagues, in the light of my long experience as a specialist in biological control!

Actually, I realize that nature's way does not always work, and that chemical pest control is frequently necessary for economical crop production. I believed that DDT was the ecologically safer chemical choice in cotton. But what I learned at the Rochester conference[1] came as a shock and convinced me that the use of DDT and certain other organochlorines should be curtailed and eventually stopped.

1. First Rochester Conference on Toxicity, University of Rochester, Rochester, New York, 4-6 June 1968.

The chemical alternatives to DDT are disturbing, but until better things come along, these appear to be the safer materials. As for a moratorium on the use of DDT, it will be interesting to see how the agricultural economy of Arizona and the health and welfare of its citizenry hold up under the recently invoked year-long ban on DDT there. The ban is no assurance that all is well with chemical pest control in Arizona. Indeed, if the situation is at all comparable to that in California, it probably borders on the chaotic. But at least Arizona has stopped pouring DDT into the biosphere and is merely tearing up its own environment with alternative materials.

In general, the synthetic organic insecticides are ecologically crude and engender serious problems: resurgence of target pests, outbreaks of nontarget species, and pest resistance to pesticides. These have contributed to a steady increase in the use of insecticides in recent years. For example, in California pest control costs of its major crops, citrus and cotton, have risen sharply over the past decade. A critical analysis nationwide would reveal a similar pattern: bollworms in Texas cotton, spider mites in deciduous fruit orchards, cabbage loopers in vegetable crops, and so forth.

For the past two decades, the pest control field has been dominated by toxicologists and chemical company sales personnel—persons often either ignorant of or indifferent to ecological principles. Fortunately, entomologists are beginning to appreciate the ecological pitfalls that attend the unilateral use of synthetic insecticides. The concept of integrated control is gaining acceptance[2]. This concept recognizes the ecological nature of pest control and has its objective pest population management rather than simple pest kill. Integrated control does not reject chemical insecticides but attempts, instead, to integrate them into pest management systems. Its advocates are not "anti-insecticide," but they do reject ecologically untenable materials and practices, and they plead for more sophisticated materials and a voice in their development. . . . Greater pesticide efficacy and reduced environmental pollution will result. . . .

2. R. F. Smith and H. T. Reynolds, *Proc. Food Agr. Organ. Symp. Integrated Control* 1, 11 (1966).

28   Mercury in Man

NEVILLE GRANT

Alamogordo, New Mexico, is not a large town. Located in the sparsely populated southern portion of the state, it has few distinctions. However, in a sense, Alamogordo is symbolic of two ongoing threats to the environment that first gained national recognition there. In 1945 the first atomic weapons were exploded in nearby White Sands. Nuclear radiation as an environmental hazard became a reality. Twenty-five years later, in late 1969, an Alamogordo family ate mercury-contaminated pork and this country awoke dramatically to the possibility of widespread mercury pollution. The paths of these two environmental contaminants—radiation and mercury—converge at the genetic material of living cells. The disruptive effects of mercury on cells—called radiomimetic because they are similar to those caused by radiation—are greater than the effects of any other known chemical. Do present mercury levels in the environment pose a threat to man? It would seem that the answer is yes. The magnitude of this threat is as uncertain as that of low levels of ionizing radiation.

In the early 1950s the Minamata Bay disaster alerted the Japanese to the sequence: mercury discharge from industrial waste into water—concentration in fish—disease in people. The lesson, however, was not sufficient. In 1964 the Agano River in Niigata Prefecture was contaminated by mercury in industrial effluent: 26 persons fell ill; 5 died.[1] Elsewhere reports appeared of poisoning in large groups of people following the ingestion of mercury-treated seed baked into food.[2] These incidents invariably occurred in underdeveloped regions where malnourishment was prevalent. Sweden critically examined the extent of mercury contamination in fish and birds in the mid-1960s, took steps to eliminate mercury as an environmental pollutant, and set guidelines to avert possible human poisoning. Reports began to appear in late 1969 of elevated levels of mercury in partridge and pheasant in various parts of Canada and the U.S.[3] The stage was set for Alamogordo.

In September 1969 Ernest Huckleby obtained floor-sweepings from a granary—millet seed treated with a methyl mercury fungicide. It has been an established practice that all treated seed is mixed with a red coloring to avoid what happened next. Huckleby fed the seed to seventeen hogs he was raising. Subsequently, several hogs became ill. He chose one that appeared to be well, butchered and froze it, and began feeding it to his family; the other hogs were sold. Several weeks later three of the Huckleby children fell ill. The diagnosis, when finally established, was acute mercury poisoning. Side meat from the hog contained 27 parts per million (ppm) of mercury. The three children suffered irreparable neurological damage and a child, born of the then pregnant but asymptomatic mother, had convulsions after birth—a common manifestation of mercury toxicity in the newborn.

Thus began a hard and still unresolved battle over the use of organomercury compounds as fungicides in agriculture, a battle that Sweden had decided some years earlier in favor of suspension. One thing seems clear; the Alamogordo incident was not unique. At the present a reappraisal of mercury compounds of all types used in agriculture is underway. Sweden has shown that more stringent rules of application of the less toxic and more easily degradable mercury compounds can markedly reduce food contamination without a significant reduction in crop yield.

In March 1970 fish in Lake St. Clair on the U.S.-Canadian border, and subsequently in many lakes and rivers in the U.S.[4] and Canada,[5] were found to be contaminated with mercury at levels (1 to 10 ppm) comparable to those implicated in the Niigata disaster. In most, but not all instances, the source of pollution could be traced to industrial effluents from chemical plants, pulp factories, and the like. Fishing industries collapsed in certain areas as news spread of high mercury levels. Economic disaster visited many whose livelihood was sport and commercial fishing. The state of Alabama prohibited commercial fishing in 51,000 miles of waterways and sought federal disaster relief. They were turned down because the situation was not the result of natural causes. The Canadian government, however, has offered low-interest loans to those fishermen who were affected by high mercury levels. The Food and Drug Administration—understaffed and unprepared—began a widespread survey of all foods. Agencies both public and private began testing programs. Symposia and congressional hearings were held. Then ocean-going tuna and swordfish were found high in mercury—the source as yet uncertain. The final injustice: some health food tablets, made from the compressed liver of seals caught in the Pacific, were loaded with mercury (36 ppm).

This staccato series of events was difficult to digest, because full information was not available on which to base an evaluation of the seriousness of the situation. Many of the pieces are still missing, but the picture is beginning to emerge. In order to evaluate new information as it appears and to formulate policy decisions, attention must be given to several broad points:

Where does mercury that contaminates the environment come from; how is it dispersed; and in what form does it reach animals and man?

How are the different forms of mercury handled by the body?

At what level of exposure does mercury pose a problem for humans, and how close are we to those levels?

What is the extent of present mercury contamination? What is an appropriate maximum permissible level of mercury contamination in food?

Mercury in the Ecosystem

Where does mercury that contaminates the environment come from; how is it dispersed; and in what form does it reach animals and man?

Mercury is present in all terrestrial soil and rock. The average amount is approximately 0.05 ppm. Certain large mercuriferous belts which occur in sediment and volcanic rock consisting largely of cinnabar (HgS) may contain from 1 to 30 ppm. During the weathering of rocks and deposits mercury may enter the sediment of streams, lakes, and oceans.[6]

Perhaps the largest quantities of mercury added to the environment by man are released with the burning of natural fuels. From available evidence it appears that U.S. coal may average between 0.5 and 3.3 ppm mercury; at present rates of coal consumption, between 275 and 1,800 tons of mercury are probably being released to the air annually.[7] Petroleum may contain from 1.9 to 21 ppm mercury; it is not known how much is released in refining and burning. Bitumens and asphalt contain 2.0 to 900 ppm mercury. The combined use of all these materials may add more mercury to the environment than intentional uses of mercury in industry and agriculture.

The extraction and use of mercury itself is a substantial source of pollution. According to one estimate, mining, smelting, and refining operations released 170,000 pounds of mercury into the environment in 1965.[8] About one-third of the annual U.S. consumption of mercury is produced by domestic mines; the remainder is either imported or released from federal stockpiles. Total demand for mercury in 1968 was 5,730,400 pounds,[4] of which a significant portion may ultimately find its way into the environment.

An analysis of the uses to which this mercury is put was recently performed by a group at Oak Ridge National Laboratory.[4] They reported that 26 percent of the total mercury demand in 1968 was required for "dissipative" uses, such as mercury fungicides for agriculture and manufacturing, in which mercury is necessarily dispersed to the environment. By far the largest consumer of mercury was the manufacture of chlorine and caustic soda. Twenty-three percent of the total mercury consumption during 1968 was released to the environment as wastes from these plants. Another 23 percent of total consumption was of unknown ultimate disposition; much of this material was fixed in electronic instruments and measuring devices, including thermometers. How and to what extent this mercury reaches the environment is not known. Only 18 percent of the mercury produced was reclaimed for further use, however, and a great percentage of the remainder probably will eventually find its way into the environment in one way or another.

Agricultural uses of mercury, although small compared to the total, are of concern because of their immediacy to man. Mercurial fungicides may enter the food chain of man in a variety of ways: through the spraying of plants; the leaching of fungicide from soil to waterways; the translocation of mercury from seed to plant (crops grown from treated seed may contain twice the mercury content of untreated crops; this level appears to be extremely low[9] and would seem to pose no significant threat); and feeding of treated seed to livestock and poultry. The real and potential threat of ingestion of methyl mercury-treated seed by birds, mammals, and their bird predators, has been well documented.[10]

Most recent concern over mercury has been focused on water pollution and the resultant contamination of fish. The degree to which this situation is manmade is still in dispute. The amount of natural mercury in streams, rivers, and lakes averages 0.03 part per billion (ppb) (range 0.01 ppb to 0.1 ppb). Oceans average 0.03 to 5.0 ppb. Waters near mercury deposits contain 5.0 to greater than 100 ppb. It has not yet been shown what percentage of this total mercury in water is in the form of the water soluble and toxic methyl mercury. Studies are in progress on this point. The conversion of inorganic mercury to organic by microorganisms ("methanogenic bacteria") has been shown[7] and this reaction appears to be ubiquitous. Thus, lakes contaminated by simple inorganic mercury act as a continuous source for the production of methyl mercury. It has been estimated that this mercury may remain in the environment for as much as 100 years.

Methyl mercury is concentrated in fish approximately 5,000-fold that in the surrounding water[11] by entering through the gills during respiration or by ingestion of mercury adsorbed on phytoplankton. Once bound to protein, the half-life (the time required for half the mercury to be eliminated) in fish has been judged to be two to three years,[12] and the binding is of such strength that it is not disrupted by freezing, boiling, or frying. Ninety-five to 100 percent of the mercury in fish is methyl mercury. That environmental pollution is the major cause of elevated levels of mercury in fish is shown by the 100-fold increase in mercury in certain species of fish in Lake St. Clair (0.07 to 0.11 ppm in 1935 to 5.0 to 7.0 ppm in 1970).[12] The natural level of mercury in fish is thought to be up to 0.2 ppm; higher concentrations are probably due to mercury contamination of water, except in water which washes over mercuriferous rock. High levels of natural mercury in water may not necessarily concentrate in fish if it is not in a methylated form. However, research is in progress on the possibility that microorganisms on fish gills may be methanogenic, that is, capable of converting inorganic mercury to an organic form. The argument that high levels (greater than 0.5 ppm) in fish are natural overlooks the fact that almost all of this is methyl mercury and therefore potentially dangerous.

Mercury in the Body

If there is dispute over the sources of mercury in the environment, its effects are still more hotly debated. These effects vary greatly with the chemical compounds of mercury to which the body is exposed.

The two general classes of mercury compounds—organic and inorganic— differ greatly in the extent to which they are absorbed by the body and the degree of damage they may do, once absorbed. As was pointed out in our previous report in May 1969, the most common form of organic mercury found in the environment, and unfortunately the most toxic for man, is methyl mercury. Most mercury compounds can be converted to this form by bacteria once they have been released to the environment; it is this form which will concern us here. Methylation is the process whereby mercury is changed from an inorganic to an organic form by combining with a one-carbon organic molecule. Methyl mercury is far more readily absorbed, and much more slowly excreted, than inorganic mercury compounds. When taken by mouth, for instance, absorption of inorganic mercury is extremely low—less than 2 percent. That some conversion of inorganic to methyl mercury by bacteria may take place in the intestine of some animals has been suggested.[13] Birds fed various nonmethylated mercury compounds (as seed-dressing on feed) produce eggs which contain methyl mercury. The extent to which methylation of mercury in the intestinal tract takes place is unknown. Indications are that it may be quite small, but studies on humans, particularly during periods of slow intestinal passage, are entirely lacking. *Intestinal absorption of methyl mercury, however, is close to 90 to 95 percent.*

Once absorbed, methyl mercury is transported by the blood throughout the body, almost entirely by the red cells. It appears to be bound to certain sulfur-containing (sulfhydryl) "binding groups."[14] Thus, measurement of mercury in red cells reflects the level of methyl mercury in whole blood. The relatively slow excretion of methyl mercury may be due to the fact that it is excreted in the bile and then almost totally reabsorbed by the small intestine.[15]

Inorganic mercury, by contrast, is transported approximately 50 percent in plasma and in this form is more readily excreted in urine. Aryl mercury (substances such as phenylmercuric acetate, or PMA—a non-methylated form of organic mercury) is largely converted to the inorganic form and handled as such by the body.

Slow conversion of methyl mercury to the inorganic form, in the liver and other organs, probably also accounts for its delayed excretion.[16] There is some evidence that the liver may contain the capability of methylating mercury, but the extent of this reaction is unknown.

Methyl mercury is excreted largely by the intestine, and evidence indicates that some may be converted to inorganic mercury in the process. Small amounts are excreted in the kidney in both the organic and inorganic form. Thus urinary levels of mercury are a poor indicator of prior methyl mercury exposure.

Mercury compounds have been shown to cause breakage and abnormal chromosome division in concentrations lower than any other known substance —as low as 0.05 ppm.[17] An area of both major concern and incomplete knowledge is how mercury may affect chromosomes—the carriers of genetic material. It is here that the dangers of low-level pollution may be the greatest. Decisions must be made regarding acceptable levels of exposure. Genetic abnormalities occur when chromosomes are damaged or their division disturbed. The derangement of chromosomes by mercury probably depends on its interaction with sulfhydryl groups essential for normal spindle formation that directs an equal division of chromosomes into each newly formed cell. Interference with this segregation will result in some cells receiving unequal numbers of chromosomes (non-disjunction). That this happens readily in plant cells and flies exposed to mercury has clearly been shown.[18] This effect has been shown with aryl as well as alkyl (methyl) mercury. A variety of human genetic abnormalities of unknown cause are the result of non-disjunction. There has been no evidence that mercury has caused chromosome damage to reproductive cells in humans such that genetically malformed offspring have resulted. However, should isolated instances occur, the evidence would be extremely difficult to detect. Recently, evidence of a slight but statistically significant increase in chromosome breakage was noted in lymphocyte (white blood cell) cultures from humans with elevated blood mercury levels due to ingestion of contaminated fish.[18] The significance of this observation is not yet clear. Vaginal application of PMA to pregnant mice resulted in fetal death and malformation.[20] The reason for this is not clear, because PMA given intravenously is not detected in the fetus (unborn offspring) despite a large concentration in the placenta (the organ which unites the fetus to the maternal uterus). This is in contrast to methyl mercury, which passes the placental barrier readily. The pertinence of these findings is heightened by the fact that many conveniently available vaginal creams contain PMA. One such product contains 0.02 percent PMA (delivering 16 milligrams of PMA in an 80-gram tube which is designed to be used within one week) and is readily absorbed through the vaginal lining. Its effect on maternal reproductive cell, sperm, and developing fetus is unknown. A further review of this problem is given by M. Shimizu in the *Journal of the Japanese Obstetric and Gynecological Society.*[28]

A most disturbing feature of methyl mercury is its demonstrated ability to penetrate the placental barrier and produce fetal damage. Toxic effects have been noted in the fetuses of experimental animals and in humans at levels that have not produced symptoms in the mother. There is an apparent concentration of methyl mercury in the fetus, as manifested by a higher concentration of mercury in umbilical cord red cells as compared to maternal blood.[29] Developing fetal nerve tissue appears to be more sensitive to the destructive effects. Some evidence suggests that placental and fetal "trapping" of methyl mercury may actually protect the mother.[21] Recently a new factor has received attention. Certain substances such as NTA (nitrilotriacetic acid—introduced as a substitute for phosphates in detergents) have been shown to form chemical complexes with mercury that appear to increase the ability of mercury to cross the placenta and produce damage in the unborn. Wisely, caution has been observed, and NTA has been removed from detergents.

Methyl mercury characteristically penetrates the blood-brain barrier and is distributed in the brain, producing specific symptoms due to the destruction of cells in the cerebellum (balance center), visual and hearing centers, and elsewhere. Inorganic mercury does not readily penetrate to brain tissue except as a vapor.[22]

Level of Exposure

At what level of exposure does mercury pose a problem for humans? In correlating the relation of estimated onset of tissue damage with concentration of mercury in (1) red blood cells and (2) brain tissue, these important assumptions are made: (1) All mercury is in the form of methyl mercury or is converted to it. (2) Exposure is continuous, or nearly so.

What is an Acceptable Daily Intake (ADI) of mercury? Calculation of an ADI (whether for mercury or any other chemical food contaminant) is an extremely difficult task. With regard to mercury, a number of factors must be considered.

The form of mercury must be known. Clearly, the more easily absorbed and more toxic alkyl mercury will require a much lower ADI than other forms of mercury.

Calculations of half-life in the body and distribution (especially to the brain) may vary. Levels observed in humans may be either falsely low (for example, blood collected at varying times after exposure ceased) or falsely high (for example, in autopsy brain tissue concentration in fatal cases) in relation to symptoms.

Damage may occur at levels much lower than can be recorded by present techniques of clinical evaluation. (This is almost certainly true with regard to brain damage and quite possibly true with regard to chromosome damage). Of great interest in this regard is a case reported by Takeuchi of an elderly man (with no symptoms of mercury poisoning) found at autopsy to have brain lesions typical of methyl mercury exposure (from frequent fish consumption).[17]

Variation in individual sensitivity appears to be extremely wide. A safety factor of 100 is generally accepted as adequate when transferring experimental results from animals to man (interspecies variation). A safety factor of ten may be adequate in relating effects in humans to other humans (intraspecies). Both safety factors are generally calculated from a "no-effect" level for the *most* sensitive species.

Considering the many areas of uncertainty to be taken into account, it is not surprising that standards for mercury levels in the diet recommended by various groups have differed widely. One of the most widely quoted "standards," however, is not really a standard at all. In 1967 the World Health Organization published a report in which it estimated a "practical residue limit" in food. This was defined as the concentration of mercury expected in the diet from natural background and natural environmental contamination, from 0.02 to 0.05 ppm mercury in its organic forms. Rather than a standard, this is the irreducible minimum of exposure to mercury that we can expect, and WHO and other organizations have recommended that all efforts be made not to exceed this minimum exposure.

The U.S. Food and Drug Administration, largely in response to concern over contamination of fish, has established an "interim guideline" of 0.5 ppm. This is predicated on a fairly modest intake of fish, as this level, if present in the diet as a whole, would result in total consumption of mercury well in excess of that generally recommended.

Based on observed blood and brain levels of mercury of the most sensitive symptomatic cases, half-life and distribution characteristics, and estimated intake of mercury in toxic cases, an intake of not more than 0.03 milligram methyl mercury per day (for a 150 pound man) has been recommended by a Swedish panel of experts.[23]

An average serving of fish of 150 to 200 grams with 1.0 ppm would yield 0.15 to 0.20 milligram methyl mercury. To maintain an ADI of 0.03 milligram per day this could be eaten only once a week. At 0.5 ppm only two meals per week could be eaten, and a daily meal of fish would reach the maximum safe level of mercury in red cells estimated by the Swedes (0.04 ppm). For unrestricted eating, a level of 0.2 ppm would be the maximum permitted by this recommended standard. On the assumption that the general American fish intake is less than two meals per week (and for other reasons), the FDA has set a level of 0.5 ppm. Clearly, with an upper limit of 0.5 ppm and careful monitoring, the average concentration in fish would be considerably lower—perhaps in the range of 0.2 to 0.3 ppm or less. This is in contrast to the estimated concentration of mercury in the fish at Niigata producing mercurialism—50 percent less than 1.0 ppm and 50 percent greater than 1.0 ppm, mostly in the range of 1.0 to 10.0 ppm.[24] This range has clearly been reached in certain lakes and rivers in North America.[25] *The only difference has been the eating habits of the two areas.* No cases of mercury poisoning from fish in North America have been reported. It is possible that minor symptoms have occurred and gone undetected or that subclinical damage has occurred.

Mercury exposure occurs from other sources in the environment. It is not yet clear how much and in what form this occurs. *If all food averaged 1.0 ppm methyl mercury,* a consumption of 500 grams of food per day would produce an intake of 0.5 milligram per day. At the end of one year, equilibrium at 5 ppm brain tissue would occur, which is clearly a toxic dose. A market basket averaging 0.5 ppm would yield an intake of 0.25 milligram per day, clearly a dangerous dose. A general level of 0.1 ppm would mean a daily intake of 0.05 milligram. 0.06 ppm in all food would give the Swedish group's recommended maximum acceptable intake of 0.03 milligram per day.

What are the current levels of mercury in food? At present, knowledge of mercury levels in food is fragmentary, scattered, and difficult to come by. No significant monitoring for the element in food in the United States was in effect before 1970. A total diet survey in Britain in 1969 showed the level of mercury to be at or below the level of detection by the method used (0.01 ppm).[26]

In Sweden most of the fish investigated from freshwater and coastal areas were in the range of 0.20 to 1.0 ppm with 1 percent greater than 1.0 ppm and the highest concentration being 9.8 ppm. Ocean-going fish generally range from 0.03 to 0.1, with the exception of tuna with a slightly higher range and swordfish frequently found to have greater than 0.5 ppm.

In Canada one survey[27] of a variety of fish sampled gave levels in a range of 0.02 to 0.42 with an average of approximately 0.1 ppm. The range was considerably higher for fish from Lake St. Clair and Lake Erie. Other surveys have shown higher concentrations in areas related to industry and pulp mills.

In the United States many states have reported areas where the content of mercury in fish was in the range of 0.5 to greater than 1.0 ppm.[11] Most fish, however, living in noncontaminated areas contain less than 0.5 ppm. At the present time a widespread survey is taking place on mercury in the foods of the market basket. These reports are not yet complete; several things, however, seem clear: (1) In general, foods contain less than 0.1 and are usually below 0.06 ppm. (2) "Hot spots" may occur along certain chains, for example, seed- and fish-eating birds which *may* accumulate significant levels.[3] Excessive use of mercury fungicides and the feeding of mercury-treated seed to poultry and livestock may increase the possibility of food contamination. A decrease in mercury content of food can be brought about by an increase in the use of non-mercurial fungicides.

In conclusion it can be said that no widespread epidemic of mercury poisoning is underway in the U.S., perhaps in large part because U.S. eating habits do not include large amounts of fish. However, there is clearly the potential for human damage at present levels of mercury pollution. Much new knowledge must be gained before a safe level of exposure can be confidently set. The difficulty, of course, is the uncertainty of levels that might cause chromosome damage. Certainly evidence of chromosome damage to white blood cells at mercury blood levels commonly found in moderate fish consumers in Sweden gives great pause. New information may well alter what is ultimately considered an acceptable daily intake. In the meantime, prudence would dictate that intensive efforts be made to reduce industrial mercury wastes, to find other, less toxic agricultural fungicides, and to pinpoint and reduce all other sources of mercury contamination of the environment.

In addition, the methods of mercury detection must be standardized in such a way that results are reliable and reproducible. Already some controversy has arisen over this point. More information is needed concerning what percentage of the mercury in the environment is methyl mercury. Finally, a program of regular monitoring of food must be maintained.

NOTES

1. Tsuchiya, K., *Keio Journal of Medicine,* 18:213-227, 1969.
2. Kantarjian, A. D., "A Syndrome Clinically Resembling Amyotrophic Lateral Sclerosis Following Chronic Mercurialism," *Neurology,* 11:639, 1961.
3. Keith, J. A., "Mercury Residues in Canadian Wildlife," Special Symposium on Mercury in Man's Environment, Ottawa, Canada, February 1971.
4. Wallace, R. A., W. Fulkerson, W. D. Shults, and W. S. Lyon, *Mercury in the Environment, the Human Element,* Oak Ridge National Laboratory, Oak Ridge, January 1971, p. 5.
5. Bligh, E. G., "Mercury Levels in Canadian Fish," Special Symposium on Mercury in Man's Environment, Ottawa, Canada, February 1971.
6. Jonasson, I. R., and R. W. Boyle, "Geochemistry of Mercury," Special Symposium on Mercury in Man's Environment, Ottawa, Canada, February 1971.
7. Wood, J. M., F. Scott Kennedy, and C. G. Rosen, *Nature,* 220:173, 1968.
8. Lutz, G. A., S. B. Gross, J. B. Boatman, P. J. Moore, R. C. Darby, W. H. Veazie, and F. A. Butrico, *Design of an Overview System for Evaluating the Public Health Hazards of Chemicals in the Environment,* Batelle Memorial Institute, July 1967, NTIS document PB194 398, p. 4.
9. Lagervall, M. and G. Westöö, *Var Foda,* 21:9-12, 1969.
10. Fimreite, N. R., W. Fyfe, and J. A. Keith, *The Canadian Field-Naturalist,* 84:269-276, 1970.
11. Johnels, S. et al., "Observed Levels and Their Dynamics in the Environment," Special Symposium on Mercury in Man's Environment, Ottawa, Canada, February 1971.
12. Wood, J. M. in press.

13. Westöö, G., *Acta. Chem. Scand.,* 22:2277-2280, 1968.
14. Takeda, *Toxicology and Applied Pharmacology,* 17:181-188, 1970.
15. Clarkson, T. W., and R. E. Shapiro, "The Absorption of Mercury from Food, Its Significance and New Methods of Removing Mercury from the Body," Special Symposium on Mercury in Man's Environment, Ottawa, Canada, February 1971.
16. Norseth, T. and T. Clarkson, *Archives of Environmental Health,* 21:717, 1970.
17. Löfroth, Göran, *A Review of Health Hazards and Side Effects Associated with the Emission of Mercury Compounds into Natural Systems,* Swedish Natural Science Research Council, Stockholm, Sweden, 2nd Edition, Sept. 1970, pp. 49, 50.
18. *Ibid.,* pp. 20, 21.
19. Skerfring, S., K. Hansson, and J. Lindston, *Archives of Environmental Health,* 21:133-139, 1970.
20. Murakami, et al., as cited by S. Keckes and J. K. Miettinen in "Review of Mercury as Marine Pollutant," FAO Technical Conference on Marine Pollution and Its Effect on Living Resources and Fishing, Rome, Dec. 9-18, 1970.
21. Clegg, D. J., "Embryotoxicity of Mercury Compounds," Special Symposium on Mercury in Man's Environment," Ottawa, Canada, February 1971.
22. Takahata, N., H. Hayashi, S. Watanabe, and T. Anso, "Accumulation of Mercury in the Brains of Two Autopsy Cases with Chronic Inorganic Mercury Poisoning," *Folia Psych. Newro, Jap.,* 24:59-69, 1970.
23. Morrison, A. B., "The Canadian Approach to Acceptable Daily Intakes of Mercury in Foods," Special Symposium on Mercury in Man's Environment, Ottawa, Canada, February 1971.
24. Tsubaki, T., "Clinical and Epidemiological Aspects of Organic Mercury Intoxication," Special Symposium on Mercury in Man's Environment, Ottawa, Canada, February 1971.
25. Wallace, et al., *ibid.,* and Bligh, *ibid.*
26. Report of the Government Chemist, 1969, H.M.S.O., 1970.
27. Jervis, R. E., et al., Summary on Progress (Canada) National Health Grant Project No. 605-7-510, revised to September 30, 1970.
28. Shimizu, M., in *Journal of the Japanese Obstetric and Gynecological Society,* 22:1209-1216, November 1970.
29. Suzuki, T., T. Miyama, and H. Katsunuma, *Bulletin of Environmental Contamination and Toxicology,* 5:502-508, 1971.

PCB's

PCB's (Polychlorinated biphenyls), chemically related to DDT, are being produced world-wide at about 50,000 tons a year. Paints and varnish are the prime sources. Wood's Hole Oceanographic Institute scientists in an extensive survey have found 0.1 to 1.5 parts per million in plankton from the open ocean. Plankton from coastal waters usually contain from .01 to .05 ppm. Surprisingly, these lower links of the food chain are more heavily contaminated than their predators. It has been estimated that PCB's last more than 100 times as long as DDT.

FERTILIZERS

Millions of dollars are required to produce, distribute and apply the chemical fertilizers needed by agriculture. Millions of dollars are also required to dispose of the natural fertilizer produced by the growing cattle feedlot industry. A 25,000 head feedlot, 70 percent full year around, will generate 150,000 tons of manure. If this waste is untreated and merely allowed to enter a public stream, the contribution is equal to that of a city of 250,000 people contributing untreated wastes. The former has been tolerable to the mind, but the latter is unthinkable. Feedlot runoff has been cited as the source of numerous and large fish kills in several mid-western states. The West Germans dry animal waste and use it as fertilizer. This has not become a widespread practice in the U. S. The application of fertilizer to upland areas will seriously affect life in a pond or lake which receives the drain-off. Eutrophication in a confined body of water often follows as readily from the run-off following fertilization of nearby fields as it would from the direct introduction of sewage into water.

Soil Pollution   29

DAVID E. ELRICK

Fertilizers are applied to the soil and it is the behavior of these chemicals both on or in the soil that will determine any subsequent transport which could lead to water pollution. Under normal conditions small amounts of some nutrients are transported. For example, fall applications of nitrogen fertilizers in the temperate climates will probably lead to an increased leaching of nitrogen as both nitrate (and nitrite) nitrogen are mobile and will move in some manner associated with the percolating water. Under normal growth conditions, microbial mineralization and nitrification will convert some of the organic and ammonium forms of nitrogen in the upper layers of the soil to the nitrate form. Phosphorus compounds are relatively immobile within the soil (movement is generally of the order of centimeters).

All of North America is involved because nitrate nitrogen is mobile within the soil and the real problem involves the long range effects of slowly increasing the nitrogen content of our groundwater supplies throughout the continent.

30

Lake Tahoe
Measured for Pollution

EDWARD S. DEEVEY, JR.

One can only have arrived at the conclusion that mineral fertilizers pose no threat to Lake Tahoe by supposing the volume of Lake Tahoe to be infinite, like God's bounty to undeserving man. This kind of notion has survived the collapse of the whaling industry and now promises to outlive Lake Erie and Lake Baikal. It has been claimed that the annual increment of fertilizer to the entire state of Nevada, 2000 tons (2×10^{15} μg) of nitrogen, could not be detected by any means, "including a biological one," if mixed all at once into Lake Tahoe. This may be true in plant food circles, but limnologists use methods appropriate to the concentrations they encounter. Although no analyses of Tahoe waters are readily available to me, (and I have not studied the lake myself), the total nitrogen in so pure a lake is unlikely to exceed 100 μg/liter and is probably closer to 20; soluble nitrogen may be presumed to vary seasonally between 1 and 20 μg/liter. Tahoe is one of the deepest lakes in the world. Its boundaries are circumscribed in a map on p. 17 of G. E. Hutchinson's *Treatise on Limnology,* vol. 1 (Wiley, New York, 1957), and its volume is 124 km^3, or 1.24×10^{14} liters. Thus the hypothetical addition of 20×10^{14} μg of soluble nitrogen (16 μg/liter) might easily double the concentration; the difference would be easily detectable by standard micromethods, and ultramicromethods are available if needed.

Commercial fertilizers usually contain as much phosphorus as nitrogen, whereas the two elements are ordinarily present in natural waters in the proportion of N:P = 7:1 by weight. Doubling the nitrogen concentration might therefore entail a sevenfold increase of phosphorus. Ignoring sewage as a source of algal nutrients, we may use the 2×10^{15} μg of nitrogen, taken as the annual increment of fertilizer to Nevada, to estimate the current input of phosphorus to the lake. The lake itself occupies 0.18 percent of the state's area, and I will suppose that the drainage basin occupies 0.3 percent. The predevelopment concentration of total phosphorus would be of the order of 5 μg/liter. If the basin received its proportionate share of Nevada's fertilizer, with phosphorus equal to nitrogen, the current rate of application of phosphorus would yield an increment of 0.05 μg/liter per year to the lake. If only half the phosphorus, or 0.025 μg/liter per year, reaches the lake, its waters would be enriched by 1 μg/liter, or 20 percent, in the course of 40 years, or a little more than one generation. The amount of the increase is probably small, compared with sewage pollution, but algae know what to do with a scarce element when it suddenly becomes available.

The present mode of harvesting Lake Tahoe's productivity—angling for salmonid fishes—is admittedly obsolete, even atavistic; technological progress could easily find more efficient ways of utilizing an enriched lake. Most citizens, however, would find the price of such progress rather high, for Lake Tahoe, apart from its quite exceptional beauty, is poorly sited, and much too deep, for an experiment in growing algae.

ORGANIC AGRICULTURE AS AN ALTERNATIVE

Before we go back to an organic agriculture in this country somebody must decide which 50 million Americans we are going to let starve or go hungry and I don't want to make that decision.

Earl L. Butz
Secretary of Agriculture
January, 1972

We have learned only recently that relative to our level of consumption that the U.S. is resource poor, outside of forests and soils. Many of us clung to the fond belief that it mattered little so long as we had the most important of all resources—our good land— to sustain us. Should we take the words of our secretary seriously? If we do, then we are skating on thinner ice than we thought.

"Recycle" may well become the key word of the seventies. New industries will likely spring up to assume the task of returning materials to the system. As things now stand, an observer from another planet might reasonably conclude, given the way products are blithely junked, that reservoirs of raw products are bottomless; or that our science is so very clever that we create materials out of nothing. In truth, however, resources are in a finite supply and we must learn to recycle them. When we do this we will immediately solve much of our disposal problem. For example, it has been estimated recently that if all the paper used in this country were recycled, sixty percent of the country's trash disposal problems would be solved. In addition, the hodgepodge of materials that usually goes into the dump makes "mining" of these materials at a future date difficult. The electric toaster, purchased at a discount store, is now thrown into the "sanitary land fill" because it is "cheaper to buy a new one than to fix the old." Reprocessing the materials in the toaster will be more difficult than was the initial process of claiming them from the system.

Part of the past and present Administration's monetary package for cleaning up the environment provides for the construction of sewage treatment plants. Such plants are designed to "detoxify" the effluent before it is discharged into waterways. Research and development is underway to find efficient methods for returning the effluent to the system free of odor and disease. The valuable nutrients contained in sewage would then be available for recycling rather than being unproductively relegated to septic tanks, river beds or the ocean.

31   # AEC Scientists Push Project
     # to Eliminate All Wastes

NEAL STANFORD

If you think splitting the atom and harnessing its power was incredible, if you think putting men on the moon is fantastic, let me tell you about something two Atomic Energy Commission scientists are working on that can only be called apocalyptic. They are working on a project to eliminate all waste! Yes, make this a wasteless world! It sounds like the millennium.

Did you know that each person in the United States produces 4.8 pounds per day of solid waste? That by the year 2000 each person will produce 6.8 pounds per day? That over the 35-year period from 1965 to 2000 almost 10 billion tons of solid refuse will have been accumulated in the United States?

If this were all compacted and disposed of in sanitary landfill, it would cover the state of Delaware 10 feet deep! It would cover the state of Rhode Island 20 feet deep! At the cost of $1 a foot (the cost of sanitary landfill in Los Angeles), this layer of solid waste would represent a total investment of about half a trillion dollars!

Industrial Wastes Added

To the solid wastes of municipal refuse has to be added the solid wastes of industrial origin—junked cars, waste material resulting from mining of solid fuels, metals. The management of waste materials, or, better, its elimination, would quite obviously be an unparalleled boon to mankind. It would be the material equivalent of perpetual motion.

At the moment, the ability to create something from basic elements, use it as a product or service, and then economically reduce it back to its basic elements for future use (with no adverse effect on nature) sounds like fantasy. It smacks of alchemy. What it would mean to mankind staggers the imagination: a pollution-free world; a wasteless society; a control over matter such as man has never had.

The process involved in this concept is called "the fusion torch." It rests upon the prospect of man being able to tame the hydrogen—or fusion—bomb, just as he tamed the nuclear—or fission—bomb. Controlled atomic fission made possible nuclear reactors.

Controlled atomic fusion would not only allow man on a large scale and economic basis to desalt water, process urban sewage, perform plasma chemistry, produce electricity through fuel cells, but also to recycle essentially all solid waste.

Return to Raw Form

That last operation constitutes the fusion-torch concept, or closing the cycle from use to reuse. What this means in layman's language is that waste products would be converted back to elemental form. There would be no waste products to dispose of. There would rather be a supply of basic raw materials for reuse.

When fusion reactors become available, a volume of materials equal to thousands of tons per day could be handled in a single plant. That would take care of urban wastes even in the volume produced today. It is said that if just 10,000 megawatts were used for processing via the fusion torch, the entire wastes of a city with a population in the millions could be converted into raw materials each day.

Who are these modern Merlins—the men working to make possible a wasteless world? Drs. Bernard J. Eastlund and William C. Gough, of the AEC's division of research, as well as the many scientists, physicists, and engineers working on the problem of controlled thermonuclear fusion.

It can be reported that at present new progress has been made both in the

United States and in the Soviet Union in this field. The Soviets, it is understood, have made particularly great strides recently.

Ultimate Solution?

In this matter of waste management, two possibilities exist today. Now the fusion-torch concept provides the third—or ultimate—solution. Waste disposal produces no economic return. Partial recycle involves some economic penalty. But this prospect of closing the cycle of use of a resource back to resource makes waste itself a resource.

The fusion-torch concept is a bit complicated for the layman, so it may be better to let the nuclear scientists working on it explain it in their own words.

This is how Drs. Eastlund and Gough describe their fusion-torch concept: "This closing the basic link from used back to resource would be accomplished by vaporizing and ionizing solids (for example, ores or waste products) in the plasma and then separating the elements from the mixture of ionized species.

A fusion plasma is able to vaporize solids easily by the propagation of shock waves. This is because of the plasma's tremendously large flux of random kinetic energy and its high thermal conductivity."

To control fusion energy, say Drs. Eastlund and Gough, "we must heat a dilute gas of fusion fuel to temperatures of hundreds of millions of degrees, then contain it long enough (and at sufficient purity) for an appreciable fraction of the fuel to react." That first goal, they say, was achieved five years ago when plasmas above the ideal ignition temperature were obtained for a self-sustaining fusion reactor. So the problem now is to confine the hot plasmas.

These two scientists say that progress to this end "has been accelerating as the result of increased correlation between theory and experiment, also the use of advanced computers for plasma simulation."

They become quite enthusiastic in explaining their fusion-torch concept: "The fusion torch would close the basic link from user back to resource. Waste products would be converted back to elemental form.

"When a solid is injected into the fusion torch, the interaction results in the transformation of an ultrahigh temperature hydrogen plasma into a low-temperature plasma composed of ionic species characteristic of the solid, irrespective of a solid's chemical composition or mechanical properties.

Attainment Held-Possible

"The number of processes needed for complete recovery of elements from waste products would equal the number of types of waste products present. The fusion torch probably would handle all species in one central recovery plan."

Drs. Eastlund and Gough, while immersed in their research on fusion and on fusion-torch physics, certainly have a vision, a vision, as they put it, "of the future—large cities, operated electrically by clean, safe fusion reactors that eliminate the city's waste products and generate the city's raw materials."

They conclude: "The vision is there. Its attainment does not appear to be blocked by nature. Its achievement depends on the will and the desire of men to see that it is brought about."

Shock at Sea   **32**

TIME MAGAZINE

When the Norwegian author-explorer Thor Heyerdahl sailed across half the Pacific on a balsawood raft 22 years ago, he recalls, "We on *Kon Tiki* were thrilled by the beauty and purity of the ocean." During his recent attempt to sail from Africa to Central America in a boat made of papyrus reeds, which he was forced to abandon last month 600 miles from his goal, Heyerdahl's old thrill was replaced by shock. In Manhattan he reported to the Norwegian Mission at the United Nations: "Large surface areas in mid-ocean as well as nearer the continental shores on both sides were visibly polluted by human activity."

Heyerdahl and his six-man crew were astonished and depressed by the quantity of jetsam bobbing hundreds of miles from land. Almost every day, plastic bottles, squeeze tubes and other signs of industrial civilization floated by the expedition's leaky boat. What most appalled Heyerdahl were sheets of "pelagic particles." At first he assumed that his craft was in the wake of an oil tanker that had just cleaned its tanks. But on five occasions he ran into the same substances covering the water so thickly, he told *Time* Researcher Nancy Williams, that "it was unpleasant to dip our toothbrushes into the sea. Once the water was too dirty to wash our dishes in."

The particles, some of which Heyerdahl collected for later analysis, are roughly the size of a pea. Oily and sometimes encrusted with tiny barnacles, they smell like a combination of putrefying fish and raw sewage. Heyerdahl hopes that his experience will stir the U.N. to propose new international regulations to keep the oceans clean. "Modern man seems to believe that he can get everything he needs from the corner drugstore," says the explorer. "He doesn't understand that everything has a source in the land or sea, and that he must respect those sources. If the indiscriminate pollution continues, we will be sawing off the branch we are sitting on."

RADIOACTIVE AND CHEMICAL AND BIOLOGICAL WARFARE MATERIALS

---

33   ## Radioiodine Fallout over the Midwest in May

LESTER MACHTA

Abstract. High concentration of radioiodine in milk, found preferentially over the midwestern United States after atmospheric nuclear tests in May 1962, 1965, and 1966, can best be explained by high-reaching intense thunderstorms that scavenge passing radioactivity from the upper troposphere and lower stratosphere.

Fallout after nuclear tests, including 8-day radioiodine, I^{131}, has been documented. Radioiodine enters man by passage from the nuclear cloud and through atmosphere, pasture, cow, and milk. I now illustrate the manner in which one atmospheric phenomenon increases the likelihood of contamination of milk in the Midwest in May or therebouts, in contrast to other parts of the country and other months.

Nuclear clouds passed over the United States during May of 3 years between 1961 and 1967. The highest concentrations of radioiodine in milk occurred in the Midwest during each episode. The air concentrations are the highest readings, preceding the peak milk concentrations, from the closest station to each milkshed. All the highest concentrations in milk, apart from Charleston, South Carolina, occurred in the Midwest. The highest values during episodes in January and in September through December 1961-67 were not preferentially in the Midwest.

Crops may be contaminated by deposition of radioiodine with precipitation or directly by ground-level radioiodine, or by both. It is argued that during the three May episodes almost all radioiodine was deposited with rainwater.

Three other episodes with little or no rain but with much I^{131} in milk were examined for their ratios of I^{131} in milk to gross beta activity in ground-level air; such ratios roughly indicate the contributions of dry fallout to contamination of milk. During dry weather the ratios are less than 3 on all but three of 17 sites; the highest is only 15, while equivalent ratios run to scores. These higher ratios suggest that a mechanism other than dry fallout enhanced the contamination of milk in May.

Nor is there correlation between milk contamination and gross beta radioactivity during the three May episodes. For example, in May 1966 the highest Midwest concentrations were 9 pc/m³ in air and more tha 100 pc/liter in milk, while Denver, Colorado, and Phoenix, Arizona, reported 14 pc/m^3 and only 20 and 30 pc/liter, respectively. Since the latter stations had little rain, the air:milk ratios agree with the previous dry-weather ratios.

Unfortunately a direct link between concentrations of radioiodine in the upper atmosphere, in rainwater falling on a milkshed, and subsequently in milk is unavailable because of the lack of appropriate measurements. The ability of rain to scavenge fission products from the atmosphere and of contaminated rainwater to enhance concentrations in milk is universally acknowledged. There are a few reports of radioiodine in rainwater in the Midwest in May 1962, and many observations of gross beta radioactivity in rainwater during all three episodes. But, because of the isolated nature of thundershowers and other difficulties, it has not always been possible to document adequately even gross beta contaminations in rainwater in all milksheds. In some instances the evidence of significant gross beta concentration in rainwater over the Midwest is clear: on 17 May 1966 Jefferson City, Missouri, reported a concentration about 30 times greater than did any non-Midwest station after the nuclear test of 9 May 1966.

The Midwest suffers severe weather in the spring. It is the severe thunderstorms from which some tornadoes spawn that concern us rather that the high incidence of tornadoes. Florida and the Southwest have the most thunderstorms in summer. Two characteristics set the Midwest in May apart from the rest of the United States: there is high incidence of nocturnal storms, and the cloud tops reach to great heights. While the nocturnal frequency is of unknown significance, one may argue that high-reaching rainclouds by day and by night account for the greater fallout of I^{131} in the Midwest during May.

Clouds from atmospheric nuclear detonations equivalent to more than about 10 kilotons rise initially into the upper troposphere or lower stratosphere or the upper atmosphere—above about 10 km. These higher altitudes contain a larger fraction of the radioactivity and stronger winds than does the lower troposphere. The stronger winds normally effect faster transit to the United States, with less decay and dilution.

Nerve Gas   34
Dugway Accident Linked to Utah Sheep Kill

PHILIP M. BOFFEY

[In March, 1968,] some 6000 sheep grazing in Skull Valley, Utah, were killed or sickened by a mysterious ailment that attacked the central nervous system. The sheep were located near the Dugway Proving Ground, the Army's chief site for field testing chemical and biological weapons, so suspicions were immediately aroused that the sheep had been felled by a lethal substance originating at Dugway. These suspicions were heightened when it was subsequently revealed that Dugway had tested highly toxic nerve agents the day before the sheep became

ill. Circumstantial evidence publicly available indicated that the primary cause
of the sheep deaths was VX, a persistent nerve agent that was used in an aircraft
spray test at Dugway the day before the sheep started dying.

Scientists have found traces of the nerve agent in the dead sheep and in
nearby vegetation and snow water; they have established that the sheep were
poisoned by an organic phosphate compound, of which the nerve agent is one;
and they have shown that low doses of the nerve agent fed to healthy sheep will
produce the same symptoms as those found in the sick Skull Valley sheep. There
is evidence that the sheep ingested the nerve agent primarily by eating contaminated vegetation, and that the toxic material persisted in the area for at least
three weeks after the incident. As a result of the unfortunate incident, a high-level
advisory committee, headed by Surgeon General William H. Stewart, has recommended stringent new safety procedures for Dugway, and the Army last week
adopted them *in toto*.

How the agent escaped from Dugway may never be known beyond doubt,
but investigators suggest that a combination of circumstances conspired to bring
about the sheep slaughter. There was an accident during the spray test at Dugway; shortly thereafter a change in weather conditions apparently carried the
agent toward the sheep and then precipitated it around them; and sheep turned
out to be unusually susceptible to the agent. Had any of these factors been absent,
it is conceivable—though unprovable—that there would have been no "Dugway
incident."

35   Academy Changes Army Gas Dump Plan

PHILIP M. BOFFEY

The Army intended to ship some 27,000 tons of chemical weapons from as
far away as Denver, Colo., to the Naval Ammunition Depot at Earle, N.J., where
they were to be loaded on four old Liberty ships, towed at least 145 miles out to
sea, and then sunk with the ships in at least 7200 feet of water. But critics in
Congress charged that a railroad accident might spew lethal chemicals over the
countryside and that the chemicals might cause serious ecological damage to the
ocean.

The Academy panel, which was headed by George B. Kistiakowsky, Harvard
chemist and science adviser to the late President Eisenhower, generally agreed
with the critics. It recommended that two of the five chemical materials involved
be deactivated and that the other three be dumped in the ocean only as a last
resort. Although the Army had previously argued that deactivation was time-
consuming, costly, and dangerous, the panel said the government should minimize risks to humans and the environment "even though this may complicate and
make more costly its own operations."

The panel said that clusters of bomblets loaded with GB, a liquid nerve gas, should be disassembled and neutralized chemically by acid or alkaline hydrolysis. It said that under the Army's original plans there was a "remote possibility" that a "catastrophic explosion" could be caused by a sniper's bullet or a railroad or ship collision. The Pentagon indicated it would carry out this recommendation.

The panel also said that liquid mustard agent, which is currently stored in bulk containers, should be burned in government establishments where local air pollution would not be a serious problem. The panel said that while there was virtually no danger of a catastrophic accident with mustard, it was concerned about possible adverse effects on the oceanic ecosphere when the mustard eventually leaked out of its containers. The Pentagon also agreed to comply with this recommendation.

The panel said the other three materials involved—namely, GB nerve gas rockets imbedded in concrete and steel "coffins," steel containers contaminated by toxic chemicals, and canisters of CS riot control agent imbedded in drums filled with concrete—could be dumped at sea without serious harm if no other suitable means of disposal can be found. However, the panel urged the Army to convene a group of technical and demolition experts to determine if it is feasible to demilitarize the nerve gas rockets, and the Army agreed to form such a group.

The Academy study, by implication, pointed to two glaring oversights on the part of the Army. It noted that while "various chemical warfare agents have been repeatedly disposed of in the oceans by the United States and other nations . . . we have no information regarding possible deleterious effects of these operations on the ecosphere of the seas." The panel also suggested that the Army should assume that all chemical weapons will require eventual disposal and should consequently build disposal facilities that will not require dumping at sea.

THE URBAN ENVIRONMENT

The greatest crime committed in American cities may not be murder, rape or robbery, but rather the wholesale and constant exposure of children to noise, ugliness and garbage in the street, thereby conditioning them to accept public squalor as the normal state of affairs . . .

Rene Dubos

The United States urban poor, 4.5 million ghetto whites and 3.1 million blacks, have understandably resisted being a part of the "new concern" for the environment. They have construed this as an alternative focus to the "real problems" of racism, war, and poverty. We need the development of a land ethic; we need to save the redwoods, to stop urban sprawl, to lower population, and to figure out ways to stop the compulsive consumption that is promoting the resource drain of our own country, as well as the siphoning from underdeveloped nations. Perhaps we can get needed help if we begin to clean up where the environment is the worst—the urban ghetto. Poor urban blacks have three times as many heart ailments as middle-class whites. Black women have a four times greater risk of dying while giving birth to a child. Piled-up solid wastes provide a substrate for the rats and insects that spread rat bite fever, leptospirosis, salmonellosis, and murine typhus fever. 400,000 ghetto children have high lead content in their blood primarily because ghetto people breathe in 50 times more lead particles than do rural residents. Noise pollution is said to contribute heavily to sexual impotency, heart attacks, headaches, insomnia, and even malformed babies. Autopsies of people that have died of liver cirrhosis, carcinoma, and hypertension have revealed high pesticide contents. Apparently, in an effort to kill the pests breeding in the solid waste heaps, ghetto residents profusely spray their living quarters. These poisons enter through the skin, get inhaled and, among undernourished children, get licked up from window sills. Polluted water around major cities comes through the tap to promote kidney disease, typhoid and mercury poisoning.

118

RESOURCES

There are two sources of long life. One is a gift of nature, and it is the pure air and clear water of the mountains, the fruit of the earth, peace, rest, the soft and warm climate of the highlands. The second source is people. He lives long who enjoys life, and who bears no jealousy of others, whose heart harbors no malice or anger, who sings a lot and cries a little, who rises and retires with the sun, who likes to work and who knows how to rest.

Shirali Mislimov on his 166 birthday
in the Azerbaijani Mountains of the Soviet
Union, 1971.

36

Energy
How Much Can We Use?

CHARLES WASHBURN

The attitude of Americans towards energy resources is in many respects similar to their attitude towards other "free goods" such as air: "It's there—let's use it." And indeed, as far as the economy goes, energy is nearly a free good. The value of the raw fuels—coal, petroleum, and natural gas—produced in the U.S. in 1970 was about 20.1 billion dollars. Thus the value of the fuels was about 2 percent of the gross national product and nearly the same as the advertising expenditure of American business which was 19.7 billion dollars! Virtually any substitution of commercial energy for manpower "pays" in economic and convenience terms—two cents worth of electricity can perform the same physical work as a laborer working a ten hour day.

The average American family consumes energy from three direct sources: gasoline for their auto (about 350 dollars per year); natural gas for water and space heating (about 130 dollars per year); and electricity for household use (about 150 dollars per year). The total direct energy cost, averaging 630 dollars per year per household, is only 6.4 percent of the median family income. However, the consumption of energy, as we have all recently learned, is accompanied by substantial detrimental environmental side effects. Furthermore, we hear much talk that the U.S. is facing an "energy crisis."

An American beginning her or his career in the early 1970's has many good reasons to ponder the American energy resource situation as well as the impact of energy use on the environment:

1. Each year the United States consumes over one-third of the total commercial energy (coal, petroleum, natural gas, hydropower, and nuclear energy) consumed on earth, although Americans constitute only 1/17th of the world's population.
2. During the period 1951 to 1970, we consumed 1.3 times as much petroleum and natural gas (on a combined energy basis) as in all time prior to 1950.
3. Over two-thirds of the common air pollutants emitted (carbon monoxide, sulfur dioxide, particulates, hydrocarbons, and nitrogen oxides) are directly attributable to the use of energy.

120

4. The exploitation and use of energy present many current and potential environmental problems of high importance: in addition to air pollution, land destruction by strip mining, ocean pollution by oil, thermal pollution of fresh water streams and lakes and of ocean bays and littoral areas, and contamination of land, air, and water with the by-products and fuels of nuclear energy.

The crucial questions regarding the energy future of the United States—questions concerning environmental effects as well as resource adequacy—all hinge on growth of our energy consumption. Since World War II the growth rate of total energy demand in the United States has not been particularly high—about 3.1 percent per year (22 year doubling time). During this same period our population has averaged an annual growth rate of 1.5 percent per year. However, the overall growth rate of energy consumption since World War II has been held down by several changes in energy use which have resulted in large improvements in the efficiency of energy utilization. Among the most important of these have been:

1. Dieselization of the railroads. Per ton-mile of freight hauled, the diesel powered train requires only about 15 percent as much energy input as the train pulled by a coal burning steam locomotive. In 1945 only 9 percent of the locomotives were diesel, whereas by 1969, 99 percent were diesel. In 1945 the railroads used 12.5 percent of all the fuel used in the U.S., but in 1969 the railroads used only about 0.8 percent of the fuel used in the U.S. (The number of ton-miles of freight hauled in 1969 was about 10 percent larger than the 1945 figure.)
2. The average efficiency of steam electric power plants has increased from 21.9 percent in 1947 to 32.7 percent in 1969. This increase in the efficiency of power plants has partially offset the rate of growth of electrical energy consumption. During the 1947-69 period, electrical power consumption averaged a 7.8 percent per year growth rate, while the fuel input for power generation grew at 6.2 percent per year.
3. In 1945 many homes and businesses were heated by coal furnaces—typically, the efficiencies of these furnaces was less than 50 percent. Now most homes and businesses are heated by gas or oil fired furnaces which have efficiencies of about 70 percent.

Correspondingly large efficiency improvements are not foreseeable in the immediate future. The railroads are completely dieselized. The average efficiency of the steam power plants has leveled off. (Average power plant efficiency increased only from 32.05 to 32.67 percent during the 1961-69 period, while the efficiency of the "best plant" in the U.S. improved only from 38.9 to 39.1 percent during the same period.) Much of the space heating has already been converted to oil or natural gas fuel.

Because large gains in the efficiency of energy use are not likely in the immediate future, the growth rate of fuel consumption will increase even if the growth rate for the application of energy does not increase above the past trends. In fact, some trends are towards lower overall efficiency in energy use. One example is electric heat—a gas furnace is typically 70-75 percent efficient (30-25 percent of the energy released goes up the chimney). A resistance electric heater is 100 percent efficient at converting electrical energy into heat, but, as we saw above, the power plants average less than 33 percent efficiency at producing the electricity. When losses of electrical power in transmission are included, the overall efficiency of resistance electrical heating is less than 30 percent.

So we can expect some acceleration in the growth of energy demand in the near future because efficiency gains which were possible in the past are now largely "saturated" and because some less efficient energy applications are becoming popular. The recent decline in our population growth rate will eventually help to slow the rate of growth in energy demand, but for many years the rate of formation of new families (family units, not children, are the large energy users) will increase at about the same rate as the population grew in the 1950s and early 1960s.

Another, more important factor, is our increasing reliance on electrical energy. As electrical power becomes a larger and larger fraction of the total energy supply, the overall growth rate of energy consumption will tend to rise from the past trend of 3.1 percent per year to approach the growth rate of electrical energy demand (recently, 7.8 percent per year).

Unless changes in attitudes and policies act to temper the demand of our society for more and more energy, it is likely that we will be using over five times as much energy in 2020 as we are using today.

Should we continue our current policy of developing resources to meet every demand for energy? Would the American public accept some form of energy rationing? What will be the environmental and resource costs of meeting an energy demand five times larger than our current demand? Can technology solve the energy resource problems and at the same time develop means of eliminating the negative environmental side effects of energy development and consumption?

Let's take a brief look at the alternatives which are likely to be available to meet our future energy demands, and consider some of the problems which must be solved if even greater environmental damage due to energy exploitation is to be avoided. Basically, three fuel resources appear to be adequate to meet, for a long period of time, an energy demand projected at five times the current level: coal, oil produced from shale oil, and uranium used in breeder reactors. In addition, there may be a possibility that large supplies of foreign petroleum will be available for importing into the U.S. in 2020 (this possibility depends on an assumption that the developing world fails to make large gains in development over the next 50 years). The U.S. domestic supplies of natural gas and petroleum are clearly not adequate to be substantially contributing to our energy supply in 2020. Two other sources, nuclear fusion using deuterium extracted from the oceans and solar power, could become important, but the first has not yet been shown to be possible (and hence can't be counted on) and the second has failed to attract enough interest to spur its development.

First consider the potential utilization of our vast coal reserves. The U.S. coal reserves could be mined and converted to liquid and gaseous fuels which could be sold for not too much more than the current energy prices in the United States. To meet a 2020 energy requirement five times larger than our current energy demand would require the mining of 13.1 billion tons of coal per year—a rate of mining twenty-two times the current rate. What about the environmental effects of producing this quantity of energy from coal? To just tread water, to merely maintain the current unsatisfactory rate of environmental damage due to the production and usage of coal—strip mine damage, water pollution from mine drainage, mine accidents, and air pollution from particulates, sulfur dioxide, and nitrogen oxides—would require an improvement in the damage rate by a factor of 22 (per ton of coal mined and used) in each of these categories. Certainly technology could produce some improvements in each of these areas of impact; perhaps an improvement by a factor of 22 or more in some of the areas, but to produce the improvement required in all of the areas would demand a tremendous effort, and even then there is no assurance that it can be done.

How about imported oil? Let's consider just the shipping problem. To provide enough oil to meet the projected energy demand in 2020 would require shipping to the United States seven times as much oil as is currently shipped in all international commerce.

America has vast deposits of oil shale underlying several states, particularly Colorado, Wyoming, and Utah. There is probably enough shale oil to meet our energy needs and demands for a considerable period of time. About 54 billion barrels of oil per year would be required to meet the total projected energy demand for 2020—a level of consumption eleven times our current level. If we were to produce this petroleum by mining and retorting oil shale which averaged 17 gallons of oil per ton (a relatively rich shale), the annual rate of mining would have to be 133 billion tons of shale. After extracting the oil, 124 billion tons of burned rock residue would remain for disposal. For comparison, the current U.S. production of sand and gravel is just about one billion tons per year and the current rate of solid waste production in our cities and towns is about 197 million tons per year.

What about nuclear energy? The exploration effort of the 1950s fairly thoroughly prospected the North American continent for uranium, and very significant strikes were made. If the uranium deposits which are known to exist or can be reasonably inferred to exist were utilized in a breeder reactor system, the energy produced would be many times the total energy content of our original fossil fuel resources. The uranium must be mined, of course, and some environmental damage is bound to be associated with any mining operation. The uranium ores currently being mined average about 0.21 percent uranium. At this concentration, four million tons of uranium ore would have to be mined each year to supply a breeder-based economy which effectively utilized half of the uranium. Of course, the richest ores would be mined first, and the average concentration of uranium in the ore would be decreasing as time went on. However, as has frequently been pointed out, very large deposits of rock exist which contain uranium or thorium (which could be used in a different type of breeder reactor) in concentrations of about two ounces of uranium (or thorium) per ton of rock. If uranium ores of this very low concentration were utilized, about 75 million tons of ore would need to be mined each year to supply the total needs of an economy demanding five times as much energy as the current level. Seventy-five million tons per year is only 0.06 percent the quantity of oil shale which would be required to provide the same energy and only 0.6 percent of the coal tonnage which would be required. On the basis of mining damage, use of even very low grade nuclear fuels has a clear advantage over the use of fossil fuels. However, many other factors must be considered before nuclear energy can be considered to be "the answer."

A breeder reactor economy using uranium ores produces and uses large quantities of plutonium which is one of the most toxic metals. In addition, about one pound of fission products will be produced for each pound of uranium mined; the fission products will have to be stored for at least 1,000 years and perhaps 20,000 years. Past civilizations have not done well at hiding their garbage; a much different orientation will be needed in the future. A workable system for assuring nearly absolute containment of plutonium and fission products will be required if long-term environmental effects due to the utilization of nuclear energy are to be avoided. This implies a zero accident rate.

The new approach which will be required is perhaps as much a matter of new economic thinking as new technology. Safety and containment requirements must be established without consideration of cost; the energy demand must readjust to the new cost levels rather than require that the new cost levels (and therefore safety standards) remain at a level which has no effect on the demand for energy. In the future, the competitiveness of fuels must be based on their total costs—including the costs of meeting necessary environmental constraints. The current system of allowing the demand to effectively determine the level of safety and environmental protection provided (through the argument that environmental and safety protection must not be too costly or they will price many energy applications out of the market) must be abandoned.

Our energy consumption cannot continue to grow forever; eventually problems of global heating will bring energy growth to a halt, even if all other problems are solved. At what point man decides to limit energy use between the current rate of energy use and the maximum rate imposed by global heating will depend more on what level of energy-produced environmental degradation we are willing to accept than on the exhaustion of our energy resources.

Whenever the growth of anything is halted, questions of equitable distribution of wealth and resources come to the front. If growth can accommodate the demands of the poor, few of the rich resent their catching up. A much tougher situation arises when the demands and needs of the poor are met by redistribution of a fixed quantity of wealth (whether wealth is dollars, jobs, or energy). On the other hand, society has become poor in terms of clean air, clear water, and natural beauty—a balancing question regarding the distribution of these forms of wealth becomes "how much of our land, air, and water resources, as well as energy resources, should those with a compulsion to consume at ever increasing rates be able to command? "

Charles Washburn has outlined the environmental consequences in the energy extraction process. Little attention has been paid to this in the past, just as insufficient attention is being paid to the disposal of the lethal products of nuclear fission plants springing up all over. The lethal garbage was to have been stored in a Kansas salt mine, until it was discovered that the mine "leaked like a sieve," quite possibly into the water table. At this time we still don't know what to do with the fission products having half-lives ranging up to 24,400 years.

Another shuddering reality is the fantastic domestic and international committment to political stability that we make as we develop these fission reactors. A clean bomb from an external enemy or a "Weatherman" could convert a "nice clean" electricity-generating nuclear reactor into a lethal heap.

But let's assume that technology really is as wonderful as our public has been led to believe, and that the clean fusion reactor comes into being, giving us essentially unlimited power. We now may be capable of "achieving" what is described by the astronomer, Fred Hoyle, in the next reading.

Isn't it possible that man simply lacks the wisdom to handle inflated energy budgets above that of hunting and gathering, including agriculture? Perhaps the worst thing that could happen to the country, or for that matter, the world, is to make energy so cheap it would not have to be metered. Perhaps Hoyle *is* dead serious, though the reading was taken from a science-fiction novel.

Consequences of Unlimited Energy   37

FRED HOYLE

The showing took upward of four hours. It was the longest documentary film I had ever seen, naturally enough for it dealt with a time span of six thousand years. We covered time at an average rate of a century to each four minutes. There was no place here for intricate involvements, or for the niceties of politics. Yet it was all too easy to follow. The black record of the human species swept remorselessly on as the minutes and hours ticked away.

It was a shock at the beginning to be very quickly out of both the twentieth and the twenty-first centuries. The first quick point was a transition from poverty to affluence in the undeveloped continents of the twentieth century, Africa and Asia. A homogeneous civilization swept with incredible speed over the whole Earth. There were brief flashes of the people, of their machines, their customs, their political leaders. It was all done visually. We sat in silence watching, our ears free of the cacophonous uproar of the usual sound track. It was easy to comment to each other on what we saw, not that we had much to say beyond the occasional exclamation.

Earth teemed with people. Cities spread out farther and farther until they became joined to each other. Urban populations covered an increasing fraction of the land surface. At first it was only one per cent, then five per cent, then twenty-five per cent. The technological drive went irresistibly on. Land became of more and more value. There was no room any longer for any animal save man. So we watched the gradual extinction of the whole animal world. Even the bird population declined and withered away.

We saw something of domestic life. We saw the standardized little boxes in which almost everybody was now living. The insistent question formed in your mind, what was it all good for? What conceivable reason could there be to prefer a thousand little boxes to one dignified house? The same of course for the people. What was the advantage of this appalling fecundity of the human species?

Soon we were in the twenty-fifth century. Angry voices began to be heard.

The pressures were mounting, competing with the technology. The technology itself was kept going by the most rigorous demands on individual freedom. It was indeed a veritable ant-heap. The average person became restricted to a life that lay somewhere between the freedom of the twentieth century and the lack of freedom of a man serving a life sentence in prison. Nobody travelled now, except on official business—I mean travelled to distant parts. Everything was provided in one's own locality, food, amusements, work. The work itself demanded little initiative. The people were leading what can only be described as a punched-card life.

The technology wasn't working too well any more. Food was mostly of poor quality, mostly factory produced. At that stage, in the twenty-fifth century, the seas were essentially swept clean of fish. The land animals had been the first to go, then the birds, now last the fish.

The first disaster happened with amazing suddenness. What had seemed a more or less homogeneous civilization split into two, like the division of an amoeba.

"It's a point of instability," whispered John. "Look, the whole thing's going to grow exponentially."

Whatever he meant, this vast gargantuan, sprawling, tasteless, in every way appalling, civilization exploded in a flash. It started with bombs and rockets, with fire. The film, so far silent, now came alive, not with any synthetic sound track, but with the crackling of the actual fire, with the shriek, instantly cut short, of a woman enveloped in a cloud of burning petrol. Then it was all over. It was quiet everywhere. Death and decay swept at an incredible speed, like some monstrous fungus, everywhere over the Earth. There was no movement, no transport, no food distribution. The intricate organization which had itself fed on the efforts of a large fraction of the whole population was dead. Everything which had depended on it, including the lives of the people, now died too. We could hear the whine of infants, the despairing cries of children. The abomination came at last to an end. It seemed as if the human species, having wiped everything else from the face of the planet, had now itself become extinct.

Miraculously this did not happen. A dozen or more specially favoured, especially lucky, small centres of population managed to survive. They were already beginning their recovery by the time we saw them, I suppose because no camera had been there to record the worst moments. Indeed the technique of photography suddenly became very crude, almost the way it had been when photography was first invented.

We saw the slow steady expansion of one centre after another. The population increased, the technology improved. We saw the people happy and smiling again. We heard them talking in a new language. We saw them attempting to recover the relics and treasures of the past, particularly books and manuscripts. We saw how they made every effort as they improved to absorb the culture of the past. Amazingly, a great deal survived.

By now we were almost a thousand years on. The new civilization was becoming exuberant. There was nothing of the deathly, machine-like quality of the situation before the first upheaval, the Great Disaster as it came to be known. People were individuals again. There was hope for the future once more.

The different centres were by now overlapping each other. They were in argument. There was a period of war, astonishingly short it seemed to us on this kaleidoscopic record. The war turned out to be no more than a kind of lubricant that allowed the hitherto separate regions to join up with each other into a coherent whole. With a growing sense of horror I realized it was all going to happen again. There was going to be a second disaster. It became so completely inevitable as one watched. Century after century went by. Each brought its contribution to the elephantine growth. Gone was the zip and zest of the first pioneers of this new civilization. We were back again in a punched-card era. It all happened with horrible predictability. The first and second catastrophes might have been interchanged and you couldn't have told the difference.

Ten Commandments of the Energy Ethic for Survival   **38** of Man in Nature

HOWARD T. ODUM

1. Thou shall not waste potential energy.
2. Thou shall know what is right by its part in survival of thy system.
3. Thou shall do unto others as best benefits the energy flows of thy system.
4. Thou shall revel in thy systems work rejoicing in happiness that only finds thee in this good service.
5. Thou shall treasure the other life of thy natural system as thine own, for only together shall thee all survive.
6. Thou shall judge value by the energies spent, the energies stored, and the energy flow which is possible, turning not to the incomplete measure of money.
7. Thou shall not unnecessarily cultivate high power, for error, destruction, noise, and excess vigilence are its evil wastes.
8. Thou shall not take from man or nature without returning service of equal value, for only then are thee one.
9. Thou shall treasure thy heritage of information, and in the uniqueness of thy good works and complex roles will thy system reap that which is new and immortal in thee.
10. Thou must find in thy religion, stability over growth, organization over competition, diversity over uniformity, system over self, and survival process over individual peace.

CONSERVING THE BIOTIC RESOURCES

Something will have gone out of us as a people if we ever let the remaining wilderness be destroyed; if we ever permit the last virgin forests to be turned into comic books and plastic cigarette cases; if we drive the few remaining wild species into zoos or extinction; if we pollute the last clear air and dirty the last clean streams and push out paved roads through the last of the silences.

Wallace Stegner
The Living Wilderness
Winter 68-69

The soul of a man, given time can put some revealing marks upon his face. The soul of a people invariably makes an indelible imprint upon their land.

Wm. O. Douglas

The sentiments expressed in the above quotations, valid and important as they are, refer only to the "soul of a people." Most conservationists of less than a decade ago were "blue sky boys." The public has recently started to become aware that conservation of our resources must be argued on more than aesthetic grounds. The selections that follow demonstrate the complexity involved in the conservation issue.

Encroachment

Frontierism will likely be long in dying since man has always been able to go "just over the hill" or "around the bend" when his nest was fouled or his resources dwindled. But now, for the first time in history, our species has been permanently turned back. Man may make occasional excursions to planets in his own solar system, but the other stars are too far away.

The greatest experiment of mankind may just be getting under way. That is, how to live on a finite spaceship with finite resources and be obliged to repair the life support system. But a mature ecosystem is self-sustaining and requires none of man's time to repair it. We call this the wilderness. Thoreau's words, "In wilderness is the preservation of the world," take on new meaning in a period of accelerated encroachment.

The Wail of Kashmir

LEE MERRIMAN TALBOT

A striking example of man's growing impact on the land is the Great Thar Desert in western India. At the time of Christ, Indian rhinoceros roamed in grass jungles in the middle of what is now desert. And for the past 80 years the desert has been advancing into the rest of India at the rate of one-half mile a year along its whole long perimeter. That means that in 80 years, an estimated 56,000 square miles, or an area equal to that of Wisconsin, has been turned into shifting sand.

The mechanics of this land degradation seem clear. The starting point is the mature forest with its wildlife, fertile soil, and abundant water. The lumber is cut, often clear-cut with young growth destroyed. The land is then cultivated for a time, then grazed and overgrazed. There can be no replacement of trees or grass, for everything green is eaten by ravenous livestock. When there is nothing left for cattle, goats take over, and when the goats have left, nothing remains but sand or blowing dust. This story holds true, with the same plot and characters, but with different stage scenery and costumes, throughout much of the world.

To illustrate the effect of this land-use pattern on wilderness, let us consider Kashmir, the ancient Moguls' "paradise on earth." This is a lovely mountain land in northernmost India, lying at about the same latitude as San Francisco, and bordered by Tibet, China, and Pakistan. The British with the local maharajah set aside magnificent wild areas here. But when independence came, here as in most former colonies, the tendency during the first burst of nationalism was to reject all that smacked of the previous "imperialism" or "colonialism." Parks and wilderness areas were thought of as something kept away from the people by the former rulers rather than as a resource maintained for them, so the first reaction was to destroy them, to take "what was rightfully ours." On top of this came political and military unrest with a side effect of a large population suddenly armed but with little discipline. Among the results have been large-scale poaching leading to the virtual extermination of the Kashmir stag, heavy forest cutting, and overgrazing.

Through much of Kashmir up to and above timberline one runs into herders and livestock. In less than ten years much of this land changed from dense conifer forest or park lands like the best of our Sierra or Rockies, to what are approaching high-altitude deserts, with the vegetation pulled apart, cut, overgrazed, and burned out—and the soil, too.

Economic need, destructive land use, and destructive nationalism form a constantly recurring pattern deadly to wilderness. Until all three of these factors are somewhat ameliorated it is hard to be optimistic about the future of wilderness lands throughout the world.

As my last example I would like to mention an area not usually thought of as living wilderness—the Middle East. Much of it is arid desert, but when Moses led the children of Israel through the Sinai wilderness, it was a live wilderness with wildlife and trees. Today one can go for days through that country and never see a living thing. The mountains above the Promised Land were cloaked with dense forest, with pine, oak, and cedar; and in the more open areas, Asiatic lions stalked abundant wildlife. Today these mountains are largely dead stone skeletons, and the last small remnant of the Asiatic lions is to be found 3,000 miles to the east. There are still two more or less living wilderness areas left—in northern Lebanon and western Syria. Until recently, protected by inaccessibility and unsettled conditions, the forest here remained intact; but within the last few years, lumbering and cultivation have begun to move into these last forests. When the land's fertility has been cropped out and the trees have been cut off, the crops will give way to grazing. Once overgrazing has gone far enough, the starving animals preventing grass, brush, and tree reproduction, the area will assume the desert aspect of most of the Middle East.

This remnant biblical wilderness illustrates one of the very real economic values of wilderness that, perhaps, is not often thought of in our country. It would be easy to say, looking at most of the desert Middle Eastern lands, that this area never did support much life, or that the old records of forests and crops are wrong, or that if there were trees here once there has since been a climactic change. But in these remaining wild forest areas we have the living proof that this was not the case. North Lebanon and western Syria provide a point of reference by which one may judge the condition of the land as it was, see what man has done to the rest of the land, and therefore see what can be done with what land is left.

40   Encroachment Of The Present

KENNETH S. NORRIS

By the time of Charlemagne, who was an enlightened ruler, the onslaught against the forests of western Europe was under way, to continue through the thirteenth century. By the end of the Middle Ages the land was largely divested of its trees, as the Mediterranean region had been before the Christian era, and stringent laws against cutting came into being. Whatever advanced ideas had been inherited from Rome were soon lost to sight. Fields were used, then abandoned. Feudal lords shifted their headquarters from one castle to another, to get away, it has been said, from the accumulated filth. But the coefficient of toleration of filth was so high in those days that the moving was more likely to have been for the purpose of tapping new sources of food as the old sections of the fief played out. Eventually, after a period of rest, the abandoned fields had to be used again. Such a system is unsound. Recuperation takes too long, and too much of the land at a time remains idle. Paintings and sculptured figures of the period portray human beings who are wan and rickety, and since these portrayals were commonest in sacred art, most of us still have the feeling that anaemia and sainthood are inseparable. Actually the trouble was due to inadequate diet and malnutrition on a huge scale, such as we find in backward rural communities.

Deserts On The March

41

PAUL B. SEARS

A casual observer might suggest that there would be no problem in carrying out a population study of desert animals by driving 5 miles or so beyond Palm Springs into the completely barren dunes, and as an added protection walking about a thousand feet off the road before beginning work. I did this and had a motel built right in the middle of my study plot. Thus, ended one half-finished doctoral thesis problem, and thus arose much concern regarding the undisturbed character of the barren dunes.

Surely one could expect to maintain a trapline of drop-can lizard traps along the margins of uninhabited austere Pisgah Crater, 35 miles out of Barstow, which is itself far out in the desert. These traps are buried flush with the ground and unobtrusively covered by a plywood sheet on top of which is sprinkled local dirt for camouflage. I did this too, and over a 2-year period about 20% of my traps were pulled from the ground, shot full of bullet holes, or carried completely away. I cannot know how many times undisturbed traps were raided of the animals I sought. An entire aspect of my work, thus, became insecure, and this project also had to be abandoned.

On my own campus, as a student and later as a staff member, I watched a magnificent natural canyon disappear under buildings and the pavement of parking lots. Deer once visited UCLA every year or so to have their fawns. A fox family used to live where the present University elementary school is now located. A colony of bats and chaparral plants and animals once lived where the music, social science, and art buildings now stand. Furthermore, near our campus urbanization has all but eliminated opportunities for teaching in nature.

The Los Angeles basin, not so many years ago, had extensive marshes, the nesting grounds for avocets and least terns, and great populations of spade-foot toads, but now it is covered with a vast slum-in-the-making of housing tracts, which is uniformly repellant to naturalists. We felt we were being excluded by social change from our lands, like the American Indians, and like them, we needed reservations to protect ourselves.

A Letter From The Arctic

42

SAM WRIGHT

Samuel Wright "A Letter From The Arctic" was written February 15, 1969, reproduced in a limited number of copies on a flat tin of gelatin, and flown out by bush pilot in a small plane. It was written on the author's second trip to the Brooks Range, where he and his wife are spending their second winter in a 12 x 12 foot log cabin at Big Lake, 200 miles from Fairbanks, north of the Arctic

Circle. On a previous trip "north of timberline," in the summer of 1967, he went for two reasons: one reason was that he "had never been there"; another was to look for white spruce which Robert Marshall had planted as seeds twenty-seven years before, north of present timber.

As I write this, a great caravan of heavily laden trucks is growling over a new winter road which yesterday reached the Eskimo village in Anaktuvuk Pass at the central top of the range. Yesterday wrote the end of Anaktuvuk Pass as it was, a small village of inland Eskimos still dependent upon migrating herds of caribou. It may have written the beginning of the end of the great caribou herds, majestic mountain sheep and the wolf. It was certainly the end of thousands of years of solitude, as the great diesel trucks thundered up the John River valley on their way to the "North Slope" and the great oil strike near Prudhoe Bay on the Arctic Ocean.

For many millenia this great range of mountains north of the Yukon in Alaska not only sheltered caribou herds and bands of mountain sheep, but provided breeding grounds for myriad birds. Athabascan Indians and inland Eskimos shared this great wilderness, living out their lives as an integral part of a balanced ecology. To the Indian and caribou hunting Eskimo, this was more than home. It was ten thousand years of Eden, where the bear and wolf gave their pelts, and the fish flashing in lakes and streams after break-up were fat and abundant.

This is the way it was in what is now called the Brooks Range, that great escarpment which stretches over 500 miles from Canada to the western coast, north of the Arctic Circle in Alaska. Because of its inaccessability and because the winters are long and cold, this last great wilderness on the American continent is still relatively pristine, a resource from which man can yet gain sustenance for his spirit, know his roots, and perhaps save his soul.

At this moment in history this great wilderness is doomed. Domestication has already begun. Until yesterday, Anaktuvuk Pass was accessible only by airplane, and just twenty years ago there was no village in this mountain sheltered valley on the route of the caribou. For hundreds of years it had been a camping place of the Nunamiut (inland people) until a school, church and airstrip drew the nomadic Eskimos into a permanent settlement. With the projection of a railroad, and a forty-eight inch crude oil pipeline over the range in the immediate future, the arrival of the road at Anaktuvuk Pass signals not only the end of a way of life for the Nunamiut but for the wilderness itself.

Who speaks for wilderness? Nearly everyone says it is a value we must not lose, and expresses regret at what seems to be the inevitable ambition of civilization to bring every niche on earth under domestication. But when a choice for wilderness or domestication is to be made, progress, money, exploitation, if not encouraged are condoned. With the North Slope oil strike already producing millionaires, and an estimate of enough reserves to make the United States virtually independent of foreign sources, few question that the fields will be brought into full production. But need we destroy a wilderness in the process?

We are fortunate in Alaska that such potential wealth lies beneath the northern tundra. The State is blessed at a time in history when such income can materially enrich the lives of all. Will we use it to create a balanced ecology for our time, and live in harmony with the land as its native population did for centuries, or will we destroy the very resource of serenity and beauty we hope to buy with our newly found wealth?

It is a question of balancing values. Today, oil may be high in our hierarchy of values, but there may come a day, closer than we realize, when the values of the wilderness will be worth more to us than all the oil on earth—as important as the issue of war and peace.

We must not think only of ourselves, but of our children and all to come. We need to reserve this last great wilderness, from the Yukon River to the North Slope, with the exception of settled areas around the Seward Peninsula. Through her aids of cold and inaccessibility, nature reserved the oil on the North Slope for our day. We can no longer count on nature to reserve for the future. It is up to us to preserve the wilderness. The issue could be life or death.

What are the values of wilderness which can be spoken of so strongly that I use terms of life and death? They are those qualities which have made us what we are as a people, a nation—qualities of self-reliance, spontaneity, and affirmation. These have been shared by others throughout the history of man, but they have been nurtured by the wilderness, which in our past history has so amply blessed us. . . .

Any reasonable person whose values are not these is beholden to nurture and protect that quality of life which comes from and is symbolized in wilderness, *wherever* he lives. There are many who do not know the wilderness first hand, but because it exists their lives are enhanced. This quality is not confined to the wilderness, but without the wilderness resource, there is a question as to how long this quality will survive. Where so much of contemporary life is dribbled second hand through many fingers, the only place where life remains unequivocally first hand is in the wilderness.

What is this quality of life which came from the wilderness and still is nurtured there? It is aliveness. Aliveness is given to those who live wild, not bred to domesticity. That the wild has taken on negative, unwarranted connotations over the years beyond the aliveness it represents is unfortunate. It is this quality of aliveness which is affirmation. In wildness is not only the preservation of the world, as Thoreau says, but it is that quality which makes of life more than existence.

It is this "more than existence," a sense of adventure, a risk-taking, which has projected man into the frontiers of both inner and outer space. The answer is not domestication, but a recognition that wildness is not predatory but a relationship. Without a quality of wildness, man ceases to be human.

There is no time left. If there is any natural resource which deserves our full attention, it is wilderness. We must preserve any wilderness area left on this planet we have now seen from the moon to be our home or the opportunity is lost forever. Fortunately, the Brooks Range is in the State of Alaska in the United States of America, and we can save it now. Next month, tomorrow, will be too late.

In our technological age, the domestication of the Eskimo village in Anak-tuvuk Pass is inevitable. But what is not inevitable is the domestication of this last great arctic wilderness, the Brooks Range. The choice is ours. Whether by action or indifference, the choice will be made.

The Public And The Wilderness

In 1968, a long-standing proposal for the creation of a nationwide system of trails was signed into law. The Appalachian trail will extend from Maine to Georgia, a distance of about 2000 miles. The Pacific Crest will run about 2350 miles, from Canada to Mexico. Additional side and connecting trails will likely be added. How much "togetherness" is possible in the wilderness before it ceases to be wilderness?

It is possible to lower the vehicle density in some established National Parks while actually increasing the Parks' accessibility to more people (reading 43). However, some naturalists strongly maintain that only the able-bodied and self-sufficient should be permitted access to the most rugged areas of the wilderness (reading 44).

43   **National Parks**

Traffic Jams Turn Attention To Roads

LUTHER J. CARTER

Many of our (national) parks are no longer a place of escape and repose, but a massive traffic jam as nerve-racking as a 5 o'clock urban rush. Senator Frank E. Moss of Utah, in a speech on 1 August in the United States Senate.

The Park Service is investigating the capabilities, costs, and possible effects on terrain and natural communities of monorails, tramways, minirails, helicopters, hydrofoils, and other systems.

Consider how this hypothetical system would operate on a tour of Yellowstone. Assume that a Chicago family of four stops off for a quick tour of a few of the park's most famous spectacles. After arriving at Gardner, at Yellowstone's north entrance, they leave their car and take one of the monorail trains which make frequent stops at park entrance points. They are now on Yellowstone's "mainline" system, designed to move people about quickly between those principal park attractions and visitor centers which earlier were linked by road. This elevated system allows them sweeping scenic views, while itself intruding far less conspicuously upon the landscape than the road it has replaced.

The Chicagoans begin their tour with stops at Old Faithful geyser and Canyon Village. At the latter, the family (which includes small children for whom rugged hikes and back-country trips are out of the question) leaves the monorail and boards a minirail train for a 6-mile round trip to Yellowstone Canyon. Some parts of the canyon may be seen from the train itself, though it passes well back from the north rim of the canyon and is not visible from the south rim. The visitors make frequent stops, however, walking to various overlooks, then boarding other trains to make their way around the circuit. Later, the family gets back on the monorail but then leaves it again briefly for an excursion by aerial tramway to the summit of Mount Washburn. The family's visit to Yellowstone ends back at Gardner—after a tour of about 150 miles in which no one had to fight traffic.

We Must Earn Again For Ourselves What We Have Inherited
(A Lesson in Wilderness Economics)

GARRETT HARDIN

To some it may seem anathema to mention wilderness and economics in the same breath. Certainly, in the past, some of the most dangerous enemies of wilderness have been men who spoke the economic lingo. Despite this historic tar I think the brush of economics is a proper one for painting a picture of wilderness as a problem in human choice.

Economics may be defined as the study of choice necessitated by scarcity. There is something improper in speaking of the "economics of abundance" as Stuart Chase once did. With true abundance all economics ceases, except for the ultimately inescapable economics of time. Of the economics of time there is no general theory, and perhaps cannot be. But for the *things* of the world there is an economics, something that can be said.

Although there really is no such thing as an economics of abundance, the belief that there is is one of the suppurating myths of our time. This belief had its origin partly in a genuine economic phenomenon, "the economy of scale." For complex artifacts in general the unit cost goes down as the scale of manufacture increases. In general, the more complex the artifact, the more striking the economy of scale: the cost per unit to build a million automobiles per year is far, far less than the cost per unit when only one is manufactured. Because artifacts are so pervasive in modern life, most of us unconsciously assume "the bigger the better," and "the more the cheaper." It takes a positive effort of imagination to realize that there are things the supply of which cannot be multiplied indefinitely. Natural resources in general, and wilderness in particular, fall in this group.

This is obvious enough to Sierra Club members. It should be obvious to everyone, but it is not. Discussing some proposed improvements in a national park the *Toronto Financial Post* recently said: "During 1968 and early 1969, campsites will be expanded and roads paved to enable the visitor to enjoy the wilderness atmosphere that was nearly inaccessible only a few years ago." This is an astonishing sentence, but I will bet you would have to argue with the writer for quite a while before he could be made to see the paradox in proposing to "build a road into the wilderness."

Wilderness cannot be multiplied; and it can be subdivided only a little. It is not increasing; we have to struggle to keep it from decreasing. But population increases steadily. The ratio of the wilderness available to each living person becomes steadily less—and bear in mind that this is only a statistical abstraction: were we to divide up the wilderness among even a small fraction of the total population there would be no wilderness available to anyone. So what should we do?

The first thing to do is to see where we stand, to see what the possibilities are, to make a calendar of possibilities without (initially) making any judgment of their desirability. On the first level of analysis there are just three possibilities.

1. The wilderness can be opened to everyone. The end result of this is completely predictable: absolute destruction. Only a nation with a small population, perhaps no greater than one percent of our present population, a nation that does not have at its disposal our rapid means of transportation could maintain a wilderness that was open to all.

2. We can close the wilderness to everyone. In a limited sense, this action would preserve the wilderness. But it would be a wilderness like Bishop Berkeley's "tree in the quad" when no one is there: does wilderness really exist if no one experiences it? Such an action would save wilderness for the future but it would do no one any good now.

3. We can allow only limited access to the wilderness. This is the only course of action that can be rationally defended. Only a small percent of a large population can ever enjoy the wilderness. With suitable standards and a detailed study of the variables, we can (in principle) work out a theory for maximizing the enjoyment of wilderness under a system of limited access.

Whatever theory we adopt we shall have to wrestle with the problem of choice, the problem of determining what small number from among a vast population shall have the opportunity to enjoy this scarce good, wilderness. It is this problem of choice that I wish to explore here.

What I have to say applies not only to wilderness in the sense in which that term is understood by all good outdoorsmen, but also to all other kinds of outdoor recreational areas—to national parks, to ski areas and the like. All of these can be destroyed by localized overpopulation. They differ in their "carrying capacity," to use a term taken from game management. The carrying capacity of a Coney Island (for those who like it, and there are such people) is very high; the carrying capacity of wilderness, in the sense defined by Howard Zahniser, is very low. In the Wilderness Bill of 1964 Zahniser's felicitous definition stands for all to admire:

A wilderness, in contrast with those areas where man and his own works dominate the landscape is hereby recognized as an area where the earth and its community of life are untrammeled by man, where man himself is a visitor who does not remain.

The carrying capacity of Coney Island is, I suppose, something like 200 people per acre; the carrying capacity of a wilderness may be less than one person per square mile. Whatever the capacity, as population inexorably increases, each type of recreational area sooner or later comes up against the problem of allocation of a scarce resource among a more than sufficient number of claimants. The problem of limited access must be faced.

How shall we limit access? How shall we choose from among the too-abundant petitioners those few who shall be allowed to come in? Let's run over the various possibilities.

First: By the market place. We can auction off the natural resource, letting the richest purchase it, or purchase tickets for admission. In our part of the world and in our time most of us unhesitatingly label this method "unfair." Perhaps it is. But don't forget that many an area of natural beauty that we enjoy today was passed down to us unspoiled in an estate of the wealthy of past times. This method of allotment has at least the virtue that it preserves natural treasures until a better, or perhaps we should merely say a more acceptable, method of distribution can be devised. The privilege of wealth has in the past carried many of the beauties of nature through the first, destructive eras of nascent democracy to the more mature stages when people are capable of appreciating beauty. A somewhat different privilege in China, the privilege of religion, preserved the "dawn red-wood" in temple gardens while all the rest of the species was being cut for timber and fuel by the impoverished people outside.

Second: By queus. Wilderness could be made available on a first come, first served basis, up to the extent of the carrying capacity. People would simply line up each day in a long queue and a few would be allowed in. It would be a fatiguing and wasteful system, but it would be "fair." But it might not be stable.

Third: By lottery. This would be eminently "fair," and it would not be terribly fatiguing or wasteful. In earlier days, the decision of a lottery was re-garded as the choice of God. We cannot recapture this consoling belief (now that "God is dead"), but we still are willing to abide by the results of a lottery. Hunting rights in several states where big game abounds are allocated by lottery.

Fourth: By merit. Whether one regards this as "unfair" or "fair" depends on the complexion of one's political beliefs. Whether it is fair or not, I will argue that it is the best system of allocation.

Anyone who argues for a merit system of determining rights immediately raises an *argumentum ad hominem.* He immediately raises the suspicion that he is about to define "merit" in such a way as to include himself in the meritorious group. The suspicion is justified, and because it is justified it must be met.

To carry conviction, he who proposes standards must show that his argu-ment is not self-serving. What I hereby propose as a criterion for admission to the wilderness is great physical vigor. I explicitly call your attention to this significant fact: *I myself cannot pass the test I propose.* I had polio at the age of four, and got around moderately well for more than 40 years, but now I require crutches. Until today, I have not traded on my infirmity. But today I must, for it is an essential part of my argument.

I am not fit for the wilderness I praise. I cannot pass the test I propose. I cannot enter the area I would restrict. Therefore I claim that I speak with objectivity. The standard I propose is not an example of special pleading in my own interest. I can speak loudly where abler men would have to hesitate. I hope that what I have the right to say can be accepted by all.

To restrict the wilderness to physically vigorous people is inherently sensible. What is the *experience* of wilderness? Surely it has two major components. The first is *the experience of being there,* the experience (to use Thoreau's words) of being refreshed "by the sight of inexhaustible vigor," of being emotionally over-whelmed by the vast and titanic forces of nature.

The experience of being there is part of the experience of wilderness, but only a part. Dropped down from a line by helicopter into the middle of a wilderness we would miss an important part of the total experience, namely *the experience of getting there.* The exquisite sight, sound and smell of wilderness is many times more powerful if it is earned through physical achievement, if it comes at the end of a long and fatiguing journey for which vigorous good health is a necessity.

Practically speaking, this means that no one should be able to enter a wilderness by mechanical means. He should have to walk many miles on his own two feet, carrying all his provisions with him. In some cases, entrance might be on horse or mule back, or in a canoe, or by snowshoes; but there should be no automobiles, no campers, no motorcycles, no tote-goats, no outboard motors, no airplanes. Just unmechanized man and nature—this is a necessary part of the prescription of the wilderness experience.

That mechanical aids threaten wilderness is already recognized by the managers of our wildernesses. Emergency roads, it is said, should be used sparingly. I submit that this cautious policy is not cautious enough. I submit that there should be *no* emergency roads, that the people who go into the wilderness should go in without radio transmitters, that they should know for certain that if an emergency arises they can get no help from the outside. If injured, they must either somehow struggle to the outside under their own power, or (if lucky) catch the attention of another rare wanderer in the wilderness and get him to help. For people who are physically prepared for it, the wilderness is not terribly dangerous —but such danger as there is, is a precious part of the total experience. The knowledge that one is *really* on one's own is a powerful tonic. It would be a sentimental cruelty to deprive the wilderness adventurer of the tonic knowledge that death is possible.

There is not even a public interest in making the wilderness safe. Making great and spectacular efforts to save the life of an individual makes sense only when there is a shortage of people. I have not lately heard that there is a shortage of people.

There is, however, a public interest in making the wilderness as difficult and dangerous as it legitimately can be. There is, I think, a well-founded suspicion that our life has become, if anything, too safe for the best psychological health, particularly among the young. The ever-greater extension of the boundaries of legal liability has produced a controlled and fenced-in environment in which it is almost impossible to hurt oneself—unless one tries. The behavior of the young clearly indicates that they really try. Drag races, road races, "rumbles," student sit-ins, marches, and tauntings of the police—all these activities look like the behavior of people looking for danger. I do not wish to deny that these activities spring from other motivations as well, e.g., idealistic political beliefs. I am only saying that it looks like a deliberate seeking of danger is part of the motivation of our obstreperous young. I think they are right to seek danger. I think we should tear down some of the fences that now deprive people of the possibility of danger. I think that a wilderness without rescue services would, in a small way, contribute to the stability of society.

There is another respect in which the interests of society could be furthered by a rigorous wilderness. From time to time a president of the United States tries to improve the physical condition of the average citizen by pummeling him with rhetoric. The verbal assault consists principally of the words "responsibility," "duty," and "patriotism." I'm afraid these rhetorical duds no longer move the young. The negative motivation of shame is, in general, not as effective as the positive motivation of prestige. A wilderness that can be entered only by a few of the most physically fit of the population will act as an incentive to myriads more to improve their physical condition. The motivation will be more effective if we have (as I think we should) a graded series of wilderness and park areas. Areas in which the carrying capacity is reckoned at one person per thousand acres should be the most difficult to enter; those with a capacity of one per hundred acres should be easier; those with one per ten, still easier, and so on. Yosemite Valley should, I suggest, be assigned a carrying capacity of about one per acre, which might mean that it could be opened to anyone who could walk ten miles. All automobile roads should come to a dead end ten miles short of the Valley. At first, of course, the ten-mile walkers would be a very small class, but once the prestige factor took effect more and more people would be willing to walk such a distance. Then the standard should be made more rigorous.

I am sure other details of such a system would eventually have to be faced and worked out. It might be necessary to combine it with a lottery. Or some independent, easily administered test of physical fitness might be instituted. These are details, and in principle can be solved, so I will not spend time on them. But whatever the details, it is clear that many of our present parks, forests, and other recreation areas should be forever closed to people on crutches, to small children, to fat people, to people with heart conditions, and to old people in their usual state of physical disrepair. On the basis of their lack of merit, such people (and remember, I am a member of this deprived group) should give up all claim of right to the wilderness experience.

The poet Goethe once said, "We must earn again for ourselves what we have inherited," recognizing that only those things that are earned can be precious. To be precious the heritage of wilderness must be open only to those who can earn it again for themselves. The rest, since they cannot gain the genuine treasure by their own efforts, must relinquish the shadow of it.

We need not be so righteous as to deny the excluded ones all experience of the out-of-doors. There is no reason in the world why we cannot expand our present practice of setting up small outdoor areas where we permit a high density of people to get a tiny whiff of the outdoors. Camping cheek by jowl with thousands of others in an outdoor slum does not appeal to me personally (I have not visited Yosemite Valley in thirty years) but there *are* people who simply love this slummy togetherness—a fact that Sierra Clubbers sometimes forget or find hard to believe. By all means, let us create some *al fresco* slums for the people —but not in the likes of Yosemite Valley, which is too good for this purpose. But there will be little loss if some of the less attractive forest areas are turned into outdoor slums to relieve the pressure on the really good areas. We must have lakes that fairly pollute with water skiers, in order that we may be able to set aside other lakes for quiet canoeing. At the terminus of six-lane highways we must have beaches that fairly writhe with oily bodies and vibrate to a steady cacaphony of transistor radios—in order to maintain other beaches, difficult of access, on which we forbid all noise makers.

The qualities we seek in wilderness can be achieved only by adopting a policy of variety in management, and selling the concept of merit as the ticket for entrance to the most restricted areas.

The idea of wilderness is a difficult one, but it is precisely because it is difficult that clarifying it is valuable. In discovering how to justify a restricted good to a growing nation of 200 million people we find a formula that extends beyond wilderness to a whole spectrum of recreational activities in the national commons. The solution of this difficult case erects a framework into which other cases can be easily fitted.

The Fate of Wildlife

What we save in the next few years is all that will ever be saved.—Allen Morgan.

Extinction is the rule. Species die out naturally through change over time or by failure to adapt. Or they are killed off by men who hunt, change habitats and introduce predators, competitors and diseases. The readings in this group are concerned exclusively with extinction through the agency of man. Fisher, Simpson and Vincent[1] have estimated that from 70 to 80 percent of extinctions and significant population declines are due to man. What is especially alarming is that the great majority of these extinctions or declines have occurred since 1600, the beginning of the age of colonization. As men more densly crowd the globe, the figures for many species' life spans will undoubtedly continue to plunge.

Fisher et al. have estimated (from fossil records) the average life of a bird species to be two million years. The average duration of a mammal species is something over 6,000,000 years. Island populations evolve faster and become extinct faster than mainland populations. In a shocking island example from the West Indies, before colonization by man, a bird species lasted about 180,000 years. After aboriginal man appeared, this number plummeted to 30,000 years. The figure dropped to 12,000 when the European colonizers came on the scene.

In the West of North America it has been estimated that a million buffalo a year were slaughtered between 1872 and 1875. Ten years later the species was almost extinct.

Major industries sprang up in New England to "harvest" whales and Atlantic salmon. Luckily, these enterprises faded before their prey became extinct.

In eastern Australia, during the 1960s, 1 million kangaroos were slaughtered each year.

In India, conservation and wildlife authorities are afraid that the Indian tiger and rhinoceros are headed for extinction. Less than 35 years ago there were 50,000 tigers, and today the official estimate is 2,000. Of the thousands of rhino's, fewer than 500 exist, 120 of these in game preserves. The guns of poachers and licensed sportsmen have taken their toll of the tiger, but so has the poison of cattlemen. The prized horn of the rhino, considered to be an aphrodisiac has been

1. *Wildlife in Danger.* James Fisher, Noel Simpson, Jack Vincent, and members and correspondents of the Survival Service Commission of the International Union for Conservation of Nature and Natural Resources. New York: Viking, 1969.

widely sought by hunters and poachers. Indian officials believe that the poachers do more damage than sportsmen and essentially cannot be stopped. In view of this, to avert the "tragedy of the commons" (see reading 66), will centralized authority, as distasteful as the idea is, be necessary and able to "enforce" uniformity of obligation and uniformity of restraint?

Animals from the Amazon Basin 45

PAUL GREGORY HELTNE

History shows that precisely the resources and species thought to be inexhaustible are those in greatest danger of misuse and extinction. Laymen and scientists alike generally consider the flow of products from the "green sea" of the Amazon Basin to be limitless. It is not.

From 19 Sept.—12 Oct. 1966, I explored the forests near the Peruvian towns of Pebas, Santa Clara, Iquitos, and Pucallpa in order to survey the area for the study of primates. I flew over or boated through the intervening miles. Wherever I inquired, army officers, missionaries, and natives insisted that animals and good forest could be found *"en el centro"* (meaning directly away from the major waterway in the area). However, after half-day treks into forests of a type in which experience led me to expect many animals, I found none, even though I had been previously assured that I was in a "good" area. The sounds of the forests where I walked were chiefly those of insects. Visible were small birds, small lizards, and colorful tree frogs, joined only occasionally by a bird of medium size. Not once did I see any mammals or any large birds or reptiles. The usually common armadillo trails were extremely rare; feces or signs of feeding or resting were extremely scattered, and no nests were spotted. A colleague who has worked the Amazon from the Colombian border into Brazil and another who has worked the headwaters of the Pachitea River confirm these observations.

Wherever land is high enough to permit farming, slash-and-burn agriculture degrades the soil, completing the depredation of the forests which was begun by lumbering. In places the destructive trend has progressed to an "anticlimax" of pastureland. The second-growth forests, soon to be recut in their turn, are of poor quality and produce mainly wind—dispersed seeds. These are probably poor or inefficient food sources and can support little animal life in comparison with the original forests, though it is true that in slashed areas the collapse of the vertical stratification contributes to the abundance of a few species. Losses of forests to lumbering and farming, and animals to hunting practices are inevitable corollaries of the burgeoning populations along the river. (Not only dried monkeys but also fresh rat-sized rodents are for sale in the open meat market in Iquitos.) Road building will soon send colonizers into frontier areas which are now inaccessible.

However, the fur and live animal export markets threaten wildlife over a wider range. Demand always exceeds the fur traders' supply, though tens of thousands of skins are shipped from Iquitos every year. Select species such as tapir, peccary, ocelot, and jaguar are being severely depleted over truly vast regions because of the desirability of their hides. All animals must be sought further and further into the forests each year. The trends set in motion by agriculture and the fur trade are compounded by exportation. Many animal exporters are unable to fill their huge orders—mostly from the U.S.—and mainly for experimental animals. The methods of hunting and capture are those most devastating to the breeding populations. My experiences lead me to conclude that through human intervention many species' ranges are being truncated, perhaps irreversibly, over large areas.

Editor's Footnote To Letter

In August, 1968, a bill was passed (HR-11618) to prohibit any species threatened with extinction from being imported unless it is to be used for educational and scientific purposes. Many pet shop owners objected to the law as it would hurt business.

46   Loss Of Wild Genetic Stocks

KENNETH S. NORRIS

Naturalists are growing increasingly aware that to let any species become extinct is a deeply serious error. The mere presumption of humans obliterating other species is reason enough to avoid this error, but a practical reason also exists for saving species. Each organism contains within it a genetic code that has been buffeted, altered, and molded through long geologic time, fitting that organism to the subtle and varied complex of environmental stresses imposed by nature. Each organism is thus a magnificently intricate response system whose subsystems and structures mesh together for survival. Each is a marvel of adaptation.

Modern genetics has revealed so much of the living blueprint in recent years that one may predict with some confidence that our means for altering the genetic constitutions of our domestic animals and plants may increase manyfold in the coming years. The raw materials will most likely be these natural systems, tested and approved by nature. Already we often return to wild plants or animals for genetic materials to diversify and strengthen our in-bred food stocks. Genetic modification will probably become a much more sophisticated applied science, placing great power in human hands, and we will need nature as its basis. The use of such a "gene bank" will likely extend far beyond application to our present domestic animals and plants, to subtle use in bringing many organisms, now useless from the human standpoint, under our control. Crops may one day thrive on salt flats or on barren desert slopes as a result.

Decline of Whales

ROGER PAYNE

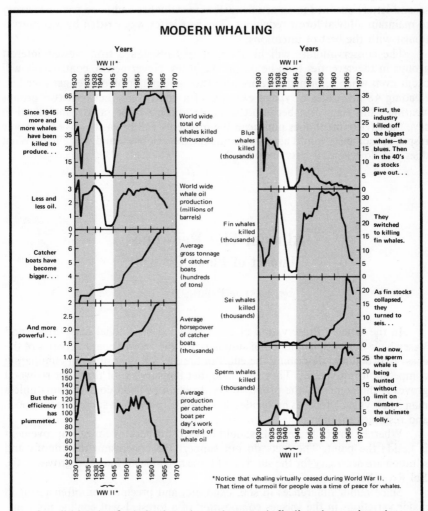

MODERN WHALING

As wild herds of whales have been destroyed, finding the survivors has become more difficult and required more effort. As larger whales are killed off, smaller species are exploited to keep the industry alive. However, since there have never been species limits, large whales are always taken wherever and whenever encountered. Thus small whales are used to subsidize the extermination of large ones.

An Example of Conservation Controversy

The two letters that follow appeared after Stone and Vasey (authors of second letter) outlined in an article in *Science* why fire and flood were necessary to maintain alluvial forest redwoods. The first letter was written by a conservationist with the best of intentions.

The conservationist will likely meet less resistance from vested interest groups in the seventies than he did in the fifties. Nevertheless, controversy will occur even when informed citizens with the same major objectives get together. Reading 48 illustrates a typical example of a controversy between two groups wearing white hats. Just because the nation appears to be rapidly mobilized to save the environment does not mean the problems will be easily solved. In some respects, ecologists would again welcome the days of black and white hats. What does one do when all hats are white?

48   Alluvial-Flat Redwoods
Impact of Flood Control

BESTOR ROBINSON

In the article "Preservation of coast redwood on alluvial flats" Stone and Vasey have done a splendid job of summarizing the growth characteristics of the coast redwood and describing the effect of fire and silt deposition in eliminating competing forest species. They conclude that the survival of the giant redwood groves is threatened by the proposed construction of flood control dams unless man employs such tools as herbicides, fire, and chainsaws as a substitute for floods and resultant siltation.

Whether any of these tools should be used for park or forest improvement is beside the point. The facts do not support the conclusion that floods and siltation are necessary for the survival of these magnificent redwood groves in the Eel River basin.

Since minor differences in soil, exposure, and precipitation often result in major variations in the species composition of a forest, I will confine my comments to the redwood forests of the Eel River basin.

First, it should be noted that large or "giant" redwoods, that is, over 150 cm in diameter at breast height, are not confined to the alluvial flats that are subject to flood and silt deposit. They are found in almost solid strands in this basin wherever the following conditions coexist:

1. Adequate soil depth for nutrition and prevention of windthrow.
2. Benches, flats, and slopes sufficiently moderate to prevent soil creep or excessive erosion.

3. Adequate summer moisture to substitute for this region's deficient rainfall. This substitute moisture is provided by either moderate depth of water table (alluvial flats), underground seepage from higher slopes, or condensation of ocean summer fogs. Most of these groves and forests are above maximum flood level and many of them show no evidence of fire scar or fire-blackened bark.

The survival vigor of the solid stands of redwood is based on the fact that although fire and siltation may help, neither of these agents is necessary.

The redwood, given proper growing conditions as previously outlined, has weapons and competitive advantages that enable it to become a climax species as against its competitors in this region—Douglas fir, tan oak, and bay. (Grand fir will not be discussed since it is not a major competitive species in the Eel River basin.)

The bay tree is slow of growth and only partially shade-tolerant. Even when given an equal start on cleared land, it is, in a few decades, shaded out by the redwood and reduced to the status of a scattered understory of weak growth.

The tan oak, like the bay tree, cannot compete with the redwood in height. Although it sprouts from the stump after a fire and is vigorous in reproduction, it has a short life on sites suitable for redwood, and usually succumbs to heart rot. It does, however, compete vigorously with the redwood for a longer period than the bay tree.

The Douglas fir, if sprouted on cleared land at the same time as the redwood, will live to maturity as a large competing tree, finally yielding to the redwood because of its shorter lifespan. But in an established redwood forest, Douglas fir, because of low shade-tolerance plus vigorous root competition by the redwood, seldom succeeds in reaching the region of sunlight.

It should also be noted that, in a dense climax forest of redwood, the mat of redwood roots in the top 15 cm of soil deprives all seedlings of moisture sufficient to survive the first summer. Floods and resulting silt deposits on alluvial flats do eliminate most of the tan oak and Douglas fir. This favorable factor in the continued survival of mature redwoods is more than outweighed by the three undesirable effects of flooding:

1. The silt deposit produces a new seed bed without a surface mat of redwood roots. For several years, depending on the depth of silt, this deposit is free of competition from redwood roots and permits competing trees to survive beyond the critical initial years.

2. The physical undermining and toppling of several thousand large trees such as occurred during the 1955 and 1964 floods are an intolerable loss.

3. The power of streams to move boulders and large cobbles increases exponentially with the volume of the flow. The Eel River bed in many places was raised a meter or more as a result of these recent floods; the raised bed was normally confined to gravel beds adjacent to the alluvial-redwood flats. This resulted in the raising of the water table and the death of many mature redwoods from what is locally known as "sour root."

If the facts and conclusions stated above are sound, there is only one answer to the basic question. The construction of flood control dams on the Eel River and its tributaries would aid in the preservation of the giant redwood groves on the adjacent alluvial flats.

EDWARD C. STONE and RICHARD B. VASEY

The greatest threat to the alluvial-flat redwoods may, in the long run, turn out to be the lay conservationists. This is ironical because they were largely responsible for getting these redwoods placed under park protection in the first place. Unfortunately, however, they have failed to fully appreciate the dynamic character of the ecosystem involved. They have focused their attention on preserving the trees now standing, ignoring the rest of the ecosystem which was responsible for these redwoods being present and upon which their replacements must depend. Protection from man, fires, and floods has been their goal. They have attached little importance to the fact that fires and floods were critical elements in the system under which the alluvial-flat redwoods developed and have actively opposed any man-generated substitutes.

It is essentially from this position that Bestor Robinson writes today. For 31 years as a director of the Sierra Club and an active conservationist, he is protection-oriented and is a strong advocate of flood control because he wants to keep the alluvial-flat redwoods from being washed away. He has dismissed as insignificant the impact such action might have on the functioning of the alluvial-flat ecosystem of which these redwoods are only part. The crux of his argument is that, because there are big trees on the slopes and benches where flooding does not occur, siltation per se is not necessary in order for the redwood to maintain its competitive position on the alluvial flats; he even goes so far as to suggest that siltation, by creating a competition-free seedbed, aids the survival of competing species and is therefore undesirable. Apparently, he is unaware that he cannot readily extrapolate from one ecosystem to another.

We are fully aware that nearly pure stands of large redwoods exist off the alluvial flats. But the ecology that has contributed to their development is not the same as that which has contributed to the development of the alluvial-flat redwoods. It was the ecology of the alluvial-flat redwood that we considered in the paper to which Robinson takes exception.

Robinson argues that because the potential competitors of redwood are short-lived they could not possibly replace redwood. Obviously he is not familiar with the facts. In the absence of floods and fires, seedlings and saplings of bay, tan oak, and grand fir will actively maintain a suppressed understory on the alluvial flats. Only an opening in the canopy is needed for these species to develop into full-fledged competitors. Thus when a redwood falls—as some do each year —these waiting competitors are on hand ready to take its place. Not always will there be a redwood seedling in the right place at the right time to compete for space when an opening occurs. It is in this way that the alluvial-flat redwoods will eventually be replaced with a mixture of bay, tan oak, and grand fir if flooding and fire are removed from the ecosystem and man fails to actively intervene. It is unimportant how big or for how long redwood can grow when once established on the alluvial flats. The important fact is that periodically a redwood tree falls and there are competing species ready to take its place.

All the evidence we have been able to collect to date suggests that time is running out for the alluvial-flat redwoods and that flood control could be the final blow unless man actively intervenes with herbicides, the ax, or the chainsaw. Strong support behind a program of active intervention is urgently needed. Our hope is that it will not be too late in coming.

How Simple Answers Backfire

To know what is ecologically correct behavior often depends on a complex weighting of an ensemble of factors. We are now discovering that many time-honored ecological dicta are inadequate, if not downright erroneous. This is illustrated in the next selection. Smokey the Bear has taught us that fire in the wilderness is bad. Is it always?

Forest Fires   49
Suppression Policy Has Its Ecological Drawbacks

MARK OBERLE

In California and the Southwest, tree-ring studies of ponderosa pine forests have indicated that ground fires—small blazes that spread through the turf and underbrush but not the treetops—swept through these areas at least once in a decade during prehistoric times. By preventing even these moderate ground fires from periodically clearing accumulations of litter from the forest floor, the policy of total fire suppression has made some woods easy targets for disastrous fires. In primitive times, periodic fires also prevented an understory of competing shade-resistant trees from developing, and thus gave the ponderosa forests an open, park-like appearance. But, in the absence of fire, understory trees have crowded the forest and weakened the taller pines through competition, Harold H. Biswell, professor of forestry at the University of California, Berkeley, told *Science*. Crown fires—the huge conflagrations that spread through the forest canopy—rarely occurred in primitive California forests, Biswell added, but this understory of trees has formed a new intermediate level of fuel between the canopy and the forest floor that encourages crown fires.

One biologist has advanced the theory that fire-exclusion policies may be a factor in the near-extinction of the California condor. Raymond B. Cowles of the University of California at Santa Barbara has suggested that the condor needs relatively long runways for takeoffs, and clearings on ridgetops for feeding. With the prevention of fires, Cowles said, dense plant growth has reclaimed these clearings and thus has narrowed the condor's ecological niche.

In Alaska, the permafrost layer complicates the relationship of fire to wildlife populations. "Fire has been an important part of the ecology of interior Alaska," said David R. Klein, leader of the Cooperative Wildlife Research Unit at the University of Alaska. When fire is excluded from many lowland sites, an insulating carpet of moss tends to accumulate and raise the permafrost level, he said, and permafrost close to the surface encourages the growth of black spruce, a low-growing species with little timber or food value. "These areas are veritable deserts," Klein said. Bear, deer, moose, and other animals depend on lightning fires to maintain a constant cycle of vegetation types for food and cover.

Harold Biswell of the University of California, Berkeley, argues that under-brush and leaf litter in ponderosa pine and some mixed conifer forests should be removed much as they were before white man came—by means of small ground fires every few years. When Biswell advanced this forest-management proposal, in the early 1950's, the idea received so much flak from government foresters that he claims he was forced to do his research on private land. His burning technique involves setting a fire on a hilltop at a time of year when only the upper layer of pine needles is dry enough to burn, and letting the fire creep down the slope under close supervision. The technique involves extensive initial cutting of underbrush in forests with thick undergrowth, and heavy investments of manpower to control the low-intensity blaze, but Biswell claims that the investment pays off in fire hazard reduction.

In 1962, a crown fire whipped through a forest adjacent to his prescribed burning plot at Hobergs, California, but as soon as the fire reached his land it dropped out of the tree-tops and crept through the forest floor, where it was easily controlled. His prescribed burning causes minimal soil erosion and has no adverse effects on long-term soil fertility or water-holding ability, Biswell says. He esti-mates that his technique may be applicable to 4 million acres in California alone.

"The public," said one administrator, "can't see why we allow a fire we set in November to burn when we'll jump in with a thousand men to put out a wildfire that starts in June."

All the Way to the End

Compare the position argued for in Peugnet's letter (reading 50) with the attitude expressed in Garrett Hardin's "We Must Earn Again for Ourselves What We Have Inherited," (reading 44). How valid is it to maintain virgin wilderness if "restoration" to its original state can occur? This raises the heated issue of how important it is to be able to say, "This has not been altered by technological man." Is it just as satisfactory to be able to say, "This has been altered by technological man, but the restoration has likely made it the way it was before man"?

Will the oceans perish from good intentions? Paul Ehrlich's article "Eco-ca-tastrophe!" (reading 51) suggests how the oceans may die. A valuable exercise would be to determine how many readings in this book contain information alluded to in Ehrlich's article.

Flyspeck on Glacier Peak   50

AMÉDÉE A. PEUGNET

The 450-acre site of the Kennecott mine is a mere flyspeck in the 458,000-acre Glacier Peak area. The region "which is largely inaccessible except by helicopter or by foot" would be made relatively accessible to the public, with a minimum expenditure of public funds, by the road which Kennecott would have to build. Also, without cost to the public, a reasonably large and potentially beautiful lake would result from the operation. A foregone conclusion cannot be made that the tailings would either pollute streams or destroy fish. It should be obvious that the excavation from which both ore and waste are derived could eventually contain the tailings. Any deleterious effect that the proposed pit might have on the wilderness area would be of short duration, especially if the rather common practice of "restoration" were put into effect, and would be more than offset by the lake created. One has only to visit the numerous abandoned mining areas in the Americas to be impressed by the rapidity with which Nature reclaims her own, even without human efforts. This, true even in arid areas, is much more rapid in areas of reasonable amounts of rainfall. On completion of mining and restoration, there would exist in this huge wilderness an ideal, ready-made, site on which appropriate authority could erect facilities for public enjoyment, and from which to exercise safety, fire protection, and other functions required in large public recreation areas. Roads, piped water, and sanitary facilities would already exist, together with a lake sufficiently large to provide recreation to many, but not so large that it could not be adequately policed for safety.

Since real "national wealth" consists of the industry of its people and its natural resources, it would be a serious error to deprive a nation of possibly a not inconsiderable portion of its natural wealth. It should not be forgotten that mining claims of the kind in question are, to a large extent, won by aching feet, backs, and heads; not infrequently at the cost of life. The fact that our country is largely self-sufficient in many of its mineral requirements is, to no small extent, a result of the lowly, unsung, prospector. The very existence of 91,000 mining claims, of any nature or worth, is mute testimony to the existence of a large highly mineralized area. The closing off of huge potential areas of mineral wealth augurs ill with respect to our deficiencies in gold, silver, and other minerals. Let us not hastily write off large portions of our national inheritance.

Eco-catastrophe!   51

PAUL R. EHRLICH

The end of the ocean came late in the summer of 1979, and it came even more rapidly than the biologists had expected. There had been signs for more than a decade, commencing with the discovery in 1968 that DDT slows down photosynthesis in marine plant life. It was announced in a short paper in the technical journal, *Science,* but to ecologists it smacked of doomsday. They knew that all life in the sea depends on photosynthesis, the chemical process by which green plants bind the sun's energy and make it available to living things. And they knew that DDT and similar chlorinated hydrocarbons had polluted the entire surface of the earth, including the sea.

But that was only the first of many signs. There had been the final gasp of the whaling industry in 1973, and the end of the Peruvian anchovy fishery in 1975. Indeed, a score of other fisheries had disappeared quietly from over—exploitation and various eco-catastrophes by 1977. The term "eco-catastrophe" was coined by a California ecologist in 1969 to describe the most spectacular of man's attacks on the systems which sustain his life. He drew his inspiration from the Santa Barbara offshore oil disaster of that year, and from the news which spread among naturalists that virtually all of the Golden State's seashore bird life was doomed because of chlorinated hydrocarbon interference with its reproduction. Eco-catastrophes in the sea became increasingly common in the early 1970's. Mysterious "blooms" of previously rare microorganisms began to appear in offshore waters. Red tides—killer outbreaks of a minute single-celled plate—returned to the Florida Gulf coast and were sometimes accompanied by tides of other exotic hues.

It was clear by 1975 that the entire ecology of the ocean was changing. A few types of phytoplankton were becoming resistant to chlorinated hydrocarbons and were gaining the upper hand. Changes in the phytoplankton community led inevitably to changes in the community of zooplankton, the tiny animals which eat the phytoplankton. These changes were passed on up the chains of life in the ocean to the herring, plaice, cod and tuna. As the diversity of life in the ocean diminished, its stability also decreased.

Other changes had taken place by 1975. Most ocean fishes that returned to fresh water to breed, like the salmon, had become extinct, their breeding streams so dammed up and polluted that their powerful homing instinct only resulted in suicide. Many fishes and shellfishes that bred in restricted areas along the coasts followed them as onshore pollution escalated.

By 1977 the annual yield of fish from the sea was down to 30 million metric tons, less than one-half the per capita catch of a decade earlier. This helped malnutrition to escalate sharply in a world where an estimated 50 million people per year were already dying of starvation. The United Nations attempted to get all chlorinated hydrocarbon insecticides banned on a worldwide basis, but the move was defeated by the United States. This opposition was generated primarily by the American petrochemical industry, operating hand in glove with its subsidiary, the United States Department of Agriculture. Together they persuaded the government to oppose the U.N. move—which was not difficult since most Americans believed that Russia and China were more in need of fish products than was the United States. The United Nations also attempted to get fishing nations to adopt strict and enforced catch limits to preserve dwindling stocks. This move was blocked by Russia, who, with the most modern electronic equipment, was in the best position to glean what was left in the sea. It was, curiously, on the very day in 1977 when the Soviet Union announced its refusal that another ominous article appeared in *Science.* It announced that incident solar radiation had been so reduced by a worldwide air pollution that serious effects on the world's vegetation could be expected.

Apparently it was a combination of ecosystem destabilization, sunlight reduction, and a rapid escalation in chlorinated hydrocarbon pollution from massive Thanodrin applications which triggered the ultimate castastrophe. Seventeen huge Soviet-financed Thanodrin plants were operating in underdeveloped countries by 1978. They had been part of a massive Russian "aid offensive" designed to fill the gap caused by the collapse of America's ballyhooed "Green Revolution".

It became apparent in the early '70s that the "Green Revolution" was more talk than substance. Distribution of high yield "miracle" grain seeds had caused temporary local spurts in agricultural production. Simultaneously, excellent weather had produced record harvests. The combination permitted bureaucrats, especially in the United States Department of Agriculture and the Agency for International Development (AID), to reverse their previous pessimism and indulge in an outburst of optimistic propaganda about staving off famine. They raved about the approaching transformation of agriculture in the underdeveloped countries (UDCs). The reason for the propaganda reversal was never made clear. Most historians agree that a combination of utter ignorance of ecology, a desire to justify past errors, and pressure from agroindustry (which was eager to sell pesticides, fertilizers, and farm machinery to the UDCs and agencies helping the UDCs) was behind the campaign. Whatever the motivation, the results were clear. Many concerned people, lacking the expertise to see through the Green Revolution drivel, relaxed. The population-food crisis was "solved."

But reality was not long in showing itself. Local famine persisted in northern India even after good weather brought an end to the ghastly Bihar famine of the mid-'60s. East Pakistan was next, followed by a resurgence of general famine in northern India. Other foci of famine rapidly developed in Indonesia, the Philippines, Malawi, the Congo, Egypt, Columbia, Ecuador, Honduras, the Dominican Republic, and Mexico.

Everywhere hard realities destroyed the illusion of the Green Revolution. Yields dropped as the progressive farmers who had first accepted the new seeds found that their higher yields brought lower prices—effective demand (hunger plus cash) was not sufficient in poor countries to keep prices up. Less progressive farmers, observing this, refused to make the extra effort required to cultivate the "miracle" grains. Transport systems proved inadequate to bring the necessary fertilizer to the fields where the new and extremely fertilizer-sensitive grains were being grown. The same systems were also inadequate to move produce to markets. Fertilizer plants were not built fast enough, and most of the underdeveloped countries could not scrape together funds to purchase supplies, even on concessional terms. Finally, the inevitable happened, and pests began to reduce yields in even the most carefully cultivated fields. Among the first were the famous "miracle rats" which invaded Philippine "miracle rice" fields early in 1969. They were quickly followed by many insects and viruses, thriving on the relatively pest-susceptible new grains, encouraged by the vast and dense plantings, and rapidly acquiring resistance to the chemicals used against them. As chaos spread until even the most obtuse agriculturists and economists realized that the Green Revolution had turned brown, the Russians stepped in.

In retrospect it seems incredible that the Russians, with the American mistakes known to them, could launch an even more incompetent program of aid to the underdeveloped world. Indeed, in the early 1970's there were cynics in the United States who claimed that outdoing the stupidity of American foreign aid would be physically impossible. Those critics were, however, obviously unaware that the Russians had been busily destroying their own environment for many years. The virtual disappearance of sturgeon from Russian rivers caused a great shortage of caviar by 1970. A standard joke among Russian scientists at that time was that they had created an artificial caviar which was indistinguishable from the real thing—except by taste. At any rate the Soviet Union, observing with interest the progressive deterioration of relations between the UDCs and the United States, came up with a solution. It had recently developed what it claimed was the ideal insecticide, a highly lethal chlorinated hydrocarbon complexed with a special agent for penetrating the external skeletal armor of insects. Announcing that the new pesticide, called Thanodrin, would truly produce a Green Revolution, the Soviets entered into negotiations with various UDCs for the construction of massive Thanodrin factories. The USSR would bear all the costs; all it wanted in return were certain trade and military concessions.

It is interesting now, with the perspective of years, to examine in some detail the reasons why the UCDs welcomed the Thanodrin plan with such open arms. Government officials in these countries ignored the protests of their own scientists that Thanodrin would not solve the problems which plagued them. The governments now knew that the basic cause of their problems was overpopulation, and that these problems had been exacerbated by the dullness, daydreaming, and cupidity endemic to all governments. They knew that only population control and limited development aimed primarily at agriculture could have spared them the horrors they now faced. They knew it, but they were not about to admit it. How much easier it was simply to accuse the Americans of failing to give them proper aid; how much simpler to accept the Russian panacea.

And then there was the general worsening of relations between the United States and the UDCs. Many things had contributed to this. The situation in America in the first half of the 1970's deserves our close scrutiny. Being more dependent on imports for raw materials than the Soviet Union, the United States had, in the early 1970's, adopted more and more heavy-handed policies in order to insure continuing supplies. Military adventures in Asia and Latin America had further lessened the international credibility of the United States as a great defender of freedom—an image which had begun to deteriorate rapidly during the pointless and fruitless Vietnam conflict. At home, acceptance of the carefully manufactured image lessened dramatically, as even the more romantic and chauvinistic citizens began to understand the role of the military and the industrial system in what John Kenneth Galbraith had aptly named "The New Industrial State."

At home in the USA the early '70s were traumatic times. Racial violence grew and the habitability of the cities diminished, as nothing substantial was done to ameliorate either racial inequities or urban blight. Welfare rolls grew as automation and general technological progress forced more and more people into the category of "unemployable." Simultaneously a taxpayers' revolt occurred. Although there was not enough money to build the schools, roads, water systems, sewage systems, jails, hospitals, urban transit lines, and all the other amenities needed to support a burgeoning population, Americans refused to tax themselves more heavily. Starting in Youngstown, Ohio in 1969 and followed closely by Richmond, California, community after community was forced to close its schools or curtail educational operations for lack of funds. Water supplies, already marginal in quality and quantity in many places by 1970, deteriorated quickly. Water rationing occurred in 1723 municipalities in the summer of 1974, and hepatitis and epidemic dysentery rates climbed about 500 percent between 1970-1974.

Air pollution continued to be the most obvious manifestation of environmental deterioration. It was, by 1972, quite literally in the eyes of all Americans. The year 1973 saw not only the New York and Los Angeles smog disasters, but also the publication of the Surgeon General's massive report on air pollution and health. The public had been partially prepared for the worst by the publicity given to the U.N. pollution conference held in 1972. Deaths in the late '60s caused by smog were well known to scientists, but the public had ignored them because they mostly involved the early demise of the old and sick rather than people dropping dead on the freeways. But suddenly our citizens were faced with nearly 200,000 corpses and massive documentation that they could be the next to die from respiratory disease. They were not ready for that scale of disaster. After all, the U.N. conference had not predicted that accumulated air pollution would make the planet uninhabitable until almost 1990. The population was terrorized as TV screens became filled with scenes of horror from the disaster areas. Especially vivid was NBC's coverage of hundreds of unattended people choking out their lives outside of New York's hospitals. Terms like nitrogen oxide, acute bronchitis and cardiac arrest began to have real meaning for most Americans.

The ultimate horror was the announcement that chlorinated hydrocarbons were now a major constituent of air pollution in all American cities. Autopsies of smog disaster victims revealed an average chlorinated hydrocarbon load in fatty tissue equivalent to 26 parts per million of DDT. In October, 1973, the Department of Health, Education and Welfare announced studies which showed unequivocally that increasing death rates from hypertension, cirrhosis of the liver, liver cancer and a series of other diseases had resulted from the chlorinated hydrocarbon load. They estimated that Americans born since 1946 (when DDT usage began) now had a life expectancy of only 49 years, and predicted that if current patterns continued, this expectancy would reach 42 years by 1980, when it might level out. Plunging insurance stocks triggered a stock market panic. The president of Velsicol, Inc., a major pesticide producer, went on television to "publicly eat a teaspoonful of DDT" (it was really powdered milk) and announce that HEW had been infiltrated by Communists. Other giants of the petrochemical industry, attempting to dispute the indisputable evidence, launched a massive pressure campaign on Congress to force HEW to "get out of agriculture's business." They were aided by the agro-chemical journals, which had decades of experience in misleading the public about the benefits and dangers of pesticides. But by now the public realized that it had been duped. The Nobel Prize for medicine and physiology was given to Drs. J.L. Radomski and W.B. Deichmann, who in the late 1960's had pioneered in the documentation of the long-term lethal effects of chlorinated hydrocarbons. A Presidential Commission with unimpeachable credentials directly accused the agrochemical complex of "condemning many millions of Americans to an early death." The year 1973 was the year in which Americans finally came to understand the direct threat to their existence posed by environmental deterioration.

And 1973 was also the year in which most people finally comprehended the indirect threat. Even the president of Union Oil Company and several other industrialists publicly stated their concern over the reduction of bird populations which had resulted from pollution by DDT and other chlorinated hydrocarbons. Insect populations boomed because they were resistant to most pesticides and had been freed, by the incompetent use of those pesticides, from most of their natural enemies. Rodents swarmed over crops, multiplying rapidly in the absence of predatory birds. The effect of pests on the wheat crop was especially disastrous in the summer of 1973, since that was also the year of the great drought. Most of us can remember the shock which greeted the announcement by atmospheric physicists that the shift of the jet stream which had caused the drought was probably permanent. It signalled the birth of the Midwestern desert. Man's air-polluting activities had by then caused gross changes in climatic patterns. The news, of course, played hell with commodity and stock markets. Food prices skyrocketed, as savings were poured into hoarded canned goods. Official assurances that food supplies would remain ample fell on deaf ears, and even the government showed signs of nervousness when California migrant field workers went out on strike again in protest against the continued use of pesticides by growers. The strike burgeoned into farm burning and riots. The workers, calling themselves "The Walking Dead," demanded immediate compensation for their shortened lives, and crash research programs to attempt to lengthen them.

It was in the same speech in which President Edward Kennedy, after much delay, finally declared a national emergency and called out the National Guard to harvest California's crops, that the first mention of population control was made. Kennedy pointed out that the United States would no longer be able to offer any food aid to other nations and was likely to suffer food shortages herself. He suggested that, in view of the manifest failure of the Green Revolution, the only hope of the UDCs lay in population control. His statement, you will recall, created an uproar in the underdeveloped countries. Newspaper editorials accused the United States of wishing to prevent small countries from becoming large countries and thus threatening American hegemony. Politicians asserted that President Kennedy was a "creature of the giant drug combine" that wished to shove its pills down every woman's throat.

Among Americans, religious opposition to population control was very slight. Industry in general also backed the idea. Increasing poverty in the UDCs was both destroying markets and threatening supplies of raw materials. The seriousness of the raw material situation had been brought home during the Congressional Hard Resources hearings in 1971. The exposure of the ignorance of the cornucopian economists had been quite a spectacle—a spectacle brought into virtually every American's home in living color. Few would forget the distinguished geologist from the University of California who suggested that economists be legally required to learn at least the most elementary facts of geology. Fewer still would forget that an equally distinguished Harvard economist added that they might be required to learn some economics, too. The overall message was clear: America's resource situation was bad and bound to get worse. The hearings had led to a bill requiring the Departments of State, Interior, and Commerce to set up a joint resource procurement council with the express purpose of "insuring that proper consideration of American resource needs be an integral part of American foreign policy."

Suddenly the United States discovered that it had a national consensus: population control was the only possible salvation of the underdeveloped world. But that same consensus led to heated debate. How could the UDCs be persuaded to limit their populations, and should not the United States lead the way by limiting its own? Members of the intellectual community wanted America to set an example. They pointed out that the United States was in the midst of a new baby boom: her birth rate, well over 20 per thousand per year, and her growth rate of one percent per annum were among the very highest of the developed countries. They detailed the deterioration of the American physical and psychic environments, the growing health threats, the impending food shortages, and the insufficiency of funds for desperately needed public works. They contended that the nation was clearly unable or unwilling to properly care for the people it already had. What possible reason could there be, they queried, for adding any more? Besides, who would listen to requests by the United States for population control when that nation did not control her own profligate reproduction?

Those who opposed population controls for the U.S. were equally vociferous. The military-industrial complex, with its all-too-human mixture of ignorance and avarice, still saw strength and prosperity in numbers. Baby food magnates, already worried by the growing nitrate pollution of their products, saw their market disappearing. Steel manufacturers saw a decrease in aggregate demand and slippage for that holy of holies, the Gross National Product. And military men saw, in the growing population-food-environment crisis, a serious threat to their carefully nurtured Cold War. In the end, of course, economic arguments held sway, and the "inalienable right of every American couple to determine the size of its family," a freedom invented for the occasion in the early '70s, was not compromised.

The population control bill, which was passed by Congress early in 1974, was quite a document, nevertheless. On the domestic front, it authorized an increase from 100 to 150 million dollars in funds for "family planning" activities. This was made possible by a general feeling in the country that the growing army on welfare needed family planning. But the gist of the bill was a series of measures designed to impress the need for population control on the UDCs. All American aid to countries with overpopulation problems was required by law to consist in part of population control assistance. In order to receive any assistance each nation was required not only to accept the population control aid, but also to match it according to a complex formula. "Overpopulation" itself was defined by a formula based on U.N. statistics, and the UDCs were required not only to accept aid, but also to show progress in reducing birth rates. Every five years the status of the aid program for each nation was to be re-evaluated.

The reaction to the announcement of this program dwarfed the response to President Kennedy's speech. A coalition of UDCs attempted to get the U.N. General Assembly to condemn the United States as a "genetic aggressor." Most damaging of all to the American cause was the famous "25 Indians and a dog" speech by Mr. Shankarnarayan, Indian Ambassador to the U.N. Shankarnarayan pointed out that for several decades the United States, with less than six percent of the people of the world had consumed roughly 50 percent of the raw materials used every year. He described vividly America's contribution to worldwide environmental deterioration, and he scathingly denounced the miserly record of United States foreign aid as "unworthy of a fourth-rate power, let alone the most powerful nation on earth."

It was the climax of his speech, however, which most historians claim once and for all destroyed the image of the United States. Shankarnarayan informed the assembly that the average American family dog was fed more animal protein per week than the average Indian got in a month. "How do you justify taking fish from protein-starved Peruvians and feeding them to your animals?" he asked. "I contend," he concluded, "that the birth of an American baby is a greater disaster for the world than that of 25 Indian babies." When the applause had died away, Mr. Sorensen, the American representative, made a speech which said essentially that "other countries look after their own self-interest, too." When the vote came, the United States was condemned.

This condemnation set the tone of U.S.-UDC relations at the time the Russian Thanodrin proposal was made. The proposal seemed to offer the masses in the UDCs an opportunity to save themselves and humiliate the United States at the same time; and in human affairs, as we all know, biological realities could never interfere with such an opportunity. The scientists were silenced, the politicans said yes, the Thanodrin plants were built, and the results were what any beginning ecology student could have predicted. At first Thanodrin seemed to offer excellent control of many pests. True, there was a rash of human fatalities from improper use of the lethal chemical, but, as Russian technical advisors were prone to note, these were more than compensated for by increased yields. Thanodrin use skyrocketed throughout the underdeveloped world. The Mikoyan design group developed a dependable , cheap agricultural aircraft which the Soviets donated to the effort in large numbers. MIG sprayers became even more common in UDCs than MIG interceptors.

Then the troubles began. Insect strains with cuticles resistant to Thanodrin penetration began to appear. And as streams, rivers, fish culture ponds and onshore waters became rich in Thanodrin, more fisheries began to disappear. Bird populations were decimated. The sequence of events was standard for broadcast use of synthetic pesticide: Great success at first, followed by removal of natural enemies and development of resistance by the pest. Populations of crop-eating insects in areas treated with Thanodrin made steady comebacks and soon became more abundant than ever. Yields plunged, while farmers in their desperation increased the Thanodrin dose and shortened the time between treatments. Death from Thanodrin poisoning became common. The first violent incident occurred in the Canete Valley of Peru, where farmers had suffered a similar chlorinated hydrocarbon disaster in the mid—'50s. A Russian advisor serving as an agricultural pilot was assaulted and killed by a mob of enraged farmers in January, 1978. Trouble spread rapidly during 1978, especially after the word got out that two years earlier Russia herself had banned the use of Thanodrin at home because of its serious effects on ecological systems. Suddenly Russia, and not the United States, was the *bete noir* in the UDCs. "Thanodrin parties" became epidemic, with farmers, in their ignorance, dumping carloads of Thanodrin concentrate into the sea. Russian advisors fled, and four of the Thanodrin plants were leveled to the ground. Destruction of the plants in Rio and Calcutta led to hundreds of thousands of gallons of Thanodrin concentrate being dumped directly into the sea.

Mr. Shankarnarayan again rose to address the U.N., but this time it was Mr. Potemkin, representative of the Soviet Union, who was on the hot seat. Mr. Potemkin heard his nation described as the greatest mass killer of all time as Shankarnarayan predicted at least 30 million deaths from crop failures due to overdependence on Thanodrin. Russia was accused of "chemical aggression," and the General Assembly, after a weak reply by Potemkin, passed a vote of censure.

It was January, 1979, that huge blooms of a previously unknown variety of diatom were reported off the coast of Peru. The blooms were accompanied by a massive die-off of sea life and of the pathetic remainder of the birds which had once feasted on the anchovies of the area. Almost immediately another huge bloom was reported in the Indian ocean, centering around the Seychelles, and then a third in the South Atlantic off the African coast. Both of these were accompanied by spectacular die-offs of marine animals. Even more ominous were growing reports of fish and bird kills at ocean points where there were no spectacular blooms. Biologists were soon able to explain the phenomena: the diatom had evolved an enzyme which broke down Thanodrin; that enzyme also produced a breakdown product which interfered with the transmission of nerve impulses, and was therefore lethal to animals. Unfortunately, the biologists could suggest no way of repressing the poisonous diatom bloom in time. By September, 1979, all important animal life in the sea was extinct. Large areas of coastline had to be evacuated, as windrows of dead fish created a monumental stench.

But stench was the least of man's problems. Japan and China were faced with almost instant starvation from a total loss of the seafood on which they were so dependent. Both blamed Russia for their situation and demanded immediate mass shipments of food. Russia had none to send. On October 13, Chinese armies attacked Russia on a broad front. . . .

A pretty grim scenario. Unfortunately, we're a long way into it already. Everything mentioned as happening before 1970 has actually occurred; much of the rest is based on projections of trends already appearing. Evidence that pesticides' harmful long-term lethal effects on human beings has started to accumulate, and recently Robert Finch, Secretary of the Department of Health, Education and Welfare expressed his extreme apprehension about the pesticide situation. Simultaneously the petrochemical industry continues its unconscionable poison-peddling. For instance, Shell Chemical has been carrying on a high-pressure campaign to sell the insecticide Azodrin to farmers as a killer of cotton pests. They continue their program even though they know that Azodrin is not only ineffective, but often *increases* the pest density. They've covered themselves nicely in an advertisement which states, "Even if an overpowering migration (sic) develops, the flexibility of Azodrin lets you gain control fast. Just increase the dosage according to label recommendations." It's a great game—get people to apply the poison and kill the natural enemies of the pests. Then blame the increased pests on "migration" and sell even more pesticides!

Right now fisheries are being wiped out by over-exploitation, made easy by modern electronic equipment. The companies producing the equipment know this. They even boast in advertising that only their equipment will keep fishermen in business until the final kill. Profits must obviously be maximized in the short run. Indeed, Western society is in the process of completing the rape and murder of the planet for economic gain. And, sadly, most of the rest of the world is eager for the opportunity to emulate our behavior. But the underdeveloped peoples will be denied that opportunity—the days of plunder are drawing inexorably to a close.

Most of the people who are going to die in the greatest cataclysm in the history of man have already been born. More than three and a half billion people already populate our moribund globe, and about half of them are hungry. Some 10 to 20 million will starve to death *this year*. In spite of this, the population of the earth will increase by 70 million souls in 1969. For mankind has artificially lowered the death rate of the human population, while in general birth rates have remained high. With the input side of the population system in high gear and the output side slowed down, our fragile planet has filled with people at an incredible rate. It took several million years for the population to reach a total of two billion people in 1930, while a *second two billion will have been added by 1975!* By that time some experts feel that food shortages will have escalated the present level of world hunger and starvation into famines of unbelievable proportions. Other experts, more optimistic, think the ultimate food-population collision will not occur until the decade of the 1980's. Of course a more massive famine may be avoided if other events cause a prior rise in the human death rate.

Both worldwide plague and thermonuclear war are made more probable as population growth continues. These, along with famine, make up the trio of potential "death rate solutions" to the population problem—solutions in which the birth rate-death rate imbalance is redressed by a rise in the death rate rather than by a lowering of the birth rate. Make no mistake about it, *the imbalance will be redressed.* The shape of the population growth curve is one familiar to the biologist. It is the outbreak part of an outbreak-crash sequence. A population grows rapidly in the presence of abundant resources, finally runs out of food or some other necessity, and crashes to a low level or extinction. Man is not only running out of food, he is also destroying the life support systems of the Spaceship Earth. The situation was recently summarized very succinctly: "It is the top of the ninth inning. Man, always a threat at the plate, has been hitting Nature hard. It is important to remember, however, that NATURE BATS LAST."

Conflicts and Guidelines

Fundamental changes in the way of looking at the environment must occur before the public can develop an eco-conscience. An "attitude toward" the environment is necessary (reading 52), perhaps even an eco-religion. Legislation alone does not change people's minds, though it may provide a necessary impetus (especially if the legislation is enforced). Once an individual is convinced of a need for action and desires to convince others, some guidelines may be helpful (reading 53).

Four Conflicts in Conservation 52

CHARLES A. DAMBACH

Because the conflicts in conservation are many, of varying degrees of complexity and importance, and derive from diverse origins, it is necessary to sort them into some kinds of sets or groups so they can be better examined. There are a variety of ways in which to do this. I suggest dividing them into *four groups*. One concerns conflicts arising out of such cultural sources as historical antecedents, concepts of ownership and rights, religious and philosophical beliefs, the way in which emotions are affected, and the conservation related legends and myths which prevail. There are many examples. Historically, we have always been on the frontier of new lands, of new discoveries, which made available new resources. Even now there is the frontier of outer space. We are thus conditioned to an infinite and expanding resource base.

I. Deep in our religious beliefs is the prevailing concept that man was created to have dominion over the earth, that he can and should master nature. The first view runs counter to the idea of a finite limit to resources; the matter runs counter to the concept of man as a part of nature.

Edward Teller stated this view cogently when he observed: "It is true that conditions are wretched in many countries, but even where life is hard people are objecting not because they look back to a happier past but rather because they demand a better future which they know can be realized. Human fertility is undoubtedly great, but so far human ingenuity has proved greater. I suspect that ultimately the population of the earth will be limited not by any scarcity but rather by our ability to put up with each other."

In a similar vein, Thomas B. Nolan (1958) during a symposium conducted by the Resources for the Future organization said, "I believe that the prospect of impending shortages or unsuitable supplies will continue to inspire research and technical advances that will make it possible to resolve such problems well in advance of the doom we often are prone to foresee. We probably need to fear not the exhaustion of physical resources but the dangers of inadequate or belated utilization of our intellectual resources. . . ." It is beliefs such as these which support confidence in planned obsolescence and the defense of waste which are the antithesis of the advocation of prudent use of resources.

There is the basic and vigorously defended concept that each individual has a right to do what he wishes with resources reduced to possession, for instance, cutting into lumber the great oak that may have been a community landmark for a century or logging the redwoods that may otherwise be enjoyed indirectly by nonowners or vicariously by an apartment dweller thousands of miles away.

Elements of such basic beliefs are evident in many of the conservation controversies which exist. Unfortunately, they are not readily resolvable by adult education. An editor of a large city daily once set me straight on this subject after I had confronted him with what I believed was overwhelming evidence concerning a local conservation controversy. The editor's answer in the press and on the air to that evidence was to quote an old but unfortunately valid cliche that "a man convinced against his will is of the same opinion still." This could be amended to say a man convinced against his basic beliefs is really not convinced at all.

II. Another broad set of conservation conflicts are those based on different economic, social, and other self-interests of individuals and groups. These are more readily identified. Sometimes they are amenable to settlement by bargaining. They also represent, however, some of the more complex and difficult problems to resolve because of the great range of interests involved. Their resolution is often elusive due to inadequate means with which to assess related public values and the lack of mechanisms whereby the interests of indirect users can be properly evaluated. The cross currents of conflicts in this category are often strong if not violent. The conflicts which fit into this category are many, and need no elaboration. Senator Gaylord Nelson stated the situation well in speaking at the annual meeting of the National Wildlife Federation in 1965, when he said, "What we have done in this country is to develop a vast network of special-interests conservation. We have lost our broad vision of the public interests, and we have fallen to quarrelling over little pieces of it."

III. There is another group of conservation conflicts which emanates from a source more difficult to describe. These are conflicts generated by dissidents who exist in virtually every community. Often they are well-meaning individuals and groups. Unfortunately, however, there are many who seek personal recognition through exploiting otherwise readily resolvable conservation conflicts. I can perhaps best illustrate the nature of this source of conflict with a personal experience. I served for 5 years as the administrative head of the Division of Wildlife of the newly organized State of Ohio Department of Natural Resources, in the period 1950 to 1955. During that tour of duty, I arrived at the office one day to find on my desk a stack of petitions sent over from the Governor's office with 3156 signatures. The petitions implored the Governor to direct the chief of the Division of Wildlife to stock nearby thirty-seven hundred acre Buckeye Lake with fish. In 1951 when this episode occurred, the scientists in the Division had records of fish populations for this body of water which indicated that stocking would be superfluous.

It is one thing for an administrator to listen to a confident group of scientists backed by filing cabinets full of data declaring the inadvisability of stocking a body of water and another to convey that message effectively to more than three thousand signers of a petition and a general public inclined to agree with them.

As a scientist trained in the management of wildlife resources, my first inclination was to stand firm on the scientific evidence and deny the petitioners. As an educator, however, it occurred to me that here was an opportunity to demonstrate the wisdom of the scientist and to gain support not only for our position in this matter but to gain respect upon which to base future actions. The decision was to choose the latter course. The method chosen involved a gamble. We proposed to stock the lake if we were unable through demonstration to convince the petitioners and their backers that the lake was adequately stocked. A public demonstration was arranged. For their part, the petitioners invited key political figures, members of their organizations, the press, the radio, and anyone interested to the demonstration. For our part, we agreed to place test nets in the water at points where fishing was reputedly at its worst and lift them publicly for all to see. To assure that the demonstration was conducted in a scientific manner, we used two standard test nets and placed them in the water just 24 hours before the appointed time for them to be lifted and witnessed. Also to assure scientific validity and for other reasons, a rotation of guards was employed for the full 24 hours.

At the appointed time for the demonstration, hundreds of people crowded on the pier to watch the lifting of the nets. Note now the following quote from an editorial which appeared in the *Newark Advocate* (1951), the local daily newspaper, a few days later:

A whispering campaign said there was no fish in Buckeye Lake. That libel has now been erased officially.... A test was made under the most unfavorable conditions near the lake's shore at the park where much boat activity and other conditions prevailed which fish don't like. In one trap 967 were taken. ... In another trap some 400 fish of a similar variety were taken. ... The fish management boys were pleased..... And now the wise boys are changing their tune. Instead of singing a doleful song of no fish, they are asking why the conservation authorities don't seine a third of the fish out of the lake. Their point is Buckeye Lake is overpopulated. As Ralph Edwards would say, 'People are indeed funny.'

Although there is much humor in the incident, one can become easily discouraged from efforts to resolve conflicts by educational methods when agitation, not conservation, is the objective.

But there is a sequel to the story which illustrates that while not many conservation conflicts can be resolved totally through adult education, much can be done to contribute to their resolution. The residents of the State of Ohio, and more recently residents of many other states, now enjoy millions of hours of virtually restriction-free recreational fishing not formerly available. This came about despite many deep-seated beliefs about over-fishing and putting little fish back and protecting fish on their spawning beds. It came about because of repeated demonstrations of this kind and educational programs which afforded interested parties an opportunity to have their questions answered. Confidence in the judgment of scientists was achieved, and a willingness to resolve conflict by experimentation, by trial, and by test was permitted.

There remain, of course, enough unanswered questions that groups still looking for a cause by which to gain recognition have plenty of room in which to operate.

IV. Let me draw your attention now to the fourth category of sources of conservation conflicts: those arising out of ignorance. There are many conservation problems for which we do not have good answers or, at best, but partial answers. Who knows, for example, the necessary physical dimensions of a unit of coastal redwoods essential to their perpetuation as man found them? Who knows with full assurance the specific cause of the degradation of the waters of Lake Erie? Who knows with certainty the cause of the great increase in red wing blackbirds which have become a scourge to crops in the Midwest? Who knows when man will, if he can, discover a substitute for silver which can be used satisfactorily in the photographic process or which will find acceptance as a medium of exchange for goods and services?

There will continue to be controversy over conservation problems which we do not understand. And understanding becomes more difficult as the problems become more complex and as individuals become more specialized. A scientist may be an expert in one resource area but no better informed than the average lay person in others. Under these circumstances, it is easy for an aggressive proponent with little knowledge to win support for a cause out of all proportion to the evidence substantiating it. Paul B. Sears had a favorite way of expressing this situation by noting that some people he knew knew a great deal about things which just aren't so.

53   Guidelines for Action in Saving the Environment

CHARLES H. W. FOSTER

In evaluating the validity of a position or the desirability of a project, the following guidelines might usefully be employed by an organization.

Be prepared. Always have the necessary facts at hand and your homework done prior to facing the issue.

Be right. Nothing is more transparent than the distortion of facts to a predetermined conclusion. Knowing when you are wrong—and being big enough to admit it—will enhance rather than hurt an organization's image.

Be practical. Natural area protectionists are frequently accused of being blue-sky advocates, and many are. Being practical, however, is *not* the same as compromising on principle.

Be wise in time. Knowing when to espouse an issue, or undertake a project, is perhaps the real key to success. A prophet achieves much personal satisfaction but rarely lives long enough to see his cause realized.

From these few remarks you should be able to sense my personal conviction that the natural area movement is important and promising—but one whose essence must be action. This will require close teamwork between governmental and private agencies, and within the private sector itself. In my judgment, private leadership must carry the main burden if the movement is to be ultimately successful.

TAXONOMY OF INTERNATIONAL
ENVIRONMENTAL PROBLEMS AND SOLUTIONS

International Environmental Problems   **54**
A Taxonomy

CLIFFORD S. RUSSELL AND HANS H. LANDSBERG

The last few years have seen an explosion of interest in environmental problems among citizens of the developed countries, both East and West. Most of this interest has focused on domestic situations and on possible changes in domestic policies designed to provide remedies. Increasingly, however, the focus has widened to embrace environmental concerns that transcend national borders. A high point may be reached in June 1972, when the United Nations Conference on the Human Environment will be held in Stockholm. Wide-ranging discussions and the signing of international treaties on specific international environmental issues are on the agenda. Even though it will not be the first conference on these subjects *(1)*, both the auspices of the United Nations and the publicity that it is bound to receive will give it special importance.

The growth of interest and enthusiasm, however, is not matched by accomplishments. That little action has been taken is perhaps easily explained, since sovereign states are involved in these issues, which are old as a class but essentially novel in degree. So far, it has even proved difficult for concerned parties to discuss the problems *(2)*.

A major reason for the lack of communication has been the general failure to look beyond the label, "international environmental problems," to the disparate elements it covers and to limit, in advance, the number of such elements that can be discussed at any one time and in any given group. A second reason may be that environmentalists have sometimes couched their arguments in terms that impugn the morality and intelligence of the parties concerned, thus guaranteeing defensive, hostile reactions *(3)*.

A third reason may be that management of international environmental problems is most often thought of in terms of "police actions" and regulatory authorities rather than as a component of growth and development. It should be realized that this component of growth and development, neglected by the now developed countries (and being paid for dearly by them), can still be built into the development of emerging countries, probably with long-lasting benefits. Finally, political problems, in terms of a lack of new institutions and mechanisms, have played a role. For example, the growing pollution of the Baltic Sea involves eight countries, three of which are in the Soviet orbit, and one of which (East

Germany) has a sufficiently undefined international status to make any international agreement difficult, at best, to achieve *(4)*.

Many environmental problems involve citizens of two or more countries and hence are "international." Confusion and controversy arise easily: an individual or a government is usually concerned with (or even aware of) only one or two specific problems and incorrectly assumes that other individuals or governments are talking about the same problem when they use the same general label. Consider, for example, the prospects for agreement when one group's mind is on the long-term buildup of carbon dioxide in the atmosphere and particulates in the lower stratosphere; another worries over the dangers associated with increasing storage of radioactive wastes; a third focuses on the ecological implications of large-scale hydroelectric developments in the tropics; a fourth is concerned with the effect of domestic air pollution controls on export prices and hence trade patterns; yet another is concerned about a specific regional problem in which one nation's pollution, or attempt at protection against pollution, imposes costs on another nation; and, finally, a group of developing nations views matters through the prism of its overwhelming interest in increasing per capita income.

Some of these situations affect all the world's people, though significant contributors may number only a handful. Others are problems of a particular region and do not concern nations outside that region. To developing nations, all environmental problems may appear to be potential threats to their domestic development. At the least, they seem to be concerns of those nations that have incomes sufficiently high to permit concern with esthetics and that have health standards high enough to permit detection of the effects on morbidity and mortality of concentrations of sulfur dioxide. To lay the basis for more successful discussion, this article suggests a first cut at a taxonomy of international environmental problems and solutions, as well as areas in which further research can contribute to this discussion. We take the point of view of the social scientist, since that view is most likely to speak directly to the concerns of those who must ultimately do the discussing and deciding, but the categories we suggest are based on characteristics of the physical world.

A Taxonomy of Problems

International environmental problems may profitably be divided into two broad categories, depending on the nature and scope of the international linkages involved: physical-linkage effects and social-linkage effects. The first may be divided again into global and regional effects, and the second into pecuniary and nonpecuniary effects.

Global problems are those problems that physically involve all or nearly all nations of the world, either as contributing parties (emitters) or damaged parties (receptors) or both. Some of the most widely discussed environmental issues fall into this category. For example, since World War II, persistent pesticides have been used all over the world in programs to control disease vectors and agricultural pests. The residues directly affect animal life and potentially affect human life, not only in the country in which a specific application is made, but also through the actions of wind, water, and living carriers, even in regions remote from the point of origin. Notice that it is the combination of persistence and mobility that makes the pesticide problem a global one. If any significant user remains outside a control agreement and continues application of pesticides, the impact on everyone may still be felt *(5)*. Even if they were applied by virtually every nation, highly toxic pesticides that were used in small quantities and that broke down quickly to inert residual chemicals might not constitute an international problem. Each nation could manage its own environmental quality problem by enacting its own laws: It would not be dependent for effectiveness on simultaneous action by all other user nations *(6)*.

Two familiar examples of global problems, the balance of carbon dioxide in the atmosphere and the particulate content of the stratosphere, are closely related to man's burning of fossil fuels, and both tend to affect the earth's temperature *(7)*. Here again, the essential elements of the problem are persistence in the atmosphere (for carbon dioxide, the extended time scale of the carbon cycle and its components) and the global span of the physical systems involved. Carbon dioxide is relatively stable, and the molecules are not removed from the atmosphere very rapidly. The very small particulates do not settle out rapidly, but tend to remain in suspension in the stratosphere over long periods. Thus global agreement will eventually be needed to assure a long-term solution. However, since the sources of fossil-fuel emissions are highly concentrated now in the developed countries (North America, Western Europe, the Soviet Union, and Japan), an agreement on limitations among this group would probably result in a solution good for several decades at least *(8)*.

Carbon monoxide and larger particulates are also produced in great quantities in some forms of fossil-fuel combustion and cause specific environmental problems. Carbon monoxide, however, is not stable; it does not survive long in that form in the air and is not a problem at some distance from the source. Similarly, larger particulates tend to settle out relatively quickly after emission. Thus, even though these products of combustion are as ubiquitous as carbon dioxide and the very small particulates, they create almost entirely intranational or local difficulties.

A fourth example of a global environmental problem is the dumping or spillage of oil on the high seas. Here, a look at the registry of the world tanker fleet makes it clear that relatively few nations are emitters. Through its effects on marine life, however, the dumping affects the much larger group of nations that engage in ocean fishing (or that, by a slightly more remote linkage, depend on another nation's catch). Ultimately, it could affect every nation directly: if, for example, the as yet controversial possibility that continued large-scale dumping could affect the photosynthetic activity of the seas and hence could threaten one of our largest sources of oxygen were to be demonstrated; or if changes in the surface reflectivity of the water affected the earth's heat balance. Once again, the global nature of the problem results from the discharge of a persistent residual into a natural system that spreads the effects of the residual over long distances. For example, Thor Heyerdahl sighted numerous, large globs of oil in a recent Atlantic crossing. The list of global environmental problems, which, prior to the nuclear test ban treaty, also included worldwide transport of radionuclides, may become longer as our ability to measure trace elements and track their movements increases and we are alerted to interdependencies as yet unseen. But for the moment, the issues listed appear to constitute the major, truly global phenomena *(9)*.

Regional Problems

Regional problems result from physical, including biological, linkages between two or more nations, with little or no spillover to the world at large because of the particular combinations of relatively low persistency of pollutants and relatively limited scope of the natural systems involved in transporting them. Regional problems often resemble the domestic environmental quality issues now facing most developed nations. That is, because geographic proximity frequently permits identification of "upstream" and "downstream" countries, the *assignment* of costs of control and the benefits from damages avoided presents no difficulty, even if the *estimation* of damages avoided may, in principle, be impossible in many cases. Many of the same analytical techniques developed for dealing with domestic quality issues are directly applicable to regional situations. Examples of such situations are most common in the highly industrialized parts of the world: their natural systems are subject to the most stress, both in quantity and variety of pollution discharges; agriculture tends to be more intensive, with the attendant use of fertilizers and pesticides *(10)*; "conventional" pollutants associated with lack of sanitary facilities (toilets, sewers, waste disposal, and so on) are at a low level, thus giving greater visability to the pollutants associated with high technology (detergents, scrapped automobiles, carbon monoxide, and so on); and incomes are high enough to permit people to concern themselves with damages to esthetic values and recreational opportunities.

There is no lack of examples of regional problems of the upstream-downstream variety. The Rhine serves France and Germany as a sewer, but it serves the Netherlands as a part of its water supply. Acid rainfall over western Sweden and eastern Norway has been attributed by some scientists to sulfur oxide emissions originating in industrial operations in Germany's Ruhr and England's Midlands *(11)*. As a result, trout fishing in southern Norway is threatened, and there is a suspicion that the growth of trees is being slowed down. The Environmental Committee of the Organization for Economic Cooperation and Development has been asked to investigate the problem, and management of the resulting project has been entrusted to Norway. The seaborne flow of pollutants from Italy to France along the Riviera is another instance of the upstream-downstream syndrome *(12)*. The use of Arctic waters by U.S. oil tankers, should this development occur, would be yet another, involving Canada, the United States, and, depending on the implication of ocean currents and the like, possibly other countries.

In other cases, because of the natural system involved, all parties become both emitters and receptors. This is true, for example, of the Baltic Sea and of Lake Erie. Countries around the Baltic are concerned, above all, about oil transportation and mercury pollution from pulp mills. The narrow link with the North Sea makes much of the Baltic practically an inland sea body, and the results of a major oil spill could bring great harm to any or all of the eight countries involved.

Other cases involve despoliation rather than pollution in the conventional sense, but still present the upstream-downstream pattern of damage. Thus, European conservationists are concerned about the effects that the Italian practice of netting will have on migratory bird populations. Large numbers of birds that winter in Africa and summer in the north of Europe are trapped each year as they migrate up the Italian peninsula *(13)*. Finally, there are the major environmental alterations that involve neither pollution nor despoliation. A case in point is the Aswan Dam. By cutting the flow of silt and organic debris in the Nile, it appears to have adversely affected the eastern Mediterranean sardine fishery *(14)* (apart from other consequences that are purely domestic at this time).

Although regional and global problems have many similarities, it is useful to distinguish between them in order to emphasize that not every international environmental problem need—or should—be grist for the mill of the United Nations. It may, in fact, be helpful in seeking a solution to involve only the smallest possible group of nations—generally those directly interested *(15)*. This is not, however, to suggest that the distinction between the two classes will always be clear. Realistically, one must expect that some large-scale regional problems will be most conveniently dealt with as global issues, while the interests of a very few powerful nations may so dominate a global problem that its solution rests, at least initially, entirely with them *(16)*.

Social-Linkage Effect

Social-linkage effect is the term we use to refer to a second class of international environmental problems in which no physical linkages exist but in which, nonetheless, the policies of one national government impinge directly on the well-being of citizens of one or more other nations. This may occur through established economic relationships between nations (that is, trade and investment, including foreign aid), or in a way that is not, in the first instance, pecuniary. We deal with the second class first and call it, for want of a better term, nonpecuniary linkage.

A classic case of nonpecuniary linkage is that of one country's possessing unique natural or historical gifts that citizens of other nations value as part of the human cultural and natural heritage *(17)*. Thus, for example, Uganda's plan to develop a hydroelectric scheme that would involve cutting by 90 percent the flow through Murchison Falls (a very narrow gorge on the Upper White Nile) has aroused considerable ire among conservationists, particularly those in Europe *(18, 19)*. The filling of Lake Nasser, behind the Aswan High Dam, stimulated an international effort to rescue a number of tombs, temples, and statues erected along that stretch of the river by early Egyptian civilizations. Similarly, the Italian government's care of remnants of antiquity has postponed the completion of Rome's subway, but has probably prevented it from becoming an international issue *(20)*.

Many countries, particularly the developing nations, have been criticized for failing to take effective action to protect animal species that are valued by conservationists around the world. Perhaps the most widely known examples are the African cats, especially the leopard, which are endangered by poachers, and the Ceylonese elephant, threatened by the large-scale clearing of forests for agriculture.

These situations are local phenomena, but they become international problems when citizens of other countries protest and attempt to obtain actions that accord with their own values rather than with those of the country concerned. Aroused citizens implicitly or explicitly involve their own governments in their efforts. Thus, the opponents of the Murchison Falls Dam would persuade the British government to renege on its promise of financing the initial construction phase *(21)*. Thus the nonpecuniary interaction can become pecuniary.

It is worth noting that motives are of the highest character in both camps; and, as is always the case when neither side is villainous, the problem appears in its purest and most difficult to solve form.

This is equally true of yet another variety of nonpecuniary interaction—international altruism, in which citizens of one nation endeavor to help citizens of another nation avoid mistakes in dealing with the environment. For example, agricultural experts in the West may be anxious to help African nations avoid exhaustion and erosion of laterite soils. This type of interaction will only lead to problems if the country to be assisted does not agree that the proposal is in its best interests, or if the outside altruists become too insistent or paternalistic.

This situation is apt to arise, above all, in large-scale, agriculture-oriented engineering works. As an example, consider the controversy over the eventual benefits of the Aswan High Dam. Leaving aside the question—often hard to judge—of whether or not some of the effects were or could reasonably have been anticipated, it is useful to distinguish between adverse effects that diminish the chances of success of the primary project objectives, and those that adversely affect some other environmental facet.

In the first instance, decreased soil fertility or increased salinity, for example, if indeed resulting from the changed characteristics of the river, would directly diminish the project's objective—that is, higher agricultural production. Provided there was no dispute on the scientific findings, it would be a straightforward computation to evaluate the size of the loss in dollars and cents. There would be no room for dispute over the consequences. By contrast, the spread of schistosomiasis, while also damaging to the country, could not, in the same sense, be calculated as a direct offset to agricultural production. Outsiders might view it as part of an ecological horror story and consider it a serious offset to the value of the project as a whole, but the national government, given the already very wide diffusion of the disease in rural Egypt, might view it less severely. Indeed, it might even consider that increased output and income might, in the long run, provide a better basis for a successful battle against the disease *anywhere.*

Weighing of environmental effects is, then, unlikely to lead to controversy in the first instance (direct relation to project objective) but apt to do so in the second (adverse side effects related only tenuously, if at all, to project objective).

Divergences of judgment, as described above, sometimes leading to the attempt to impose some kind of sanctions on another country, are not new. Boycotts, embargoes, and other measures have been used in the past to express disapproval of a country's behavior and force it to comply with more acceptable standards. What is new here is the issue that gives rise to such conflict and pressures; and as that issue gains increased status among the aspirations of mankind, the opportunities for intervention, as well as the felt justification, are bound to rise.

Pecuniary Effects

The issue becomes at once more pedestrian and more pointed when we turn to another class of social linkage—namely, the pecuniary effects upon country B of specific environmental policies followed in country A. Here the cases shade into well-known phenomena in foreign trade, even though the impetus lies in a newly prominent field, the environment.

Thus, when the United States adopts strict automobile emission standards, it raises the costs of European and Japanese auto manufacturers who wish to export to this country. Even if the sales price of U.S. automobiles should rise in proportion, foreign manufacturers will need to make special provisions for cars sold in the U.S. market. This fact, together with the likelihood of a proportionately greater financial burden on smaller cars, will directly affect the income of the owners and employees of foreign firms, and will indirectly affect the income of other citizens of those nations. Similarly, limits on the permissible sulfur content of fuels burned in U.S. and European cities imply gains for those nations that own low-sulfur fuel reserves, and lost markets or decreased profits (because of the costs of desulfurization) for others. These examples are only extensions of long-standing regulations in food imports, for example, where tolerances for specific ingredients or impurities, or observation of stated sanitary procedures, are prerequisites for admission to the U.S. market. They bring us squarely up against trade effects as international environmental problems; and for many people trade effects are the most immediate and important of such problems. Thus, it will be valuable to pause and consider how trade effects fit into the taxonomy we are proposing.

There are generally two kinds of trade effects: (i) loss of export markets as a consequence of the increased costs of maintaining high environmental quality in the exporting country, or (ii) the erection of barriers to imports in line with the importing country's policies on environmental quality *(22)*. In the first case, by forcing domestic manufacturers to absorb the costs of disposing of production residuals, environmental quality legislation will tend to diminish the competitiveness of domestic products in the world market. This, in turn, will lead to a decline in domestic income and employment and to losses in the value of invested capital *(23)*. The second effect is exemplified by the standards on auto emissions and sulfur content of fuels. Here the major losses will arise through action in the importer's country, which raises the additional specter of retaliation.

There is no doubt that both situations can create friction between nations and be the subject of negotiation, unilateral action, and so on. Hence, both are international problems. This is obvious with barriers to imports, but the implications of the loss of export markets are no less disconcerting. As put by Germany's Minister of the Interior Genscher *(24)*:

We must ... avoid a situation in which individual countries exclude themselves from making investments for environmental protection, thereby securing competitive advantages for their own economy vis-à-vis those countries who do meet their responsibilities.

What is noteworthy here is the use of the term "responsibility," placing environmental effects in a context beyond voluntary action.

It is important to realize, however, that trade effects are quite different from the direct, physical-linkage effects. The loss of export markets due to action in the exporting country is simply an international facet of the classical adjustment process necessary within an economy when tastes or ground rules shift markedly, causing capital and labor to move out of some industries and into others. Some owners of capital suffer unanticipated losses, and, in the short run, lower incomes and some unemployment will result. But the real cost of producing the same goods (or of obtaining the goods internationally) has increased by what it costs to achieve the higher level of environmental quality. Hence, given government policies designed to maintain aggregate demand, there is no reason that full employment cannot again be obtained *(25)*. In the long run, and in the absence of similar environmental policies by other governments, the nation will tend to import those goods that involve the greatest environmental costs and to export those involving the least. It will, in effect, be exporting pollution *(26)*.

The emergence of so-called "pollution havens" is not a theoretical consideration. For example, air pollution standards have led to reductions in copper smelting operations in Arizona, Texas, Montana, and Washington, and to an increase in shipments of ore to smelters in West Germany, Canada, and Japan. Japan is reported to be shipping ore to Indonesia for smelting, though on a very small scale. A movement in the opposite direction is our export of coal and lumber to Japan. To the extent that those exports are stimulated by lower prices, made possible by a lack of strip-mining regulation and of control of timber overcutting, the United States is functioning as a pollution haven, suffering land erosion, acid mine drainage, reduction of wildlife stocks, and disruption of natural vistas in order to support domestic employment in export industries.

Environmental policies that act as direct obstacles to trade affect the outside world as do other nontariff barriers such as product quotas or import prohibitions. For the domestic economy of the importing countries, the higher real cost of imports is, again, the one facet of the overall cost of reaching the desired level of environmental quality.

Because international trade problems have been dealt with extensively elsewhere, little need be said about them here, even though they arise in a novel context. However, the novelty must be qualified. Nontariff barriers that confer large gains on specific industries are frequently justified in terms of noble objectives—to further health or some other aspect of the well-being of some or all citizens. When environmental objectives act as trade barriers, it is not, therefore, surprising that the motives of those who are responsible for them will be suspected.

It is difficult to predict the effects on international trade of domestic environmental quality policies that are imposed unilaterally. The one attempt with which we are familiar is limited to five major developed countries (France, Japan, West Germany, the United States, and the United Kingdom). The reported results must be interpreted with caution because of the rather strict assumptions and limited data on which they are based *(27)*. Nevertheless, this study does indicate the order of magnitude of the short-term impact on national income and the balance of payments of domestic environmental control policies, if it is assumed that each nation, in turn, acts alone while others continue present policies and that the government of the nation imposing the controls does not pursue policies designed to reduce the resulting economic dislocations. In this situation, the predicted effect on the balance of payments and national income of the United States is quite small; on those of West Germany, moderate; and on those of the other three nations, substantial. These results suggest that U.S. environmental policy need not be constrained by fears of serious national income and balance of payments implications, but that other major developed nations will probably be extremely cautious about acting, except in concert with their major trading partners, in such a way as to force domestic industry to take account of environmental damages. There is the additional complication that the degree to which adjustments are borne by society as a whole (for example, through subsidies paid out of general revenue), as against being reflected in the price of the affected commodity, will impinge upon relative prices and thus competitiveness in international markets.

Environmental considerations are equally likely to affect the allied field of investment. We have pointed out the tendency to import, rather than produce at home, goods that have a highly adverse effect on the environment. In addition, some countries do not impose strict regulations, either because conditions (whether natural or otherwise) do not yet require them, or because they wish to attract capital. As a result of these two factors, investments may be shifted to those countries. It is easy to see how such moves can lead to international friction.

These investment effects also appear in the field of foreign aid, whether bilateral or multilateral, except that here the reverse situation obtains. By U.S. law, development projects financed by the U.S. government must now be evaluated for their impact on the environment. In a parallel development, the World Bank has recently established a program designed to look into adverse effects of foreign aid on the environment. From such evaluations are likely to come actions to prevent or remedy adverse environmental consequences. Hence, the cost of a given project is likely to be higher than it would otherwise have been, and the host country will be concerned over the competitive status of the goods and services that will result from the investment. Recipients of aid do not look kindly on the need for additional foreign exchange, perhaps foreign technicians, and further delay in achieving economic independence—all for benefits often little understood or valued.

Shared Experiences

Before abandoning the taxonomy of problems and proceeding to that of solutions, a comment is needed on a range of matters that are not in any real sense international environmental problems but that do relate to them. These are the domestic environmental experiences common to most countries at specific stages in their growth.

Problems of human settlement, especially those of large urban areas, come to mind at once. These are not new problems. Most of them have merely been given a new label. Thus Calcutta, Rio de Janeiro, Lima, Tokyo, and New York all suffer from problems related to large concentrations of population. Similar problems were noted in London 150 years ago. The international aspect lies in the commonality of such problems, not in any interaction. And so it is with matters like soil erosion, poor drainage and resulting salinity (encountered many thousands of years ago in the plains of the Tigris and Euphrates), deforestation to meet the needs of shipbuilders (Rome), or settlers (United States), and a host of other environmental problems. Here the opportunities for international cooperation are greatest: in the exchange of information, technology, and so forth. In short, here is the possibility of progress without conflict. But, by the same token, it is not here that truly perplexing international issues are found.

A final comment is in order on the above taxonomy. A problem in any of the three categories may be—and usually is—complicated by considerations of the income distribution among the nations (and their citizens) involved. These will be particularly obvious and important when one or more of the interested parties are developing nations, but they will also be present when only developed nations are concerned. Any particular solution to an international environmental problem will involve transfers of real income from nation to nation. These can generally be identified and at least partially quantified at a technical level. But the desirable direction and size of such income transfers become two variables for consideration in the political process of choosing between alternative outcomes.

A Taxonomy of Solutions

Solutions to international environmental problems may be either negotiated or imposed. If negotiated, the appropriate group of interested parties will, as we have suggested, be defined by the scale of the natural system involved, although considerable improvement may be obtained over a fairly long period through agreements among the smaller group of nations responsible for most of the problem.

Solutions may be imposed by a single nation or by a group of nations that has the required economic—or, in extreme cases, military—power. The imposition may be directly by force; for example, if one nation invades another to destroy a dam that has changed the flow of a river (27). More likely are impositions based on the terms of foreign aid (as in the Murchison Falls example mentioned above), trade restrictions (as in auto emission standards for imported vehicles and the prohibition against importing certain furs), or by internal law operating as a trade restriction (restrictions on the sulfur content of fuels or prohibitions against the landing of SST's at domestic airports).

An imposed solution generally implies that the costs and benefits have been assessed by the imposing nation from its own point of view. But if negotiation is to be attempted, the problem of evaluating alternative solutions becomes extremely difficult. There are the usual problems of making cost comparisons among nations with different internal factor-cost structures and correcting the nominal rate of exchange to reflect at least the most serious distortions. In addition, the task of getting any real notion of the benefits will be all but impossible. Nations' preferences for the changes in environmental quality being sought will vary in accordance with their stage of economic development, cultural matrix, political structure, and so on. Moreover, these changes are associated not with private goods, where the market provides a test of preferences, but with public goods, which are consumed willy-nilly in equal amounts by all. Therefore, there exists an opportunity, if not an incentive, to conceal true preferences (for a nation as much as for an individual) and report falsely on the evaluation of benefits (28). Solutions may be implemented through the setting of standards or through levying charges on contributing nations, although there are tremendous difficulties in achieving either on an international scale.

Standards, in turn, may be "ambient" (that is, applying to the quality of the environment of the receptor nations) or "discharge" (applying only to the contributing nations) (29). If the mechanisms of the natural world are sufficiently understood, a set of ambient standards, if attainable at all, can be translated into a set of discharge standards *(30)*.

Because demands for "minimum standards" crop up so frequently in proposals for safeguarding the environment, it is well to stress that such minimums are unlikely to be either unambiguously defined or easily agreed upon. For example, is the minimum standard for oil tanker design simply to require hull thickness and tank sizes such that at least tankers won't break up in storms for their first 10 years? Or is it to require some minimum of oil spillage resulting from a design collision or grounding incident? Who chooses the design incident and the minimum acceptable spillage? Or, consider minimum standards for mercury contamination of foods. For any particular food, the level of contamination that a nation will be willing to tolerate will vary with the importance of that food in the diet of its citizens, *and* with the incidence of poisoning it finds acceptable. Since individual susceptibility to mercury undoubtedly varies, any given minimum standard is likely to result in some (albeit very few) cases of poisoning. The only minimum standard that can, with certainty, prevent poisoning is a zero level. Any nonzero level implies choices of probabilities of incidence; and any level high enough to be a minimum (in the sense that no nation would insist that a higher tolerance be agreed on) would undoubtedly lead to significant incidence in one or more nations.

Notice also that *any* standard which changes the status quo will create costs for some nations and benefits for others. Thus, in the tanker example, nations whose citizens own tanker fleets or ship oil will absorb costs if tankers are made more expensive. Nations with coastlines near busy international shipping lanes will reap obvious benefits from stronger construction, smaller tank size, and soon. Similarly for the mercury example, nations producing and consuming a particular food are likely to differ on the desirability of any standard, even a very low one.

The point is that minimum standards are no more objectively determined than would be optimum standards, and attempting to find and agree on a set of global minimum standards will not make the negotiating problems appreciably easier. Any standard that finds immediate and nearly unanimous international support is likely to be quite meaningless.

The term "monitoring" also tends to give rise to much confusion, even though it is a prominent activity apt to draw nations together rather than push them apart. One kind of monitoring is directed toward exploring basic processes and flows in natural systems, setting baselines, discovering what needs to be measured, and assuring comparability of measurements carried on by different nations. Some of this activity is underway. A second sense of the term refers to compliance with set standards and is used in the context of regulation. In terms of sequence, the second sense follows the first. A clear distinction between the two meanings is helpful for avoiding unnecessary conflict and suspicion.

Other Dimensions of Variation

International environmental problems differ in a number of dimensions other than the one we have chosen for our basic taxonomy. Thus, problems may involve different time scales between cause and effect and, hence, a different level of immediacy for the present population of the world. For example, the buildup of carbon dioxide is a long-term problem, with the possibility of any detrimental global effects many decades in the future, if they occur at all. This is apart from the fact that the environmental effects of fuel combustion and energy conversion and use generally are as yet poorly understood. Thus, any attempts at timing are highly speculative.

The persistent pesticide problem, on the other hand, is much more immediate, with consequences of past applications observable today and with every indication that the situation will worsen unless action is taken now. Related to this dimension of timing is the degree of certainty with which an event will or will not occur. Generally, the further in advance effects are predicted, the more uncertain the outcome; on the other hand, the continuation of presently observable effects is far more certain.

Two other important dimensions of environmental problems are magnitude and degree of irreversibility of effects. Because the effects will be of different types, occur in different places, and affect different facets of human life, the relative magnitude of particular problems is not easily determined, except in the infrequent cases where some estimates of monetary damages can be obtained.

The scope of effects, however, can roughly be compared: For example, a global warming trend is a "greater" effect than is the extinction of a species. However, this approach is too intuitive, and it becomes progressively less useful as one moves away from extremes.

Reversibility refers to the possibility of returning the world, or one of its subsystems, to the state it was in before some effect occurred. Thus, sulfur dioxide pollution in the atmosphere, because of the speed with which it is scrubbed out, is highly reversible. The construction of a dam, on the other hand, is generally considered to be irreversible. As a matter of fact, many effects are reversible *at some cost;* irreversibility, in everyday parlance, generally means that the cost of returning to an earlier state is very high. True irreversibility can be seen in species extinction, destruction of scenic areas, and changes in global climate and weather (except sub specie aeternitatis).

The dimensions of timing, certainty, magnitude, and reversibility of effects all contribute to the broader dimension of urgency. A situation that produces immediate (thus certain), serious, and irreversible effects is perceived as more urgent than a situation that produces long-deferred (hence uncertain), minor, or reversible effects. There is, of course, no one scale on which all environmental problems may be ranked according to urgency, but individuals and governments make subjective evaluations of this sort all the time, and these evaluations help to determine willingness to negotiate solutions.

The ability to proceed from some mutual willingness to negotiate to an acceptable settlement will depend, in general, on the number of interested parties, the degree of diversity in their development and needs, and the nature of the issues involved. For example, if "national pride" somehow becomes an issue in its own right, negotiation will be far more difficult than if only economic or esthetic questions were involved (though in practice it will be hard to make distinctions). More important, objectives differ. Thus, developing countries will generally desire to exploit their natural resources more rapidly and process more of them at home, in order to earn foreign exchange and raise per capita income. "Some of us would rather see smoke coming out of a factory and men employed than no factory at all. It is, after all, a matter of priority," commented the president of the Consumer

Association of Malaysia at the recent meeting of the International Organization of Consumers Unions *(31)*. At the same conference, the director of the Consumer Council of India is quoted with this remark: "The wealthy countries worry about car fumes. We worry about starvation." *(31)*. Presence or creation of appropriate institutions will also make a difference. The pooling of the Scandinavian countries' research efforts in "Nordforsk" is likely to promote internationally advantageous action, just as failure to do so in the context of the Baltic will retard action. Thus, building institutions is an important element of progress in negotiated settlements.

Some Research Needs

We have attempted simply to outline and categorize the range of issues subsumed in the broad heading "international environmental problems." Solutions to these problems must rest on difficult international negotiations, but social scientists can play a useful role in setting the stage for such negotiations by undertaking research to answer questions that are currently being answered, without sound data or analysis, by advocates of one or another solution. The following are examples of such questions:

(1) What are the pitfalls of various types of international agreements as revealed by previous experience, for example, in the field of marine fisheries or international communications via the radio spectrum? What forms and safeguards have proven to be successful in, for instance, international control of uses of nuclear energy? in control of the movement of toxic materials, such as drugs?

(2) What are the costs of altering the behavior currently giving rise to the problems? For example, what would be the costs (economic, political, and in terms of additional radiation hazard) of the widespread substitution of atomic energy for fossil fuel in generating electricity, in order to cut down on global emissions of carbon dioxide and particulates *(8)*? What would be the cost of abandoning the use of DDT in specified areas and for specified purposes, and of replacing it with a range of alternatives? What would be the costs of undertaking alternatives to the schemes giving rise to the direct nonpecuniary interactions defined above? As a specific example, what would be the additional costs to Uganda of obtaining the generating capacity of the Murchison Falls project by some other method? Or how valuable is the generating capacity that would be lost in some compromise scheme to preserve a flow through Murchison Falls?

(3) What policies could be devised to assure that the cost differences calculated above could be made up by nations voicing concern? As a subproblem, how could one effectively assure the country making the substitution—as one would have to—that the cost difference would not come out of development funds that had already been committed? And how would it be possible to erect safeguards against "ecological blackmail" (that is, the threat of an adverse undertaking as a means of securing financial indemnity for acceptable modifications, or abstention from action)?

(4) What are the costs of meeting various objective sets of ambient environmental quality standards in such classic cases as the Rhine and the Baltic? Who would bear these costs in the first instance? And what mechanism could encourage payments from nations deriving benefits to those bearing costs?

This list is not meant to be comprehensive, but to outline a set of specific problems that can be tackled by social scientists with, for the most part, techniques that have already been developed in the context of domestic problems. It is purposely confined to the cost side of the problems and is designed to modify arguments about these problems, at least to the extent that proponents of change know what costs they are imposing on other nations. The task of quantifying benefits is probably beyond the competence of any scientist and must remain a matter for political judgment as exercised in the process of negotiation.

REFERENCES AND NOTES

1. Notable examples are the Study on Critical Environmental Problems held at Williams College during 1970, the results of which have quickly become available in an initial report [*Man's Impact on the Global Environment: Assessments and Recommendations for Action* (M.I.T. Press, Cambridge, Mass., 1970], and the Prague Conference this spring, sponsored by the United Nation's Economic Commission for Europe.
2. The exception has been the increasing activity by international scholarly bodies. For example, the Scientific Committee on Problems of the Environment was formally established late in 1970 by the International Council of Scientific Unions and so far has set up at least three study groups. These have begun to conduct research on matters ranging from the effect of chlorinated aromatic compounds on human tissue to the scope and methods of worldwide environmental monitoring systems and the structure and functioning of ecosystems as influenced by man. Specialized agencies like the World Meteorological Organization (with its World Weather Watch) or the planned Global Atmospheric Research Program (to be undertaken as part of the World Weather Program) are similar ambitious programs. The International Biological Programme has been functioning for some years now. Others, such as UNESCO's Man and Biosphere, have barely begun to function. Below the global level, study programs are under way in the Organization for Economic Cooperation and Development, at NATO, at the Council of Europe, and others, but none of these are at this time action-oriented.
3. Thus, some scientists appear to feel that the setting of environmental standards is a "scientific" question, like that of understanding environmental mechanisms. One set of standards is then "correct"; others are "wrong." In fact, however, scientific inquiry only furnishes society with the understanding and the data on which to base decisions. Given identical facts, the differing tastes, preferences, and prejudices of different members of society will lead them to advocate different standards. Because of the impossibility of trading the results of environmental standards in a private market, the problem of combining individual preferences to arrive at a social decision becomes a political problem. Politicians make these decisions not by default, but because such decisions are the very substance of democratic government.
4. *New York Times,* 4 October 1970, p. 15.
5. Persistence alone is not sufficient to cause a global problem. A discarded tire is extremely persistent and creates a visual blight that is surely an environmental quality problem. But the tire is not subject to global transportation by the natural system into which it is discharged. Similarly, mobility without persistence would not create the problem discussed.
6. How subtle are the distinctions involved is evidenced by the possibility that even nonmobile, nonpersistent pesticides could have affects beyond national borders if (i) they affected migratory birds, for example, and thus broke the food chain, or (ii) they were used near international boundaries. But control of these cases would require agreement among a much smaller set of nations.
7. For a recent comprehensive survey of the subject, see H. E. Landsberg [*Science* 170, 1265 (1970)].
8. See W. O. Spofford, "Decision-making under uncertainty: The case of carbon dioxide build-up in the atmosphere," paper prepared for the Study of Critical Environmental Problems, Williams College, July 1970.
9. Dealing with global issues is, in one sense, not a totally new experience. Control of infectious diseases affecting human, animal, and plant life has long been practiced on a worldwide basis with considerable success, since in many instances carriers could be identified and thus isolated. Note also that global "concern," of course, extends far beyond this list, to include population growth, the nuclear threat, and so on.
10. Even this situation is not without its fuzzy edges. Agriculture in the developed countries is conducted with more care for soil erosion: thus, dispersion of nutrients into the environment is lessened. On the other hand, poor farming practices in the less developed countries may be the cause of the major portion of particulates in the atmosphere, according to the Williams College report *(1)*. If so, poor agricultural practices would have to be considered a true global environmental issue.

11. *New York Times,* 27 November 1970, p. 64.
12. J. Cornwell, *New York Times Magazine* 21 February 1971, p. 24.
13. *New York Times,* 19 April 1970, p. 17; *ibid.,* 27 December 1970, p. 16. This is not a new phenomenon, but a new attitude, arising in the context of general concern for the environment.
14. C. J. George, "The role of the Sadd El Aali [Aswan High Dam] in the fisheries of the southeastern Mediterranean," paper presented at the conference on Ecological Aspects of International Development, Airlie House, Warrenton, Virginia, 9–11 December 1968. See also C. Sterling, Washington *Post,* 15, 17, 20, and 24 February 1971; *Life,* 12 February 1971, p. 46.
15. Recent work in political theory on legislatures, individual preferences, and social decisions suggests that it is preferable not to have a decision made on an issue by a legislature in which few individual legislators have a direct interest in that issue [see E. Haefele, *Amer. Econ. Rev.* 61, 217 (1971)]. An analogy between legislators and national government representatives in international organizations does not seem far-fetched.
16. This is true of nuclear disarmament, the extreme case of a threat to life on earth. On a less extreme level, G. F. Kennan has suggested that global problems are best handled by the developed nations in any event—not only because they are the principal polluters but because it will be too much to expect the rest of the world to take an interest in a problem that does not loom large at that stage of economic development [*Foreign Aff.* 48, 401 (April 1970)].
17. J. V. Krutilla, C. J. Cicchetti, A. M. Freeman, C. S. Russell, in *Environmental Quality Analysis; Theory and Method in the Social Sciences,* V. Kneese and B. T. Bower, Eds. (Johns Hopkins Press, Baltimore, in press).
18. P. Géroudet, *Biol. Conserv.* 2, 309 (1970).
19. C. S. Russell, *ibid.,* in press. '
20. *New York Times,* 23 January 1971, p. 2. The economics of the preservation of unique historical and geological sites is discussed in *(17).*
21. A translation of a public letter from three prominent British scientist-naturalists (F. Darling, J. S. Huxley, and P. Scott) calling for this action is in *(18).*
22. Both manifestations are mentioned in *Bus. Week,* 23 January 1971, p. 72.
23. We emphasize that income, as measured by such market-based indices as gross national product, will decline relative to what it would have been in the absence of the domestic policies. The fact that the policies were adopted, however, shows that the society judged it would be better off with them than without them. Nonmarket income has increased enough to offset the decline in market income.
24. *J. Commer.,* 15 January 1971.
25. Even in the short run, wise government policies may ᴄase the transition considerably. For example, worker retraining allowances and expanded unemployment coverage, as well as subsidized loans for machinery conversions, can cut the frictional costs of the required employment shifts. Such policies to offset trade effects are possible under the current tariff law but have almost never been used. There are signs that this situation is changing. For a discussion of assistance being given the Massachusetts shoe industry, see *New York Times,* 21 February 1971, section F, p. 2.
26. R. C. d'Arge, Appendix F, in A. V. Kneese. "The economics of environmental pollution in the United States," paper prepared for a meeting of the Atlantic Council, Washington, D.C., 1970.
27. It is hard to visualize anything less drastic, such as water pollution, as a cause belli, even though the consequences in the long run may be just as damaging. But, of course, the invocation of an environmental insult may merely mask a more traditional objective of foreign policy, economic or otherwise.
28. P. Bohm, *Swed. J. Econ.,* in press. The fundamental papers in the theory of public goods are P. A. Samuelson, *Rev. Econ. Stat.* 36, 387 (1954); *ibid.,* 37, 350 (1955); *ibid.,* 40, 332 (1958).
29. We place the words "ambient" and "discharge" in quotes to indicate that the same notions may be used more broadly. Thus, for example, in the trapping of migrating birds, a discharge standard would require that the trapping nation allow some number or percentage of the flock to escape. An "ambient" standard would require the maintenance of some population in each of the host countries.
30. In addition, of course, the ground rules chosen in translating "ambient" to "discharge" standards will make a difference to economic efficiency. If all individual dischargers may be subject to different discharge constraints, an ambient standard may be attained most efficiently. On the other hand, if notions of "equity" seem to require a uniform standard, then some dischargers will be cutting back too far when the ambient standard is just attained. In any event, however, we are a long way from approaching such sophistication in domestic affairs, let alone international conduct.
31. *New York Times,* 3 July 1970, p. 4.
32. We wish to express our appreciation to L. Carter, M. Clawson, J. L. Fisher, A. V. Kneese, and W. O. Spofford, all of Resources for the Future, for useful criticism and comments on early drafts.

POPULATION and FOOD

The growth curve so familiar to the biologist describes the pattern of development of living units from the relatively simple cellular level of organization on through the complexly structured individuals, populations, and the ecosystem. Growth experiences a series of stages. At the population level, the initial stage is characterized by both a high birth and a high death rate. Growth progresses slowly. The next stage finds the death rate falling with the birth rate remaining high. Now the mass of individuals expands explosively. As the food energy supply becomes more difficult for the population to obtain, the third stage is ushered in. This final stage witnesses an acceleration in the death rate, a decrease in the birth rate, or both. At any rate, the growth rate will eventually become stable unless an energy input in the form of food occurs.

THE POPULATION CRISIS

Unless we solve the population problem, we solve no other.

Ashley Montagu

The current world-wide population of 3.8 billion will swell to 5.03 billion in 1985 if present population increase trends continue. Even with effective family planning, the earth will know 4.65 billion that year. The difference between effective planning and no planning, then, is a mere 385 million.

In the year 2000, effective family planning may allow us to hold the population down to 6 billion; but if current trends persist, the population will nearly double and stand at 7.25 billion.

Clearly, "too many people" is the most crucial problem facing us during the remaining three decades of this century. This somber prospect demands a fundamental—not trifling—modification of our child-bearing attitudes and behavior. Yet, as Henry David Thoreau said, "There are a thousand hacking at the branches of evil to one who is striking at the root."

55   The Population Crisis Is Here Now

WALTER E. HOWARD

Preface

At the present world rate of population growth of 2% per year, a mere dozen people a thousand years ago could have produced the present world population, and in another thousand years each one of us could have 300 million living descendants. Obviously, that cannot be—something must be done. Either the birth rate must be significantly curtailed or the death rate drastically increased.

The world's overpopulation crisis is of a magnitude beyond human comprehension, yet the government and the public remain seemingly indifferent. Better awareness and a more forthright leadership are obviously needed, from biologists and politicians alike. Will you help? A vastly increased rate of involuntary premature deaths can be prevented only by an informed public, here and abroad, following dynamic leadership. No population can continue to increase indefinitely, no matter how much food there is. If civilization is to be viable, we must end the arrogant assumption that there are unlimited resources and infinite air and water. People must develop much greater voluntary restraint in reproduction —or conception itself will have to come under government control.

This earth does not have the resources necessary to provide even the present world population with the degree of affluence that the middle-class citizen enjoys. Even though the average birth rate in the United States has declined during the past decade from about seven children per family to fewer than three, the population density has been growing much more rapidly than before. The reason is the high population base level; there are now so many more women that their "small" families add a greater number of new people to the population each year than did their grandmothers, even with much larger families.

No population can continue to grow beyond certain limits; eventually, involuntary self-limitation—in the form of premature deaths from starvation, pestilence, and wars—will prevent any further increase in density. Since all finite space is limited, it is an indisputable fact that birth rates and death rates must someday be balanced. Already the rich are devouring the poor—the survival of the fittest.

Introduction

The intent of this article is not to alarm the reader unnecessarily. But how is that possible? Alarm is called for; man should be alarmed. Man must be aware of his dilemma, for if he attempts to feed the world without effective control of the birth rate, he actually is only deferring the starvation of an even greater number of people to a later date.

The world is facing this acute overpopulation situation specifically because of advances in agriculture and health, through science and technology, and a lack of similar progress in the field of sensible birth control. Families are not having more babies, it is just that more now survive.

Passion between the sexes must, of course, remain a basic human right, but it cannot include the having of children at will. While intercourse remains an individual and private matter, procreation must become of public concern. Conception should not be a euphemism for sexual relations. The obvious goal for all societies wishing an abundant life and freedom from want should be a low-birth-rate, low-death-rate culture. Man's responsibility to the next generation includes a primary duty of limiting the size of that generation.

Our problem is uncontrolled human fertility—not underproduction and maldistribution—and corrective action is being dangerously delayed by wishful thinking that some miracle will solve the problem. There is a prodigious need for immediate public awareness of the current critical situation, since overpopulation is intimately involved with political, economic, and sociological problems—in fact, with everyone's peace, security, and general well-being. All of the world's desperate needs—ample food, permanent peace, good health, and high-quality living—are unattainable for all human beings both now and in the foreseeable future for one obvious reason: there are too many people. A soaring population means a shrinking of man's space on this earth.

Not only is population growth the most basic conservation problem of today, but its dominating influence will affect the ultimate survival of mankind. Man can no longer be indifferent to this basic population problem. Its severity behooves all to act now. Hunger and overpopulation will not go away if we do not discuss them, and the bringing of too many babies into this world is not just someone else's problem; it is everyone's concern. The destiny of overpopulation is erosion of civilized life.

The World's Population

To appreciate the recent rapidity with which the world's population has grown—it took from the beginning of man until 1850 to reach a population of one billion people, only 80 years more (1930) to reach two billion, then only 30 years (1960) to reach the three billion mark, and in less than 15 years after 1960 we expect four billion. In the next 25 years after that, the population is expected to increase by another three and one-half billion people. If there have been about 77 billion births since the Stone Age, then about 1 out of every 22 persons born since then is alive today. But in only 30 or 40 years from now, if current rates of increase continue, 1 out of every 10 people ever born will be living at that time. The youth of today might see the United States with a population equal to what India has now.

Only a small proportion of the world's population has made the demographic transition of attaining both a lower fertility and a lower mortality; most have decreased only the premature death rate. The population has continued to increase rapidly because reductions in fertility have not been sufficient to offset the effects of current reductions in mortality produced by technological sanitation, disease control, and pesticide use.

The reproductive potential of the world is grim, for 40 to 45% of the people alive today are under 15 years old. How can this tremendous number of babies soon be fed solid foods? And look how soon those who survive will be breeding.

Even though technology exists that could manufacture enough intrauterine devices for every woman, the problems of distribution and the shortage of doctors make it impossible for the devices to be inserted fast enough to control the world's population growth. Within a few years the number of people dying each year from causes related to poor nutrition will equal what is now the entire population of the United States.

In the United States if the fertility and mortality trends of 1950-60 should be reestablished, replacing the 1968 low birth rate, in only 150 years our country alone could exceed the current world population of over 3.3 billion, and in 650 years there would be about one person per square foot. This will not happen, of course, because either the birth rate will decline, or more likely, the death rate will increase.

Rate of Population Increase

The basic factor is the difference between birth and death rates, not what the levels of births and deaths happen to be. Continued doubling of a population soon leads to astronomical numbers. If the world population increase continued at the low rate of only 2%, the weight of human bodies would equal the weight of the earth in about 1500 years.

The world population is reported to be currently growing by 180,000 a day, more than a million a week, or about 65 million a year, and each year it increases in greater amounts. If current trends continue, the population will reach about 25 billion in only 100 years.

Prior to Christ, it took about 40,000 years to double the population, but the current growth rate of about 2% would require only 35 years to double the present population. Populations that grow by 3% per year double within a generation and increase eighteen-fold in 100 years.

Population Dynamics

If 90% of a population survives long enough to reproduce, an average of 2.3 children per family will keep the population stable. Only a very slight increase to 2.5 children would produce an increase of 10% per generation, and 3.0 children per family would cause an increase of 31% per generation. If child-bearing families averaged 3.0 children, about one woman in four would need to be childless for the population to remain stable.

A sustained geometric increase in human beings is, of course, impossible; once the population's base level of density is high, as it now is, birth rates cannot continue much above the death rates for long without a truly impossible density being produced. As the base population density rises, even a lower birth rate can still mean that there will be a greater absolute increase in total numbers than was occurring before, when population was less and birth rates were higher.

Obviously, if input (natality) continues to exceed outgo (mortality), any finite space must eventually fill up and overflow. Populations increase geometrically, whereas food and subsistence increase arithmetically. The geometric ratio of population growth is also known as the ever-accelerating growth rate, the logistic curve, the well-known S-shaped or sigmoid growth curve, and compound interest.

When populations of people are exposed to stressing pressures, including those due to overpopulation, they may respond in a strange way of breeding earlier and more prolifically, further aggravating the situation. The principal way in which man differs from other animals is in his intellect, his ability to read and communicate, to learn, to use tools, and his society; and he also differs from other species in that he attempts to protect the unfit and all "surplus" births.

Predisposition to Overpopulate

Nature has seen to it that all organisms are obsessed with a breeding urge and provided with the biological capacity to overproduce, thereby ensuring survival of the species. Since man now exercises considerable control over so many of the natural factors which once controlled his population, he must also learn to control his innate trait to reproduce excessively.

It is not a question of whether this earth has the resources for feeding a much greater population than is now present—of course, it has. The point is that the human population is now growing too fast for food production ever to catch up without stringent birth control.

Carrying Capacity and Self-Limitation

No matter how far science and technology raise the carrying capacity of the earth for people, involuntary self-limiting forces will continue to determine man's upper population density. Surplus populations do not just quietly fade away—quite the contrary. Before surplus individuals die, they consume resources and contribute in general to other population stresses, all of which make the environment less suitable, thus lowering its carrying capacity. Man needs space to live as much as do plants and animals.

The balance of nature is governed primarily by the suitability of the habitat and species-specific self-limitation, where members of each species involuntarily prevent any further increase in their kind. This self-limitation consists of undesirable stresses which cause individual births in a family to be unwanted or cause a compensating increase in death rates. Members of the population become their own worst enemy in the sense that they are responsible for the increased rates of mortality and, perhaps, also some reduction in natality.

Nearly all organisms that are well-adapted to their environment have built-in mechanisms for checking population growth before the necessary food and cover are permanently destroyed. But nature's population control processes are unemotional, impartial, and truly ruthless, a set of conditions that educated men will surely wish to avoid.

Instead of man learning how to conquer nature, he may annihilate it, destroying himself in the process. In current times at least, there is no hope that man as a species will voluntarily limit his birth rate to the low level (zero or even minus replacement) that the overall population must have. Also, unfortunately, when a population level is below carrying capacity the innate desire to have larger families then becomes very strong, making human husbandry difficult to practice.

Nature does not practice good husbandry—all its components are predisposed to overpopulate and, in fact, attempt to do so, thus causing a high rate of premature deaths. If food supply alone were the principal factor limiting the number of people, man would long ago have increased to a density where all of the food would have been consumed and he would have become an extinct species.

When other organisms follow a population growth curve similar to what man is currently experiencing—and they do this only in disturbed (usually man-modified) environments—they can then become so destructive to their habitat that the subsequent carrying capacity may be dramatically reduced if not completely destroyed, thus causing not only mass individual suffering and a high rate of premature deaths but also a permanent destruction of the ecosystem.

Whenever man's population density has been markedly reduced through some catastrophe, or his technology has appreciably increased the carrying capacity of his habitat (environment), the growth rate of his population increases. The population then tends to overcompensate, temporarily growing beyond the upper limits of the carrying capacity of the environment. The excess growth is eventually checked, however, by the interaction of a number of different kinds of self-limiting population stress factors. These include such forces as inadequate food and shelter, social stress factors, competition for space, wars, an increase in pestilence, or any of many other subtle vicissitudes of life that either increase the death rate, reduce successful births, or cause individuals to move elsewhere. Unfortunately, in the developed countries, science and technology are developing at an exponential rate, so the population growth may not again be sufficiently halted by self-limitation until the earth's resources are largely exploited or a world famine or other drastic mortality factor appears.

Although nature practices survival of the fittest, man believes that all who are born should be given every opportunity to live to an old age. If this is to be our objective, and I am sure it will, then we have only one other alternative, i.e., to restrict the number of births. And to accomplish this, it seems better to reduce conception rather than to rely on abortions. Abortions are a solution, however, when other means of preventing conceptions have broken down. Surprising to most people, abortions induced by a doctor are safer than childbearing.

There is a need too for man to establish a stable relationship with the environment. Man must recognize that he also responds to many, in fact, most of the laws of nature. And his population checks are largely famine, pestilence, and war. Man has transferred himself from being just a member of the ecosystem to a dominant position, where he now mistakenly assumes that the ecosystem is his to control at will. He forgets that he is part of nature. To see his true place in the world he must not attempt to transcend too much over nature, but to discover and assimilate all he can about the truth of nature and his own role in nature.

Only self-limitation can stem the population tide, and the only voice man has in the matter is whether it will be done involuntarily by nature's undesirable stresses, as witnessed by the history of civilization, or will be done consciously by not allowing his kind to exceed an optimum carrying capacity.

Socio-Economic Situations

It is incongruous that student unrest is so great and race problems so much in the front, yet almost everyone seems unaware that the basic cause of most of these socio-economic stresses is overpopulation, about which almost nothing is said by all of these energetic and sometimes vociferous groups. The daily economic pressures of individuals attempting to provide a decent civilization, especially for themselves, may lead to the ultimate destruction of all ecosystems. Surplus individuals do not quietly fade away.

In spite of man's power of conscious thought, the only species so endowed, he seldom thinks beyond his lifetime or his own family's particular needs. The great desire of most people to provide their children and themselves with all of today's advantages is an important factor in reducing family size. That is not enough, however, for these families are still raising the population level.

At the same time that the world's population is increasing, both the number and the percentage of the "have-nots" increase and, in addition, the gap widens between the "haves" and "have-nots." As tragic as it may sound, when an underdeveloped country's population density is growing rapidly, both health and agricultural aid from the United States may not only be wasted but may severly aggravate the already deplorable social and economic situation in that country.

In industrially developed countries, middle-class couples often have fewer children than they would like (if they only had more money, domestic help, etc.), whereas in underdeveloped countries and ghettos the reverse is too frequently true. High birth rates tend to nullify national efforts to raise average per capita income since there is less money for savings and developmental investments. Neither families nor a nation can escape when life is held close to the margin of subsistence.

Overpopulation inevitably commits too many people to poverty and despair.

With perpetual pregnancies the bonds of welfare become inescapable, for un-skilled parents cannot feed a large family from the wages they can earn. No matter how you look at it, families of more than two or three children intensify the problem of national development, and this happens whether the parents are poor, middle class, or wealthy.

A complete reorientation of social values and attitudes regarding births is urgently needed now. We need new baby ethics, an awareness of the tragedies associated with too many babies. Bringing births and deaths into balance will demand great social, economic, and political changes.

With reference to our affluence, we cannot turn back—if for no other reason than the fact that there are now too many people to permit going back—to a less materialistic existence without cars, pesticides, diesel exhaust, sewage and gar-bage disposal, etc. The stork has passed the plow. Food prices in developing nations are rising faster than the purchasing power.

Economic Interests

Man seems to be governed by economic self-interest. Societies become condi-tioned to the tenets of the economists—that money can buy anything. Without the basic resources there can be no wealth and affluence; but, unfortunately, the exploitation of resources seems to be considered the very foundation of all "pro-gress."

"Progress" is the magic word. It means to increase property values and returns on one's investment; it is the deity of modern civilization. Yet, do any of us really know what we are progressing toward? Too often, the chamber-of-commerce form of "progress" is the next man's destruction.

Man seems to be more concerned with the quality of his goals than with the quantity of his goods. The more slowly a population increases the more rapid is the growth of both its gross and per capita income.

The harmful consequences of overpopulation are blindly overlooked by those who favor an expanding population for reasons of military strength, economic progress, scientific and agricultural development, and eugenics.

Man's economic dreams, his selfishness, and his materialism interfere with his awareness of the fate of the unborn. He is too busy in the United States in covering two acres per minute with houses, factories, and stores. His highways are now equivalent to paving the entire state of Indiana. Every day, California loses 300 acres of agricultural land.

Unfortunately, little planning has been done on how the socio-economic problems can be handled once the population growth is stopped. If the rush of today's living and industrial development or defense spending just slows down, a painful recession is upon us. We have no government study on how the nation could exist without a growing population.

Resource Management

Insidious economic pressures seem to prevent any effective management of resources in a manner that would provide for their utilization in perpetuity. Concrete and pavement surely are not the epitome of the human species' fulfillment. An ecological appreciation of resource management is needed, and ecological ethics must replace ecological atrocities.

Man is rapidly depleting the nonreplenishable resources. Half of the energy used by man during the past 2000 years was used in the last century. Man is reported to have mined more in the past 100 years than during all previous time. But, every barrel has a bottom; unbridled technology promises to speed us faster toward that bottom. Our planet's resources diminish faster as society's affluence is increased. Our qualitative sense of appreciation of our environment seems to be replaced by mere quantitative values. Why cannot civilization fulfill its obligation of being a competent steward of all resources?

It is inevitable that the limited legacy of natural resources must steadily yield in the face of the current explosion in the world population. As the population swells, open spaces are inundated by a flood of housing, and resources shrink faster. The United States and other developed nations are consuming a disproportionately large share of the world's nonrenewable and other resources at an ever-accelerating rate, perhaps 20 to 30 times as much on a per capita basis as are individuals in undeveloped countries. In 1954, the United States was reported to be using about 50% of the raw-material resources consumed in the world each year, and by 1980 it might be 80%. But we do not have an endless earth of boundless bounty. Any finite resource is subject to eventual exhaustion.

Effect of Science and Technology

The world may have sufficient resources, but it has never provided enough food and other necessities of life for all people at any one time. As technology improved, enabling better utilization of resources, the population similarly increased, so that there have always been many who died prematurely, as Malthus predicted.

No one anticipated the scope and rapidity of the technological changes that have occurred in Western society. About one-third of the people now consume about two-thirds of the world's food production, while the other two-thirds go undernourished. But, unfortunately, these starving people reproduce at a high rate. As individual aspirations rise and per capita resources fall, the widening gap between the haves and the have-nots could well generate some serious social and political pressures.

In recent times spectacular gains have been made in controlling mass killers such as typhus, malaria, yellow fever, small pox, cholera, plague, and influenza; but no corresponding checks have been made on birth rates. It is ironic that the root of our overpopulation problem is technical advances brought about by our increasing intellect (the knowledge explosion of the last hundred years).

Technology can produce almost anything, but only at the usually recognized high price of resource consumption and waste accumulation. As our technology advances, the amount of resources utilized per person also increases, and the supply is not endless.

Technology and science can and do progress at an ever-increasing rate, but can social, political, and religious views change rapidly enough to cope with this "progress"? The fruits of all our scientific and technological advances will be ephemeral if the world's population continues to explode. Our intelligence is so powerful that it may destroy us because we lack the wisdom and insight to recognize and correct what we are doing to ourselves and, especially, to future generations. We are passing on an enormous population problem to the next generation.

Pollution and Waste Disposal

Affluent societies have also been labeled "effluent" societies. That man is a highly adaptable species that can live in polluted environments, in extremely crowded conditions, in situations of acute malnutrition, and in some of the most depressing of environments is well exemplified today. But why should he? And how much lower can he sink and still survive as a "successful" species?

Mushrooming with the population are pollution and litter. We produce 70% of the world's solid wastes but have only 10% of the world's population. There is a need to make the reuse and disposal of rubbish more economical.

Popular Solutions and Misconceptions

Hopeful but inadequate panaceas include synthetic foods (proteins and vitamins), hydroponics, desalinization of seawater, food from the ocean, more agricultural research, fertilizers, irrigation, the vast unused lands, land reforms, government regulation, price support, migrations, redistribution of food and wealth, and private enterprise.

Science and technology may find a way to produce more food and to accommodate more people, but in the end this, of course, will only make matters that much worse if birth control is not effective. It should be obvious that the only solution is a drastically reduced birth rate or a greatly increased death rate. The one inescapable fact about a country's population—about the world's population —is that the death rate must someday equal the birth rate, regardless of how plentiful food may be.

Unfortunately, a basic American philosophy is the belief that our free-enterprise system can produce anything that is necessary, a false cornucopian faith that our population growth is not a real threat. Our overpopulation-under-development dilemma is not a matter of increasing production to meet the demand for more food; rather, the only solution is to limit demand for food so that production may someday catch up to the population's needs.

Role of Family Planning

There is no question that family planning has made great progress. But today's society and religious groups must recognize the urgency for adopting the pill, IUD, other chemical and mechanical devices (both undependable), sterilization, abortion—in fact, any means of limiting childbirth. The promotion of some form of effective means of artificial birth control is the only moral, human, and political approach available to prevent the misery and suffering which will result if people are permitted to have as many "planned" children as they want.

Despite the great benefits of family planning programs, especially the benefits to the families concerned, family planning is not a euphemism for birth control.

We need to develop a social and cultural philosophy that even a family of three children is too large and to overcome the fear of some ethic and religious sects that other groups may multiply faster, becoming more dominant. Family planning per se has little relevance to the underdeveloped countries of the world or to poverty groups in the more advanced countries. Therefore anything other than government control of conception may be self-defeating.

Sexual Desire and Love of Children

The basic conflict with the overpopulation problem is that of desires— actually drives—and the fact that most young women are fecund; without either the strong drives or the ability of women to conceive, there would be no problem. As with all organisms, man's potential fecundity and predisposition to over-produce are the basic causes for his excess fertility over deaths. Most babies are the consequence of passion, not love. But children are loved.

Motherhood must become a less significant role for women. We must forego some of our love for children and learn to be content with fewer numbers. What is needed in the way of governmental control of births is not control of an individual's behavior but control of the consequence of such behavior, the prevention of intemperate breeding.

There is no question that children make family ties more intimate, but man has already done too well toward "fathering" the country. Compassionate relations between spouses, not the having of children, must become the primary goal of marriages in the future. There is no need to find drugs that destroy sexual desire; the objective is to control the conception rate, not frequency of intercourse.

Is Having Children a Basic Right?

One price that society must be willing to pay for sustained world peace is a stringent universal birth-control program, which will require revolutionary revisions of modes of thought about our basic human rights with regard to family planning.

The increasing disparity between population density and food supply, by itself, justifies effective birth control regardless of the "morality" associated with depriving parents of the right to have as many planned children as they choose.

Having too many children can no longer be dismissed as an act of God, for it is now truly the consequence of a complacent society that is unwilling to take any of many steps available for preventing surplus births. Our primitive reproductive instincts cannot be condoned in the face of modern survival rates. The two are no longer in balance.

To say that the opportunity to decide the number and spacing of children is a basic human right is to say that man may do whatever he wants with nature without thought of its inevitable consequence to future generations. Our legal and ethical right should be to have only enough children to replace ourselves.

No longer can we consider procreation an individual and private matter. Intercourse, yes, but not unregulated numbers of conceptions since they affect the welfare of all other individuals living at that time plus those to be born in the future.

Religious Complications

It needs to be said over and over again that the bringing of surplus children into this world, whether from personal desire or from religious edicts, destines not only some of these children but many others to a premature death. Overproduction actually lowers the maximum density that can be sustained for normal life spans, thereby increasing the number of souls in need of salvation.

The "morality" of birth control in today's burgeoning human population has taken on an entirely new aspect. God clearly never meant for man to overpopulate this earth to the point where he would destroy many other forms of life and perhaps even himself. The religious doctrines we lean on today were established before science and technology had dramatically raised the carrying capacity for man.

The question of complete abstinence as the only acceptable means of family regulation is as ludicrous as compulsory euthanasia. The mortal sin, if there is one, in God's eyes surely would be associated with those who do *not* practice birth control, for to let babies come "as they naturally do" will prove to be a form of murder—through starvation, pestilence, and wars resulting from excess babies. It must be recognized that the number of children can no longer be left to "the will of God" or to our own desires and family plans, and if population controls are to be successful, they may have to be determined by government regulations.

Religious views that do not condone rigorous birth control must realize that every surplus birth their philosophy promotes will guarantee, on the average, a horrible death some day to more than one individual.

Although the Christian attitude implies that everything on this earth was created for man's use, in reality man is inescapably also part of nature.

Some form of compulsory control of birth rates is essential, although I see no reason why various religious groups cannot be permitted to achieve birth limitations in whatever manner they choose. If a woman or a couple exceeds the limit set by society, however, then they must be dealt with by law compelling them to be sterilized, to have an abortion, or by some other repayment to society.

Birth control is not murder, as some claim, but lack of it in today's overpopulated world most surely will be. For those who strongly oppose the setting of any limit on the number of children a family can have, I ask them to tell the rest of us just how they think the premature death rate should be increased to offset their extra births.

Wealth vs. Number of Children

Civilization can no longer endure a way of life in which people believe they have the right to have as many children as they can afford. This is hypocritical, for those who can "afford" luxurious living are already utilizing many times their share of the limited food and other resources, and also they are contributing much more pollution to the environment than are the have-nots. The affluent population needs to be made aware of the overpopulation problems, for they often desire to have more children per family than those who are in poverty.

Too much of today's religious climate makes birth control a politically sensitive area, thus constraining public officials. But, as citizens, are we not justified in asking why our governmental officials have not done more to make us aware of the urgency of population control—political sensitivities notwithstanding?

Governments should be guiding the development of a better life and world to live in, but if it does not recognize the need for human husbandry, then it will be fostering the ultimate destruction of the earth rather than the goals it seeks.

Man, in spite of his intellect, is so concerned with the present that he too often turns a deaf ear to alarming sounds of the future. Another difficulty in stabilizing the population is that our standard of living and our economy cannot survive in a static state.

Limiting Size of Families

We can no longer be prophets and philosophers; we must act. The biomagnification of births must be brought to an abrupt halt. Procreation must come under governmental control if no other way can be found. Perhaps what is needed is a system of permits for the privilege of conceiving, or compulsory vasectomies of all man and sterilization of all women who have been responsible for two births.

Since the taboo against birth control is inviolable to some, regardless of the dire consequences of overpopulation, laws must be passed to regulate conceptions and births. Each individual needs to have the right to produce or adopt only a replacement for himself or herself.

The general public must be made to realize that from now on, for a married couple to have more than two children or three at most, is a very socially irresponsible act. We must advocate small families. When business is good and living has quality, marriages will naturally tend to be earlier and births more numerous; therefore, only through the development of new nonfamilial rewards can later marriages be made to appear attractive to people. Taxes now subsidize children, whereas we should be taxed for the privilege of having children.

A rising age at marriage is an effective way of reducing births, and, sociologically and economically, it gives women more time to become better educated, acquire nonfamily sorts of interests, and develop greater cautions toward pregnancy.

Up to now, only death has been of public concern; procreation has remained an individual and highly cherished private matter. But this privilege cannot continue, and regulation of the number of conceptions, or at least births, must also become a government function.

Population Control or Premature Deaths

Man must decide whether the future growth of populations will be governed by famine, pestilence, and war, or whether he will use his intellect to control birth rates artificially. If the population growth is not controlled by lower birth rates, hundreds of millions of people must soon die prematurely each year.

Man must use his intellect to counteract his excessive fertility, for all species have been endowed by nature to be overfecund. If he does not, the extra individuals will be eliminated by the natural process of "struggle for existence—survival of the fittest," which causes all surplus individuals to die prematurely as a result of nature's ruthless laws of involuntary "self-limitation" whenever the carrying capacity has been exceeded. That territoriality and aggression are life-preserving functions of the social order of animals is frightening when man applies these same principles to his own species.

There have always been hungry people in the world, but both the total number of individuals and the percentage of the total population that are destined to go hungry in the future will be dramatically increased if birth rates are not drastically checked. Many like to think that nature will somehow take care of things. They fail to remember how nature has taken care of many species that were no longer adaptable to existence on this earth—they are now preserved as fossils.

Modern public-health methods and medical technology have lessened the chronic hunger, general economic misery, and other vicissitudes that once caused high mortality rates. But, sooner or later, any increase in births over deaths will be balanced by an increase in the rate of premature deaths.

Human Husbandry and Quality Living

Human husbandry implies that we regulate the population density before the natural self-limiting demographic and societal stress factors do it for us. But human motivation will always work against good human husbandry, because to each individual who has quality living, a large family will seem desirable.

The population of the world is so great that what used to be a ripple when it doubled now means catastrophic effects because of the great numbers involved and the lack of this earth's ability to support them. Man is not practicing good husbandry when he lets his population density expand beyond the carrying capacity.

The most important thesis regarding the need for human husbandry is that human beings will not voluntarily restrict their number of children to just two when economic, social, and political conditions appear to be personally favorable. A quality society with quality existence is now unattainable in many parts of the world, and may soon be unattainable any place in the world. The "economic" struggle of overpopulation is the world's greatest threat to quality living, enriched leisure, and even man's ultimate existence.

Conclusion

The ultimate goal must be a zero population growth. To achieve "quality living" instead of nature's "survival of the fittest," as has persisted throughout the history of mankind, the birth rate must not continue to exceed the death rate. If the birth rate of nations and the world are not greatly reduced, an ever-increasing amount of starvation and other types of premature deaths are inevitable. There is a prodigious need for mankind to practice human husbandry (Human Husbandry, a guest editorial in *BioScience.* 18: 372-373, 1968, by Walter E. Howard).

A conscientious regulation of fertility is needed, or a calamitous rise in premature mortality rates is inevitable. Without this tremendous voluntary re-straint or the development of a strong social stigma against bearing more than two or three children, the rate of conceptions must come under some form of governmental control. It can no longer be a basic human right to have as many children as one wants, especially if such action dooms others to a premature death.

Even though the above picture is bleak, the world is not going to come to an end. In fact, none of the people who read this article are going to starve, but their very existence is going to cause others who are less well off to perish. As overpopulation becomes worse, the percentage of the people who will fall into this nonsurviving unfit category must obviously increase. If babies of the future are to live, there must be fewer of them now.

In the early part of 1971, drought ravaged northeast Brazil. Crops dried up and cattle herds were decimated. People were observed in such extreme activity as fighting off buzzards and one another for the carcass of an ox. Bands of peasants left their land for the towns; many camped on the main square where they were given food, but no jobs. An Associated Press article mentioned that in Sergipe State alone, 100,000 of the 877,000 residents were hungry. In the entire AP article there was never mention of overpopulation. Apparently the writer felt that there was merely a bad drought in the area. Garrett Hardin comments on this state of mind in the next reading.

Also see readings 57, 58, 89, and 90 for more on the problems in Latin America.

Nobody Ever Dies of Overpopulation   56

GARRETT HARDIN

Those of us who are deeply concerned about population and the environment —"econuts," we're called—are accused of seeing herbicides in trees, pollution in running brooks, radiation in rocks, and overpopulation everywhere. There is merit in the accusation.

I was in Calcutta when the cyclone struck East Bengal in November 1970. Early dispatches spoke of 15,000 dead, but the estimates rapidly escalated to 2,000,000 and then dropped back to 500,000. A nice round number: it will do as well as any, for we will never know. The nameless ones who died, "unimportant" people far beyond the fringes of the social power structure, left no trace of their existence. Pakistani parents repaired the population loss in just 40 days, and the world turned its attention to other matters.

What killed those unfortunate people? The cyclone, newspapers said. But one can just as logically say that overpopulation killed them. The Gangetic delta is barely above sea level. Every year several thousand people are killed in quite ordinary storms. If Pakistan were not overcrowded, no sane man would bring his family to such a place. Ecologically speaking, a delta belongs to the river and the sea; man obtrudes there at his peril.

In the web of life every event has many antecedents. Only by an arbitrary decision can we designate a single antecedent as "cause." Our choice is biased—biased to protect our egos against the onslaught of unwelcome truths. As T. S. Eliot put it in *Burns Norton:*

Go, go, go, said the bird: human kind
Cannot bear very much reality.

Were we to identify overpopulation as the cause of a half-million deaths, we would threaten ourselves with a question to which we do not know the answer: *How can we control population without recourse to repugnant measures?* Fearfully we close our minds to an inventory of possibilities. Instead, we say that a cyclone caused the deaths, thus relieving ourselves of responsibility for this and future catastrophes. "Fate" is *so* comforting.

Every year we list tuberculosis, leprosy, enteric diseases, or animal parasites as the "cause of death" of millions of people. It is well known that malnutrition is an important antecedent of death in all these categories; and that malnutrition is connected with overpopulation. But overpopulation is not called the cause of death. We cannot bear the thought.

People are dying now of respiratory diseases in Tokyo, Birmingham, and Gary, because of the "need" for more industry. The "need" for more food justifies overfertilization of the land, leading to eutrophication of the waters, and lessened fish production—which leads to more "need" for food.

What will we say when the power shuts down some fine summer on our eastern seaboard and several thousand people die of heat prostration? Will we blame the weather? Or the power companies for not building enough generators? Or the econuts for insisting on pollution controls?

One thing is certain: we won't blame the deaths on overpopulation. No one ever dies of overpopulation. It is unthinkable.

Some Consequences of Population Growth

57   The Social Consequences Of Population Growth

BENJAMIN VIEL

It has been demonstrated that families lacking access to contraceptive means of birth control, particularly in Latin America, often turn in desperation to the harsh alternative of abortion. Some evidence for this fact is presented in the following provocative essay by a distinguished Chilean physician. According to Dr. Viel, the rate of induced abortion in Latin America is highest among the middle classes, which do not practice contraception on a wide scale. Extremely poor families, he asserts, seldom resort to abortion or contraception because "ignorance and demoralization probably destroy the capacity of poor women to combat family growth." Under such circumstances, birth rates are very high.

The most disturbing part of Dr. Viel's essay is his hypothesis that women in large, poor families may unconsciously wish for the death of their newest-born children. While the evidence for this hypothesis is still inconclusive, it merits further attention. The degree to which unconscious infanticide exists in Latin America—and the degree to which it may occur among large families in the United States and elsewhere—can only be ascertained through research. Such research is urgently needed.

When we refer to population growth and its effects, we should differentiate clearly between normal growth, which parallels the increase in the means of subsistence, and accelerated growth, which takes place more rapidly than the increase in resources available to support life. Far from stimulating progress and giving rise to evolutionary processes, accelerated growth has been the cradle of wars and revolutions. It has slowed down production and vastly increased human misery and hunger.

Starting somewhat arbitrarily with the year 1930, we have had normal growth in the developed regions of the world and accelerated growth in all the regions we call underdeveloped or developing. In the latter areas, mortality rates have dropped swiftly as a result of techniques imported from the industrialized world. Populations have consequently grown fast, but there has been no parallel growth in productivity or in the sources of employment.

Latin America today is a typical victim of this speedup in population growth. Its predicament has been caused largely by the reduction of infectious diseases through new drugs and more effective methods of administering and distributing medical resources. Both the new drugs and the improved methods are imports from abroad. Instead of creating a biological balance between the South American and his environment, they have helped to destroy the equilibrium already in existence. Death rates have dropped much faster than they would have fallen through improvements in nutrition brought about by an increase in the means of subsistence.

Between 1930 and 1968, the population of Latin America more than doubled, and at the present rate of growth, it will have tripled between 1960 and the end of this century.

What are the social implications of this enormously rapid growth? In offering an analysis, I will, as a doctor, start with those effects which lie closest to the field of medicine.

Unconscious Infanticide

It comes as a shock to realize that infanticide has grown more widespread during the twentieth century. This phenomenon exists at a frequency and in a form that is unknown to the great majority of people in Latin America.

I do not speak of deliberate infanticide such as the outright killing of the newborn, which is very rare, or the abandonment of infants, which is tragically on the increase, at least in Chile. Rather, I refer to infanticide of the unconscious type, in which the mother allows her child to die without even admitting to herself that she desires the child's death.

In a careful study in Santiago, Dr. Aníbal Faúndes found that for first-born infants, 60 of every 1,000 died during their first year. Among the third- or fourth-born, however, infant deaths rose to about 100. After 10 or more children were born to the same couples, the number of deaths during the first year of life

reached 300 for every 1,000 infants. Since there is no biological phenomenon that
entirely explains this increase in mortality, we must consider the possibility that
a major cause is the growing lack of concern on the part of the mother towards
additional children who burden her with more work than she can endure.

This hypothesis is supported by the experience of almost any pediatrician.
Mothers come to him when they detect the least symptoms of illness in their
first-born children. After they have had five or six children, however, these same
mothers bring in their infants only when they are seriously ill.

In developing countries such as those of Latin America, the multiplicity of
births per family may provoke unconscious infanticide and thereby serve as an
important cause of high infant mortality rates. High mortality, moreover, continues through the preschool years. We must face the shameful fact that out of every
100 deaths in Latin America, 44 are of persons less than five years old. In
Argentina and Uruguay, where birth rates are lower than elsewhere in the continent, mortality rates in the younger ages are also lower. Only 18 out of every 100
deaths in these two countries occur among children under five.

Induced Abortion

When the mother's life is not imperiled by pregnancy or childbirth, induced
abortion is considered illegal throughout Latin America. Both the mother who
submits to such an abortion and the person who performs it are liable to punishment. Yet we have had an extremely high rate of induced abortion. The result
has been widespread non-enforcement of the law. If the law *were* enforced, we
would soon face a grave shortage of police, judges and jails.

How common are induced abortions in Latin America? Their illegal status
has led to vast underreporting, and we must therefore resort to indirect means
of evaluating their frequency.

Assuming that in 1960 the use of reliable contraceptives was very rare among
Latin American women and that the age distribution was "young" in all Latin
American countries except Argentina and Uruguay, we may then state that the
theoretical birth rate (without abortion) in these countries could not have been
lower than 50*. From the differences between this theoretical rate and the actual
birth rates in 1960, as shown in Table 1, we can obtain a rough idea of the
frequency of induced abortion.

This table indicates that induced abortion is more frequent in Brazil, Chile
and Peru than in other countries. Although the relationship is not very close, the
table also suggests that the actual birth rate tends to be higher where the percentage of urban population is smaller. In other words, the incidence of provoked
abortion rises with urbanization.

In 1964, the U.N. Regional Center for Demographic Training and Research
(CELADE) conducted a random-sample survey of abortion and contraception
among women of reproductive age in several Latin American cities. Table 2 gives
the results. San Jose, the capital of Costa Rica, had an abortion rate of 33 per
1,000 woman-years; Caracas and Mexico City also had very high rates. Comparing these results with those of Table 1, we may state that where the frequency
of abortion is low at the national level, it is very often high in urban areas. The

*Birth and death rates are given per 1,000 people per year.

TABLE 1: Difference Between Theoretical and Actual Birth Rates, 1960.

Country	Actual Birth Rate	Difference from Theoretical Birth Rate of 50	Percentage of Population Urban
Brazil	33.0	−17.0	40.4
Chile	33.0	−17.0	66.2
Peru	38.2	−11.8	47.1
Venezuela	42.8	− 7.2	63.7
Colombia	44.6	− 5.4	50.6
Mexico	44.7	− 5.3	50.7
Honduras	47.2	− 2.8	22.5
Salvador	48.5	− 1.5	38.5
Costa Rica	49.2	− 0.8	34.5

varying rates of abortion in different countries therefore tend to reflect the varying degrees of urbanization.

Table 2 also reveals an inverse relationship between the abortion rate and the percentage of women in each sample using contraceptives.

Other investigations bear out the urban-rural differential in provoked abortion. Surveys by the population department of the Colombian Association of Medical Schools reveal that the rate of induced abortions reached 16 per 100 pregnant women in Bagotá and 20 or more in other cities, while in rural communities it averaged only about 8. Likewise, in Santiago, Chile, the induced abortion rate as determined by surveys reached 35, while in the rural community of Calera it was less than 7.

What are some of the reasons for this urban-rural differential? In the rural areas, particularly where the climate is favorable as it is in most of Latin America, children do not constitute a great housing problem; they use the home mainly for sleeping. Even before they reach the age of 15, moreover, they help with the farm work. But in the cities, conditions are much different. Children remain in the home for a much longer time, creating a serious housing problem. Far from

TABLE 2: Abortion, Contraception and Family Size in Seven Latin American Countries, 1964.

City	Abortions per 1,000 Woman-Years	Percentage of Women Using Contraceptives	Average Number of Children
Mexico City	37	13.7	3.3
Caracas	34	24.4	3.0
San José of Costa Rica	33	27.2	3.0
Bogotá	26	21.8	3.2
Panama City	24	na	2.7
Rio de Janeiro	21	na	2.3
Buenos Aires	21	41.8	1.5

contributing substantially to the family's income, they constitute a financial burden even after the age of 15. Moreover, they are increasingly born into families where the mother works outside the home. It is under such circumstances that women turn to abortion when they lack effective contraceptive devices. In the cities, too, it is much easier to find the facilities for abortion.

Considering the fact that in Latin America there is a growing trend towards urbanization, it is easy to conclude that, unless an attempt is made to prevent them, induced abortions will become tragically more prevalent in the next decade.

The trend towards a gradual increase in illegal abortions in Chile can be traced as far back as 1937. In that year, records first became available of the number of women hospitalized for complications which arose from illegal abortions performed outside the hospital. Certainly such cases represent only a fraction of all illegal abortions, since illegal abortions without complications are not recorded. It should also be noted that these hospital cases do not represent all the socioeconomic classes. They are heavily weighted towards the low-income groups. When complications of abortion arise in women who are economically well off, the patients are usually hospitalized in private clinics where it is easy to falsify the diagnosis.

The Chilean record reveals a gradual increase in hospital abortion rates, nationwide, and in Santiago, between 1937 and 1967. It also reveals that abortion is more frequent in Santiago than in the rest of the country. Outside Santiago, the problem appears to have been minimized by the low rate of abortion in the rural areas, even though the rate in other Chilean cities is as high as in Santiago —sometimes even higher. Since 1966, the level of hospital abortions has stabilized, particularly in Santiago. This stabilization appears to have been caused by a birth control program which has been in effect since 1965 and which has been applied more extensively in Santiago than elsewhere.

In conjunction with studies of hospital abortions in Chile between 1937 and 1967, a decrease has also been observed in infant mortality rates. It is thus clear that there is an inverse relationship between abortion and infant mortality. While infant mortality rates have dropped, the frequency of illegal abortion has risen. There is a logical explanation to this relationship. Years ago, high infant mortality severely limited the size of families. In recent decades, however, medical advances and the availability of powdered milk have decreased infant mortality without stimulating any significant change in the economic conditions of the home. Women, the most responsible members of Latin American society, are attacking the problem of excessive family size by resorting more and more to illegal abortions.

It is interesting to note that the greatest frequency of induced abortion exists among married women. From studies recently conducted in Santiago and San José, we can see that the yearly rate of induced abortions for married women was 49 per 1,000 women in Santiago and 26.5 in Costa Rica, while for single girls it was only 19 in Santiago and 11.5 in Costa Rica. The old belief that illegal abortion is resorted to mainly by single women who wish to hide premarital relationships is erroneous. This practice undoubtedly exists, but its extent is very small compared with the number of married women with children who seek abortion to prevent a further increase in family size.

Abortion and Socioeconomic Class

It has been shown that a definite relationship exists between socioeconomic class and the frequency of abortions. If we assume that fertility is roughly equal in all classes, then abortion must be considered a rare phenomenon in the extreme classes and a very common one in the middle-income classes. Wealthy women resort less often to abortion for the simple reason that they use contraceptive methods to a much greater extent than other women. Middle-income women submit to illegal abortion much more frequently because they seldom use contraceptives to prevent unwanted births. In the very low-income classes, however, abortion is rare and the birth rate is extremely high. The ignorance and demoralization caused by destitution probably destroy the capacity of the poor woman to combat family growth.

In studying the frequency of abortion, researchers use the degree of education as a measure of socioeconomic status. Table 3 shows the percentage of women in three educational groups who have resorted to abortion in three Latin American cities.

If we assume that educational levels roughly coincide with economic classes, then Table 3 bears out the statement that abortions are sought primarily by women in the middle socioeconomic classes.

Throughout Latin America, women in these classes generally hire domestics who, in addition to receiving a salary, live in the homes of their employers. Practically every middle-class family has one or more domestic workers. For this type of hired help, abortion can be called a professional disease. Faced with pregnancy, domestics must choose between losing their jobs and resorting to induced abortion. Most well-off families will not hire domestics who are mothers.

In the methods as well as the frequency of abortion, we can discern distinct differences according to socioeconomic class. When a woman from the high-income group decides to have an abortion, she seeks out a professionally trained doctor and she generally pays an expensive fee. At a somewhat lower economic level, however, the woman resorts to a non-professional whose competance is as low as the fee he charges. This woman may suffer complications from the methods used by the unskilled practitioner.

In the poorest classes, a woman is likely to perform a crude abortion on herself by inserting a stiff implement or sewing needle through the neck of the uterus. She seeks help only when hemorrhaging begins.

While complications requiring hospitalization may result from abortions performed by unskilled "specialists," they almost always follow from abortions performed by the pregnant woman herself.

TABLE 3: Abortion and Educational Status

Level of Education	Percentage of women having resorted to one or more abortions		
	Santiago	Bogotá	Mexico City
None	27.3	26.0	29.6
Primary School	39.3	28.8	34.2
Secondary School and above	24.3	19.1	24.8

The foregoing conclusions, based on research in Chile, reflect practices throughout Latin America. Illegally induced abortions result in the deaths of many young women. They are the cause of an incalculable number of gynecological infections that lead to a serious interruption of medical practice, because proper attention for women during childbirth and for newborn children is made difficult by the need to care for so many complications of abortion. Medical care for these complications drains a large fraction of the funds allocated to health programs by the Latin American countries.

We may conclude that unless something is done to reduce the problem, abortion will continue to increase in direct proportion both to the rate of urbanization in our countries and to the expected drop in infant mortality.

Control of Illegal Abortion

The punishment of abortion by law in Chile has failed miserably, even though authorities have long had access to the names and addresses of women who are hospitalized each year because of complications of illegal abortion. Since no attempt has even been made to initiate court proceedings, many people ask: "Why not adopt the policy of Japan and make all abortions legal?" This proposal reflects a very superficial analysis of the problem. First of all, there are strong moral objections to making abortions legal. Secondly, such a policy would be completely impractical. It is true that the Soviet Union and Japan, among many other countries, have legalized abortions, but in the Soviet Union there is a doctor for every 460 people, and in Japan the ratio of doctors to the total population is only slightly smaller. In Chile, one of the medically more advanced countries in Latin America, there is only one doctor for every 1,600 persons. If doctors were authorized to practice abortion, and even more importantly, if they had the legal *obligation* to practice abortion on request, Chile would not have enough doctors to handle the demand. Nor would there be enough hospital beds—even for one day of hospitalization—unless Chile accepted a significant reduction in the present insufficient number of beds used for normal obstetric care.

There is, finally, a strong medical objection to legalizing abortion. Giving a woman the means to exercise very high fertility is incompatible with her good health and with the normalcy of her last-born children. Therefore, an indiscriminate policy of legalizing abortion is not an acceptable solution.

What about other proposed remedies? There is no doubt that reducing abortion by abstinence would require a return to the harsh times of Malthus. No one could seriously consider such an approach. It is equally wrong to maintain that abortion can be prevented by improving the living standards of the family and guaranteeing the education of children. Housing space is becoming continuously smaller because every day there are more people to be housed. Education is expensive, and government programs are seldom on par with the educational requirements of countries having high birth rates.

The truth is that a humane, effective solution to the very serious problem of illegal abortion cannot be other than the use of contraceptives. This brings together the two demographic goals which must be sought in today's world—first, the reduction of the rate of population increase to the point where it parallels the rise in production, and second, the reduction of the population explosion within the family which forces women to expose themselves to a cruel operation.

Those persons who are against birth control join forces with those seeking legalized abortion to maintain that the contraceptive methods known today are incapable of replacing abortion and reducing the birth rate to any significant extent. It is even argued that illegal abortion tends to increase when a birth control plan based on contraception is started. The evidence, however, is to the contrary.

In our own experience with a birth control program in the western district of Santiago between 1964 and 1968, we observed a considerable drop in the number of induced abortions that resulted in complications requiring hospital care. Table 4 shows the estimated population of fertile women (aged 15-44) in the area studied, the cumulative number and percentage of women using intrauterine devices, the number of hospitalized abortions, and the percentage of women in the 15-44 age group who resorted to abortion.

TABLE 4: Abortion and Contraception in West Santiago, 1964-1968.

Year	Females Aged 15-44	Women Using IUD's (Cumulative Number)	Per-cent	Hospi-talized Abortions	Percent of 15-44 Age Group
1964	81,642	4,073	5.0	5,282	6.5
1965	84,747	8,222	9.9	6,237	7.4
1966	87,994	14,579	17.1	4,731	5.4
1967	101,909	26,147	28.5	4,265	4.2
1968	104,283	36,377	38.3	3,727	3.6

The number of hospitalized abortions in 1968 amounted to only about 70 percent of those in 1964. This drop can only be attributed to the free distribution and use of the intrauterine device and other effective contraceptives.

In maintaining that a contraceptive program can reduce the number of illegally induced abortions to the extent shown in Table 4, we do not claim that abortion can be eliminated. The contraceptives available today, even the most effective ones, involve a certain percentage of failure and are not suitable for all women.

Abortion will therefore continue to be a serious problem. Nevertheless, a reduction in abortions to the point where they do not require the use of over 10 percent of the beds in gyneco-obstetric wards would be a real triumph.

Population Growth and Employment

Despite high infant mortality and the increasing use of illegal abortions, Latin American countries are experiencing very rapid population growth at rates which, with the exception of Argentina and Uruguay, range between 2 and 3.5 percent annually.

Sustained high fertility has raised the percentage of young people in Latin America, and the majority of the Latin American nations find that over half their people are under 20. Every year the number of new job candidates is so great that the labor market cannot absorb all of them. The consequence of this phenomenon is increasing unemployment.

When Europe experienced a decline in its mortality rates as a result of better hygiene and improved nutrition, she also enjoyed the benefits of an extraordinary economic expansion arising from a successful industrial revolution. Furthermore, Europe had a safety-valve—emigration—which enabled her to colonize other continents when her own labor market failed to absorb all the new candidates for employment. Conditions in Latin America today are much different.

Latin America's labor market is growing too slowly to absorb all the workers which modern medicine and public health measures have saved from premature death. Furthermore, the continent lacks almost completely the migratory outlet which Europe long enjoyed.

There is another point of comparison which is unfavorable to Latin America. When the population growth rates of the European nations increased—and they were never as high as those occurring today in Latin America—the industrial machinery of that time required a large number of human laborers. But the slow economic expansion of Latin America today is being achieved through more automated industrial machines which are continuously replacing muscle power. Every day we see how factories which once employed 1,000 workers are modernizing their machinery and producing more and better products with only half as many workers.

The mechanization of agriculture has increased productivity and reduced the number of farm laborers. Those who do not find new jobs in the rural environment must migrate to the cities, where they face very serious problems created by a type of industrial production which requires fewer and fewer workers and which selects only the most qualified persons. Skills are demanded which cannot be acquired in the rural environment.

The continent's cities are growing, partly as a result of their own natural increase, but largely because of rural migration caused by the mechanization of agriculture. The growing mass of urban unemployed is seriously inflating the service expenditures of the Latin American countries, and it is disturbing the social peace.

This trend affects not only the city laborer and the farm worker. Intellectuals are also victims of technological progress. Without a doubt, if Latin America had the capital to purchase many more electronic computers, the middle classes would be as seriously riddled with unemployment as the classes of blue-collar workers and farm workers are now.

What are the political consequences of population growth which is too rapid for the economy to absorb? If a young man cannot find work, his natural reaction is to blame the socioeconomic system. It is not strange that energy is spent in resisting the economic and social structures prevalent today.

The intense and growing political activity of the youth of Latin America, which has assumed more and more violent forms in recent times, is the natural reaction to the uncertain future which is faced by young people who cannot find employment in the labor market.

For young intellectuals, the circumstances of the unemployed man give further incentive to protest and rebellion. Universities join in the violence. Strike after strike interrupts the periods of study. Students who should leave our universities technically trained are handicapped by an inadequate preparation, and thus they help widen the gap between the high-technology developed world and the low-technology underdeveloped world.

The Loss of Values

Youth has always been rebellious, but perhaps in no period of history has its rebellion been more vehement than now. In former times, fathers spoke to their sons with absolute faith in the moral and intellectual values which had guided their own lives. Today, men who are approaching 50—the generation holding power—sense that their faith is wavering. They can no longer hand down a given set of values to their sons with complete sincerity.

The multicellular family which constituted the basis of Latin American life in the past has been swept away by the population increase. The ancestral home of the grandparents, parents and grandchildren has been replaced by the apartment in the cooperative which the new generation views less as a home than as a bedroom.

We were taught in the cradle that work was a virtue, and that every person should cultivate his talents to the maximum. But we are living in a world in which overzealous work, far from being virtuous, is anti-social. One man's excessive work leaves another man unemployed.

We were taught that savings would guarantee the education of our children, that they would be an insurance against our old age. But we are living at a time when inflation has so thoroughly destroyed savings that anyone who saves what he earns is destined to be poor.

Having lost faith in the moral values which were absolute pillars of our upbringing, we do not understand the upcoming generation. We have lost the confidence to promote an evolutionary movement which will deliver us from a revolutionary force of dire consequences. If the Latin American population continues to grow ever more rapidly, a revolution led by illiterate and impoverished masses will be the logical result.

Given this dangerous prospect, it is very difficult to understand those traditional elements of Latin American society which so vehemently resist the effort to reduce the rate of population growth. Yet this rate must come down if we are to relieve the family tensions that lead mothers to unconscious infanticide and abortion. And it must come down if we are to relieve the social tensions which lead men to rebellion and violence, seeking changes which are possible only in a climate of peaceful dialogue.

President Nixon is quoted as having told Brazil's military president, General Emilio Garrastazu Medici, "We know that as Brazil goes, so will the rest of the Latin American continent."

Currently Brazil has more than half of the Latin American population and land area. Economic growth is presently galloping at a 9 percent increase per year. As Wright's contribution will show, this "healthy" economic increase is not enough to keep up with the four horsemen of the apocalypse. If Latin America has as many people as Red China has now by the year 2000, does this mean that other countries will go as Brazil, toward a military dictatorship? Is a repressive regime the best way of coping with too many people and too few resources? Can democracy be afforded only in a land of plenty for all?

58   Living With Overpopulation

ANGUS WRIGHT

Most Americans have never had the experience of living in a society where masses of people are in excess, without work, without income, without social services, without hope. In much of Latin America, Asia, and Africa the permanent crisis of national economies and rapid population growth make massive unemployment and human misery commonplace. A year of research in the Brazilian state of Bahia gave me as a historian a glimpse of Brazil's centuries-old struggle with poverty, but it also provided a frightening view of a world of the future. A world of scarce resources, excessive population, and a form of social organization better designed to exploit misery than to end it.

The thirty-five plus percent of the population in Bahia which is unemployed is by no means idle. There is the constant and wearing search for steady employment; work as a laborer, a laundress, a maid, a janitor, a dishwasher, a cook in a private home. Perhaps several wealthy people can be found who will pay to have their cars washed regularly. In 1960, 25 percent of the working population of Salvador, the Bahian state capital and city of one million people, were domestic servants.

Better even than a simple job is to find, through one's cleverness and charm, a *patrão,* a relatively powerful man who will protect and find a job for a man down on his luck in exchange for future loyalty and returned favors. But this happens only once or twice in a lifetime, if one is lucky, and for the majority of poor people it is a vain hope. Some say that Bahian politics is built on the exchange of favors and loyalties of the *patrão* system. If that is true, it is another example of the exclusion of poor people from the system, the reason they are called *marginalizados.* Marginalized people are people who try to survive at the edge of society rather than in it.

At the edge there is scrap to be gathered. Tin cans can be smashed and used to build walls for a house. Straw is worth gathering to be mixed with mud for a type of adobe. A cardboard box can be a dresser, a table, or, spread flat, the basis for a bed. A cast-off newspaper also makes a good bed when nothing else is available. Folded carefully each day, it may give some protection from the hard ground or a city sidewalk for several nights of sleep. An old shoe for the right foot may complement the cast-off rubber sandal that was found a few days before to protect the left. Old bottles are gathered to be sold at market, and virtually any piece of scrap, from bent-up rusty nails to a piece of a bicycle chain, will eventually find a buyer on market day, or any day of the week at the market of Agua dos Meninos. Pieces of wood are valuable for cooking fuel or for saving for just that right and yet unknown purpose which may arise some day.

There is begging, with a style to suit every personality and degree of desperation. There is systematic begging, with a regular route or a well-chosen spot downtown or near some tourist attraction. Church steps are a favorite location. Only if one is blind is he permitted the most lucrative form of begging, riding free on the city buses, where almost everyone is embarrassed to seem to be less charitable than the fellow sitting next to him. Another form of systematic begging on the buses requires a small investment. A man buys little cards with a brightly colored picture of Jesus, the Virgin Mary, or a much-loved saint. He jumps onto a bus and gives a picture to each passenger. Then he returns to each passenger asking for a small sum of money in return for the card. If the passenger simply hands back the card he is left with the feeling that he has insulted the religious figure portrayed, that he has spit in the face of Jesus or Saint Anthony. At the very least he feels that he has displayed his lack of charity where he can hardly help but be observed by whatever cosmic forces may exist.

For thousands of women, and for a few men, there is prostitution. If there were not so many pimps and police to be paid off, if there weren't so much competition, it might be a relatively lucrative profession. The thorough professional works out of a carefully managed house in a red-light district more or less officially recognized by the city authorities as long as appropriate pay-offs and favors are made available. The wages are not high, especially for the less-than-pretty, and the dangers of disease and violence are only slightly diminished by the protection of the house. In some areas where the customers are nearly as poor as the prostitutes the houses reek of urine and mildew and are in hopeless disrepair. Still, there is a roof and the very small comfort that the environment in the more expensive areas is probably more regular, hygienic, and comforting for one's children than most neighborhoods which could be considered as alternatives by the prostitutes. The privileges of the lower middle class—a television set shared with twenty other people, some glass vases with plastic flowers, a vinyl-covered sofa—may be some consolation. Contraceptives and abortions are so much more easily available here than elsewhere that it is one of the few places where "family planning" is a realistic possibility for the poor. Exceptionally good-looking girls find it more profitable to work on one's own, waiting along a busy beach side boulevard for wealthy men in cars or a taxi-driver who has had a good day to take them out of the city and have relations in the car or on a lonely stretch of beach. The woman who hooks a steady customer may enjoy favors and advantages for herself and her children that other women of her class would never dream of. There are obvious and terrible dangers, including venereal disease. From the point of view of the habitually privileged there ought to be psychological problems, but in a world where one in three has no real work and where more than seventy percent live in unrelieved poverty, perhaps one learns to be less sentimental about life and love. It is impossible to say.

Under some circumstances one can make use of family ties. A cousin or an uncle who has a job may be willing to supply a bed for a while and may even tolerate one's presence at the dinner table. After all, he knows that at any moment the positions may be reversed. Perhaps he can even use some help in improving his house; adding running water or electricity bought or pirated from nearby lines, putting a galvanized roof or an extra room on the house, gathering stones for a patio. Because everyone in this world of the poor is living at such close proximity to the deathly grey of utter destitution the slightest touch of beauty or imagination may be considered a great favor for which some return in a meal or night's lodging is only fair trade. A man can sing and play the guitar very well and still be unable to make a living out of it, but he can turn his skill to advantage from time to time to make himself welcome where he would otherwise be greeted with nothing but hostility. Even a gift for storytelling or flirtation can be vital in winning a few meals and a place to stay.

Handicrafts are another way of dealing with underemployment or unemployment. Women make lace, do seamstress jobs wherever they can be found, do fancy embroidery for the tourist market or a well-to-do acquaintance, or make home-made delicacies for sale on the street. Men do wood sculpture, leather work, toy making. For some who are highly skilled or well-connected such work can be a real profession. For most it is a matter of filling up hours, making a few pennies to stay alive. On the streets of most Brazilian cities vendors offer a variety of home-made toys and decorative items conceived and fashioned in the city's slums. Mice with a roller mechanism and string; pull the string and the mouse scurries along the pavement. Snakes that curl and strike. Whirligigs, sandals, place-mats, paper flowers. All of these are offered by vendors along with cheaply made factory goods of every description. As little as there is to profit from these products, there is always the chance for a little bit of cash income and the chance to keep utter despair from taking over.

None of these ways of surviving can be called having a job, with the possible exception of prostitution (one Brazilian city is subsidizing prostitution as a growth industry), and most of them return a tiny sum for an enormous amount of work. There is little or no guarantee of making anything at all; everything depends on luck and the good will of other people. There is no hospitalization, no insurance, no fringe benefits, no vacation, no union, no group of fellow workers to help you out. About the only thing this kind of activity shares with that paradise known as having a job is work, in many cases harder work for the unemployed than for the employed.

If work is one main feature of the life of people in excess, horrible and well-justified fear is its Siamese twin. The anthropologist Allen Holmberg once wrote an article on fear as the dominant motif in the life of the Peruvian peasant. Fear of the landlord, fear of the overseer, fear of the Christian god and saints, fear of local deities, fear of starvation, fear of disease, fear of storms, fear of falling off cliffs, fear of wild animals; in short, a complex of fear expressive of the extreme insecurity of life for a man who lives on the margin of society and at the edge of death and knows it. The same could be said for Brazilian peasants and urban slum dwellers as well.

The fear of disease is a good example of the terror and the reality of insecurity for the Brazilian without a secure income. There is the whole range of temperate climate diseases: measles, mumps, chicken pox, small pox, rheumatic fever, tuberculosis, among others. Even the milder of these, as our own ancestors knew very well, can be fatal when proper medical care and drugs are not available or are too expensive. Then there are diseases which are peculiar now to poor countries or tropical countries, always encouraged by overcrowding and poor housing.

One of the most serious in Brazil is Chagas disease, heart disease which can kill in anything from two to thirty years after contracting it. The victim gradually feels weaker and more uncomfortable, plagued by aches and pains. It is transmitted by the bite of a beetle which lives in the mud construction material of most poor people's houses. There is no known cure and none in sight. Some estimates state that more than half of the Brazilian population suffers from Chagas disease. Leptospirosis is another frequent killer in Bahia, again with no known cure. It is carried to humans by rat urine, and even the Bahian government admits that there are at least 10 rats for every person in the city of Salvador. Bubonic plague is another disease which gets at Bahians through the high rat population. Amoebic dysentery is endemic to some neighborhoods. Various types of intestinal worms are quite familiar to Bahians, and sometimes even attack upper-class people insufficiently wary about the handling of the food they eat or the sanitary conditions in their houses. Poor families lose many babies to worms.

Death of small children by "dehydration" sometimes reaches a rate of twenty to thirty deaths per day in the city of Salvador. Dehydration usually occurs in small children who are undernourished. They pick up an intestinal infection, most often in the summer months when flies are unusually numerous, which causes diarrhea. Mal-nourishment has already left them with little fluid content in their bodies, and within less than twenty-four hours the resulting dehydration causes death. The treatment, once the infection has begun in an undernourished child, is both expensive and unreliable. Death by dehydration is one of the ways in which people die before they actually starve to death.

We have been talking mostly about the urban poor, but for the rural poor the situation is similar. The upland cocoa-growing region is a good example. In the 1880s the southern portion of the state of Bahia began to enjoy a boom in the production of cocoa as a result of the increased demand for chocolate by the mass consumer markets created by rapid industrialization in the United States and Western Europe. People migrated to work in the plantations from other areas of the Brazilian Northeast where booms in other export crops had died out and given way to chronic regional depression. The first few decades were difficult, and the fluctuations of the world market, as well as local battles over the best land, periodically threw people out of work. The worst was yet to come, however, as foreign-owned export houses and powerful planters consolidated their positions on the best land and their control over credit and marketing. As overproduction and speculation became a constant in the cocoa market, as African cocoa farming boomed even faster than Brazil's, many of the migrants and their descendants faced the same problem they had fled from farther north. They were dismissed from plantations, forced onto marginal lands to produce subsistence crops or low quality cocoa with a high labor input. The bus trip through the region confirms the statistics. A highland population humiliated, prostituted, forgotten, contrasts with the relatively prosperous people fortunate enough to remain on the best land or in the bustling lowland cocoa towns. Laborers on the best farms work for little pay, live in mud shacks or dreary workers' barracks, and are denied the right to organize effectively or to receive social services. Those left to beg work mass together on isolated, unproductive land or migrate to the cities, where factory work holds an illusive promise for the escape from the cycle of export-crop migration their ancestors have engaged in for the four centuries of the history of the Brazilian economy. Agricultural production and mining have failed them for generations. Can industrialization save them, in a world quickly using up its resources, chronically incapable of arranging terms of trade of simple justice for poor nations, unable to plan humane industrial cities, strangling the environment with waste?

59   Birth Control and Economic Development

STEPHEN ENKE

Most less-developed countries have population increases approaching 3 percent a year. Death rates have fallen dramatically in the past several decades, but annual birthrates remain at around 4 percent of population. Income per head is rising slowly.

Enough is known about the main parameters that a demographic-economic computer model can be used to assess the effects of declining fertility rates on various indices of economic welfare in a typical less-developed country. Thus halving in 30 years a 3.025 gross rate of reproduction results in income per head increasing 3.0 percent a year instead of 1.7 percent a year with no fertility change. Halving fertility also results in a third more capital per worker after 30 years.

A large birth-control program might directly cost about $5 a year per "acceptor." About 25 percent of the population aged 15 through 49 would have to practice contraception on an average to halve the gross reproduction rate in 30 years. During this period the total cost might be roughly $200 million for a less-developed country that started with a population of 10 million. Accumulated benefits could be $16 billion. The benefit to cost ratio is roughly 80 to 1.

Population Policy

Two myths have been too long in dying regarding the population question in the United States. The myth that the poor want no more children than the non-poor has become the basis for government policy. Birth control programs have been "poverty oriented" with the assumption generally made that lack of education and family planning services are at the root of the large family. However, Judith Blake Davis, Department of Demography, University of California at Berkeley, writing in Science in 1969, has presented data supporting the position that poor families do indeed want more children than non-poor ones. Apparently when there is little else to live for, children serve as a means of obtaining fulfillment.

The following paper by Kingsley Davis (reading 60) deals with the second myth. Professor Davis makes a distinction between population planning and population control. This now classic document emphasizes that "planning" may be successful while "control" fails.

Population Policy

Will Current Programs Succeed?

KINGSLEY DAVIS

Throughout history the growth of population has been identified with prosperity and strength. If today an increasing number of nations are seeking to curb rapid population growth by reducing their birth rates, they must be driven to do so by an urgent crisis. My purpose here is not to discuss the crisis itself but rather to assess the present and prospective measures used to meet it. Most observers are surprised by the swiftness with which concern over the population problem has turned from intellectual analysis and debate to policy and action. Such action is welcome relief from the long opposition, or timidity, which seemed to block forever any governmental attempt to restrain population growth, but relief that "at last something is being done" is no guarantee that what is being done is adequate. On the face of it, one could hardly expect such a fundamental reorientation to be quickly and successfully implemented. I therefore propose to review the nature and (as I see them) limitations of the present policies and to suggest lines of possible improvement.

The Nature of Current Policies

With more than 30 nations now trying or planning to reduce population growth and with numerous private and international organizations helping, the degree of unanimity as to the kind of measures needed is impressive. The consensus can be summed up in the phrase "family planning." President Johnson declared in 1965 that the United States will "assist family planning programs in nations which request such help." The Prime Minister of India said a year later, "We must press forward with family planning. This is a programme of the highest importance." The Republic of Singapore created in 1966 the Singapore Family Planning and Population Board "to initiate and undertake population control programmes" (1).

As is well known, "family planning" is a euphemism for contraception. The family-planning approach to population limitation, therefore, concentrates on providing new and efficient contraceptives on a national basis through mass programs under public health auspices. The nature of these programs is shown by the following enthusiastic report from the Population Council (2):

No single year has seen so many forward steps in population control as 1965. Effective national programs have at last emerged, international organizations have decided to become engaged, a new contraceptive has proved its value in mass application, ... and surveys have confirmed a popular desire for family limitation ...

An accounting of notable events must begin with Korea and Taiwan ... Taiwan's program is not yet two years old, and already it has inserted one IUD (intrauterine device) for every 4-6 target women (those who are not pregnant, lactating, already sterile, already using contraceptives effectively, or desirous of more children). Korea has done almost as well ... has put 2,200 full-time workers into the field, ... has reached operational levels for a network of IUD quotas, supply lines, local manufacture of contraceptives, training of hundreds of M.D.'s and nurses, and mass propaganda ...

Here one can see the implication that "population control" is being achieved through the dissemination of new contraceptives, and the fact that the "target women" exclude those who want more children. One can also note the technological emphasis and the medical orientation.

What is wrong with such programs? The answer is, "Nothing at all, if they work." Whether or not they work depends on what they are expected to do as well as on how they try to do it. Let us discuss the goal first, then the means.

Goals

Curiously, it is hard to find in the population-policy movement any explicit discussion of long-range goals. By implication the policies seem to promise a great deal. This is shown by the use of expressions like *population control* and *population planning* (as in the passages quoted above). It is also shown by the characteristic style of reasoning. Expositions of current policy usually start off by lamenting the speed and the consequences of runaway population growth. This growth, it is then stated, must be curbed—by pursuing a vigorous family-planning program. That family planning can solve the problem of population growth seems to be taken as self-evident.

For instance, the much-heralded statement by 12 heads of state, issued by Secretary-General U Thant on 10 December 1966 (a statement initiated by John D. Rockefeller III, Chairman of the Board of the Population Council), devotes half its space to discussing the harmfulness of population growth and the other half to recommending family planning (3). A more succinct example of the typical reasoning is given in the Provisional Scheme for a Nationwide Family Planning Programme in Ceylon (4):

The population of Ceylon is fast increasing. . . . (The) figures reveal that a serious situation will be created within a few years. In order to cope with it a Family Planning programme on a nationwide scale should be launched by the Government.

The promised goal—to limit population growth so as to solve population problems—is a large order. One would expect it to be carefully analyzed, but it is left imprecise and taken for granted, as is the way in which family planning will achieve it.

When the terms *population control* and *population planning* are used, as they frequently are, as synonyms for current family-planning programs, they are misleading. Technically, they would mean deliberate influence over all attributes of a population, including its age-sex structure, geographical distribution, racial composition, genetic quality, and total size. No government attempts such full control. By tacit understanding, current population policies are concerned with only the *growth* and *size* of populations. These attributes, however, result from the death rate and migration as well as from the birth rate; their control would require deliberate influence over the factors giving rise to all three determinants. Actually, current policies labeled population control do not deal with mortality and migration, but deal only with the birth input. This is why another term, *fertility control,* is frequently used to describe current policies. But, as I show below, family planning (and hence current policy) does not undertake to influence most of the determinants of human reproduction. Thus the programs should not be referred to as population control or planning, because they do not attempt to influence the factors responsible for the attributes of human populations, taken generally; nor should they be called fertility control, because they do not try to affect most of the determinants of reproductive performance.

The ambiguity does not stop here, however. When one speaks of controlling population size, any inquiring person naturally asks, What is "control"? Who is to control whom? Precisely what population size, or what rate of population growth, is to be achieved? Do the policies aim to produce a growth rate that is nil, one that is very slight, or one that is like that of the industrial nations? Unless such questions are dealt with and clarified, it is impossible to evaluate current population policies.

The actual programs seem to be aiming simply to achieve a reduction in the birth rate. Success is therefore interpreted as the accomplishment of such a reduction, on the assumption that the reduction will lessen population growth. In those rare cases where a specific demographic aim is stated, the goal is said to be a short-run decline within a given period. The Pakistan plan adopted in 1966 (5, p. 889) aims to reduce the birth rate from 50 to 40 per thousand by 1970; the Indian plan (6) aims to reduce the rate from 40 to 25 "as soon as possible"; and the Korean aim (7) is to cut population growth from 2.9 to 1.2 percent by 1980. A significant feature of such stated aims is the rapid population growth they would permit. Under conditions of modern mortality, a crude birth rate of 25 to 30 per thousand will represent such a multiplication of people as to make use of the term *population control* ironic. A rate of increase of 1.2 percent per year would allow South Korea's already dense population to double in less than 60 years.

One can of course defend the programs by saying that the present goals and measures are merely interim ones. A start must be made somewhere. But we do not find this answer in the population-policy literature. Such a defense, if convincing, would require a presentation of the *next* steps, and these are not considered. One suspects that the entire question of goals is instinctively left vague because thorough limitation of population growth would run counter to national and group aspirations. A consideration of hypothetical goals throws further light on the matter.

Industrialized nations as the model. Since current policies are confined to family planning, their maximum demographic effect would be to give the underdeveloped countries the same level of reproductive performance that the industrial nations now have. The latter, long oriented toward family planning, provide a good yardstick for determining what the availability of contraceptives can do to population growth. Indeed, they provide more than a yardstick; they are actually the model which inspired the present population policies.

What does this goal mean in practice? Among the advanced nations there is considerable diversity in the level of fertility (8). At one extreme are countries such as New Zealand, with an average gross reproduction rate (GRR) of 1.91 during the period 1960-64; at the other extreme are countries such as Hungary, with a rate of 0.91 during the same period. To a considerable extent, however, such divergencies are matters of timing. The birth rates of most industrial nations have shown, since about 1940, a wave-like movement, with no secular trend.

The average level of reproduction during this long period has been high enough to give these countries, with their low mortality, an extremely rapid population growth. If this level is maintained, their population will double in just over 50 years—a rate higher than that of world population growth at any time prior to 1950, at which time the growth in numbers of human beings was already considered fantastic. The advanced nations are suffering acutely from the effects of rapid population growth in combination with the production of ever more goods per person (9). A rising share of their supposedly high per capita income, which itself draws increasingly upon the resources of the underdeveloped countries (who fall farther behind in relative economic position), is spent simply to meet the costs, and alleviate the nuisances, of the unrelenting production of more and more goods by more people. Such facts indicate that the industrial nations provide neither a suitable demographic model for the nonindustrial peoples to follow nor the leadership to plan and organize effective population-control for them.

Zero population growth as a goal. Most discussions of the population crisis lead logically to zero population growth as the ultimate goal, because *any* growth rate, if continued, will eventually use up the earth. Yet hardly ever do arguments for population policy consider such a goal, and current policies do not dream of it. Why not? The answer is evidently that zero population growth is unacceptable to most nations and to most religious and ethnic communities. To argue for this goal would be to alienate possible support for action programs.

Goal peculiarities inherent in family planning. Turning to the actual measures taken, we see that the very use of family planning as the means for implementing population policy poses serious but unacknowledged limits on the intended reduction in fertility. The family-planning movement, clearly devoted to the improvement and dissemination of contraceptive devices, states again and again that its purpose is that of enabling couples to have the number of children they want. "The opportunity to decide the number and spacing of children is a basic human right," say the 12 heads of state in the United Nations declaration. The 1965 Turkish Law Concerning Population Planning declares (10):

Article 1. Population Planning means that individuals can have as many children as they wish, whenever they want to. This can be ensured through preventive measures taken against pregnancy. . . .

Logically, it does not make sense to use *family* planning to provide *national* population control or planning. The "planning" in family planning is that of each separate couple. The only control they exercise is control over the size of *their* family. Obviously, couples do not plan the size of the nation's population, any more than they plan the growth of the national income or the form of the highway network. There is no reason to expect that the millions of decisions about family size made by couples in their own interest will automatically control population for the benefit of society. On the contrary, there are good reasons to think they will not do so. At most, family planning can reduce reproduction to the extent that unwanted births exceed wanted births. In industrial countries the balance is often negative—that is, people have fewer children as a rule than they would like to have. In underdeveloped countries the reverse is normally true, but the elimination of unwanted births would still leave an extremely high rate of multiplication.

Actually, the family-planning movement does not pursue even the limited goals it professes. It does not fully empower couples to have only the number of offspring they want because it either condemns or disregards certain tabooed but nevertheless effective means to this goal. One of its tenets is that "there shall be freedom of choice of method so that individuals can choose in accordance with the dictates of their consciences" (11), but in practice this amounts to limiting the individual's choice, because the "conscience" dictating the method is usually not his but that of religious and government officials. Moreover, not every individual may choose: even the so-called recommended methods are ordinarily not offered to single women, or not all offered to women professing a given religious faith.

Thus, despite its emphasis on technology, current policy does not utilize all available means of contraception, much less all birth-control measures. The Indian government wasted valuable years in the early stages of its population-control program by experimenting exclusively with the "rhythm" method, long after this technique had been demonstrated to be one of the least effective. A greater limitation on means is the exclusive emphasis on contraception itself. Induced abortion, for example, is one of the surest means of controlling reproduction, and one that has been proved capable of reducing birth rates rapidly. It seems peculiarly suited to the threshold stage of a population-control program —the stage when new conditions of life first make large families disadvantageous. It was the principal factor in the halving of the Japanese birth rate, a major factor in the declines in birth rate of East-European satellite countries after legalization of abortions in the early 1950s, and an important factor in the reduction of fertility in industrializing nations from 1870 to the 1930s (12). Today, according to *Studies in Family Planning* (13), "abortion is probably the foremost method of birth control throughout Latin America." Yet this method is rejected in nearly all national and international population-control programs. American foreign aid is used to help *stop* abortion (14). The United Nations excludes abortion from family planning, and in fact justifies the latter by presenting it as a means of combating abortion (15). Studies of abortion are being made in Latin America under the presumed auspices of population-control groups, not with the intention of legalizing it and thus making it safe, cheap, available, and hence more effective for population control, but with the avowed purpose of reducing it (16).

Although few would prefer abortion to efficient contraception (other things being equal), the fact is that both permit a woman to control the size of her family. The main drawbacks to abortion arise from its illegality. When performed, as a legal procedure, by a skilled physician, it is safer than childbirth. It does not compete with contraception but serves as a backstop when the latter fails or when contraceptive devices or information are not available. As contraception becomes customary, the incidence of abortion recedes even without its being banned. If, therefore, abortions enable women to have only the number of children they want, and if family planners do not advocate—in fact decry—legalization of abortion, they are to that extent denying the central tenet of their own movement. The irony of anti-abortionism in family-planning circles is seen particularly in hair-splitting arguments over whether or not some contraceptive agent (for example, the IUD) is in reality an abortifacient. A Mexican leader in family planning writes (17):

One of the chief objectives of our program in Mexico is to prevent abortions. If we could be sure that the mode of action (of the IUD) was not interference with nidification, we could easily use the method in Mexico.

The questions of sterilization and unnatural forms of sexual intercourse usually meet with similar silent treatment or disapproval, although nobody doubts the effectiveness of these measures in avoiding conception. Sterilization has proved popular in Puerto Rico and has had some vogue in India (where the new health minister hopes to make it compulsory for those with a certain number of children), but in both these areas it has been for the most part ignored or condemned by the family-planning movement.

On the side of goals, then, we see that a family-planning orientation limits the aims of current population policy. Despite reference to "population control" and "fertility control," which presumably means determination of demographic results by and for the nation as a whole, the movement gives control only to couples, and does this only if they use "respectable" contraceptives.

The Neglect of Motivation

By sanctifying the doctrine that each woman should have the number of children she wants, and by assuming that if she has only that number this will automatically curb population growth to the necessary degree, the leaders of current policies escape the necessity of asking why women desire so many children and how this desire can be influenced (18, p. 41; 19). Instead, they claim that satisfactory motivation is shown by the popular desire (shown by opinion surveys in all countries) to have the means of family limitation, and that therefore the problem is one of inventing and distributing the best possible contraceptive devices. Overlooked is the fact that a desire for availability of contraceptives is compatible with *high* fertility.

Given the best of means, there remain the questions of how many children couples want and of whether this is the requisite number from the standpoint of population size. That it is not is indicated by continued rapid population growth in industrial countries, and by the very surveys showing that people want contraception—for these show, too, that people also want numerous children.

The family planners do not ignore motivation. They are forever talking about "attitudes" and "needs." But they pose the issue in terms of the "acceptance" of birth control devices. At the most naive level, they assume that lack of acceptance is a function of the contraceptive device itself. This reduces the motive problem to a technological question. The task of population control then becomes simply the invention of a device that *will* be acceptable (20). The plastic IUD is acclaimed because, once in place, it does not depend on repeated *acceptance* by the woman, and thus it "solves" the problem of motivation (21).

But suppose a woman does not want to use *any* contraceptive until after she has had four children. This is the type of question that is seldom raised in the family-planning literature. In that literature, wanting a specific number of children is taken as complete motivation, for it implies a wish to control the size of one's family. The problem woman, from the standpoint of family planners, is the one who wants "as many as come," or "as many as God sends." Her attitude is construed as due to ignorance and "cultural values," and the policy deemed necessary to change it is "education." No compulsion can be used, because the movement is committed to free choice, but movie strips, posters, comic books, public lectures, interviews, and discussions are in order. These supply information and supposedly change values by discounting superstitions and showing that unrestrained procreation is harmful to both mother and children. The effort is considered successful when the woman decides she wants only a certain number of children and uses an effective contraceptive.

In viewing negative attitudes toward birth control as due to ignorance, apathy, and outworn tradition, and "mass-communication" as the solution to the motivation problem (22), family planners tend to ignore the power and complexity of social life. If it were admitted that the creation and care of new human beings is socially motivated, like other forms of behavior, by being a part of the system of rewards and punishments that is built into human relationships, and thus is bound up with the individual's economic and personal interests, it would be apparent that the social structure and economy must be changed before a deliberate reduction in the birth rate can be achieved. As it is, reliance on family planning allows people to feel that "something is being done about the population problem" without the need for painful social changes.

Designation of population control as a medical or public health task leads to a similar evasion. This categorization assures popular support because it puts population policy in the hands of respected medical personnel, but, by the same token, it gives responsibility for leadership to people who think in terms of clinics and patients, of pills and IUD's, and who bring to the handling of economic and social phenomena a self-confident naiveté. The study of social organization is a technical field; an action program based on intuition is no more apt to succeed in the control of human beings than it is in the area of bacterial or viral control. Moreover, to alter a social system, by deliberate policy, so as to regulate births in accord with the demands of the collective welfare would require political power, and this is not likely to inhere in public health officials, nurses, midwives, and social workers. To entrust population policy to them is "to take action," but not dangerous "effective action."

Similarly, the Janus-faced position on birth-control technology represents an escape from the necessity, and onus, of grappling with the social and economic determinants of reproductive behavior. On the one side, the rejection or avoidance of religiously tabooed but otherwise effective means of birth prevention enables the family-planning movement to avoid official condemnation. On the other side, an intense preoccupation with contraceptive technology (apart from the tabooed means) also helps the family planners to avoid censure. By implying that the only need is the invention and distribution of effective devices, they allay fears, on the part of religious and governmental officials, that fundamental changes in social organization are contemplated. Changes basic enough to affect motivation for having children would be changes in the structure of the family, in the position of women, and in the sexual mores. Far from proposing such radicalism, spokesmen for family planning frequently state their purpose as "protection" of the family—that is, closer observance of family norms. In addition, by concentrating on *new* and *scientific* contraceptives, the movement escapes taboos attached to old ones (the Pope will hardly authorize the condom, but may sanction the pill) and allows family planning to be regarded as a branch of medicine: over-population becomes a disease, to be treated by a pill or a coil.

We thus see that the inadequacy of current population policies with respect to motivation is inherent in their overwhelmingly family-planning character.

Since family planning is by definition private planning, it eschews any societal control over motivation. It merely furnishes the means, and, among possible means, only the most respectable. Its leaders, in avoiding social complexities and seeking official favor, are obviously activated not solely by expediency but also by their own sentiments as members of society and by their background as persons attracted to the family-planning movement. Unacquainted for the most part with technical economics, sociology, and demography, they tend honestly and instinctively to believe that something they vaguely call population control can be achieved by making better contraceptives available.

The Evidence of Ineffectiveness

If this characterization is accurate, we can conclude that current programs will not enable a government to control population size. In countries where couples have numerous offspring that they do not want, such programs may possibly accelerate a birth-rate decline that would occur anyway, but the conditions that cause births to be wanted or unwanted are beyond the control of family planning, hence beyond the control of any nation which relies on family planning alone as its population policy.

This conclusion is confirmed by demographic facts. As I have noted above, the widespread use of family planning in industrial countries has not given their governments control over the birth rate. In backward countries today, taken as a whole, birth rates are rising, not falling; in those with population policies, there is no indication that the government is controlling the rate of reproduction. The main "successes" cited in the well-publicized policy literature are cases where a large number of contraceptives have been distributed or where the program has been accompanied by some decline in the birth rate. Popular enthusiasm for family planning is found mainly in the cities, or in advanced countries such as Japan and Taiwan, where the people would adopt contraception in any case, program or no program. It is difficult to prove that present population policies have even speeded up a lowering of the birth rate (the least that could have been expected), much less that they have provided national "fertility control."

Let us next briefly review the facts concerning the level and trend of population in underdeveloped nations generally, in order to understand the magnitude of the task of genuine control.

Rising Birthrates in Underdeveloped Countries

In ten Latin-American countries, between 1940 and 1959 (23), the average birth rates (age-standardized), as estimated by our research office at the University of California, rose as follows: 1940-44, 43.4 annual births per 1000 population; 1945-49, 44.6; 1950-54, 46.4; 1955-59, 47.7.

In another study made in our office, in which estimating methods derived from the theory of quasi-stable populations were used, the recent trend was found to be upward in 27 underdeveloped countries, downward in six, and unchanged in one (24). Some of the rises have been substantial, and most have occurred where the birth rate was already extremely high. For instance, the gross reproduction rate rose in Jamaica from 1.8 per thousand in 1947 to 2.7 in 1960; among the natives of Fiji, from 2.0 in 1951 to 2.4 in 1964; and in Albania, from 3.0 in the period 1950-54 to 3.4 in 1960.

The general rise in fertility in backward regions is evidently not due to failure of population-control efforts, because most of the countries either have no such effort or have programs too new to show much effect. Instead, the rise is due, ironically, to the very circumstance that brought on the population crisis in the first place—to improved health and lowered mortality. Better health increases the probability that a woman will conceive and retain the fetus to term; lowered mortality raises the proportion of babies who survive to the age of reproduction and reduces the probability of widowhood during that age (25). The significance of the general rise in fertility, in the context of this discussion, is that it is giving would-be population planners a harder task than many of them realize. Some of the upward pressure on birth rates is independent of what couples do about family planning, for it arises from the fact that, with lowered mortality, there are simply more couples.

Underdeveloped Countries with Population Policies

In discussions of population policy there is often confusion as to which cases are relevant. Japan, for instance, has been widely praised for the effectiveness of its measures, but it is a very advanced industrial nation and, besides, its government policy had little or nothing to do with the decline in the birth rate, except unintentionally. It therefore offers no test of population policy under peasant-agrarian conditions. Another case of questionable relevance is that of Taiwan, because Taiwan is sufficiently developed to be placed in the urban-industrial class of nations. However, since Taiwan is offered as the main showpiece by the sponsors of current policies in under-developed areas, and since the data are excellent, it merits examination.

Taiwan is acclaimed as a showpiece because it has responded favorably to a highly organized program for distributing up-to-date contraceptives and has also had a rapidly dropping birthrate. Some observers have carelessly attributed the decline in birth rate—from 50.0 in 1951 to 32.7 in 1965—to the family-planning campaign (26), but the campaign began only in 1963 and could have affected only the end of the trend. Rather, the decline represents a response to modernization similar to that made by all countries that have become industrialized (27). By 1950 over half of Taiwan's population was urban, and by 1964 nearly two-thirds were urban, with 29 percent of the population living in cities of 100,000 or more. The pace of economic development has been extremely rapid. Between 1951 and 1963, per capita income increased by 4.05 percent per year. Yet the island is closely packed, having 870 persons per square mile (a population density higher than that of Belgium). The combination of fast economic growth and rapid population increase in limited space has put parents of large families at a relative disadvantage and has created a brisk demand for abortions and contraceptives. Thus the favorable response to the current campaign to encourage use of the IUD is not a good example of what birth-control technology can do for a genuinely backward country. In fact, when the program was started, one reason for expecting receptivity was that the island was already on its way to modernization and family planning (28).

At most, the recent family-planning campaign—which reached significant proportions only in 1964, when some 46,000 IUD's were inserted (in 1965 the number was 99,253, and in 1966, 111,242) (29; 30, p. 45)—could have caused the increase observable after 1963 in the rate of decline. Between 1951 and 1963 the average drop in the birth rate per 1000 women (see Table 1) was 1.73 percent per year; in the period 1964-66 it was 4.35 percent. But one hesitates to assign all of the acceleration in decline since 1963 to the family-planning campaign. The rapid economic development has been precisely of a type likely to accelerate a drop in reproduction. The rise in manufacturing has been much greater than the rise in either agriculture or construction. The agricultural labor force has thus been squeezed, and migration to the cities has skyrocketed (31). Since housing has not kept pace, urban families have had to restrict reproduction in order to take advantage of career opportunities and avoid domestic inconvenience. Such conditions have historically tended to accelerate a decline in birthrate. The most rapid decline came late in the United States (1921-33) and in Japan (1947-55). A plot of the Japanese and Taiwanese birth rates (Fig. 1) shows marked similarity of the two curves, despite a difference in level. All told, one should not attribute all of the post-1963 acceleration in the decline of Taiwan's birthrate to the family-planning campaign.

The main evidence that *some* of this acceleration is due to the campaign comes from the fact that Taichung, the city in which the family-planning effort was first concentrated, showed subsequently a much faster drop in fertility than other cities (30, p. 69; 32). But the campaign has not reached throughout the

TABLE 1: Decline in Taiwan's Fertility Rate, 1951 Through 1966.

Year	Registered births per 1000 women aged 15-49	Change in rate (percent)*
1951	211	
1952	198	−5.6
1953	194	−2.2
1954	193	−0.5
1955	197	+ 2.1
1956	196	−0.4
1957	182	−7.1
1958	185	+ 1.3
1959	184	−0.1
1960	180	−2.5
1961	177	−1.5
1962	174	−1.5
1963	170	−2.6
1964	162	−4.9
1965	152	−6.0
1966	149	−2.1

*The percentages were calculated on unrounded figures. Source of data through 1965, *Taiwan* Demographic Fact Book (1964, 1965); for 1966, *Monthly Bulletin of Population Registration Statistics of Taiwan* (1966, 1967).

FIGURE 1. Birth rates per 1000 women aged 15 through 49 in Japan and Taiwan.

island. By the end of 1966, only 260,745 women had been fitted with an IUD under auspices of the campaign, whereas the women of reproductive age on the island numbered 2.86 million. Most of the reduction in fertility has therefore been a matter of individual initiative. To some extent the campaign may be simply substituting sponsored (and cheaper) services for those that would otherwise come through private and commercial channels. An island-wide survey in 1964 showed that over 150,000 women were already using the traditional Ota ring (a metallic intrauterine device popular in Japan); almost as many had been sterilized; about 40,000 were using foam tablets; some 50,000 admitted to having had at least one abortion; and many were using other methods of birth control (30, pp. 18, 31).

The important question, however, is not whether the present campaign is somewhat hastening the downward trend in the birth rate but whether, even if it is, it will provide population control for the nation. Actually, the campaign is not designed to provide such control and shows no sign of doing so. It takes for granted existing reproductive goals. Its aim is "to integrate, through education and information, the idea of family limitation *within the existing attitudes, values, and goals* of the people" [30, p. 8 (italics mine)]. Its target is *married* women who do not want any more children; it ignores girls not yet married, and women married and wanting more children.

With such an approach, what is the maximum impact possible? It is the difference between the number of children women have been having and the number they want to have. A study in 1957 found a median figure of 3.75 for the number of children wanted by women aged 15 to 29 in Taipei, Taiwan's largest city; the corresponding figure for women from a satellite town was 3.93; for women from a fishing village, 4.90; and for women from a farming village, 5.03. Over 60 percent of the women in Taipei and over 90 percent of those in farming villages wanted 4 or more children (33). In a sample of wives aged 25 to 29 in Taichung, a city of over 300,000, Freedman and his co-workers found the average number of children wanted was 4; only 9 percent wanted less than 3, 20 percent wanted 5 or more (34). If, therefore, Taiwanese women used contraceptives that were 100 percent effective and had the number of children they desire, they would have about 4.5 each. The goal of the family-planning effort would be achieved. In the past the Taiwanese woman who married and lived through the reproductive period had, on the average, approximately 6.5 children; thus, a figure of 4.5 would represent a substantial decline in fertility. Since mortality would continue to decline, the population growth rate would decline somewhat less than individual reproduction would. With 4.5 births per woman and a life expectancy of 70 years, the rate of natural increase would be close to 3 percent per year (35).

In the future, Taiwanese views concerning reproduction will doubtless change, in response to social change and economic modernization. But how far will they change? A good indication is the number of children desired by couples in an already modernized country long oriented toward family planning. In the United States in 1966, an average of 3.4 children was considered ideal by white women aged 21 or over (36). This average number of births would give Taiwan, with only a slight decrease in mortality, a long-run rate of natural increase of 1.7 percent per year and a doubling of population in 41 years.

Detailed data confirm the interpretation that Taiwanese women are in the process of shifting from a "peasant-agrarian" to an "industrial" level of reproduction. They are, in typical fashion, cutting off higher-order births at age 30 and beyond (37). Among young wives, fertility has risen, not fallen. In sum, the widely acclaimed family-planning program in Taiwan may, at most, have somewhat speeded the later phase of fertility decline which would have occurred anyway because of modernization.

Moving down the scale of modernization, to countries most in need of population control, one finds the family-planning approach even more inadequate. In South Korea, second only to Taiwan in the frequency with which it is cited as a model of current policy, a recent birthrate decline of unknown extent is assumed by leaders to be due overwhelmingly to the government's family-planning program. However, it is just as plausible to say that the net effect of government involvement in population control has been, so far, to delay rather than hasten a decline in reproduction made inevitable by social and economic changes. Although the government is advocating vasectomies and providing IUD's and pills, it refuses to legalize abortions, despite the rapid rise in the rate of illegal abortions and despite the fact that, in a recent survey, 72 percent of the people who stated an opinion favored legalization. Also, the program is presented in the context of maternal and child health; it thus emphasizes motherhood and the family rather than alternative roles for women. Much is made of the fact that opinion surveys show an overwhelming majority of Koreans (89 percent in 1965) favoring contraception (38, p. 27), but this means only that Koreans are like other people in wishing to have the means to get what they want. Unfortunately, they want sizable families: "The records indicate that the program appeals mainly to women in the 30-39 year age bracket who have four or more children, including at least two sons . . ." (38, p. 25).

In areas less developed than Korea the degree of acceptance of contraception tends to be disappointing, especially among the rural majority. Faced with this discouragement, the leaders of current policy, instead of reexamining their assumptions, tend to redouble their effort to find a contraceptive that will appeal to the most illiterate peasant, forgetting that he wants a good-sized family. In the rural Punjab, for example, "a disturbing feature . . . is that the females start to seek advice and adopt family planning techniques at the fag end of their reproductive period" (39). Among 5196 women coming to rural Punjabi family-planning centers, 38 percent were over 35 years old, 67 percent over 30. These women had married early, nearly a third of them before the age of 15 (40); some 14 percent had eight or more *living* children when they reached the clinic, 51 percent six or more.

A survey in Tunisia showed that 68 percent of the married couples were willing to use birth-control measures, but the average number of children they considered ideal was 4.3 (41). The corresponding averages for a village in eastern Java, a village near New Delhi, and a village in Mysore were 4.3, 4.0, and 4.2, respectively (42, 43). In the cities of the regions women are more ready to accept birth control and they want fewer children than village women do, but the number they consider desirable is still wholly unsatisfactory from the standpoint of population control. In an urban family-planning center in Tunisia, more than 600 of 900 women accepting contraceptives had four living children already (44). In Bangalore, a city of nearly a million at the time (1952), the number of offspring desired by married women was 3.7 on the average; by married men, 4.1 (43). In the metropolitan area of San Salvador (350,000 inhabitants) a 1964 survey (45) showed the number desired by women of reproductive age to be 3.9, and in seven other capital cities of Latin America the number ranged from 2.7 to 4.2. If women in the cities of underdeveloped countries used birth-control measures with 100 percent efficiency, they would have enough babies to expand the city populations senselessly, quite apart from the added contribution of rural-urban migration. In many of the cities the difference between actual and ideal number of children is not great; for instance, in the seven Latin-American capitals mentioned above, the ideal was 3.4 whereas the actual births per women in the age range 35 to 39 was 3.7 (46). Bombay City has had birth-control clinics for many years, yet its birthrate (standardized for age, sex, and marital distribution) is still 34 per 1000 inhabitants and is tending to rise rather than fall. Although this rate is about 13 percent lower than that for India generally, it has been about that much lower since at least 1951 (47).

Is Family Planning the "First Step" in Population Control?

To acknowledge that family planning does not achieve population control is not to impugn its value for other purposes. Freeing women from the need to have more children than they want is of great benefit to them and their children and to society at large. My argument is therefore directed not against family-planning programs as such but against the assumption that they are an effective means of controlling population growth.

But what difference does it make? Why not go along for awhile with family planning as an initial approach to the problem of population control? The answer is that any policy on which millions of dollars are being spent should be designed to achieve the goal it purports to achieve. If it is only a first step, it should be so labeled, and its connection with the next step (and the nature of that next step) should be carefully explained. In the present case, since no "next step" seems ever to be mentioned, the question arises, Is reliance of family planning in fact a basis for dangerous postponement of effective steps? To continue to offer a remedy as a cure long after it has been shown merely to ameliorate the disease is either quackery or wishful thinking, and it thrives most where the need is greatest. Today the desire to solve the population problem is so intense that we are all ready to embrace any "action program" that promises relief. But postponement of effective measures allows the situation to worsen.

Unfortunately, the issue is confused by a matter of semantics. "Family *planning*" and "fertility *control*" suggest that reproduction is being regulated according to some rational plan. And so it is, but only from the standpoint of the individual couple, not from that of the community. What is rational in the light of a couple's situation may be totally irrational from the standpoint of society's welfare.

The need for societal regulation of individual behavior is readily recognized in other spheres—those of explosives, dangerous drugs, public property, natural resources. But in the sphere of reproduction, complete individual initiative is generally favored even by those liberal intellectuals who, in other spheres, most favor economic and social planning. Social reformers who would not hesitate to force all owners of rental property to rent to anyone who can pay, or to force all workers in an industry to join a union, balk at any suggestion that couples be permitted to have only a certain number of offspring. Invariably they interpret societal control of reproduction as meaning direct police supervision of individual behavior. Put the word *compulsory* in front of any term describing a means of limiting births—*compulsory sterilization, compulsory abortion, compulsory contraception*—and you guarantee violent opposition. Fortunately, such direct controls need not be invoked, but conservatives and radicals alike overlook this in their blind opposition to the idea of collective determination of a society's birth rate.

That the exclusive emphasis on family planning in current population policies is not a "first step" but an escape from the real issues is suggested by two facts. (i) No country has taken the "next step." The industrialized countries have had family planning for half a century without acquiring control over either the birth rate or population increase. (ii) Support and encouragement of research on population policy other than family planning is negligible. It is precisely this blocking of alternative thinking and experimentation that makes the emphasis on family planning a major obstacle to population control. The need is not to abandon family-planning programs but to put equal or greater resources into other approaches.

New Directions in Population Policy

In thinking about other approaches, one can start with known facts. In the past, all surviving societies had institutional incentives for marriage, procreation, and child care which were powerful enough to keep the birth rate equal to or in excess of a high death rate. Despite the drop in death rates during the last century and a half, the incentives tended to remain intact because the social structure (especially in regard to the family) changed little. At most, particularly in industrial societies, children became less productive and more expensive (48). In present-day agrarian societies, where the drop in death rate has been more recent, precipitate, and independent of social change (49), motivation for having children has changed little. Here, even more than in industrialized nations, the family has kept on producing abundant offspring, even though only a fraction of these children are now needed.

If excessive population growth is to be prevented, the obvious requirement is somehow to impose restraints on the family. However, because family roles are reinforced by society's system of rewards, punishments, sentiments, and norms, any proposal to demote the family is viewed as a threat by conservatives and liberals alike, and certainly by people with enough social responsibility to work for population control. One is charged with trying to "abolish" the family, but what is required is selective restructuring of the family in relation to the rest of society.

The lines of such restructuring are suggested by two existing limitations on fertility. (i) Nearly all societies succeed in drastically discouraging reproduction among unmarried women. (ii) Advanced societies unintentionally reduce reproduction among married women when conditions worsen in such a way as to penalize childbearing more severely than it was penalized before. In both cases the causes are motivational and economic rather than technological.

It follows that population-control policy can de-emphasize the family in two ways: (i) by keeping present controls over illegitimate childbirth yet making the most of factors that lead people to postpone or avoid marriage, and (ii) by instituting conditions that motivate those who do marry to keep their families small.

Postponement of Marriage

Since the female reproductive span is short and generally more fecund in its first than in its second half, postponement of marriage to ages beyond 20 tends biologically to reduce births. Sociologically, it gives women time to get a better eduction, acquire interests unrelated to the family, and develop a cautious attitude toward pregnancy (50). Individuals who have not married by the time they are in their late twenties often do not marry at all. For these reasons, for the world as a whole, the average age of marriage for women is negatively associated with the birth rate: a rising age at marriage is a frequent cause of declining fertility during the middle phase of the demographic transition; and, in the late phase, the "baby boom" is usually associated with a return to younger marriages.

Any suggestion that age at marriage be raised as a part of population policy is usually met with the argument that "even if a law were passed, it would not be obeyed." Interestingly, this objection implies that the only way to control the age at marriage is by direct legislation, but other factors govern the actual age. Roman Catholic countries generally follow canon law in stipulating 12 years as the minimum *legal* age at which girls may marry, but the actual average age at marriage in these countries (at least in Europe) is characteristically more like 25 to 28 years. The actual age is determined, not by law, but by social and economic conditions. In agrarian societies, postponement of marriage (when postponement occurs) is apparently caused by difficulties in meeting the economic prerequisite for matrimony, as stipulated by custom and opinion. In industrial societies it is caused by housing shortages, unemployment, the requirement for overseas military service, high costs of education, and inadequacy of consumer services. Since almost no research has been devoted to the subject, it is difficult to assess the relative weight of the factors that govern the age at marriage.

Encouraging Limitation of Births Within Marriage

As a means of encouraging the limitation of reproduction within marriage, as well as postponement of marriage, a greater rewarding of nonfamilial than of familial roles would probably help. A simple way of accomplishing this would be to allow economic advantages to accrue to the single as opposed to the married individual, and to the small as opposed to the large family. For instance, the government could pay people to permit themselves to be sterilized (51); all costs of abortion could be paid by the government; a substantial fee could be charged for a marriage license; a "child-tax" (52) could be levied; and there could be a requirement that illegitimate pregnancies be aborted. Less sensationally, governments could simply reverse some existing policies that encourage childbearing. They could, for example, cease taxing single persons more than married ones; stop giving parents special tax exemptions; abandon income-tax policy that discriminates against couples when the wife works; reduce paid maternity leaves; reduce family allowances (53); stop awarding public housing on the basis of family size;

stop granting fellowships and other educational aids (including special allowances for wives and children) to married students; cease outlawing abortions and sterilizations; and relax rules that allow use of harmless contraceptives only with medical permission. Some of these policy reversals would be beneficial in other than demographic respects and some would be harmful unless special precautions were taken. The aim would be to reduce the number, not the quality, of the next generation.

A closely related method of de-emphasizing the family would be modification of the complementarity of the roles of men and women. Men are now able to participate in the wider world yet enjoy the satisfaction of having several children because the housework and childcare fall mainly on their wives. Women are impelled to seek this role by their idealized view of marriage and motherhood and by either the scarcity of alternative roles or the difficulty of combining them with family roles. To change this situation women could be required to work outside the home, or compelled by circumstances to do so. If, at the same time, women were paid as well as men and given equal educational and occupational opportunities, and if social life were organized around the place of work rather than around the home or neighborhood, many women would develop interests that would compete with family interests. Approximately this policy is now followed in several Communist countries, and even the less developed of these currently have extremely low birthrates (54).

That inclusion of women in the labor force has a negative effect on reproduction is indicated by regional comparisons (18, p. 1195; 55). But in most countries the wife's employment is subordinate, economically and emotionally, to her family role, and is readily sacrificed for the latter. No society has restructured both the occupational system and the domestic establishment to the point of permanently modifying the old division of labor by sex.

In any deliberate effort to control the birth rate along these lines, a government has two powerful instruments—its command over economic planning and its authority (real or potential) over education. The first determines (as far as policy can) the economic conditions and circumstances affecting the lives of all citizens; the second provides the knowledge and attitudes necessary to implement the plans. The economic system largely determines who shall work, what can be bought, what rearing children will cost, how much individuals can spend. The schools define family roles and develop vocational and recreational interests; they could, if it were desired, redefine the sex roles, develop interests that transcend the home, and transmit realistic (as opposed to moralistic) knowledge concerning marriage, sexual behavior, and population problems. When the problem is viewed in this light, it is clear that the ministries of economics and education, not the ministry of health, should be the source of population policy.

The Dilemma of Population Policy

It should now be apparent why, despite strong anxiety over runaway population growth, the actual programs purporting to control it are limited to family planning and are therefore ineffective. (i) The goal of zero, or even slight, population growth is one that nations and groups find difficult to accept. (ii) The measures that would be required to implement such a goal, though not so revolutionary as a Brave New World or a Communist Utopia, nevertheless tend to offend most people reared in existing societies. As a consequence, the goal of so-called population control is implicit and vague; the method is only family planning. This method, far from de-emphasizing the family, is familistic. One of its stated goals is that of helping sterile couples to *have* children. It stresses parental aspirations and responsibilities. It goes along with most aspects of conventional morality, such as condemnation of abortion, disapproval of premarital intercourse, respect for religious teachings and cultural taboos, and obeisance to medical and clerical authority. It deflects hostility by refusing to recommend any change other than the one it stands for: availability of contraceptives.

The things that make family planning acceptable are the very things that make it ineffective for population control. By stressing the right of parents to have the number of children they want, it evades the basic question of population policy, which is how to give societies the number of children they need. By offering only the means for *couples* to control fertility, it neglects the means for societies to do so.

Because of the predominantly pro-family character of existing societies, individual interest ordinarily leads to the production of enough offspring to constitute rapid population growth under conditions of low mortality. Childless or single-child homes are considered indicative of personal failure, whereas having three to five living children gives a family a sense of continuity and substantiality (56).

Given the existing desire to have moderate-sized rather than small families, the only countries in which fertility has been reduced to match reduction in mortality are advanced ones temporarily experiencing worsened economic conditions. In Sweden, for instance, the net reproduction rate (NRR) has been below replacement for 34 years (1930-63), if the period is taken as a whole, but this is because of the economic depression. The average replacement rate was below unity (NRR = 0.81) for the period 1930-42, but from 1942 through 1963 it was above unity (NRR = 1.08). Hardships that seem particularly conducive to deliberate lowering of the birth rate are (in managed economies) scarcity of housing and other consumer goods despite full employment, and required high participation of women in the labor force, or (in freer economies) a great deal of unemployment and economic insecurity. When conditions are good, any nation tends to have a growing population.

It follows that, in countries where contraception is used, a realistic proposal for a government policy of lowering the birthrate reads like a catalogue of horrors: squeeze consumers through taxation and inflation; make housing very scarce by limiting construction; force wives and mothers to work outside the home to offset the inadequacy of male wages, yet provide few childcare facilities; encourage migration to the city by paying low wages in the country and providing few rural jobs; increase congestion in cities by starving the transit system; increase personal insecurity by encouraging conditions that produce unemployment and by haphazard political arrests. No government will institute such hardships simply for the purpose of controlling population growth. Clearly, therefore, the task of contemporary population policy is to develop attractive substitutes for family interests, so as to avoid having to turn to hardship as a corrective. The specific measures required for developing such substitutes are not easy to determine in the absence of research on the question.

In short, the world's population problem cannot be solved by pretense and wishful thinking. The unthinking identification of family planning with population control is an ostrich-like approach in that it permits people to hide from themselves the enormity and unconventionality of the task. There is no reason to abandon family-planning programs; contraception is a valuable technological instrument. But such programs must be supplemented with equal or greater investments in research and experimentation to determine the required socioeconomic measures.

REFERENCES AND NOTES

1. *Studies in Family Planning, No. 16* (1967).
2. *Ibid., No. 9* (1966), p. 1.
3. The statement is given in *Studies in Family Planning (I*, p. 1), and in *Population Bull.* 23, 6 (1967).
4. The statement is quoted in *Studies in Family Planning* (*I*, p. 2).
5. *Hearings on S. 1676, U.S. Senate, Subcommittee on Foreign Aid Expenditures, 89th Congress, Second Session, April 7, 8, 11* (1966), pt. 4.
6. B. L. Raina, in *Family Planning and Population Programs.* B. Berelson, R. K. Anderson, O. Harkavy, G. Maier, W. P. Mauldin, S. G. Segal, Eds. (Univ. of Chicago Press, Chicago, 1966).
7. D. Kirk, *Ann. Amer. Acad. Polit. Soc. Sci.* 369, 53 (1967).
8. As used by English-speaking demographers, the world *fertility* designates actual reproductive performance, not a theoretical capacity.
9. K. Davis, *Rotarian* 94, 10 (1959); *Health Educ. Monographs* 9, 2 (1960); L. Day and A. Day, *Too Many Americans* (Houghton Mifflin, Boston, 1964); R. A. Piddington, *Limits of Mankind* (Wright, Bristol, England, 1956).
10. *Official Gazette* (15 Apr. 1965); quoted in *Studies in Family Planning* (*I*, p. 7).
11. J. W. Gardner, Secretary of Health, Education, and Welfare, "Memorandum to Heads of Operating Agencies" (Jan. 1966), reproduced in *Hearings on S. 1676 (5),* p. 783.
12. C. Tietze, *Demography* 1, 119 (1964); *J. Chronic Diseases* 18, 1161 (1964); M. Muramatsu, *Milbank Mem. Fund Quart.* 38, 153 (1960); K. Davis, *Population Index* 29, 345 (1963); R. Armijo and T. Monreal, *J. Sex Res.* 1964, 143 (1964); Proceedings World Population Conference, Belgrade, 1965; Proceedings International Planned Parenthood Federation.
13. *Studies in Family Planning, No. 4* (1964), p. 3.
14. D. Bell (then administrator for Agency for International Development), in *Hearings on S. 1676 (5),* p. 862.
15. *Asian Population Conference* (United Nations, New York, 1964), p. 30.
16. R. Armijo and T. Monreal, in *Components of Population Change in Latin America* (Milbank Fund, New York, 1965), p. 272; E. Rice-Wray, *Amer. J. Public Health* 54, 313 (1964).
17. E. Rice-Wray, in "Intra-Uterine Contraceptive Devices," *Excerpta Med. Intern. Congr. Ser. No. 54* (1962), p. 135.
18. J. Blake, in *Public Health and Population Change,* M. C. Sheps and J. C. Ridley, Eds. (Univ. of Pittsburgh Press, Pittsburgh, 1965).
19. J. Blake and K. Davis, *Amer. Behavioral Scientist,* 5, 24 (1963).
20. See "Panel discussion on comparative acceptability of different methods of contraception," in *Research in Family Planning,* C. V. Kiser, Ed. (Princeton Univ. Press, Princeton, 1962), pp. 373-86.
21. "From the point of view of the woman concerned, the whole problem of continuing motivation disappears, . . ." [D. Kirk, in *Population Dynamics,* M. Muramatsu and P. A. Harper, Eds. (Johns Hopkins Press, Baltimore, 1965)].
22. "For influencing family size norms, certainly the examples and statements of public figures are of great significance . . . also . . . use of mass-communication methods which help to legitimize the small-family style, to provoke conversation, and to establish a vocabulary for discussion of family planning." [M. W. Freymann, in *Population Dynamics,* M. Muramatsu and P. A. Harper, Eds. (Johns Hopkins Press, Baltimore, 1965)].
23. O. A. Collver, *Birth Rates in Latin America* (International Population and Urban Research, Berkeley, Calif., 1965), pp. 27-28; the ten countries were Colombia, Costa Rica, El Salvador, Ecuador, Guatemala, Honduras, Mexico, Panamá, Peru, and Venezuela.
24. J. R. Rele, *Fertility Analysis through Extension of Stable Population Concepts.* (International Population and Urban Research, Berkeley, Calif., 1967).
25. J. C. Ridley, M. C. Sheps, J. W. Lingner, J. A. Menken, *Milbank Mem. Fund Quart.* 45, 77 (1967); E. Arriaga, unpublished paper.

26. "South Korea and Taiwan appear successfully to have checked population growth by the use of intrauterine contraceptive devices" [U. Borell, *Hearings on S. 1676* (5), p. 556].
27. K. Davis, *Population Index* 29, 345 (1963).
28. R. Freedman, *ibid.* 31, 421 (1965).
29. Before 1964 the Family Planning Association had given advice to fewer than 60,000 wives in 10 years and a Pre-Pregnancy Health Program had reached some 10,000, and, in the current campaign, 3650 IUD's were inserted in 1965, in a total population of 2 1/2 million women of reproductive age. See *Studies in Family Planning No. 19* (1967), p. 4, and R. Freedman *et al., Population Studies* 16, 231 (1963).
30. R. W. Gillespie, *Family Planning on Taiwan* (Population Council, Taichung, 1965).
31. During the period 1950-60 the ratio of growth in the city to growth of the noncity population was 5:3; during the period 1960-64 the ratio was 5:2; these ratios are based on data of Shaohsing Chen, *J. Sociol. Taiwan* 1, 74 (1963) and data in the United Nations *Demographic Yearbooks.*
32. R. Freedman, *Population Index* 31, 434 (1965). Taichung's rate of decline in 1963-64 was roughly double the average in four other cities, whereas just prior to the campaign its rate of decline had been much less than theirs.
33. S. H. Chen, *J. Soc. Sci. Taipei* 13, 72 (1963).
34. R. Freedman *et al., Population Studies* 16, 227 (1963); *ibid.,* p. 232.
35. In 1964 the life expectancy at birth was already 66 years in Taiwan, as compared to 70 for the United States.
36. J. Blake, *Eugenics Quart.* 14, 68 (1967).
37. Women accepting IUD's in the family-planning program are typically 30 to 34 years old and have already had four children. [*Studies in Family Planning No. 19* (1967), p. 5].
38. Y. K. Cha, in *Family Planning and Population Programs,* B. Berelson *et al.,* Eds. (Univ. of Chicago Press, Chicago, 1966).
39. H. S. Ayalvi and S. S. Johl, *J. Family Welfare* 12, 60 (1965).
40. Sixty percent of the women had borne their first child before age 19. Early marriage is strongly supported by public opinion. Of couples polled in the Punjab, 48 percent said that girls *should* marry before age 16, and 94 percent said they should marry before age 20 (H. S. Ayalvi and S. S. Johl, *ibid.,* p. 57). A study of 2380 couples in 60 villages of Uttar Pradesh found that the women had consummated their marriage at an average age of 14.6 years [J. R. Rele, *Population Studies* 15, 268 (1962)].
41. J. Morsa, in *Family Planning and Population Programs,* B. Berelson *et al.,* Eds. (Univ. of Chicago Press, Chicago, 1966).
42. H. Gille and R. J. Pardoko, *ibid.,* p. 515; S. N. Agarwala, *Med. Dig. Bombay* 4, 653 (1961).
43. *Mysore Population Study* (United Nations, New York, 1961), p. 140.
44. A. Daly, in *Family Planning and Population Programs,* B. Berelson *et al.,* Eds. (Univ. of Chicago Press, Chicago, 1966).
45. C. J. Goméz, paper presented at the World Population Conference, Belgrade, 1965.
46. C. Miro, in *Family Planning and Population Programs,* B. Berelson *et al.,* Eds. (Univ. of Chicago Press, Chicago, 1966).
47. *Demographic Training and Research Centre (India) Newsletter* 20, 4 (Aug. 1966).
48. K. Davis, *Population Index* 29, 345 (1963). For economic and sociological theory of motivation for having children, see J. Blake [Univ. of California (Berkeley)], in preparation.
49. K. Davis, *Amer. Economic Rev.* 46, 305 (1956); *Sci. Amer.* 209, 68 (1963).
50. J. Blake, *World Population Conference [Belgrade, 1965]* (United Nations, New York, 1967), vol. 2, pp. 132-36.
51. S. Enke, *Rev. Economics Statistics* 42, 175 (1960);———, *Econ. Develop. Cult. Change* 8, 339 (1960);———, *ibid.* 10, 427 (1962); A. O. Krueger and L. A. Sjaastad, *ibid.,* p. 423.
52. T. J. Samuel, *J. Family Welfare India* 13, 12 (1966).
53. Sixty-two countries, including 27 in Europe, give cash payments to people for having children [U.S. Social Security Administration, *Social Security Programs Throughout the World, 1967* (Government Printing Office, Washington, D.C., 1967), pp. xxvii-xxviii].
54. Average gross reproduction rates in the early 1960's were as follows: Hungary, 0.91; Bulgaria, 1.09; Romania, 1.15; Yugoslavia, 1.32.
55. O. A. Collver and E. Langlois, *Econ. Develop. Cult. Change* 10, 367 (1962); J. Weeks, [Univ. of California (Berkeley)], unpublished paper.
56. Roman Catholic textbooks condemn the "small" family (one with fewer than four children as being abnormal [J. Blake, *Population Studies* 20, 27 (1966)].
57. Judith Blake's critical readings and discussions have greatly helped in the preparation of this article.

61   **Parenthood**
                         Right or Privilege?

GARRETT HARDIN

Birth control is not population control. Individual goals, not community needs, motivate individual actions. In every nation women want more children than the community needs.

How can we reduce reproduction? Persuasion must be tried first. Tomorrow's mothers must be educated to seek careers other than multiple motherhood. Community nurseries are needed to free women for careers outside the home. Mild coercion may soon be accepted—for example, tax rewards for reproductive nonproliferation.

But in the long run a purely voluntary system selects for its own failure: noncooperators outbreed cooperators. So what restraints shall we employ? A policeman under every bed? Jail sentences? Compulsory abortion? Infanticide? . . . Memories of Nazi Germany rise and obscure our vision.

We need not titillate our minds with such horrors, for we already have at hand an acceptable technology: sterilization. The taboo on this subject is fast dissolving, thanks to Arthur Godfrey and Paul Ehrlich, who have confessed their sterilizations in public. Fear (mostly unjustified) about the safety of the "pill" has motivated multitudes to follow in their footsteps.

It should be easy to limit a woman's reproduction by sterilizing her at the birth of her nth child. Is this a shocking idea? If so, try this "thought-experiment": let $n = 20$. Since this is not shocking, let n diminish until population control is achievable. The Women's Liberation Movement may not like it, but control must be exerted through females. Divorce and remarriage play havoc with assigning responsibility to couples or to men. Biology makes women responsible.

Many who want no third child would fight resolutely for the freedom to have that which they do not want. But what is freedom? Hegel said that "Freedom is the recognition of necessity." People need to recognize that population control is needed to protect the quality of life for our children.

The "right" to breed implies *ownership* of children. This concept is no longer tenable. Society pays an ever larger share of the cost of raising and educating children. The idea of ownership is surely affected by the thrust of the saying that "He who pays the piper calls the tune." On a biological level the idea of ownership of children has not been defensible for almost a century, not since August Weismann drew his celebrated diagram of the relationship of germ plasm to somatoplasm.

Biologically, all that I give "my" child is a set of chromosomes. Are they *my* chromosomes? Hardly. Sequestered in the germinal area long before *my* birth, "my" gonadal chromosomes have lived a life of their own, beyond my control. Mutation has altered them. In reproduction, "my" germ plasm is assembled in a new combination and mixed with another assortment with a similar history. "My" child's germ plasm is not *mine;* it is really only part of the community's store. I was merely the temporary custodian of part of it.

If parenthood is a right, population control is impossible. If parenthood is only a privilege, and if parents see themselves as trustees of the germ plasm and guardians of the rights of future generations, then there is hope for mankind.

Faith and Birthrates

Do Roman Catholic Countries Have   **62**
the Highest Birthrates?

POPULATION REFERENCE BUREAU, INC.

Recently the Population Reference Bureau released a 1968 "World Population Data Sheet" containing up-to-date demographic information for 136 countries. This information was widely reported by the press. Amid the commentary,
however, an old misconception reappeared—namely, that Roman Catholic countries have the world's highest birthrates. Typical was one editorial which said:
"The birth rate in the 'havenot' and Catholic nations soars while the literacy rate
and per capita income level remain stagnant."

Several errors cloud this brief statement. Not only do United Nations figures
show that birth rates are not soaring anywhere in the world, but many Roman
Catholic nations have achieved some of the lowest such rates on record. Furthermore, per capita incomes in European Catholic nations range from $350 to
$1,500; their weighted average is higher than per capita income in all but a very
few countries of non-Catholic Asia or Africa. And if the literacy rate remains
stagnant in most of Europe's Catholic countries, it is mainly because they con-
quered illiteracy long ago.

The big difference between high and low birthrate nations, according to
demographers, is not whether they are Catholic or non-Catholic but whether they
are economically underdeveloped or advanced. In the advanced countries of the
West, the industrial revolution spurred a gradual reduction of mortality and a
gradual spread of literacy—two trends followed by a slow, spontaneous decline
in birthrates. As a rule this downtrend in natality proceeded only a generation
or so after the drop in mortality, and the excess of births over deaths was therefore

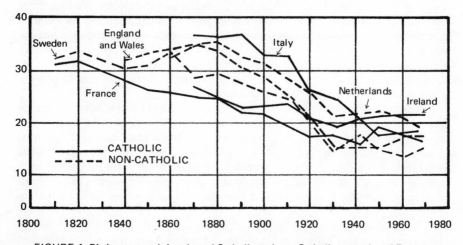

FIGURE 1. Birth rate trends in selected Catholic and non-Catholic countries of Europe.

not great enough to cause a "population explosion" in the sense of that term today. The annual rate of population growth in Europe in the nineteenth century never reached 1 percent a year. In some developing countries today, growth exceeds 3 percent. This contrast is strikingly shown in Figure 2, which compares trends in births and deaths in highly developed Sweden and still developing Mexico.

Despite such discrepancies, some observers have speculated that a European-style demographic transition will occur in the underdeveloped countries. The facts, however, run contrary to such an assumption.

In the economically depressed regions of Asia, Africa and Latin America, two demographic realities stand out as distinctly different from their counterparts in the West. First, illiteracy remains very high, and in many countries the number of illiterates is actually growing. No widespread or marked decline in birth rates has ever been recorded under such conditions. Secondly, the death rate in these regions has been drastically reduced within just a few decades through a highly effective infusion of modern public health techniques. People there have not had time to adjust to the fact that many more children and adults are surviving than before, and they continue to produce babies at a very high rate. This widening gap between births and deaths is the direct cause of the world's accelerating population growth. It can be seen in both Catholic and non-Catholic nations. But so can the modern pattern of low death rates and *low* birth rates be seen in both Catholic and non-Catholic nations.

The European Example

Europe offers a clear example of modern demographic trends. What is the impact of Roman Catholicism on the birthrates there?

Based on population, the Roman Catholic countries of Europe are Ireland, Austria, Belgium, France, Luxembourg, Czechoslovakia, Hungary, Poland, Italy, Portugal and Spain. (West Germany, with a population evenly divided between Catholics and Protestants, is not counted in this tabulation.) Experts within the Catholic Church, the World Council of Churches and the United Nations differ markedly in their definitions of a Catholic country. Some rule out any nation with a communist government, others accept certain communist governments but not all, and still others accept any nation in which over half the people are Roman Catholics. We have used this last definition because it leads to the fewest contradictions and because in Europe, at least, birth rates have run counter to government policy as often as they have reflected it.

Taken together, the 11 Roman Catholic countries of Europe have an average annual birth rate of only 18.1 babies per 1,000 people. The birth rate for the 15 non-Roman Catholic countries averages out to virtually the same: 18.0. In short, there is no evidence in Europe for the widely-held belief that Roman Catholic ism exerts a buoyant force on overall birthrates. Even when compared by a more sensitive gauge of natality—birthrates specifically for women in the child-bearing ages of 15-44—Catholic and non-Catholic nations are very much alike (Figure 3).

Looking at the statistics in more detail, one finds that considerably lower-than-average natality rates occur in the three European countries where branches

FIGURE 2. Natural increase trends, Sweden vs. Mexico.

of the Greek Orthodox Catholic religion claim a majority following. For these countries—Romania, Bulgaria and Greece—the average birth rate is only 15.4. Three nations with heavily Roman Catholic populations—Ireland, Portugal and Spain—are among the least industrialized in Europe, but even they have birth rates just barely above the low European average of 18.0. And they are low indeed when compared with the figures of 35 to 50 that prevail in Asia, Africa and Latin America.

Particularly interesting are two countries at the extremes of Europe's birth-rate spectrum, both under communist control. Roman Catholic Hungary, where abortions are easily and legally obtained, has the world's lowest birth rate at 13.6, while non-Catholic Albania's rate is a lofty 34.0. Abortions, incidentally, are legal merely on the grounds of a woman's wishes in Hungary and Bulgaria; they are legal for a liberal variety of medical, eugenic and social reasons in Czechoslovakia, Poland, Yugoslavia, Norway, Sweden, Iceland, Denmark and Finland; they are harder to get but still permissible in Switzerland, Romania, East Germany and the United Kingdom; they are severely limited to urgent medical reasons in West Germany, Italy, Greece, the Netherlands, Portugal, Austria, France and Belgium; and they are legally forbidden in Ireland and Spain. Despite the varying strictures against them, however, abortions do take place in great numbers throughout Europe. The International Planned Parenthood Federation estimates that at least a one-to-one ratio exists between illegal abortions and live births in Austria, Belgium, France, West Germany and Italy.

Significantly, the historic transition from large to small families in the West began in two Roman Catholic nations—France and Ireland. In the former country, birth rates began falling nearly 200 years ago, long before the trend was observed elsewhere. (France's head start is shown in Figure 1, which clearly reveals the similarity in birth trends for both the Catholic and non-Catholic nations of Europe). The decline in France was caused by "the prevention of births within marriage by contraceptive means," according to Alfred Sauvy, former Director of the French National Institute for Demographic Studies. It occurred despite a strongly pro-natalist government policy and it quickly spread across all class lines, with much less discrepancy between city and rural fertility than is common in most countries today. The French experience of the late 18th and early 19th centuries was a classic example of population restraint that is spontaneously exercised by the people in the face of governmental and ecclesiastical opposition.

Crisis Area: Latin America

One region where Roman Catholicism coincides with high birth rates is, of course, Latin America. Here birth rates range from the low 20's for two temperate

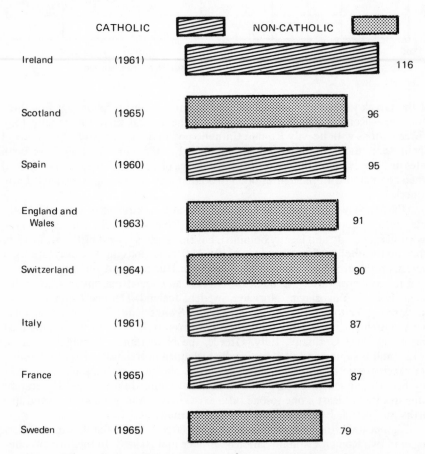

FIGURE 3. Birth rates per 1000 women aged 15-44 in selected Catholic and non-Catholic countries of Europe.

countries to above 45 for several nations in Central America, the Caribbean and tropical South America. The continental average is 40. Responding to modern medicine and public health measures, moreover, Latin America's death rate has dropped from over 20 to 10 in just a few decades—and is now only a fraction higher than that of the United States. These death rates are not directly comparable because of the higher proportion of young people in the developing world. When widely differing age distributions are taken into account, mortality rates in Latin America turn out to be somewhat higher than those of the developed countries. Still, no other large area of the world so dramatically combines a modern low death rate with a traditional high birth rate. Tropical Latin America's population is growing explosively by over three percent a year, and if present trends continue the number of people throughout the continent will double to some 536 million by 1992.

Even in heavily Roman Catholic Latin America, however, there are valid reasons for attributing high birthrates less to religious doctrine than to economic levels of living. Church influence against formal birth control programs is quite strong, but its control over sexual behavior within families is usually overrated. Surveys conducted by the United Nations Latin American Demographic Center (CELADE) and Cornell University, for example, have demonstrated a striking lack of religious influence on the number of children born to women in six Latin American cities. Using the frequency of attendance at Mass as a gauge of religiosity, the studies show that "devout" Catholic women have slightly *fewer* children, on the average, than women who are only "nominally" Catholic. There is, on the other hand, a strong link between education and fertility. In some of the cities surveyed by CELADE, women with less than a primary school education have at least one more child than their better educated counterparts—regardless of the degree of their religious conviction.

Thus it is Latin America's economic and educational levels, rather than its formal religious beliefs, that put it on common ground with the high-fertility regions of Africa and Asia. National per capita incomes on the continent range from $80 to $960 but still average only $350 a year, and illiteracy still holds a third of the population in its grasp. Thus, it is significant to note that the only major Latin American nations with birth rates under 30—Argentina (21.5) and Uruguay (23-25)—are also the two with the highest literacy levels. Furthermore they have the continent's highest per capita incomes ($740 and $540) outside of heavily subsidized Puerto Rico and oil-rich Venezuela, where the distribution of wealth is extremely uneven. As with many of their Latin neighbors, Argentines and Uruguayans frequently resort to birth control in its most extreme form— abortion. The ratio of aborted to live births in Uruguay, according to some sources, may be as high as three to one. In Chile, where statistics are more reliable, studies show that of every 100 pregnancies 25 end in artificially induced abortions.

The Policy of the Church

Italy, home of the Vatican, did not experience the transition to modern low birth rates until quite recently. At the insistence of the dictator Mussolini, a series of laws was passed in the 1920's which encouraged, through strong incentives and severe penalties, an *increase* in the national birthrate. Italians promptly responded to this suasion by *reducing* their output of bambinos. Under Il Duce the birth rate fell from about 26 in 1922 to 21 in 1940. Today it hovers just slightly above the European average at 18.9, and large areas of northern Italy record some of the lowest regional birth rates in the world. Since the Italian limitation of natural increase is being practiced around the very headquarters of the Roman Catholic Church, it raises a central question: What *is* the attitude of the Church toward population growth?

Today the Vatican finds itself in the rather paradoxical position of recognizing the dangers of the population explosion while barring the use of reliable contraceptives. Even this delicate balancing act, however, is a major advance over the traditional doctrines espoused in Pope Pius XI's famous 1930 Encyclical, "Casti Connubii."

This Encyclical warned that "since the conjugal act is destined primarily for the begetting of children, those who in exercising it deliberately frustrate its natural power and purpose sin against nature and commit a deed which is shameful and intrinsically vicious."

The harsh tone of "Casti Connubii" sounds medieval compared with that of Papal Representative the Reverend Father Stanislas de Lestapis, who addressed a United Nations meeting in Rome only 24 years later. "The choice of the number of children in the bosom of the family," he said in 1954, "is the sole personal responsibility of the spouses . . . who not only take into consideration their personal welfare but also the welfare of their children . . . and finally the general welfare of the human community, present and future."

It was this public statement, more than any other, which recognized the moral obligation of married couples to assure that hyperfertility does not endanger the family or the wider society. Subsequent announcements from the Holy See, notably the 1967 Encyclical, "On the Development of Peoples," have enlarged the theme adumbrated by Father Lestapis. This recent Encyclical from Pope Paul displays a truly broad and penetrating concern for demographic trends.

"It is true," the Pope announced, "that too frequently an accelerated demographic increase adds its own difficulties to the problems of development: the size of the population increases more rapidly than the available resources, and things are found to have reached apparently an impasse. . . . It is certain that public authorities can intervene, within the limit of their competence, by favoring the availability of appropriate information and by adopting suitable measures, provided that these be in conformity with the moral law."

Pope Paul also stressed the obligation of Catholic couples not to have more children than they can adequately provide for. "It is for the parents to decide on the number of their children," he said, "taking into account their responsibilities towards God, themselves, the children they have already brought into the world, and the community to which they belong."

The spirit of this message is one with which reasonable people around the world can feel at home. As it reveals quite clearly, the Roman Catholic Church is now directing the concern of its followers to the population problem. The Church is unrealistic only in that it offers conscientious Catholics just two means of birth control—complete or periodic abstinence. No chemical, physiological or mechanical methods have yet been approved. But while these limitations are profound, it is unfair to indict Roman Catholicism for encouraging oversized families or for promoting high birthrates. Even with respect to the means of birth control, the Church is not monolithically consistent. Richard Cardinal Cushing of Boston has several times declared that U.S. Catholics "do not seek to impose by law their moral views on other members" of a pluralistic society. The Reverend Father Dexter Hanley, S. J., a prominent Jesuit scholar who directs the Institute of Law, Human Rights and Social Values at Georgetown University, likewise affirms that "the government must allow each individual to choose the most adequate method of family planning in accord with his moral standards." These liberal views echo the expressed thought of many other Roman Catholic priests around the world.

The demographic evidence, finally, will not support a broad indictment of Church influence against population restraint. In Europe, where birth rates are low, there is virtually no differential between Catholic and non-Catholic countries. In Latin America, where birth rates are still high, religion is demonstrably less of a factor than levels of literacy and income. The figures speak for themselves.

Population Control and "The Aware Youth"

Population Control, Sterilization, and Ignorance   63

THOMAS EISNER
ARI VAN TIENHOVEN
FRANK ROSENBLATT

We recently submitted a questionnaire to students and faculty at Cornell University designed to test attitudes and preferences concerning family size and contraceptive technique. The 1059 respondents (74 percent males) were a mixed lot who represented the physical and biological sciences, humanities, and social sciences and who included faculty (294), graduate students (174), upperclassmen (264), and freshmen (327). Given the level of education of the sample, the results were unexpected in several respects.

First, although there was general agreement (84 percent) on the desirability of limiting family size, a substantial majority (65 percent) said it wanted three children (39 percent) or more (26 percent). Only 30 percent favored two children, and a mere 5 percent expressed preference for one or none. Choice was in no major way affected by age, sex, marital status, parenthood, or professional specialty. Even the respondents whom we expected to be most concerned about the population crisis (for example, graduate students and young faculty in biology) included a minimum of 50 percent with a desire for three children or more.

As regards contraception, about one-half favored "the pill" over all other available means as a way both to space children (53 percent) and to maintain family size at its desired limit (50 percent). Other contraceptive appliances such as condoms, diaphragms, and intrauterine devices were each given top preference by no more than 13 percent of the sample. Voluntary sterilization, either of man or woman, was judged as decidedly undesirable. Only 6 percent opted in favor of vasectomy as the preferred form of contraception once full family size had been achieved; the corresponding number favoring ligation of the oviducts was 2 percent. A majority (52 percent of males and 61 percent of females) said they would *never* undergo sterilization, even after having had the desired number of children. The operation was judged to be as undesirable as abortion and abstinence for prevention of family growth beyond the set limit. It is of interest in this connection that the consequences of sterilization are not generally understood. For example, asked whether vasectomy would abolish the ability to ejaculate, nearly half the respondents (49 percent) confessed to ignorance or expressed either certainty or probability that emission would no longer accompany orgasm. Biology students scored no better than nonbiologists, and graduate students, even after marriage and parenthood, seemed to be no better informed than freshmen. The only exceptional group was the biology faculty, but, even there, 30 percent were either misinformed or uninformed on this point. Comparable ignorance prevails with respect to oviduct ligation: 37 percent of respondents were certain, or thought it probable, that the operation would interfere with the menstrual cycle.

We are bothered by these results. Perhaps of least general concern is the probability that proponents of voluntary sterilization are backing a hopeless or nearly hopeless cause. But what are we to make of the educated youth growing up among us that is either unconcerned about population growth or, at the very least, unable or unwilling to apply to itself the simple arithmetic of compound interest? And what, if any, are the prospects for improved sex education when ignorance about the reproductive system is widespread even among those who should know best?

Controlling Births

64   **From Magic to Science**
                                    A History of Contraception

                                    MEDCOM

Primitive man believed that with prayer and magic he could control the fertility of his fields, livestock, and the animals he hunted. Even before he made the connection between sexual intercourse and human babies, he probably tried to control his own fertility, too.

Out of magic and out of trial and error came hundreds of gadgets, concoctions, spells, amulets—to induce conception or to prevent it.

Most of the magic stayed in folklore—but some of it, and some results of trial and error, found their way into early philosophic and medical writings. These are our first records of contraceptives.

Until only 20 years ago, contraceptive measures all fell into a few types:

Potions taken by mouth—animal, vegetable, or mineral products, often harmful, usually ineffective, and usually based on magic or superstition or erroneous medicine.

Sheaths for the penis—made of various materials, to prevent sperm from reaching the womb.

Pessaries and tampons—objects placed in the vagina to absorb or block sperm or obstruct the entrance to the uterus. Pessary literally means "oval pebble."

Timing of intercourse—to coincide with various periods considered to be safe. The actual "safe" period was not determined until this century.

Lubricants, spermicides, and presumably spermicidal concoctions—believed to inhibit or destroy spermatozoa when introduced into the vagina or applied to the penis before, during, or after coitus.

The Egyptians

Egyptian papyri dating back to 1850 BC provide the earliest records of contraceptive efforts. One papyrus from that time includes a prescription for a pessary made of crocodile dung, and another for irrigating or plugging the vagina with honey and natron (sodium carbonate). Sticky material presumably was expected to catch sperm.

A papyrus dated 1550 BC describes a medicated lint tampon. The recipe for the medication includes fermented acacia tips, which release lactic acid—acid was a common ingredient of spermicides into the 20th century. In the history of contraception, because of trial and error, the right thing was occasionally done —for the wrong reasons.

The Hebrews

The Old Testament, which reports an oral tradition much more ancient than the text, condemns "the sin of Onan"—coitus interruptus—a prime contraceptive measure. The story of Onan has long been used as a religious argument against contraception, and against masturbation as well.

Herbs, and especially the mandrake plant, were used both to induce and to prevent conception, as well as to cause abortion. The mandrake has some chemical similarity to the Mexican yams which are now important in synthesizing hormones for drugs that are used both to induce and to prevent conception.

The ancient Hebrews also used the "cup of roots" to render women sterile. This may have consisted, among other things, of liquid alum and garden crocus. Taken with two cups of beer, it was said to cause female sterility—and cure jaundice. With wine, it was said to cure gonorrhea. From at least the 3rd century AD until the 20th, a sponge inserted in the vagina was a popular type of pessary.

Among the Jews, female contraceptives were considered to be more "moral" than coitus interruptus, since, according to the rabbis, only men were enjoined by God to propagate, whereas women could bypass the commandment.

The Greeks and Romans

Aristotle comments that conception can be prevented by "anointing that part of the womb where the seeds fall with oil of cedar, ointment of lead, or with frankincense commingled with olive oil"—oil does reduce the motility of sperm. Cedar gum, alum, and crushed willow leaves, taken orally or spread on the genitals, were also believed to prevent conception.

Roman women wore asparagus amulets as insurance.

In his *Natural History,* written in the first century AD, Pliny the Elder suggested that two worms extracted from the hairy body of "the spider called Phalangium" should be attached to a piece of deerskin before sunrise, and then to a woman's body. Just how this contraceptive operated is unclear.

During the second century AD, Soranus, a Greek gynecologist practicing in Rome, distinguished clearly between contraceptives and abortifacients. He listed the indications and contraindications for both, and added a list of well-selected contraceptive measures: occlusive pessaries, vaginal plugs of wool and gummy substances, astringent solutions, and acidic fruits.

He also suggested abstention from coitus at the "dangerous" time—"directly before and after menstruation." It is possible, though not proven, that the Romans knew how to use animal membranes as condoms.

Other Ancient Societies

An ancient French cave painting in the Dordogne has been interpreted by some viewers as showing a man's penis covered by a sheath during coitus.

A 6th century Byzantine physician mentions the use of vinegar and brine, both highly spermicidal, for washing the genitals before intercourse. Like many bits of useful knowledge that survived in folklore, this one seems to have been forgotten by medicine until the 19th century.

Indian erotic literature includes many contraceptive hints—herbs and amulets, anointment with honey and oil, passivity in the female during coitus. Coitus obstructus, or the prevention of ejaculation, physically or magically, was also recommended.

Chinese women fried quicksilver in oil and drank it. They also believed it useful to swallow 14 live tadpoles three days after menstruation.

The wives of North African desert tribesmen mixed gunpowder solution and foam from a camel's mouth and drank the potion—proving that birth control can always be attempted with the materials at hand.

Islam knew pills or pessaries made of "cabbage, tamarisk dew, pitch, ox gall, pomegranate, animals' ear wax, elephant dung . . . used either alone or in combination," to prevent conception.

A Mohammedan writer recommended jumping seven or nine times—jumping forward to increase fertility, and backward to decrease it.

A 12th century physician at Saladin's court declared that eating beans on an empty stomach would cause female sterility, but also suggested tampons and pessaries and anointing the penis with oil or onion juice.

European ladies prevented pregnancy by spitting three times into the mouth of a frog or by eating bees. Others associated sterile animals, such as mules, with human infertility. One formula called for fumigating the vulva with the smoke resulting from holding a mule's hoof over burning prunes. Still others ate pieces of a mule's uterus or kidneys.

An appetizing instruction was to place roasted walnuts in the bosom, one nut for every barren year a bride desired. Or the bride might sit on her fingers while riding in a coach—one finger per barren year. The Middle Ages were not a time of progress for birth control.

The Renaissance

The first known published description of the condom, by the Italian anatomist Gabriel Fallopius, appeared in 1564. The renaissance of science naturally affected contraception along with other medical fields. Fallopius recommended a linen sheath to guard against syphilis, which had recently invaded Europe from the New World. It may be that some medieval slaughterhouse worker actually invented the condom made of the thin membranes of an animal. The origin of the name condom is also mysterious, but item and name became notorious in England in the 17th and 18th centuries. It was soon used for contraception as well as protection against disease. A British bishop's son wrote a poem celebrating the liberation of women by the condom. A comparable achievement is today attributed to the pill.

The Age of Reason

In the 18th century condoms were made of linen or of dried sheep gut, and the bottom was "generally bound round with a scarlet ribbon" for ornament.

Boswell, the companion of Dr. Johnson, described himself as in "complete armour" and "safely sheathed" for an amatory adventure.

But Madame de Sévigné called the sheaths "armour against enjoyment, and a spider web against danger."

The great lover Casanova sided with Boswell and used condoms to prevent infection as well as impregnation. He tested the merchandise by making sure each sheath held air. Casanova also suggested to his paramours the use of one of three gold balls he bought as pessaries for their protection.

Through the microscopic lens he developed, Anton van Leeuwenhoek studied semen, and, in 1677, discovered "animaliculi" therein.

These were sperm cells, and being able to see them made it possible for others to experiment and understand their nature—and work scientifically on chemical contraceptives. It was soon learned that seminal fluid could be diluted, with adverse effect on the animaliculi. They could be filtered and rendered impotent. Acids like vinegar, and the salts of certain heavy metals, were found to inactivate them.

Now that birth control was becoming feasible, puritanism, propaganda, and politics began to affect the development of contraceptives.

In the late 18th century Jeremy Bentham and others began to advocate birth control as a way of reducing poverty. Thus far, the rich had had access to what contraceptives there were, while the poor were left with folklore, dangerous abortions, and the pressures of large families. Now contraception became a social issue.

In 1798 Thomas Malthus introduced his theory that population tends to multiply faster than means of subsistence. He advocated "moral restraint" as the solution to overpopulation, feeling that the dole only increased the problem, and that poverty was inevitable for the poor, who deserved no better. Nevertheless his theory and name became watchwords for later advocates of family planning, and Malthus is remembered with more affection than he deserves.

The Victorians

Humanitarian reformers began to spread the word about contraception, birth control, and population control. In the early 19th century these "free-thinkers" were recommending the sponge, condoms, coitus interruptus, and tampons of lint, wool, cotton, or flax. A manual called *Every Woman's Book* gave contraception snob appeal with such examples as "the Prudent English Duchess who never goes out to dinner without being prepared with the sponge."

Queen Victoria with her nine children did not set a good example as far as the birth control movement was concerned. But the 19th century contributed other suggested solutions to the poverty and population problem—infanticide, surgery for men with insufficient income to support families, and eugenics and euthenics. Contraception still seemed the most practical solution.

In 1838 a gynecologist, F. A. Wilde, published a treatise promoting a rubber pessary, fitted to the individual lady and completely covering the cervix, as the only effective means of contraception. Rubber diaphragms were not yet available, and he was probably right—but his contribution was forgotten until nearly a hundred years later.

Coitus reservatus. At this time, intercourse without male ejaculation came into some vogue. It is one of the few "contraceptive" measures acceptable even today to the Roman Catholic Church.

The rhythm method. The Greeks and various societies after them had tried to discover and compute the "safe" period as a means of contraception, but until the 1920s most of the guesses were wrong, the right guesses went unheard, and no safe period for the menstrual cycle was ever established.

During the mid-19th century ovulation was believed to coincide with menstruation. Later the unsafe period was thought to last for 12 days after menstruation, though some observant physicians noted that this couldn't be quite accurate.

The birth control issue continued to simmer quietly all over the world—with some hot moments when writers or reformers were too direct, or when pamphlets and products were "too inexpensive" and therefore "too easily available" to the masses. Anthony Comstock (at right) took up the cudgel against the reformers. His Society for the Suppression of Vice pushed through the New York law named after him. It permitted prosecution and punishment of anyone who tried to disseminate knowledge about contraception. Atheism and obscenity, in his opinion, "occupied the same bed," and birth control, the epitome of both, was the Devil's work.

But in England in 1877 the "New Malthusian League" sprang up, and other organizations devoted to family planning were formed thereafter in many countries—France, the Netherlands, Spain, Brazil, Cuba, Switzerland, Sweden, Belgium. Clinics were opened to give advice on infant care as well as on contraception to working-class women. The first diaphragms were given to women in a Netherlands clinic; the device had been invented in the 1880s by a German, Dr. Mensinga.

The 20th Century

In this country the long hard struggle for family planning was led by Margaret Sanger (1883–1966). Her dedication was based on her experience as a public health nurse in poor neighborhoods, where she saw fatally botched abortions and the effects of overcrowding and large families. Mrs. Sanger became an ardent feminist, believing it was a woman's basic right to decide how many children she would have, and when she would have them, for economic, social, and medical reasons. Mrs. Sanger opened the first U.S. clinic in New York City; it was closed after nine days by the Vice Squad. Released on bail, she reopened it, and was promptly sent to jail for 30 days. Her career included many such incidents and culminated in the formation of the Planned Parenthood Federation. All over the world birth control movements experienced similar ups and downs, but by the 1930s contraception had become legal in many countries and states and tacitly accepted in many others.

Contraception remains part of the age-old search for control over our destinies—the chance to choose.

Contraceptive Failure

Coping with Contraceptive Failure   **65**

GARRETT HARDIN

Every unintended pregnancy represents a failure of birth control. It is important to state this truism explicitly so that we can get on with the business of studying the system of birth control. Every system has its failures; what do we do about them? In general, we react in two ways: (1) we study the system and seek to improve it; and (2) we employ remedial actions for the failures we cannot avoid.

Let us take up the second aspect first. Of remedial measures for the unwanted child, there are only two important ones: infanticide and adoption. Infanticide has been practiced openly in many societies, though not in ours:—not openly, that is. The historical studies of William Langer have shown that infanticide was institutionalized in a cryptic way in the Western world, being particularly important in the nineteenth century. The institution was that of the "baby farmer," the obliging person of flexible conscience who took care of your unwanted child for a fee, with the implicit understanding that it would not be for long. It is this understanding that gives new meaning to the scene in Gilbert and Sullivan's *H.M.S. Pinafore* in which Little Buttercup reveals the dread secret she had hinted at earlier:

> A many years ago
> When I was young and charming,
> As some of you may know
> I practised baby-farming.

To which the chorus replies:

> Now this is most alarming!
> When she was young and charming,
> She practised baby-farming,
> A many years ago.

Why did they say "this is most alarming"? Because "alarming" rhymes with "charming," of course; and to create the mood for the coming revelation that Buttercup had mixed two babies up. But Langer's study suggests that the "alarm" had another source: Baby-farming in the Victorian world was no more respectable than bootlegging was in Prohibition days. It was an institutionalized way of dealing with failures in birth control. Many of the "best people" knew this; but they didn't speak of it. It was under taboo. In writing this scene, Gilbert was drawing on an ambiguous feeling of dread that no longer exists. He was not *merely* being funny.

Does baby-farming, in this sense, still exist? I have been informed by some who lived in Germany in the pre-Hitler days that they still had their "angel-makers," as they were called. I suspect the profession has declined since. It used to be easy to make angels: All you had to do was crowd the babies together, underfeed them somewhat, expose them a bit, and let "nature" (that is, crowd diseases) take over. With the coming of antibiotics and government inspection of nurseries, baby-farming on the old scale is hardly possible.

What used to be done professionally is now done by amateurs, less efficiently and more brutally. Parents have now taken over the executioner's role—not many parents, but *too* many. Child-ridden, impoverished, and desperate parents are responsible for thousands of "battered babies" every year and perhaps some hundreds of dead ones. Statistics are hard to come by because it is difficult to distinguish between accidents and homicides in this population.

Solving The Problem

The Tragedy Of The Commons 66

GARRETT HARDIN

At the end of a thoughtful article on the future of nuclear war, Wiesner and York (1) concluded that: "Both sides in the arms race are . . . confronted by the dilemma of steadily increasing military power and steadily decreasing national security. *It is our considered professional judgment that this dilemma has no technical solution.* If the great powers continue to look for solutions in the area of science and technology only, the result will be to worsen the situation."

I would like to focus your attention not on the subject of the article (national security in a nuclear world) but on the kind of conclusion they reached, namely that there is no technical solution to the problem. An implicit and almost universal assumption of discussions published in professional and semipopular scientific journals is that the problem under discussion has a technical solution. A technical solution may be defined as one that requires a change only in the techniques of the natural sciences, demanding little or nothing in the way of change in human values or ideas of morality.

In our day (though not in earlier times) technical solutions are always welcome. Because of previous failures in prophecy, it takes courage to assert that a desired technical solution is not possible. Wiesner and York exhibited this courage; publishing in a science journal, they insisted that the solution to the problem was not to be found in the natural sciences. They cautiously qualified their statement with the phrase, "It is our considered professional judgment . . . " Whether they were right or not is not the concern of the present article. Rather, the concern here is with the important concept of a class of human problems which can be called "no technical solution problems," and, more specifically, with the identification and discussion of one of these.

It is easy to show that the class is not a null class. Recall the game of tick-tack-toe. Consider the problem, "How can I win the game of tick-tack-toe?" It is well known that I cannot, if I assume (in keeping with the conventions of game theory) that my opponent understands the game perfectly. Put another way, there is no "technical solution" to the problem. I can win only by giving a radical meaning to the word "win." I can hit my opponent over the head; or I can drug him; or I can falsify the records. Every way in which I "win" involves, in some sense, an abandonment of the game, as we intuitively understand it. (I can also, of course, openly abandon the game—refuse to play it. This is what most adults do.)

The class of "No technical solution problems" has members. My thesis is that the "population problem," as conventionally conceived, is a member of this class. How it is conventionally conceived needs some comment. It is fair to say that most people who anguish over the population problem are trying to find a way to avoid the evils of overpopulation without relinquishing any of the privileges they now enjoy. They think that farming the seas or developing new strains of wheat will solve the problem—technologically. I try to show here that the solution they seek cannot be found. The population problem cannot be solved in a technical way, any more than can the problem of winning the game of tick-tack-toe.

What Shall We Maximize?

Population, as Malthus said, naturally tends to grow "geometrically," or, as we would now say, exponentially. In a finite world this means that the per capita share of the world's goods must steadily decrease. Is ours a finite world?

A fair defense can be put forward for the view that the world is infinite; or that we do not know that it is not. But, in terms of the practical problems that we must face in the next few generations with the foreseeable technology, it is clear that we will greatly increase human misery if we do not, during the immediate future, assume that the world available to the terrestrial human population is finite. "Space" is no escape (2).

A finite world can support only a finite population; therefore, population growth must eventually equal zero. (The case of perpetual wide fluctuations above and below zero is a trivial variant that need not be discussed.) When this condition is met, what will be the situation of mankind? Specifically, can Bentham's goal of "the greatest good for the greatest number" be realized?

No—for two reasons, each sufficient by itself. The first is a theoretical one. It is not mathematically possible to maximize for two (or more) variables at the same time. This was clearly stated by von Neumann and Morgenstern (3), but the principle is implicit in the theory of partial differential equations, dating back at least to D'Alembert (1717-1783).

The second reason springs directly from biological facts. To live, any organism must have a source of energy (for example, food). This energy is utilized for two purposes: mere maintenance and work. For man, maintenance of life requires about 1600 kilocalories a day ("maintenance calories"). Anything that he does over and above merely staying alive will be defined as work, and is supported by "work calories" which he takes in. Work calories are used not only for what we call work in common speech; they are also required for all forms of enjoyment, from swimming and automobile racing to playing music and writing poetry. If our goal is to maximize population it is obvious what we must do: We must make the work calories per person approach as close to zero as possible. No gourmet meals, no vacations, no sports, no music, no literature, no art ... I think that everyone will grant, without argument or proof, that maximizing population does not maximize goods. Bentham's goal is impossible.

In reaching this conclusion I have made the usual assumption that it is the acquisition of energy that is the problem. The appearance of atomic energy has led some to question this assumption. However, given an infinite source of energy, population growth still produces an inescapable problem. The problem of the acquisition of energy is replaced by the problem of its dissipation, as J. H. Fremlin has so wittily shown (4). The arithmetic signs in the analysis are, as it were, reversed; but Bentham's goal is still unobtainable.

The optimum population is, then, less than the maximum. The difficulty of defining the optimum is enormous; so far as I know, no one has seriously tackled this problem. Reaching an acceptable and stable solution will surely require more than one generation of hard analytical work—and much persuasion.

We want the maximum good per person; but what is good? To one person it is wilderness, to another it is ski lodges for thousands. To one it is estuaries to nourish ducks for hunters to shoot; to another it is factory land. Comparing one good with another is, we usually say, impossible because goods are incommensurable. Incommensurables cannot be compared.

Theoretically this may be true; but in real life incommensurables are commensurable. Only a criterion of judgment and a system of weighting are needed. In nature the criterion is survival. Is it better for a species to be small and hideable, or large and powerful? Natural selection commensurates the incommensurables. The compromise achieved depends on a natural weighting of the values of the variables.

Man must imitate this process. There is no doubt that in fact he already does, but unconsciously. It is when the hidden decisions are made explicit that the arguments begin. The problem for the years ahead is to work out an acceptable theory of weighting. Synergistic effects, nonlinear variation, and difficulties in discounting the future make the intellectual problem difficult, but not (in principle) insoluble.

Has any cultural group solved this practical problem at the present time, even on an intuitive level? One simple fact proves that none has: there is no prosperous population in the world today that has, and has had for sometime, a growth rate of zero. Any people that has intuitively identified its optimum point will soon reach it, after which its growth rate becomes and remains zero.

Of course, a positive growth rate might be taken as evidence that a population is below its optimum. However, by any reasonable standards, the most rapidly growing populations on earth today are (in general) the most miserable. This association (which need not be invariable) casts doubt on the optimistic assumption that the positive growth rate of a population is evidence that it has yet to reach its optimum.

We can make little progress in working toward optimum population size until we explicitly exorcize the spirit of Adam Smith in the field of practical demography. In economic affairs, *The Wealth of Nations* (1776) popularized the "invisible hand," the idea that an individual who "intends only his own gain," is, as it were, "led by an invisible hand to promote . . . the public interest" (5). Adam Smith did not assert that this was invariably true, and perhaps neither did any of his followers. But he contributed to a dominant tendency of thought that has ever since interfered with positive action based on rational analysis, namely, the tendency to assume that decisions reached individually will, in fact, be the best decisions for an entire society. If this assumption is correct it justifies the continuance of our present policy of laissez-faire in reproduction. If it is correct we can assume that men will control their individual fecundity so as to produce the optimum population. If the assumption is not correct, we need to reexamine our individual freedoms to see which ones are defensible.

Tragedy of Freedom in a Commons

The rebuttal to the invisible hand in population control is to be found in a scenario first sketched in a little-known pamphlet (6) in 1833 by a mathematical amateur named William Forster Lloyd (1794-1852). We may well call it "the tragedy of the commons," using the word "tragedy" as the philosopher Whitehead used it (7): "The essence of dramatic tragedy is not unhappiness. It resides in the solemnity of the remorseless working of things." He then goes on to say, "This inevitableness of destiny can only be illustrated in terms of human life by incidents which in fact involve unhappiness. For it is only by them that the futility of escape can be made evident in the drama."

The tragedy of the commons develops in this way. Picture a pasture open to all. It is to be expected that each herdsman will try to keep as many cattle as possible on the commons. Such an arrangement may work reasonably satisfactorily for centuries because tribal wars, poaching, and disease keep the numbers of both man and beast well below the carrying capacity of the land. Finally, however, comes the day of reckoning, that is, the day when the long-desired goal of social stability becomes a reality. At this point, the inherent logic of the commons remorselessly generates tragedy.

As a rational being, each herdsman seeks to maximize his gain. Explicitly or implicitly, more or less consciously, he asks, "What is the utility *to me* of adding one more animal to my herd?" This utility has one negative and one positive component.

1) The positive component is a function of the increment of one animal. Since the herdsman receives all the proceeds from the sale of the additional animal, the positive utility is nearly $+1$.

2) The negative component is a function of the additional overgrazing created by one more animal. Since, however, the effects of overgrazing are shared by all the herdsmen, the negative utility for any particular decision-making herdsman is only a fraction of -1.

Adding together the component partial utilities, the rational herdsman concludes that the only sensible course for him to pursue is to add another animal to his herd. And another; and another . . . But this is the conclusion reached by each and every rational herdsman sharing a commons. Therein is the tragedy. Each man is locked into a system that compels him to increase his herd without limit—in a world that is limited. Ruin is the destination toward which all men rush, each pursuing his own best interest in a society that believes in the freedom of the commons. Freedom in a commons brings ruin to all.

Some would say that this is a platitude. Would that it were! In a sense, it was learned thousands of years ago, but natural selection favors the forces of psychological denial (8). The individual benefits as an individual from his ability to deny the truth even though society as a whole, of which he is a part, suffers. Education can counteract the natural tendency to do the wrong thing, but the inexorable succession of generations requires that the basis for this knowledge be constantly refreshed.

A simple incident that occurred a few years ago in Leominster, Massachusetts, shows how perishable the knowledge is. During the Christmas shopping season the parking meters downtown were covered with plastic bags that bore tags reading: "Do not open until after Christmas. Free parking courtesy of the mayor and city council." In other words, facing the prospect of an increased demand for already scarce space, the city fathers reinstituted the system of the commons. (Cynically, we suspect that they gained more votes than they lost by this retrogressive act.)

In an approximate way, the logic of the commons has been understood for a long time, perhaps since the discovery of agriculture or the invention of private property in real estate. But it is understood mostly only in special cases which are not sufficiently generalized. Even at this late date, cattlemen leasing national land on the western ranges demonstrate no more than an ambivalent understanding, in constantly pressuring federal authorities to increase the head count to the point where overgrazing produces erosion and weed-dominance. Likewise, the oceans of the world continue to suffer from the survival of the philosophy of the commons. Maritime nations still respond automatically to the shibboleth of the "freedom of the seas." Professing to believe in the "inexhaustible resources of the oceans," they bring species after species of fish and whales closer to extinction (9).

The National Parks present another instance of the working out of the tragedy of the commons. At present, they are open to all, without limit. The parks themselves are limited in extent—there is only one Yosemite Valley—whereas population seems to grow without limit. The values that visitors seek in the parks are steadily eroded. Plainly, we must soon cease to treat the parks as commons or they will be of no value to anyone.

What shall we do? We have several options. We might sell them off as private property. We might keep them as public property, but allocate the right to enter them. The allocation might be on the basis of wealth, by the use of an auction system. It might be on the basis of merit, as defined by some agreed-upon standards. It might be by lottery. Or it might be on a first-come, first-served basis, administered to long queues. These, I think, are all the reasonable possibilities. They are all objectionable. But we must choose—or acquiesce in the destruction of the commons that we call our National Parks.

Pollution

In a reverse way, the tragedy of the commons reappears in problems of pollution. Here it is not a question of taking something out of the commons, but of putting something in—sewage, or chemical, radioactive, and heat wastes into water; noxious and dangerous fumes into the air; and distracting and unpleasant advertising signs into the line of sight. The calculations of utility are much the same as before. The rational man finds that his share of the cost of the wastes he discharges into the commons is less than the cost of purifying his wastes before releasing them. Since this is true for everyone, we are locked into a system of "fouling our own nest," so long as we behave only as independent, rational, free-enterprisers.

The tragedy of the commons as a food basket is averted by private property, or something formally like it. But the air and waters surrounding us cannot readily be fenced, and so the tragedy of the commons as a cesspool must be prevented by different means, by coercive laws or taxing devices that make it cheaper for the polluter to treat his pollutants than to discharge them untreated. We have not progressed as far with the solution of this problem as we have with the first. Indeed, our particular concept of private property, which deters us from exhausting the positive resources of the earth, favors pollution. The owner of a factory on the bank of a stream—whose property extends to the middle of the stream—often has difficulty seeing why it is not his natural right to muddy the waters flowing past his door. The law, always behind the times, requires elaborate stitching and fitting to adapt it to this newly perceived aspect of the commons.

The pollution problem is a consequence of population. It did not much matter how a lonely American frontiersman disposed of his waste. "Flowing water purifies itself every 10 miles," my grandfather used to say, and the myth was near enough to the truth when he was a boy, for there were not too many people. But as population became denser, the natural chemical and biological recycling processes became overloaded, calling for a redefinition of property rights.

How To Legislate Temperance?

Analysis of the pollution problem as a function of population density uncovers a not generally recognized principle of morality, namely: *the morality of an act is a function of the state of the system at the time it is performed* (10). Using the commons as a cesspool does not harm the general public under frontier conditions, because there is no public; the same behavior in a metropolis is unbearable. A hundred and fifty years ago a plainsman could kill an American bison, cut out only the tongue for his dinner, and discard the rest of the animal. He was not in any important sense being wasteful. Today, with only a few thousand bison left, we would be appalled at such behavior.

In passing, it is worth noting that the morality of an act cannot be determined from a photograph. One does not know whether a man killing an elephant or setting fire to the grassland is harming others until one knows the total system in which his act appears. "One picture is worth a thousand words," said an ancient Chinese; but it may take 10,000 words to validate it. It is as tempting to ecologists as it is to reformers in general to try to persuade others by way of the photographic shortcut. But the essense of an argument cannot be photographed: it must be presented rationally—in words.

That morality is system-sensitive escaped the attention of most codifiers of ethics in the past. "Thou shalt not . . . " is the form of traditional ethical directives which make no allowance for particular circumstances. The laws of our society follow the pattern of ancient ethics, and therefore are poorly suited to governing a complex, crowded, changeable world. Our epicyclic solution is to augment statutory law with administrative law. Since it is practically impossible to spell out all the conditions under which it is safe to burn trash in the back yard or to run an automobile without smog-control, by law we delegate the details to bureaus. The result is administrative law, which is rightly feared for an ancient reason—*Quis custodiet ipsos custodes?* —"Who shall watch the watchers themselves?" John Adams said that we must have "a government of laws and not men." Bureau administrators, trying to evaluate the morality of acts in the total system, are singularly liable to corruption, producing a government by men, not laws.

Prohibition is easy to legislate (though not necessarily to enforce); but how do we legislate temperance? Experience indicates that it can be accomplished best through the mediation of administrative law. We limit possibilities unnecessarily if we suppose that the sentiment of *Quis custodiet* denies us the use of administrative law. We should rather retain the phrase as a perpetual reminder of fearful dangers we cannot avoid. The great challenge facing us now is to invent the corrective feedbacks that are needed to keep custodians honest. We must find ways to legitimate the needed authority of both the custodians and the corrective feedbacks.

Freedom To Breed Is Intolerable

The tragedy of the commons is involved in population problems in another way. In a world governed solely by the principle of "dog eat dog"—if indeed there ever was such a world—how many children a family had would not be a matter of public concern. Parents who bred too exuberantly would leave fewer descendants, not more, because they would be unable to care adequately for their children. David Lack and others have found that such a negative feedback demonstrably controls the fecundity of birds (11). But men are not birds, and have not acted like them for millenniums, at least.

If each human family were dependent only on its own resources; *if* the children of improvident parents starved to death; *if*, thus, overbreeding brought its own "punishment" to the germ line—*then* there would be no public interest in controlling the breeding of families. But our society is deeply committed to the welfare state (12), and hence is confronted with another aspect of the tragedy of the commons.

In a welfare state, how shall we deal with the family, the religion, the race, or the class (or indeed any distinguishable and cohesive group) that adopts overbreeding as a policy to secure its own aggrandizement (13)? To couple the concept of freedom to breed with the belief that everyone born has an equal right to the commons is to lock the world into a tragic course of action.

Unfortunately this is just the course of action that is being pursued by the United Nations. In late 1967, some 30 nations agreed to the following (14):

The Universal Declaration of Human Rights describes the family as the natural and fundamental unit of society. It follows that any choice and decision with regard to the size of the family must irrevocably rest with the family itself, and cannot be made by anyone else.

It is painful to have to deny categorically the validity of this right; denying it, one feels as uncomfortable as a resident of Salem, Massachusetts, who denied the reality of witches in the 17th century. At the present time, in liberal quarters, something like a taboo acts to inhibit criticism of the United Nations. There is a feeling that the United Nations is "our last and best hope," that we shouldn't find fault with it; we shouldn't play into the hands of the archconservatives. However, let us not forget what Robert Louis Stevenson said: "The truth that is suppressed by friends is the readiest weapon of the enemy." If we love the truth we must openly deny the validity of the Universal Declaration of Human Rights, even though it is promoted by the United Nations. We should also join with Kingsley Davis (15) in attempting to get Planned Parenthood-World Population to see the error of its ways in embracing the same tragic ideal.

Conscience Is Self-Eliminating

It is a mistake to think that we can control the breeding of mankind in the long run by an appeal to conscience. Charles Galton Darwin made this point when he spoke on the centennial of the publication of his grandfather's great book. The argument is straightforward and Darwinian.

People vary. Confronted with appeals to limit breeding, some people will undoubtedly respond to the plea more than others. Those who have more children will produce a larger fraction of the next generation than those with more susceptible consciences. The difference will be accentuated, generation by generation.

In C. G. Darwin's words: "It may well be that it would take hundreds of generations for the progenitive instinct to develop in this way, but if it should do so, nature would have taken her revenge, and the variety *Homo contracipiens* would become extinct and would be replaced by the variety *Homo progenitivus*" (16).

The argument assumes that conscience or the desire for children (no matter which) is hereditary—but hereditary only in the most general formal sense. The result will be the same whether the attitude is transmitted through germ cells, or exosomatically, to use A. J. Lotka's term. (If one denies the latter possibility as well as the former, then what's the point of education?) The argument has here been stated in the context of the population problem, but it applies equally well to any instance in which society appeals to an individual exploiting a commons to restrain himself for the general good—by means of his conscience. To make such an appeal is to set up a selective system that works toward the elimination of conscience from the race.

Pathogenic Effects of Conscience

The long-term disadvantage of an appeal to conscience should be enough to condemn it; but has serious short-term disadvantages as well. If we ask a man who is exploiting a commons to desist "in the name of conscience," what are we saying to him? What does he hear?—not only at the moment but also in the wee small hours of the night when, half asleep, he remembers not merely the words we used but also the nonverbal communication cues we gave him unawares? Sooner or later, consciously or subconsciously, he senses that he has received two communications, and that they are contradictory: (i) (intended communication) "If you don't do as we ask, we will openly condemn you for not acting like a responsible citizen"; (ii) (the unintended communication) "If you *do* behave as we ask, we will secretly condemn you for a simpleton who can be shamed into standing aside while the rest of us exploit the commons."

Everyman then is caught in what Bateson has called a "double bind." Bateson and his co-workers have made a plausible case for viewing the double bind as an important causative factor in the genesis of schizophrenia (17). The double bind may not always be so damaging, but it always endangers the mental health of anyone to whom it is applied. "A bad conscience," said Nietzsche, "is a kind of illness."

To conjure up a conscience in others is tempting to anyone who wishes to extend his control beyond the legal limits. Leaders at the highest level succumb to this temptation. Has any President during the past generation failed to call on labor unions to moderate voluntarily their demands for higher wages, or to steel companies to honor voluntary guidelines on prices? I can recall none. The rhetoric used on such occasions is designed to produce feelings of guilt in noncooperators.

For centuries it was assumed without proof that guilt was a valuable, perhaps even an indispensable, ingredient of the civilized life. Now, in this post-Freudian world, we doubt it.

Paul Goodman speaks from the modern point of view when he says: "No good has ever come from feeling guilty, neither intelligence, policy, nor compassion. The guilty do not pay attention to the object but only to themselves, and not even to their own interests, which might make sense, but to their anxieties" (18).

One does not have to be a professional psychiatrist to see the consequences of anxiety. We in the Western world are just emerging from a dreadful two-centuries-long Dark Ages of Eros that was sustained partly by prohibition laws, but perhaps more effectively by the anxiety-generating mechanisms of education. Alex Comfort has told the story well in *The Anxiety Makers* (19); it is not a pretty one.

Since proof is difficult, we may even concede that the results of anxiety may sometimes, from certain points of view, be desirable. The larger question we should ask is whether, as a matter of policy, we should ever encourage the use of a technique the tendency (if not the intention) of which is psychologically pathogenic. We hear much talk these days of responsible parenthood; the coupled words are incorporated into the titles of some organizations devoted to birth control. Some people have proposed massive propaganda campaigns to instill responsibility into the nation's (or the world's) breeders. But what is the meaning of the word responsibility in this context? Is it not merely a synonym for the word conscience? When we use the word responsibility in the absence of substantial functions are we not trying to browbeat a free man in a commons into acting against his own interest? Responsibility is a verbal counterfeit for a substantial *quid pro quo*. It is an attempt to get something for nothing.

If the word responsibility is to be used at all, I suggest that it be in the sense Charles Frankel uses it (20). "Responsibility," says this philosopher, "is the product of definite social arrangements." Notice that Frankel calls for social arrangements—not propaganda.

Mutual Coercion Mutually Agreed Upon

The social arrangements that produce responsibility are arrangements that create coercion, of some sort. Consider bank-robbing. The man who takes money from a bank acts as if the bank were a commons. How do we prevent such action? Certainly not by trying to control his behavior solely by a verbal appeal to his sense of responsibility. Rather than rely on propaganda we follow Frankel's lead and insist that a bank is not a commons; we seek the definite social arrangements that will keep it from becoming a commons. That we thereby infringe on the freedom of would-be robbers we neither deny nor regret.

The morality of bank-robbing is particularly easy to understand because we accept complete prohibition of this activity. We are willing to say "Thou shalt not rob banks," without providing for exceptions. But temperance also can be created by coercion. Taxing is a good coercive device. To keep downtown shoppers temperate in their use of parking space we introduce parking meters for short periods, and traffic fines for longer ones. We need not actually forbid a citizen to park as long as he wants to; we need merely make it increasingly expensive for him to do so. Not prohibition, but carefully biased options are what we offer him. A Madison Avenue man might call this persuasion; I prefer the greater candor of the word coercion.

Coercion is a dirty word to most liberals now, but it need not forever be so. As with the four-letter words, its dirtiness can be cleansed away by exposure to the light, by saying it over and over without apology or embarrassment. To many, the word coercion implies arbitrary decisions of distant and irresponsible bureaucrats; but this is not a necessary part of its meaning. The only kind of coercion I recommend is mutual coercion, mutually agreed upon by the majority of the people affected.

To say that we mutually agree to coercion is not to say that we are required to enjoy it, or even to pretend we enjoy it. Who enjoys taxes? We all grumble about them. But we accept compulsory taxes because we recognize that voluntary taxes would favor the conscienceless. We institute and (grumblingly) support taxes and other coercive devices to escape the horror of the commons.

An alternative to the commons need not be perfectly just to be preferable. With real estate and other material goods, the alternative we have chosen is the institution of private property coupled with legal inheritance. Is this system perfectly just? As a genetically trained biologist I deny that it is. It seems to me that, if there are to be differences in individual inheritance, legal possession should be perfectly correlated with biological inheritance—that those who are biologically more fit to be the custodians of property and power should legally inherit more. But genetic recombination continually makes a mockery of the doctrine of "like father, like son" implicit in our laws of legal inheritance. An idiot can inherit millions, and a trust fund can keep his estate intact. We must admit that our legal system of private property plus inheritance is unjust—but we put up with it because we are not convinced, at the moment, that anyone has invented a better system. The alternative of the commons is too horrifying to contemplate. Injustice is preferable to total ruin.

It is one of the peculiarities of the warfare between reform and the status quo that it is thoughtlessly governed by a double standard. Whenever a reform measure is proposed it is often defeated when its opponents triumphantly discover a flaw in it. As Kingsley Davis has pointed out (21), worshippers of the status quo sometimes imply that no reform is possible without unanimous agreement, an implication contrary to historical fact. As nearly as I can make out, automatic rejection of proposed reforms is based on one of two unconscious assumptions: (i) that the status quo is perfect; or (ii) that the choice we face is between reform and no action; if the proposed reform is imperfect, we presumably should take no action at all, while we wait for a perfect proposal.

But we can never do nothing. That which we have done for thousands of years is also action. It also produces evils. Once we are aware that the status quo is action, we can then compare its discoverable advantages and disadvantages with the predicted advantages and disadvantages of the proposed reform, discounting as best we can for our lack of experience. On the basis of such a comparison, we can make a rational decision which will not involve the unworkable assumption that only perfect systems are tolerable.

Recognition of Necessity
Perhaps the simplest summary of this analysis of man's population problems is this: the commons, if justifiable at all, is justifiable only under conditions of

low-population density. As the human population has increased, the commons has had to be abandoned in one aspect after another.

First we abandoned the commons in food gathering, enclosing farm land and restricting pastures and hunting and fishing areas. These restrictions are still not complete throughout the world.

Somewhat later we saw that the commons as a place for waste disposal would also have to be abandoned. Restrictions on the disposal of domestic sewage are widely accepted in the Western world; we are still struggling to close the commons to pollution by automobiles, factories, insecticide sprayers, fertilizing operations, and atomic energy installations.

In a still more embryonic state is our recognition of the evils of the commons in matters of pleasure. There is almost no restriction on the propagation of sound waves in the public medium. The shopping public is assaulted with mindless music, without its consent. Our government is paying out billions of dollars to create supersonic transport which will disturb 50,000 people for every one person who is whisked from coast to coast 3 hours faster. Advertisers muddy the airwaves of radio and television and pollute the view of travelers. We are a long way from outlawing the commons in matters of pleasure. Is this because our Puritan inheritance makes us view pleasure as something of a sin, and pain (that is, the pollution of advertising) as the sign of virtue?

Every new enclosure of the commons involves the infringement of somebody's personal liberty. Infringements made in the distant past are accepted because no contemporary complains of a loss. It is the newly proposed infringements that we vigorously oppose; cries of "rights" and "freedom" fill the air. But what does "freedom" mean? When men mutually agreed to pass laws against robbing, mankind became more free, not less so. Individuals locked into the logic of the commons are free only to bring on universal ruin; once they see the necessity of mutual coercion, they become free to pursue other goals. I believe it was Hegel who said, "Freedom is the recognition of necessity."

The most important aspect of necessity that we must now recognize, is the necessity of abandoning the commons in breeding. No technical solution can rescue us from the misery of overpopulation. Freedom to breed will bring ruin to all. At the moment, to avoid hard decisions many of us are tempted to propagandize for conscience and responsible parenthood. The temptation must be resisted, because an appeal to independently acting consciences selects for the disappearance of all conscience in the long run, and an increase in anxiety in the short.

The only way we can preserve and nurture other and more precious freedoms is by relinquishing the freedom to breed, and that very soon. "Freedom is the recognition of necessity"—and it is the role of education to reveal to all the necessity of abandoning the freedom to breed. Only so, can we put an end to this aspect of the tragedy of the commons.

REFERENCES

1. J. B. Wiesner and H. F. York, *Sci. Amer.* 211 (No. 4), 27 (1964).
2. G. Hardin, *J. Hered.* 50, 68 (1959); S. von Hoernor, *Science* 137, 18 (1962).
3. J. von Neumann and O. Morgenstern. *Theory of Games and Economic Behavior* (Princeton Univ. Press, Princeton, N.J., 1947), p. 11.
4. J. H. Fremlin, *New Sci.,* No. 415 (1964), p. 285.

5. A. Smith, *The Wealth of Nations* (Modern Library, New York, 1937), p. 423.
6. W. F. Lloyd, *Two Lectures on the Checks to Population* (Oxford Univ. Press, Oxford, England, 1833), reprinted (in part) in *Population, Evolution, and Birth Control*, G. Hardin, Ed. (Freeman, San Francisco, 1964), p. 37.
7. A. N. Whitehead, *Science and the Modern World* (Mentor, New York, 1948), p. 17.
8. G. Hardin, Ed. *Population, Evolution, and Birth Control* (Freeman, San Francisco, 1964), p. 56.
9. S. McVay, *Sci. Amer.* 216 (No. 8), 13 (1966).
10. J. Fletcher, *Situation Ethics* (Westminster, Philadelphia, 1966).
11. D. Lack, *The Natural Regulation of Animal Numbers* (Clarendon Press, Oxford, 1954).
12. H. Girvetz, *From Wealth to Welfare* (Stanford Univ. Press, Stanford, Calif., 1950).
13. G. Hardin, *Perspec. Biol. Med.* 6, 366 (1963).
14. U. Thant, *Int. Planned Parenthood News*, No. 168 (February 1968), p. 3.
15. K. Davis, *Science* 158, 730 (1967).
16. S. Tax, Ed., *Evolution after Darwin* (Univ. of Chicago Press, Chicago, 1960), vol. 2, p. 469.
17. G. Bateson, D. D. Jackson, J. Haley, J. Weakland, *Behav. Sci.* 1, 251 (1956).
18. P. Goodman, *New York Rev. Books* 10 (8), 22 (23 May 1968).
19. A. Comfort, *The Anxiety Makers* (Nelson, London, 1967).
20. C. Frankel, *The Case for Modern Man* (Harper, New York, 1955), p. 203.
21. J. D. Roslansky, *Genetics and the Future of Man* (Appleton-Century-Crofts, New York, 1966), p. 177.

67   The Tragedy of the Commons Revisited

BERYL L. CROWE

There has developed in the contemporary natural sciences a recognition that there is a subset of problems, such as population, atomic war, and environmental corruption, for which there are no technical solutions (1, 2). There is also an increasing recognition among contemporary social scientists that there is a subset of problems, such as population, atomic war, environmental corruption, and the recovery of a livable urban environment, for which there are no current political solutions (3). The thesis of this article is that the common area shared by these two subsets contains most of the critical problems that threaten the very existence of contemporary man.

The importance of this area has not been raised previously because of the very structure of modern society. This society, with its emphasis on differentiation and specialization, has led to the development of two insular scientific communities—the natural and the social—between which there is very little communication and a great deal of envy, suspicion, disdain, and competition for scarce resources. Indeed, these two communities more closely resemble tribes living in close geographic proximity on university campuses than they resemble the "scientific culture" that C. P. Snow placed in contrast to and opposition to the "humanistic culture" (4).

Perhaps the major problems of modern society have, in large part, been allowed to develop and intensify through this structure of insularity and specialization because it serves both psychological and professional functions for both scientific communities. Under such conditions, the natural sciences can recognize that some problems are not technically soluble and relegate them to the nether land of politics, while the social sciences recognize that some problems have no current political solutions and then postpone a search for solutions while they wait for new technologies with which to attack the problem. Both sciences can thus avoid responsibility and protect their respective myths of competence and relevance, while they avoid having to face the awesome and awful possibility that each has independently isolated the same subset of problems and given them different names. Thus, both never have to face the consequences of their respective findings. Meanwhile, due to the specialization and insularity of modern society, man's most critical problems lie in limbo, while the specialists in problem-solving go on to less critical problems for which they can find technical or political solutions.

In this circumstance, one psychologically brave, but professionally foolhardy soul, Garrett Hardin, has dared to cross the tribal boundaries in his article "The Tragedy of the Commons" (1). In it, he gives vivid proof of the insularity of the two scientific tribes in at least two respects: first, his "rediscovery" of the tragedy was in part wasted effort, for the knowledge of this tragedy is so common in the social sciences that it has generated some fairly sophisticated mathematical models (5); second, the recognition of the existence of a subset of problems for which science neither offers nor aspires to offer technical solutions is not likely, under the contemporary conditions of insularity, to gain wide currency in the social sciences. Like Hardin, I will attempt to avoid the psychological and professional benefits of this insularity by tracing some of the political and social implications of his proposed solution to the tragedy of the commons.

The commons is a fundamental social institution that has a history going back through our own colonial experience to a body of English common law which antidates the Roman conquest. That law recognized that in societies there are some environmental objects which have never been, and should never be, exclusively appropriated to any individual or group of individuals. In England the classic example of the commons is the pasturage set aside for public use, and the "tragedy of the commons" to which Hardin refers was a tragedy of overgrazing and lack of care and fertilization which resulted in erosion and underproduction so destructive that there developed in the late 19th century an enclosure movement. Hardin applies this social institution to other environmental objects such as water, atmosphere, and living space.

The cause of this tragedy is exposed by a very simple mathematical model, utilizing the concept of utility drawn from economics. Allowing the utilities to range between a positive value of 1 and a negative value of 1, we may ask, as did the individual English herdsman, what is the utility to me of adding one more animal to my herd that grazes on the commons? His answer is that the positive utility is near 1 and the negative utility is only a fraction of minus 1. Adding together the component partial utilities, the herdsman concludes that it is rational for him to add another animal to his herd; then another, and so on. The tragedy to which Hardin refers develops because the same rational conclusion is reached by each and every herdsman sharing the commons.

Assumptions Necessary To Avoid the Tragedy

In passing the technically insoluble problems over to the political and social realm for solution, Hardin has made three critical assumptions: (i) that there exists, or can be developed, a "criterion of judgment and a system of weighting . . . " that will "render the incommensurables . . . commensurable . . . " in real life; (ii) that, possessing this criterion of judgment, "coercion can be mutually agreed upon," and that the application of coercion to effect a solution to problems will be effective in modern society; and (iii) that the administrative system, supported by the criterion of judgment and access to coercion, can and will protect the commons from further desecration.

If all three of these assumptions were correct, the tragedy which Hardin has recognized would dissolve into a rather facile melodrama of setting up administrative agencies. I believe these three assumptions are so questionable in contemporary society that a tragedy remains in the full sense in which Hardin used the term. Under contemporary conditions, the subset of technically insoluble problems is also politically insoluble, and thus we witness a full-blown tragedy wherein "the essence of dramatic tragedy is not unhappiness. It resides in the remorseless working of things."

The remorseless working of things in modern society is the erosion of three social myths which form the basis for Hardin's assumptions, and this erosion is proceeding at such a swift rate that perhaps the myths can neither revitalize nor reformulate in time to prevent the "population bomb" from going off, or before an accelerating "pollution immersion," or perhaps even an "atomic fallout."

Eroding Myth of the Common Value System

Hardin is theoretically correct, from the point of view of the behavioral sciences, in his argument that "in real life incommensurables *are* commensurable." He is, moreover, on firm ground in his assertion that to fulfill this condition in real life one needs only "a criterion of judgment and a system of weighting." In real life, however, values are the criteria of judgment, and the system of weighting is dependent upon the ranging of a number of conflicting values in a hierarchy. That such a system of values exists beyond the confines of the nation-state is hardly tenable. At this point in time one is more likely to find such a system of values within the boundaries of the nation-state. Moreover, the nation-state is the only political unit of sufficient dimension to find and enforce political solutions to Hardin's subset of "technically insoluble problems." It is on this political unit that we will fix our attention.

In America there existed, until very recently, a set of conditions which perhaps made the solution to Hardin's problem subset possible: we lived with the myth that we were "one people, indivisible . . . " This myth postulated that we were the great "melting pot" of the world wherein the diverse cultural ores of Europe were poured into the crucible of the frontier experience to produce a new alloy—an American civilization. This new civilization was presumably united by a common value system that was democratic, equalitarian, and existing under universally enforceable rules contained in the Constitution and the Bill of Rights.

In the United States today, however, there is emerging a new set of behavior patterns which suggest that the myth is either dead or dying. Instead of believing and behaving in accordance with the myth, large sectors of the population are developing life-styles and value hierarchies that give contemporary Americans an appearance more closely analogous to the particularistic, primitive forms of "tribal" organizations living in geographic proximity than to that shining new alloy, the American civilization.

With respect to American politics, for example, it is increasingly evident that the 1960 election was the last election in the United States to be played out according to the rules of pluralistic politics in a two-party system. Certainly 1964 was, even in terms of voting behavior, a contest between the larger tribe that was still committed to the pluralistic model of compromise and accommodation within a winning coalition, and an emerging tribe that is best seen as a millennial revitalization movement directed against mass society—a movement so committed to the revitalization of old values that it would rather lose the election than compromise its values. Under such circumstances former real-life commensurables within the Republican Party suddenly became incommensurable.

In 1968 it was the Democratic Party's turn to suffer the degeneration of commensurables into incommensurables as both the Wallace tribe and the McCarthy tribe refused to play by the old rules of compromise, accommodation, and exchange of interests. Indeed, as one looks back on the 1968 election, there seems to be a common theme in both these camps—a theme of return to more simple and direct participation in decision-making that is only possible in the tribal setting. Yet, despite that similarity, both the Wallaceites and the McCarthyites responded with a value perspective that ruled out compromise and they both demanded a drastic change in the dimension in which politics is played. So firm were the value commitments in both of these tribes that neither (as was the case with the Goldwater forces in 1964) was willing to settle for a modicum of power that could accrue through the processes of compromise with the national party leadership.

Still another dimension of this radical change in behavior is to be seen in the black community where the main trend of the argument seems to be, not in the direction of accommodation, compromise, and integration, but rather in the direction of fragmentation from the larger community, intransigence in the areas where black values and black culture are concerned, and the structuring of a new community of like-minded and like-colored people. But to all appearances even the concept of color is not enough to sustain commensurables in their emerging community as it fragments into religious nationalism, secular nationalism, integrationists, separationists, and so forth. Thus those problems which were commensurable, both interracial and intracial, in the era of integration become incommensurable in the era of Black Nationalism.

Nor can the growth of commensurable views be seen in the contemporary youth movements. On most of the American campuses today there are at least ten tribes involved in "tribal wars" among themselves and against the "imperialistic" powers of those "over 30." Just to tick them off, without any attempt to be comprehensive, there are: the up-tight protectors of the status quo who are looking for middle-class union cards, the revitalization movements of the Young Americans for Freedom, the reformists of pluralism represented by the Young Democrats and the Young Republicans, those committed to New Politics, the Students for a Democratic Society, the Yippies, the Flower Children, the Black Students Union, and the Third World Liberation Front. The critical change in this instance is not the rise of new groups; this is expected within the pluralistic model of politics. What is new are value positions assumed by these groups which lead them to make demands, not as points for bargaining and compromise with the opposition, but rather as points which are "not negotiable." Hence, they consciously set the stage for either confrontation or surrender, but not for rendering incommensurables commensurable.

Moving out of formalized politics and off the campus, we see the remnants of the "hippie" movement which show clear-cut tribal overtones in their commune movements. This movement has, moreover, already fragmented into an urban tribe which can talk of guerrilla warfare against the city fathers, while another tribe finds accommodation to urban life untenable without sacrificing its values and therefore moves out to the "Hog Farm," "Morning Star," or "Big Sur." Both hippie tribes have reduced the commensurables with the dominant WASP tribe to the point at which one of the cities on the Monterey Peninsula felt sufficiently threatened to pass a city ordinance against sleeping in trees, and the city of San Francisco passed a law against sitting on sidewalks.

Even among those who still adhere to the pluralistic middle-class American image, we can observe an increasing demand for a change in the dimension of life and politics that has disrupted the elementary social processes: the demand for neighborhood (tribal?) schools, control over redevelopment projects, and autonomy in the setting and payment of rents to slumlords. All of these trends are more suggestive of tribalism than of the growth of the range of commensurables with respect to the commons.

We are, moreover, rediscovering other kinds of tribes in some very odd ways. For example, in the educational process, we have found that one of our first and best empirical measures in terms both of validity and reproducibility—the I.Q. test—is a much better measure of the existence of different linguistic tribes than it is a measure of "native intellect" (6). In the elementary school, the different languages and different values of these diverse tribal children have even rendered the commensurables that obtained in the educational system suddenly incommensurable.

Nor are the empirical contradictions of the common value myth as new as one might suspect. For example, with respect to the urban environment, at least 7 years ago Scott Greer was arguing that the core city was sick and would remain sick until a basic sociological movement took place in our urban environment that would move all the middle classes to the suburbs and surrender the core city to the " . . . segregated, the insulted, and the injured" (7). This argument by Greer came at a time when most of us were still talking about compromise and accommodation of interests, and was based upon a perception that the life styles, values, and needs of these two groups were so disparate that a healthy, creative restructuring of life in the core city could not take place until pluralism had been replaced by what amounted to geographic or territorial tribalism; only when this occurred would urban incommensurables become commensurable.

Looking at a more recent analysis of the sickness of the core city, Wallace F. Smith has argued that the productive model of the city is no longer viable for the purposes of economic analysis (8). Instead, he develops a model of the city as a site for leisure consumption, and then seems to suggest that the nature of this model is such that the city cannot regain its health because it cannot make decisions, and that it cannot make decisions because the leisure demands are value-based and, hence, do not admit of compromise and accommodation; consequently there is no way of deciding among these various value-oriented demands that are being made on the core city.

In looking for the cause of the erosion of the myth of a common value system, it seems to me that so long as our perceptions and knowledge of other groups were formed largely through the written media of communication, the American myth that we were a giant melting pot of equalitarians could be sustained. In such a perceptual field it is tenable, if not obvious, that men are motivated by interests. Interests can always be compromised and accommodated without undermining our very being by sacrificing values. Under the impact of the electronic media, however, this psychological distance has broken down and we now discover that these people with whom we could formerly compromise on interests are not, after all, really motivated by interests but by values. Their behavior in our very living room betrays a set of values, moreover, that are incompatible with our own, and consequently the compromises that we make are not those of contract but of culture. While the former are acceptable, any form of compromise on the latter is not a form of rational behavior but is rather a clear case of either apostasy or heresy. Thus, we have arrived not at an age of accommodation but one of confrontation. In such an age "incommensurables" remain "incommensurable" in real life.

Erosion of the Myth of the Monopoly of Coercive Force

In the past, those who no longer subscribed to the values of the dominant culture were held in check by the myth that the state possessed a monopoly on coercive force. This myth has undergone continual erosion since the end of World War II owing to the success of the strategy of guerrilla warfare, as first revealed to the French in Indochina, and later conclusively demonstrated in Algeria. Suffering as we do from what Senator Fulbright has called "the arrogance of power," we have been extremely slow to learn the lesson in Vietnam, although we now realize that war is political and cannot be won by military means. It is apparent that the myth of the monopoly of coercive force as it was first qualified in the civil rights conflict in the South, then in our urban ghettos, next on the streets of Chicago, and now on our college campuses has lost its hold over the minds of Americans. The technology of guerrilla warfare has made it evident that, while the state can win battles, it cannot win wars of values. Coercive force which is centered in the modern state cannot be sustained in the face of the active resistance of some 10 percent of its population unless the state is willing to embark on a deliberate policy of genocide directed against the value dissident groups. The factor that sustained the myth of coercive force in the past was the acceptance of a common value system. Whether the latter exists is questionable in the modern nation-state. But, even if most members of the nation-state remain united around a common value system which makes incommensurables for the majority commensurable, that majority is incapable of enforcing its decisions upon the minority in the face of the diminished coercive power of the governing body of the nation-state.

Erosion of the Myth of Administrators of the Commons

Hardin's thesis that the administrative arm of the state is capable of legislating temperance accords with current administrative theory in political science and touches on one of the concerns of that body of theory when he suggests that the " . . . great challenge facing us now is to invent the corrective feedbacks that are needed to keep the custodians honest."

Our best empirical answers to the question—*Quis custodiet ipsos custodes?* —"Who shall watch the watchers themselves?"—have shown fairly conclusively (9) that the decisions, orders, hearings, and press releases of the custodians of the commons, such as the Federal Communications Commission, the Interstate Commerce Commission, the Federal Trade Commission, and even the Bureau of Internal Revenue, give the large but unorganized groups in American society symbolic satisfaction and assurances. Yet, the actual day-to-day decisions and operations of these administrative agencies contribute, foster, aid, and indeed legitimate the special claims of small but highly organized groups to differential access to tangible resources which are extracted from the commons. This has been so well documented in the social sciences that the best answer to the question of who watches over the custodians of the commons is the regulated interests that make incursions on the commons.

Indeed, the process has been so widely commented upon that one writer has postulated a common life cycle for all of the attempts to develop regulatory policies (10). This life cycle is launched by an outcry so widespread and demanding that it generates enough political force to bring about the establishment of a regulatory agency to insure the equitable, just, and rational distribution of the advantages among all holders of interest in the commons. This phase is followed by the symbolic reassurance of the offended as the agency goes into operation, developing a period of political quiescence among the great majority of those who hold a general but unorganized interest in the commons. Once this political quiescence has developed, the highly organized and specifically interested groups who wish to make incursions into the commons bring sufficient pressure to bear through other political processes to convert the agency to the protection and furthering of their interests. In the last phase even staffing of the regulating agency is accomplished by drawing the agency administrators from the ranks of the regulated.

Thus, it would seem that, even with the existence of a common value system accompanied by a viable myth of the monopoly of coercive force, the prospects are very dim for saving the commons from differential exploitation or spoliation by the administrative devices in which Hardin places his hope. This being the case, the natural sciences may absolve themselves of responsibility for meeting the environmental challenges of the contemporary world by relegating those problems for which there are no technical solutions to the political or social realm. This action will, however, make little contribution to the solution of the problem.

Are the Critical Problems of Modern Society Insoluble?

Earlier in this article I agreed that perhaps until very recently, there existed a set of conditions which made the solution of Hardin's problem subset possible; now I suggest that the concession is questionable. There is evidence of structural as well as value problems which make comprehensive solutions impossible and these conditions have been present for some time.

For example, Aaron Wildavsky, in a comprehensive study of the budgetary process, has found that in the absence of a calculus for resolving "intrapersonal comparison of utilities," the governmental budgetary process proceeds by a calculus that is sequential and incremental rather than comprehensive. This being the case " ... if one looks at politics as a process by which the government mobilizes resources to meet pressing problems" (11), the budget is the focus of these problem responses and the responses to problems in contemporary America are not the sort of comprehensive responses required to bring order to a disordered environment. Another example of the operation of this type of rationality is the American involvement in Vietnam; for, what is the policy of escalation but the policy of sequential incrementalism given a new Madison Avenue euphemism? The question facing us all is the question of whether incremental rationality is sufficient to deal with 20th-century problems.

The operational requirements of modern institutions make incremental rationality the only viable form of decision-making, but this only raises the prior question of whether there are solutions to any of the major problems raised in modern society. It may well be that the emerging forms of tribal behavior noted in this article are the last hope of reducing political and social institutions to a level where incommensurables become commensurable in terms of values *and* in terms of comprehensive responses to problems. After all, in the history of man on earth we might well assume that the departure from the tribal experience is a short-run deviant experiment that failed. As we stand "on the eve of destruction," it may well be that the return to the face-to-face life in the small community unmediated by the electronic media is a very functional response in terms of the perpetuation of the species.

There is, I believe, a significant sense in which the human environment is directly in conflict with the source of man's ascendancy among the other species of the earth. Man's evolutionary position hinges, not on specialization, but rather on generalized adaptability. Modern social and political institutions, however, hinge on specialized, sequential, incremental decision-making and not on generalized adaptability. This being the case, life in the nation-state will continue to require a singleness of purpose for success but in a very critical sense this singleness of purpose becomes a straightjacket that makes generalized adaptation impossible. Nowhere is this conflict more evident than in our urban centers where there has been a decline in the livability of the total environment that is almost directly proportionate to the rise of special purpose districts. Nowhere is this conflict between institutional singleness of purpose and the human dimension of the modern environment more evident than in the recent warning of S. Goran Lofroth, chairman of a committee studying pesticides for the Swedish National Research Council, that many breast-fed children ingest from their mother's milk "more than the recommended daily intake of DDT" (12) and should perhaps be switched to cow's milk because cows secrete only 2 to 10 percent of the DDT they ingest.

How Can Science Contribute to the Saving of the Commons?

It would seem that, despite the nearly remorseless working of things, science has some interim contributions to make to the alleviation of those problems of the commons which Hardin has pointed out.

These contributions can come at two levels:

1) Science can concentrate more of its attention on the development of

technological responses which at once alleviate those problems and reward those people who no longer desecrate the commons. This approach would seem more likely to be successful than the " . . . fundamental extension in morality . . . " by administrative law; the engagement of interest seems to be a more reliable and consistent motivator of advantage-seeking groups than does administrative wrist-slapping or constituency pressure from the general public.

2) Science can perhaps, by using the widely proposed environmental monitoring systems, use them in such a way as to sustain a high level of "symbolic disassurance" among the holders of generalized interests in the commons—thus sustaining their political interest to a point where they would provide a constituency for the administrator other than those bent on denuding the commons. This latter approach would seem to be a first step toward the " . . . invention of the corrective feedbacks that are needed to keep custodians honest." This would require a major change in the behavior of science, however, for it could no longer rest content with development of the technology of monitoring and with turning the technology over to some new agency. Past administrative experience suggests that the use of technology to sustain a high level of "dis-assurance" among the general population would also require science to take up the role and the responsibility for maintaining, controlling, and disseminating the information.

Neither of these contributions to maintaining a habitable environment will be made by science unless there is a significant break in the insularity of the two scientific tribes. For, if science must, in its own insularity, embark on the independent discovery of "the tragedy of the commons," along with the parameters that produce the tragedy, it may be too slow a process to save us from the total destruction of the planet. Just as important, however, science will, by pursuing such a course, divert its attention from the production of technical tools, information, and solutions which will contribute to the political and social solutions for the problems of the commons.

Because I remain very suspicious of the success of either demands or pleas for fundamental extensions in morality, I would suggest that such a conscious turning by both the social and the natural sciences is, at this time, in their immediate self-interest. As Michael Polanyi has pointed out, " . . . encircled today between the crude utilitarianism of the philistine and the ideological utilitarianism of the modern revolutionary movement, the love of pure science may falter and die" (13). The sciences, both social and natural, can function only in a very special intellectual environment that is neither universal nor unchanging, and that environment is in jeopardy. The questions of humanistic relevance raised by the students at M.I.T., Stanford Research Institute, Berkeley, and wherever the headlines may carry us tomorrow, pose serious threats to the maintenance of that intellectual environment. However ill-founded *some* of the questions raised by the new generation may be, it behooves us to be ready with at least some collective, tentative answers—if only to maintain an environment in which both sciences will be allowed and fostered. This will not be accomplished so long as the social sciences continue to defer the most critical problems that face mankind to future technical advances, while the natural sciences continue to defer those same problems which are about to overwhelm all mankind to false expectations in the political realm.

REFERENCES AND NOTES

1. G. Hardin, *Science* 162, 1243 (1968).
2. J. B. Wiesner and H. F. York, *Sci. Amer.* 211 (No. 4), 27 (1964).
3. C. Woodbury, *Amer. J. Public Health* 45, 1 (1955); S. Marquis, *Amer. Behav. Sci.* 11, 11 (1968); W. H. Ferry, *Center Mag.* 2, 2 (1969).
4. C. P. Snow, *The Two Cultures and the Scientific Revolution* (Cambridge Univ. Press, New York, 1959).
5. M. Olson, Jr., *The Logic of Collective Action* (Harvard Univ. Press, Cambridge, Mass., 1965).
6. G. A. Harrison *et al., Human Biology* (Oxford Univ. Press, New York, 1964). p. 292; W. W. Charters, Jr. in *School Children in the Urban Slum* (Free Press, New York, 1967).
7. S. Greer, *Governing the Metropolis* (Wiley, New York, 1962), p. 148.
8. W. F. Smith, "The Class Struggle and the Disquieted City," a paper presented at the 1969 annual meeting of the Western Economic Association, Oregon State University, Corvallis.
9. M. Bernstein, *Regulating Business by Independent Commissions* (Princeton Univ. Press, Princeton, N.J., 1955); E. P. Herring, *Public Administration and the Public Interest* (McGraw-Hill, New York, 1936); E. M. Redford, *Administration of National Economic Control* (Macmillan, New York, 1952).
10. M. Edelman, *The Symbolic Uses of Politics* (Univ. of Illinois Press, Urbana, 1964).
11. A. Wildavsky, *The Politics of the Budgetary Process* (Little Brown, Boston, Mass., 1964).
12. Corvallis *Gazette-Times,* 6 May 1969, p. 6.
13. M. Polanyi, *Personal Knowledge* (Harper & Row, New York, 1964), p. 182.

THE FOOD CRISIS

The Hunting Culture vs
The Agricultural Treadmill or
(Who Can Afford Waste?)

The earth is now on a fossil fuel and photosynthetic energy budget. However, there is a finite supply of fossil fuel. If we turn to nuclear power as our supply dwindles, numerous problems stand in the way of development. Prior to the industrial revolution the life support system was powered almost exclusively by the green plant. How many people could the earth support now on a strictly photosynthetic energy budget?

Agriculture inflated the energy budget of man as a species. Energy budget standards established during nearly two million years of history as a hunter were decidedly raised when agriculture began about 8,000 years ago. While we are examining a depreciated energy budget, one might consider how many people the earth could support on a hunting-only energy budget.

Does man have the wisdom to handle the energy level above that of hunting? Once man got hooked on the inflated agricultural budget and later fossil fuel, there was no turning back. This is the historical background of an expansive economy. Not only does growth promote growth, but more importantly, growth requires more growth. Japan, a crowded nation that has effectively lowered the birthrate, has recently announced the need to increase its population. This nation of 102 million in an area about the size of Montana must increase the number of producers to be economically sound in twenty years or so.

It is likely that in our not too distant past, hunting was a way of life. Abundant rainfall for several seasons in an area produced lush vegetation, an increase in the number of primary consumers and an increase in the number of humans. When drought came, man starved, migrated or began to plant the weeds that followed his campfires. In breaking the ground and reducing the diversity of species in the region, he reduced the total energy moving through the system but increased the energy available to him by growing only plants he cared to eat. Agriculture, a temporary development, became a way of life because food supply is the primary determiner of man's numbers.

The agricultural treadmill moves even faster on a heavily subsidized fossil fuel budget. This fuel which drives our technology has been destroying our biosphere. Can we save ourselves only by de-escalating our numbers to a level that can be supported by a hunting way of life?

An Indian Method of Hunting Buffalo   **68**

MERIWETHER LEWIS

today we passed on the Stard. side the remains of a vast many mangled carcases of Buffalow which had been driven over a precipice of 120 feet by the Indians and perished; the water appeared to have washed away a part of this immence pile of slaughter and still their remained the fragments of at least a hundred carcases   they created a most horrid stench. In this manner the Indians of the Missouri distroy vast herds of buffaloe at a stroke;   for this purpose one of the most active and fleet young men is scelected and disguised in a robe of buffaloe skin, having also the skin of the buffaloe's head with the years and horns fastened on his head in form of a cap, thus caparisoned he places himself at a convenient distance between a herd of buffaloe and a precipice proper for the prupose, which happens in many places on this river for miles together; the other indians now surround the herd on the back and flanks and at a signal agreed on all shew themselves at the same time moving forward towards the buffaloe;   the disguised indian or decoy has taken care to place himself sufficiently nigh the buffaloe to be noticed by them when they take to flight and runing before them they follow him in full speede to the precipice, the cattle behind driving those in front over and seeing them go do not look or hesitate about following untill the whole are precipitated down the precepice forming one common mass of dead and mangled carcases: the decoy in the mean time has taken care to secure himself in some cranney or crivice of the clift which he had previously prepared for that purpose. the part of the decoy I am informed is extreamly dangerous, if they are not very fleet runers the buffaloe tread them under foot and crush them to death, and sometimes drive them over the precipice also, where they perish in common with the buffaloe.

Food Production in Prehistoric Europe   **69**

H. T. WATERBOLK

By about 3000 B.C. all the plains south of the Scandinavian mountains were inhabited by people who lived together in villages of a more or less permanent character. These settlers cut the deciduous forest with stone axes, cultivated a variety of crops, and raised cattle, sheep, goats, and pigs. Hunting was of little importance.

The art of pottery was known everywhere. From highly varied shape and ornamentation, archeologists have been able to distinguish a number of cultures of limited geographical and chronological occurrence and various degrees of relation.

How different is the picture if we go back in time another 5000 years, to about 8000 B.C. The last cold spell of the Ice Age was then almost over. Hunting and gathering were the major means of subsistence. Animal domestication and plant cultivation were unknown. Camp sites were relatively impermanent, shifting from one place to another.

From 8000 to 3000 B.C. in southwestern Asia there was a progression from food collecting to urban civilization, through the levels of incipient cultivation and domestication, of primary effective village farming and of developed village farming and town life.

70   The Tehuacan Story

ROBERT CLAIBORNE

The Tehuacan story begins around 10,000 B.C. Then and for some 3000 years thereafter, the valley was occupied by a few families of nomadic hunters, totaling perhaps twenty men, women, and children. Their lives resembled those of today's South African Bushmen. Season by season, each family group wandered from one camp to another, hunting game with stone weapons and collecting the fruits, seeds, and roots of wild plants. Their meat diet came chiefly from small game—jackrabbits, gophers, rats, birds, and turtles. These people were not the "mammoth hunters" whose remains have been found elsewhere in North America. The first Tehuacanos, commented one expert, "probably found one mammoth in a lifetime and—like some archaeologists—never got over talking about it."

Slowly, these primitive people evolved a slightly more complex culture. The valley's population increased, though by 7000 B.C. it still numbered less than 100. Meat was scarcer, perhaps because there were more people, perhaps because the valley, growing drier, had become less hospitable to animal life. When the spring rains came, the families now congregated in somewhat larger bands to gather the briefly burgeoning wild plants. To prepare these increasingly important plant foods, they hammered out a variety of stone scrapers, choppers, and grinding stones. Their diet now included a kind of squash, amaranth, tiny avocadoes with pea-sized pits, and chili peppers—all of which were subsequently cultivated in Mexico, and still are. They wove nets, perhaps for snaring animals, and baskets, as well as colorful blankets of dyed wild cotton.

Along with these richer material goods, they had developed a fairly complex ceremonial and spiritual life. They may have practiced human sacrifice (a motif that crops up repeatedly in Middle American culture) and unquestionably buried their dead elaborately.

Though the Tehuacanos had clearly progressed beyond the bare subsistence level, by Old World standards they were still terribly primitive. Their contemporaries in Mesopotamia and Asia Minor were already full-time farmers, raising grain and vegetables and herding cows, sheep, goats, and pigs.

Sometime around 5500 B.C. these ancestral Mexicans seem to have conceived the notion that if you drop a seed in the ground at the proper time, a plant will grow up. The archaeological record shows that by that date the avocado pits are no longer pea-sized but acorn-sized, presumably as a result of cultivation. A little later, a new type of squash has appeared in the valley—and one that had no wild counterpart there. The prevalence of its seeds leaves little doubt that the "import" was sown and harvested in Tehuacan.

Around 5000 B.C. corn makes its first appearance among the relics. It was far from the corn we know today. Its skinny cobs, most of them less than an inch long, bore some fifty small kernels. These were rather loosely attached to the cob, and, unlike modern corn, were not completely enclosed in a husk, so that at maturity they could be jarred loose by a gust of wind and scattered to reproduce themselves. (Modern corn could not survive if it were not sown by man.) These remnants are true wild corn. Gathering it must have been a rather unprofitable business. The open husk gave free rein to birds and rodents, and the loosely attached kernels could too easily be scattered by a careless harvester.

By 4000 B.C. the Tehuacanos are quite definitely growing two kinds of squash, gourds, beans, and several other food plants. And they are growing corn. But this corn hardly differs from the wild variety. Its cobs are merely a little bigger.

Altogether, these cultivated plants supply only about a quarter of the Tehuacanos' diet. Though the people can now gather in large groups during the growing season, in the dry season they must still hit the foraging trail in small, family bands. The valley's population, in 300 generations, has grown only to about 200. (In Mesopotamia, men are already living in towns and building mud temples; before very long they will invent writing and the wheel.)

Now the pace of progress in Tehuacan begins to speed up a little. As the people harvested their corn patches, they must have selected the larger, more productive ears for next year's seed. Moreover, a new variety of corn makes its appearance. Called "early tripsacoid," it seems to represent a cross between corn and related wild grasses. The hybrid yielded ears considerably larger than those of the original Tehuacan strain; moreover, its kernels were more firmly attached to the cob, making for easier harvesting.

By 2000 B.C., the valley is dotted with half-a-dozen little villages, each surrounded by patches of corn, beans, squash, and pumpkins; dogs scavenge among the refuse heaps (and are doubtless served up as the *piece de resistance* on feast days). The population still raises less than half its food, but it is a considerably bigger population—800 or so. It is also more skilled—its basketry, weaving, and stonework are more sophisticated, and it has learned how to make pottery, albeit still crude and poorly fired.

The corn crop continues to improve. The tripsacoid strain has crossed with the original Tehuacan strain, and some of the crosses are yielding fat ears, three inches or more long, bearing several hundred kernels. The ears are beginning to reach maturity enclosed in tight husks, which help ensure that men, rather than animals, will reap the crop—and which also make corn wholly dependent on man for propagation. It was this strain of corn that eventually replaced its wild ancestor.

By 1500 B.C. Tehuacan's transition toward an agricultural way of life is nearly complete. The population, farmers all, has passed the 2,000 mark, and is grouped in permanent villages of perhaps 200 souls. Before many generations have passed, these villages will begin to group together around small towns, each with its mud or mud-brick temple.

Around 800 B.C.—about the time that Homer was writing the Iliad—the Tehuacanos reach another milestone: they begin to irrigate their fields, constructing earth dams and crude ditches. With this systematic use of water, plus continued improvement in crop strains, the food supply leaps, and with it the population, to perhaps 8,000. The villages are larger, the temples are beginning to be built in stone rather than mud. Moreover, the valley is now in regular contact with other peoples. Chief among these—judging from the new patterns of tools and pottery—are the already-civilized Olmecs, who live several hundred miles to the east along the Gulf of Mexico.

By the time of Christ, other peoples have contributed additional food resources: peanuts, sunflowers, tomatoes, guavas, and turkeys. Agriculture is almost certainly regulated by some sort of calendar. One of the irrigation dams is now a masonry structure 70 feet high and a quarter-mile long. Anticipating the design of the most sophisticated modern dams, it is curved against the pressure of stored water, and has stone breakwaters upstream to protect it from the summer's flash floods. The population has swelled to around 20,000, and some of the villages have grown into sizable hilltop towns.

In the reigns of Charlemagne and Alfred the Great, the Tehuacanos number close to 100,000, supported by an agriculture based on large-scale irrigation. The valley is divided up into four or five little city-states, each consisting of a half-dozen farming villages centered around a city. The states may already be—as they certainly become later—feudal dependencies of the Mixtec Empire. Trade is thriving. Specialist craftsmen produce cotton textiles, pottery, and salt for export.

To coordinate and enforce this complex social structure, other classes of specialists have grown up: professional priest-bureaucrats who keep records in picture writing, professional soldiers of a standing army, and perhaps a god-king or emperor over all. These, in turn, were undoubtedly supported by some system of taxation. Tehuacan has become thoroughly civilized.

71   Japan
           A Crowded Nation Wants To Boost Its Birthrate

                          PHILIP M. BOFFEY

Japan is the most crowded nation in the world. It has 102 million people—half as many as the United States—all crammed into a string of narrow islands that are smaller in total area than Montana. Moreover, 85 percent of Japan's territory is mountainous—a scenic splendor but ill-suited for habitation—so the huge population is actually squeezed into a series of narrow valleys and coastal plains. Japan far exceeds any other country in population density per inhabitable area. As of 1968, Japan had 1333 inhabitants per square kilometer of cultivable land, compared with 565 for runner-up Holland.

The resulting congestion seems unbelievable to many Westerners. Farmland is so scarce that one finds crops growing everywhere—up the sides of steep hills, in the narrow alleys between adjacent railroad tracks, even at the front stoop, where one ordinarily expects to find a lawn. In the cities, and even in rural villages, tiny houses are jammed side by side, with little or no yard space and barely enough room to walk between. Living is so close that privacy is difficult. As one Japanese physician expressed it: "It's a standing joke among us that you can always tell what a neighbor is cooking. If you can't smell it, you can hear the conversation."

Thus it came as a shock to many Westerners last summer when Prime Minister Eisaku Sato publicly advocated an *increase* in Japan's birthrate. Sato's statement, made in a speech to Japanese newspaper editors, seemed to mark a major reversal of Japan's population policy. For the past two decades, Japan has struggled to curb its population growth, and to a large extent it has succeeded. But now, the Prime Minister indicated, the population control effort may have gone too far. Sato noted that Japan's birthrate had fallen below the average for other advanced nations, and he said the government would strive to bring it back up to that average level. Thus, while other world leaders are struggling to curb the widely feared "population explosion," Japan seems to have embarked on a somewhat contrary course.

The Prime Minister's remarks caused great consternation in family planning circles in Japan, for even at the current rate of expansion, Japan's population is expected to rise to 131 million by early next century before starting to decline. Takuma Terao, an economist who is chairman of the Family Planning Federation of Japan, told *Science:* "I am entirely against the idea of raising the birthrate. Japan already has too large a population." Similarly, Minoru Muramatsu, one of Japan's leading authorities on the public health aspects of population growth, said in an interview: "In terms of space, Japan already has too many people. If you live in Tokyo, all you can find is a place to eat and a place to earn money. There is no green, no trees. I don't feel that people are living a very human life."

A High-Level Recommendation

Yet Sato's statement was no irrational, off-the-cuff remark by an uninformed politician. It was based on some cautiously worded recommendations made by the Population Problems Inquiry Council, a cabinet-level advisory group which includes some of Japan's leading demographers. Moreover, the recommendations are aimed at alleviating some potentially serious economic and social problems that are related, at least in part, to Japan's success at curbing its population growth. One such problem is a worsening labor shortage that threatens to undermine Japan's "economic miracle"; another is an increasing number of elderly people who will have to be cared for somehow, particularly now that Japan's traditional descendant family system, in which the younger generations cared for the older, is breaking up.

This article will make no attempt to prescribe what Japan's population policy should be, for the Japanese, one of the world's most highly educated and industrious peoples, are certainly capable of deciding for themselves what sort of future environment they want. But the Japanese situation is worth examining in some detail because the same problems—and the same political and economic pressures

—may well arise in this country as the population growth here is brought under tighter control.

Japan has undeniably achieved remarkable success at controlling its birthrate. In the early 1920's, the birthrate stood above 36 per 1000 population, but then it declined moderately and steadily, a phenomenon that usually accompanies the transition from an agricultural to an industrial society. The rate fell as low as 26.6 in the late 1930's before the trend was reversed by the pronatal policy of Japan's military leaders. After the Second World War the rate soared back up as Japan experienced the normal "baby boom" that occurs when soldiers and overseas civilians return home. The birthrate reached 34.3 in 1947 (an intermediate level by world standards) and stayed above 33 in 1948 and 1949, before beginning the precipitous drop that has brought Japan such praise for its "population miracle." By 1957 Japan's birthrate had fallen to 17.2, a historically unprecedented drop of 50 percent in just 10 years. The decline seems especially sharp when measured from the peak of the postwar baby boom, but even compared with prewar trends, the reduction is considered significant.

What was the secret of Japan's success? Interestingly enough, many Japanese demographers describe the achievement as largely "spontaneous" in the sense that the Japanese people, faced with near-starvation economic conditions after the war, concluded on their own that they should limit the number of children. The news media and women's magazines issued dire warnings, particularly at the height of the baby boom, about the bleak future faced by a nation with too many mouths and a war-ravaged economy, and the highly literate Japanese population obviously got the message. The national government unquestionably helped the population control effort, chiefly by reversing its pronatal policy of the war period. A national Eugenic Protection Law, passed in 1948 and subsequently amended, removed the previous obstacles to birth control, abortion, and sterilization. But many Japanese experts believe the government was always at least one step behind what the people were already doing. One reason for the Eugenic Protection Law, for example, was that so many women were obtaining illegal abortions that the government decided it should protect their health by legalizing the procedure. "The government had no definite policy to bring about population control," says Toshio Kuroda, chief of the migration research division at the government's Institute for Population Problems. "It just happened under the very extraordinary situation after the war. Ten years later people looked back and said we were successful at controlling our population. But no expert in Japan predicted it would happen."

The chief method for curbing the birthrate was induced abortion. The Japanese do not seem to have the strong religious scruples against "taking a life" that have hobbled efforts to increase the use of abortion in this country. Indeed, during the 18th and 19th centuries Japanese peasants often resorted to infanticide to get rid of unwanted children at times of crop failure. Today, abortions are legally obtainable for a number of health and economic reasons. In practice, they are said to be obtainable almost at will. The vast majority of abortions are performed by private physicians within the first 3 months of pregnancy, and most of these take place without overnight admission to a hospital or another medical facility. The operations are quite inexpensive, costing an average of $10 to $15, according to one estimate published in 1967. Health insurance benefits often bring the out-of-pocket cost down much faster—sometimes even below $1.

Abortions Declining

The number of officially reported abortions (which is believed to represent about half the total number of abortions) reached a high of 1.17 million in 1955 but has since declined to 757,000 in 1968, largely because of government efforts to encourage contraception as an alternative to abortion. In the early 1950's, according to studies by the Institute for Population Problems, abortion accounted for roughly 70 percent of the decline in Japan's fertility while family planning accounted for 30 percent, but in recent years the percentages have been reversed.

The percentage of couples practicing contraception in Japan seems to be somewhat lower than the figure for comparable populations elsewhere. A 1965 survey indicated that about 67 percent of all Japanese couples either had practiced or were then practicing contraception, compared with perhaps 80 to 90 percent for Great Britain and for the white population of the United States. The most popular contraceptive methods have consistently been the condom and the "safe period" or a combination of both. The Japanese make little use of the "pill" or the intrauterine device (IUD), which are mainstays of the population control effort elsewhere, largely because conservative medical opinion in Japan believes it is not wholesome to introduce foreign materials into a healthy body. The government officially prohibits the insertion of IUD's and the sale of oral contraceptives, and while there are large loopholes in these laws, few Japanese use either of the methods.

Japan's success at curbing its population growth is believed to have contributed significantly to the fantastic economic boom that has propelled Japan's gross national product to third rank in the world. If Japan had not curbed its birthrate so sharply, some analysts say, then a sizable portion of the nations's capital resources would have been used to support new additions to the population and would not have been available for economic recovery and industrial investment. Yet the curbing of population growth has not been an unmixed blessing. As conditions have changed in recent years, industry has increasingly complained about a labor shortage, particularly a shortage of young laborers.

I found considerable disagreement as to whether Japan is really suffering from a labor shortage and, if so, what should be done about it. The age composition of the Japanese population has changed considerably over the past decade or two. There has been a sharp decrease, both absolute and relative, in the population of children below the age of 15, and a sharp increase, both absolute and relative, in the population over 65. Meanwhile, the working age population, from 15 to 64, has continued to increase, but at a slower and slower rate. The average annual increase in the working age population exceeded 1 million for the 1965-70 period, but it will drop to 620,000 for the next 5 years and will become negative by the end of the century. When viewed against the needs of a rapidly expanding economy, the labor pool appears to be shrinking.

"The labor supply has changed rather remarkably from surplus to shortage," says Saburo Okita, director of the Japan Economic Research Center and a member of the Population Problems Inquiry Council. "There is already a shortage of young workers, and while there is still some surplus of middle-aged workers and women, many of us predict there will be a serious labor shortage in the coming years." Some Japanese economists contend that a decline in West Germany's economic growth rate in the late 1950's was caused primarily by a drop in the growth rate for Germany's labor population, and they suggest that Japan's "economic miracle" may be stalled by the same problem.

Seeking Cheap Labor?

Yet Takuma Terao, the economist who heads the Family Planning Federation of Japan, offers a much different analysis. "The industrialists say the labor shortage is very severe," he says. "But I say what is deficient is young labor, which is very cheap. So all we can say is that we lack cheap labor, only that." Terao and most other experts agree that the chief factor behind the shortage of young labor has not been the low birthrates, but rather the great growth in the number of young people who now go on to high school or college instead of beginning work at an early age. Terao believes it would be "rash to raise fertility" simply to assure more laborers. He believes it would be more sensible for Japan to "rationalize" its traditionally inefficient business enterprises so as to gain greater labor productivity. "We already have an abundance of laborers," he says, "but they are not well utilized."

The Population Problems Inquiry Council—the cabinet-level advisory group whose recommendations provided the basis for Prime Minister Sato's remarks—took a middle-of-the-road position. The council which is made up of some 40 public and private members, including academics and business and labor leaders, was asked in April 1967 to study the implications of Japan's low birthrate. Last August a subcommittee of the council issued an interim report on its findings; a final report is due this year [1970]. According to Kuroda, who sat on the council, the interim report represents a "compromise between those who are worried about a labor shortage and those who think Japan is already too populated." The report is said to have been drafted by Minoru Tachi, an eminent demographer who heads the government's Institute of Population Problems. An unofficial English translation was prepared by the U.S. State Department.

The report, if read carefully, does not seem especially earth-shaking. It notes that Japan's population, by some measures, is no longer replacing itself; it warns that this is causing certain problems; and it recommends that Japan seek to achieve a "stationary" population in terms of both total size and age distribution. The reports makes no mention of what the ideal population for Japan should be, and as far as I could tell from talking to two members of the council—namely, Kuroda and Okita—there was little discussion of optimum population size. Instead, the report focused its attention on indicators that measure the changing growth rate and age composition of the Japanese population.

The report expressed particular concern over trends in the net reproduction rate, a measure of the extent to which the female population of child-bearing age is reproducing itself with female babies. If the net reproduction rate is 1, the population will potentially become stationary one generation later. If the rate exceeds 1, the population will continuously increase, and if it falls below 1, the population is expected to begin to decrease one generation later. Japan's rate is currently the lowest in the world except for some East European Communist bloc nations. It has remained slightly below 1 almost every year since 1956, generally ranging between 0.9 and 1.

A Rare Occurrence

The report states that while the rate has occasionally dipped below 1 in other countries, "it is very rare for such a situation to continue for more than ten years." (The net reproduction rate for the United States was 1.2 in 1967 and has not dropped below 1 since the 1930's.) The report suggests that Japan's population reproductivity is now "too low," and while it acknowledges that "a high population increase rate cannot be welcomed," it nevertheless believes it would be "desirable" for the net reproduction rate to return to 1 "in the near future" in order to ease the "severe changes in population composition by age."

But the report is very careful not to suggest any direct intervention by the government, such as subsidies to support additional children. Instead, the report simply urges the government to improve social conditions so that Japanese couples will spontaneously decide to have more children. The report also recommends that Japan improve its old-age welfare system and increase the productivity of its labor system.

The report gives no hint as to how its recommendations would affect the size of Japan's population, but there is no question that the population will continue to rise substantially. Government estimates for Japan's population in the year 2025 range from a minimum of 129 million (if the net reproduction rate remains below 1) to a maximum of 152 million, with the median projection being 140 million.

The report is so cautiously written that even such critics as Muramatsu acknowledge there is "nothing really wrong with it if you read the text very carefully." After all, who can object to the government improving social conditions? But opponents of the report are upset that mass media stressed the need for more births and largely ignored the question of social improvement. Some also feel the government was premature in its announcement, since they believe the net reproduction rate is already heading back toward 1, or even higher, without any encouragement. Other critics fear the government will eventually decide to intervene in a very direct way to encourage more births, and some even fear that the government's action was partly motivated by a desire to grow soldiers for a future large army.

At bottom, the disagreement is one of priorities. Those who regard economic expansion as the greatest good want more bodies to man the assembly lines. Those who are worried about overcrowding are willing to sacrifice some economic growth in return for more living space. The question of how much living space is desirable, however, is a knotty one. My own reaction to Japan was to be appalled at the overcrowding. But there is some evidence that the Japanese have grown accustomed to their close living conditions and actually even like them. Ichiro Kawasaki, a former Japanese diplomat, has written that the massive stone buildings of the West "overwhelm" Japanese travelers, and they soon "begin to miss the light wooden structures and small landscape gardens to which they have so long been accustomed." Similarly, Maramatsu, who spent several years at Johns Hopkins University and who frequently travels abroad, laments that many Japanese have no idea what he is talking about when he extols the "spacious way of living" in other countries. "For generations," he says, "many of our people have been living under the same conditions, so they don't question whether it is wrong or right."

Such differing attitudes toward space needs make it difficult for the experts in one advanced nation to suggest the best population policy for another advanced nation. Such differences also make it difficult to visualize how much of a burden population growth in any one country would really impose on future generations in that country. Perhaps future generations will enjoy living shoulder to shoulder.

The Lesson of Japan's Experience

Japan's decision to boost its birthrate slightly may have an impact and significance beyond its own borders. Some family planning advocates fear Japan's action may throw a monkey wrench in worldwide efforts to curb population growth by somehow downgrading the importance of birth control. Others fear Japan demonstrates that radical population control can never succeed, for the minute a nation reaches the point where its population is apt to level off and then decline, various pressures—political, economic, and nationalistic—build up to reverse the trend. Both views are probably too apocalyptic, for Japan is merely trying to boost its net reproduction rate by a modest amount until it returns to 1—a level that is considered the desirable goal by planners in many other countries. Some U.S. experts, for example, have called for a stationary population and a zero rate of growth, and that is precisely what Japan is seeking.

The real significance of Japan's experience may be that it underlines the costs involved in achieving population control. Some experts in this country, such as Ansley J. Coale, director of the Office of Population Research at Princeton University, have pointed out that a stationary population and a zero growth rate have unfavorable as well as advantageous effects. Coale suggests, for example, that a stationary population "is not likely to be receptive to change and indeed would have a strong tendency towards nostalgia and conservatism." He also suggests that such a society would no longer offer "a reasonable expectation of advancement in authority with age," since there would be essentially the same number of 50-year-olds as 20-year-olds. Zero growth is unquestionably desirable at some point before crowding becomes painful, but in the current rush to jump on the population control bandwagon, it is well to remember that population control is not an unmixed blessing. There are costs involved, and someone will have to pay them.

The Global Challenge of Health and Hunger

How soon will the crisis come? What will be the consequences? Will governments topple and anarchy reign? What is it like to starve and how does starvation affect the observer of the starving? How will the United States react to the inevitable catastrophes?

We have time to plan and prepare for some of the predictables, but do we have the foresight and will to do so?

On The Balance 72

. . . and lo a black horse; and he that sat on him had a pair of balances in his hand. And I heard a voice say, A measure of wheat for a penny, and three measures of barley for a penny; and see thou hurt not the oil and the wine.

Revelation 6:5, 6

The Locomotive and the Mudslide 73

WILLIAM AND PAUL PADDOCK

A locomotive is roaring full throttle down the track. Just around the bend an impenetrable mudslide has oozed across the track. There it lies, inert, static, deadly. Nothing can stop the locomotive in time. Collision is inevitable. Catastrophe is foredoomed. Miles back up the track the locomotive could have been warned and stopped. Years ago the mud-soaked hill could have been shored up to forestall the landslide. Now it is too late.

The locomotive roaring straight at us is the population explosion. The unmovable landslide across the tracks is the stagnant production of food in the undeveloped nations, the nations where the population increases are greatest.

The collision is inevitable. The famines are inevitable.

The Time For Rhetoric Is Over 74

LYNDON B. JOHNSON

State of the Union Message
January 10, 1967

Next to the pursuit of peace, the really greatest challenge to the human family is the race between food supply and population increase. That race tonight is being lost.

The time for rhetoric has clearly passed. The time for concerted action is here and we must get on with the job.

75   The Starving as a Race Apart

JAMES BONNER

We will, I suspect, begin to regard the starving populace of the underdeveloped nations as a race or species apart, people totally different from us, as
indeed they will be. "They are just animals," we will say, "and a serious reservoir
of disease." The inevitable culmination of the two cultures will be that one culture
will devour the other. I would think that it would turn out that the rich and strong
will devour the poor and weak.

76   Agricultural Production in the Developing Countries

G. F. SPRAGUE

At least half the world's population endures some degree of malnutrition.
The gap between food production and world population is constantly widening.
It has been estimated that by 1985 this situation could become catastrophic. Two
approaches appear obligatory: (i) a substantial decrease in the rate of population
growth, and (ii) full utilization of our biological technology to increase food
production on all economically arable lands. The utilization of microorganisms,
algae, or petrochemicals to produce protein has been suggested by many. These
and other possibilities should be actively explored and, where feasible, utilized.
However, the total impact of such possible developments cannot greatly lessen
the need for an expanded agriculture limited only by the ecological potential.

This article is concerned primarily with the possibilities for increasing
agricultural production in the developing countries through improvement in
varieties, in fertilization, and in management practices. As background, a brief
review of selected examples of progress achieved in the developed countries with
the three most important food crops—rice, wheat, and corn—during the past 35
years seems desirable.

Rice Production in Japan

Japan has the highest acre yields of paddy rice among the major rice-
producing countries. There is evidence that rice was cultivated in Japan as early
as 300 B.C. Through the centuries there has been a gradual expansion in acreage,
improvement in varieties, and modification of cultural and production practices.

The major developments, however, have occurred since about 1885, when
the national average yield was approximately 1800 kilograms per hectare. Average yields had increased to approximately 4000 kilograms per hectare by 1963.
Somewhat greater percentage gains have been achieved in the cool northeast
portions of Honshu and in Hokkaido.

As is typically the case, this increase in yield is the result of many factors: improvement in varieties, increased use of fertilizer, modification of cultural and production practices, and better control of disease, insect pests, and weeds.

In the earlier days varietal improvement was limited to selection among the various land-race populations. Later, intensive selection for pure lines was practiced by the National and Prefectural Experiment Stations. Since about 1927 breeding efforts have been centered on crossing of selected parents, followed by the isolation and evaluation of true-breeding types from among the resulting progeny. All the varieties now in use have resulted from this breeding method. In the development of new varieties major attention has been given to short, stiff-strawed types able to make effective use of large quantities of fertilizer.

The first artificial fertilizers to be used extensively were fish-scrap and soybean cake. These were replaced by ammonium sulfate, superphosphate, and other chemical fertilizers. Attention has also been given to soil-dressing, deep plowing, and a more liberal use of iron and other minor elements. Current rates of application of nitrogen, phosphorus, and potassium are higher for Japan than for any other rice-producing country.

With the expansion and intensification of rice production, both disease and insect infestation became increasingly important. Efforts toward disease control have been continuing, use having been made of resistant varieties and of fungicides ranging from Bordeaux mixture to the new mercury and phosphorus compounds. The earlier measures for controlling stem borer and leafhoppers ranged from the burning of refuse to applications of whale oil. Extensive use is now being made of the many organic insecticides.

Wheat Production in the United States

Wheat is the world's second most important food crop. Approximately 15 percent of the total supply is produced within the United States, where five main types are grown: soft red winter, hard red winter, hard red spring, white, and durum. Each of these types has its maximum concentration in a different geographical area, each fills a special commercial need, and each presents unique problems with respect to quality evaluation, resistance to disease and to insect infestation, and hazards of production.

Wheat is not native to the United States. The varieties grown during the colonial period and the era of expansion were direct importations from abroad or selections of deviant types within the imported strains. The scientific approach to the improvement of wheat dates from about 1900. The first efforts were directed toward selection of pure lines within the better adapted strains. The possibilities of improvement under this method were soon exhausted. Increased genetic variability was obtained through hybridization, followed by intensive selection within the segregating populations. This breeding method is responsible for all of our modern varieties of wheat.

Average per-acre yields have doubled in the past 30 years. The impact on the economy has been greater than this rate of increase would suggest. Severe losses from stem rust were experienced in 6 of the 20 years between 1920 and 1940, and measurable losses occurred in many of the remaining years. Rust-resistant types in a continuous succession have been developed, and used extensively for a time, only to be replaced by newer strains in the continuing battle to cope with the ever-changing biotypes of the pathogen. In comparisons involving old and new varieties, in the absence of rust epiphytotics the newer varieties exhibit only moderate superiority, suggesting that the greater selective pressure has been for resistivity to disease.

This situation has been drastically changed in the Pacific Northwest in recent years with the development of new semi-dwarf varieties. These types have a tremendous capacity to respond to improved cultural practices, particularly to increased levels of nitrogen fertilization. Yields of 200 bushels per acre (13,450 kilograms per hectare) have been recorded. Comparative yields for the area and for the nation were 38 and 23 bushels, respectively. Northwestern Europe provides a more favorable climate for wheat, and average yields for the same period would approximate 60 bushels per acre. Unfortunately the semi-dwarf types adapted to the Pacific Northwest do not appear to have the same yield potential in other major wheat-producing areas of the United States. Work is progressing, however, on the development of semi-dwarf types adapted to other geographical areas.

Corn Production in the United States

The development and utilization of hybrid corn has had an important impact on our agricultural economy. In the early 1930's, before hybrid corn was used, the United States produced approximately 2.5 billion bushels of corn per year on roughly 100 million acres. In 1963 we produced over 4 billion bushels on 60 million acres—that is, 70 percent more corn on 40 percent fewer acres. In other words, the average per-acre yield of corn has nearly tripled in the past 30 years. In this same period the percentage of our corn acreage planted to hybrids has increased from 0.1 to more than 95 percent. The pertinent data are presented in Table 1.

I do not mean to imply that the increases in production, just detailed, have resulted solely from genetic improvements. Genetic improvements, however, have been one of the components of what may be described as an agricultural revolution. Other components include the use of increasing quantities of fertilizer; an increase in plant populations; improved means of controlling weeds, insects, and disease; and better timing of all farming operations, made possible by the availability of more efficient machinery. It would be extremely difficult to assign realistic weights to these individual components, inasmuch as their relative importance would vary for different crops.

In the case of corn, however, the development and adoption of hybrids in the major production areas preceded and made economically feasible the utilization or improvement of the other components. Only limited quantities of fertilizer were used on open-pollinated varieties because yield response from such applications was limited. The open-pollinated varieties were susceptible to root-lodging and stalk-breaking, thus mechanical harvesting was both costly and inefficient. Population densities were low, by current standards, because the varieties could not tolerate heavier planting without reductions in yield.

Many farmers felt that the public research agencies had little real knowledge of agricultural problems and were slow to accept new recommendations. This general attitude accounts for the initial reluctance to accept hybrid corn. The superiority of this product was readily apparent, however, and after the first few years the rate of utilization was limited only by the availability of seed. In the Corn Belt the transition from open-pollinated varieties to hybrids was essentially completed in a 10-year period. Hybrid corn and the many other more recent innovations have resulted in a drastic change in the farmer's viewpoint.

Farmers now recognize the value of research, do a considerable amount of experimentation on their own initiative, and tend to adopt new practices before their value has been adequately established. This historical sequence must be kept in mind in any attempt to extrapolate from our highly developed agricultural economy to the agricultural economy of the developing countries.

Most of the developing countries lie outside the latitudes of the United States. Although basic principles know no geographical boundaries, the practices flowing from such research have strong ecological limitations. In general the improved crop varieties grown in the United States are unsuited to the requirements of the developing countries. When grown in Kenya, a hybrid from the Corn Belt may be inferior to a local unimproved variety. A fertilizer regime suited to the southeastern United States may be quite inappropriate in Nigeria. Improved crop varieties and management and cultural practices suitable for the developing countries must be developed through locally conducted research.

International Rice Research Institute

The International Rice Research Institute was established at Los Banos, the Philippines, in 1961. The research program organized possibly represents the most extensive effort yet made, within a developing country, to study all factors affecting production of a single crop. The institute is jointly sponsored by the Ford and Rockefeller foundations and has a senior staff of approximately 20 scientists, representing all major areas which affect production capabilities. These areas include genetics and breeding, physiology, pathology, soil science, agricultural engineering, entomology, crop production, management and rotations, economics, and extension. It became apparent almost immediately that neither the technology nor the varieties developed in Japan or the United States were suited to tropical regions.

TABLE 1: Corn Acreage, Production, Average Yields Per Acre, and Percentage of Acreage Planted to Hybrids for Selected Years During the Period 1933 to 1964. [*Agricultural Statistics* (U.S. Department of Agriculture)].

Year	Acreage harvested (1000 acres)	Total production (1000 bushels)	Average yield (bushels/ acre)	Percent of acreage planted to hybrids
1933	105,918	2,397,593	22.6	0.1
1938	92,160	2,548,753	27.7	14.9
1943	92,060	2,965,980	32.2	52.4
1948	83,778	3,605,078	42.5	76.0
1953	80,459	3,209,896	39.9	86.5
1958	63,549	3,356,205	52.8	93.9
1963	60,549	4,091,785	67.6	95.0+

Marked progress has been achieved in several areas. Information has been accumulated on growth form, on efficient utilization of sunlight, on short-statured types with erect leaves, and on the minimizing of shading effects. Through the use of insecticides and insect-resistant plant varieties, damage caused by the major insect pests has been materially reduced. In some experimental plantings, control of the stem borer through the use of the insecticide gamma BHC has given yield increases of 150 percent. Extensive screening within the world rice collection, maintained at Los Banos, has revealed types resistant to some virus diseases, to leaf blight, to certain strains of rice blast, and to other important diseases. Resistance is being incorporated into high-yielding types. Striking increases in yield have been achieved through nitrogen fertilization. In some instances the return on investment in fertilizer has been as high as 600 percent, as calculated on the assumption that nitrogen costs about four times as much as paddy rice.

The opportunities for growing two or more crops of rice per year depend upon the availability of water and the growth requirements of the varieties used. The early short-statured varieties are well suited for this purpose. Where water is limiting, sorghum, mung beans, and other short-season crops may follow rice. Some form of multiple cropping appears to offer great promise for increasing total production.

Perhaps the most striking of the short-term developments has been development of the variety IR-8. This short-statured type has many of the characteristics desired, and has given yields of over 10 metric tons of rough rice under conditions in which the tall *Oryza indica* types produced less than 6 tons. Yields of IR-8 have also been high in experimental tests in Pakistan, Thailand, Malaysia, and India. In some cases yields of IR-8 have been double those of local varieties. Production of seed of IR-8 has been increased, so that additional comparative trials may be made and planting of IR-8 may be started in these countries. At the same time, work on breeding is going forward in an effort to incorporate greater resistance to disease, improved milling characteristics, and improved quality of the rice.

Rockefeller Agricultural Program in Mexico

A research program involving the Rockefeller Foundation and the Mexican Ministry of Agriculture was initiated in 1943. This was a broad-based program, designed to improve the agriculture of Mexico and to provide opportunity for the training of Mexican scientists who would eventually assume leadership of all phases of research. The operation has been so successful that it has served as a model for other assistance programs. Although work was initiated with several crops, here I consider only one phase—wheat research.

In 1943, when the program was initiated, Mexico imported half of the wheat consumed. At present, in spite of the high rate of population increase during the past 20 years, Mexico is a wheat-exporting nation. The progress achieved is shown in Table 2.

This increase in production has been achieved through a combination of research developments in several disciplines: genetics and breeding, soil fertility, irrigation management, plant pathology, entomology, and cereal technology. Stem rust *(Puccinia graminis* var. *tritici)* and stripe rust *(P. glumarum)* were the diseases of primary importance. Extensive use was made of known sources of resistance, and new sources were identified. The first of many improved varieties was released in 1947. A continuing succession of new varieties followed, each superior in productive capacity to those it replaced. The most spectacular developments have been achieved in recent years with the release and rapid adoption of several semi-dwarf varieties.

As is often the case with new varieties, the maximum utilization of genetic potential can be achieved only through a complete reevaluation of production practices. The new semi-dwarf types could make effective use of up to 140 to 160 pounds of nitrogen per acre. Similarly, under the heavy cropping practices followed, applications of 40 pounds of phosphoric acid became profitable. Four irrigations were required where two had previously been adequate. With this combination of improved varieties and modified management practices, yields of 80 to 100 bushels per acre were achieved. This is in contrast to the 7- to 10-bushel yields that were common with the varieties and cultural practices used in 1943.

In addition to the increase in total production which has been achieved in Mexico, this program has made other outstanding contributions.

The new varieties developed in this program are relatively insensitive to day length and therefore exhibit wide adaptability. One strain, designated Mexipak, is currently being grown extensively in Pakistan.

When stem rust is a serious problem, new resistant varieties resist rust for approximately 5 years, after which time a new race of rust, to which the variety is susceptible, becomes predominant. The concept of controlled backcross derivatives (multilineal varieties) was developed, in which each component of the mixture would possess resistance to a different race or constellation of races of rust. Practical results with the method have been satisfactory. Recently, the concept has been extended to include hybrid seed production, when this becomes feasible in wheat.

Techniques for early-generation testing of gluten quality, which should simplify the evaluation of quality, have been developed.

Important as these developments have been, they are probably overshadowed by the extensive training aspects which have been an integral part of the program. In the 20 years from 1943 to 1963, more than 700 young men and women, representing many different countries, received inservice training. Many of these received advanced degrees and are now contributing to agricultural progress in their respective countries.

TABLE 2: The Impact of Research on Wheat Production in Mexico. [N.E. Borlaug, *Phytopathol. 55*, 1088 (1965)].

Year	Cultivated area (1000 hectares)	Yield (kg/ hectare)	Production (1000 metric tons)
1945	500	750	330
1950	625	900	600
1955	790	1,100	850
1960	840	1,417	1,200
1964	846	2,600	2,200

Maize Improvement in Kenya

The maize-improvement program of Kenya (*maize* is the common term for corn outside the United States) provides a striking illustration of the genetic improvement that is possible when other technological requirements are met. Support for this program is provided by the Kenya Government, the Kenya Maize and Produce Marketing Board, the Ministry of Overseas Development (Great Britain), the Rockefeller Foundation, and the United States AID-ARS Major Cereals in Africa Project. The research staff includes both geneticists and agronomists. Excellent and widespread extension support has been provided by the Kenya Ministry of Agriculture.

This maize-breeding program was initiated in 1958 as a conventional in-breeding-hybridization program based on use of the local variety, Kenya Flat White. By 1963 a double-cross hybrid which gave yield increases of 25 percent had been developed; the percentage increase was roughly equivalent to that achieved in the United States with the first hybrids produced commercially.

During the early stages of this program it became apparent that lack of genetic diversity was limiting progress. Extensive introductions were made from the United States, from Central America, and from northern South America. The great bulk of this introduced material was unadapted and was discarded. A few of the high-altitude types from Central and South America appeared worthy of further evaluation. This exotic material was crossed with the local variety, and the resulting hybrids were evaluated in yield trials. One of these, Kenya Flat White X Ecuador 573, gave yields equal or superior to those of the double-cross hybrid, depending upon altitude and fertility level. As the varietal hybrid possessed the greater potential for yield enhancement, breeding efforts were increasingly directed toward improvement of the two base populations.

Agronomic research had established optimum planting densities and planting dates, as well as efficient fertilization practices. The Ministry of Agriculture established an effective demonstration program, showing the advantages of hybrids over the local variety of maize and the relative importance of the major management practices. The Kenya Seed Company, which had specialized in grass-seed production, was induced to undertake large-scale production and distribution of hybrid maize.

Hybrid seed was first offered under a package plan. Each purchaser of seed was obliged to buy fertilizer of the recommended formulation and amount, and each agreed to follow certain minimum cultural recommendations. The utilization of hybrid seed which has been attained is shown in Table 3.

Each year the acreage of hybrid grown has been limited by shortage of seed rather than by lack of demand. After an initial lag, acceptance by the small-scale native farmer has been as great as acceptance by the large-scale farmer. Because of the procedures followed, the farmers consider hybrid maize to be a new crop, and the saving of seed from the hybrid planting, F_2 seed, has not been a problem.

This program involving use of hybrid seed, proper fertilization, and improved cultural practices has already had an important impact on total production. Further increases appear to be quite feasible. The genetic variance of the two parental varieties has been found to be primarily additive. Simple selection schemes have resulted in yield increases of 10 percent in the parental populations, and this improvement is retained in their F_1 hybrids.

TABLE 3: Acreages of Hybrid Maize Grown in Kenya.
["Major Cereals in Africa" Project, Third Annual Report].

Year	Large-scale farms (acres)	Small-scale farms (acres)
1963	300	10
1964	27,000	3,000
1965	52,000	18,000
1966	50,000	50,000
1967*	100,000	350,000

*This projection is based on seed produced and seed orders currently in hand.

Breeding programs such as the one in Kenya are admirably designed to fulfill both short- and long-range needs. Short-term needs are met by the rapid development and utilization of improved hybrids. Substantial improvement of the parental types is possible through simple selection schemes which pose minimum demands for trained manpower, financial support, or operational facilities. The improvement achieved in the base parental populations increases their potential value as sources of inbred lines, should a conventional inbreeding-hybridization program later become desirable.

Similar programs are feasible in many of the developing countries. Varietal hybrids, superior to the best available double crosses, have been identified in Mexico, India, and Thailand, but, outside of Kenya, little commercial use is being made of such material. This appears to be largely a problem of seed-production capabilities and of status. Because single and double crosses constitute the hybrids of commerce within the United States and other developed countries, the developing countries feel that commercial utilization of heterosis should be deferred until they can market hybrids of similar types. Thus substantial, immediate, and potential progress is being sacrificed to prestige.

These examples of success need not be unique. The improved varieties of rice, wheat, and maize, developed in the programs cited, are being extensively used outside the area of their development. Similar programs could develop new types of these or other crops to satisfy different ecological requirements. A total increase in food production of 50 percent in the developing countries appears to be a completely realistic goal. An increase in wheat yields of this magnitude in India would represent over 6.5 million metric tons.

Requirements for an Effective Assistance Program

A consideration of programs exhibiting varying degrees of success suggests that significant progress requires the fulfillment of certain minimum conditions. (i) A realistic system of research priorities must be developed. Under food-deficit conditions emphasis should be given to one or two of the major food crops of the area. (ii) The program must include research scientists representing several disciplines (genetics, agronomy, plant pathology, entomology, and so on) if the program is to achieve continuing success. The concept of "critical mass" in nuclear physics provides a useful analogy. A vigorous extension program must complement research activities. (iii) The scientific staff must actively participate in the research. Consultative and advisory functions have their place, but an adequate program cannot be developed on the basis of these alone. (iv) Adequate financial support must be provided, and operations in a foreign country are always expensive. (v) Provision must be made for the training of nationals. Such persons must be assigned responsibility as rapidly as their training and aptitude will permit. (vi) Governmental policies must be favorable to agricultural development. Provision must be made for satisfying a wide variety of needs—adequate supplies of fertilizers and other agricultural chemicals, a realistic pricing policy for agricultural produce to make the adoption of improved techniques attractive to farmers, and policies which will permit the development of an effective seed production and distribution industry responsive to local needs, to name only a few.

The importance of the first five requirements is generally recognized. The necessity for the sixth is often overlooked. The achievement of increased agricultural productivity in the developing countries requires more than the improvement of crop plants and associated management practices. Favorable economic, political, and social conditions and policies also are essential.

The food shortage in India has been much in the news and may thus serve as a useful illustration. It should be stressed that the situation in India is not unique. Detailed consideration of governmental policies and priorities lies outside the scope of this article and of my capabilities. It is readily apparent, however, that, had agriculture received a higher priority, the current situation would be much less critical than it is.

India uses about 4 pounds of fertilizer per acre (4 1/2 kilograms per hectare). Local varieties of wheat, rice, and corn have a limited capacity to respond to high levels of fertilization. The new varieties of wheat introduced from Mexico, however, are much more responsive to application of fertilizer. Yield increases of at least 50 percent are possible, under adequate management. If all the fertilizer currently available in India were used on such varieties, only a fraction of the wheat acreage could be fertilized at the optimum rate. Similar situations prevail for the new varieties of rice and for corn hybrids. Thus, potential gain in food production has not been realized because of inadequate supplies and the high cost of fertilizers.

India produces some nitrogenous fertilizer and imports more. Importation costs represent a serious drain on the supply of hard currency. Nitrogenous fertilizers could be produced locally from either naphtha or natural gas. The need for a major expansion of this industry has been recognized in the successive 5-year plans, but the goals established fall short of the need, and no decision has yet been reached on the production process to be used.

An effective seed industry is essential to agricultural progress. Historically, government-controlled operations have been unsatisfactory. The quality of seed produced is often inferior, distribution is inadequate, and seed-production goals are relatively insensitive to local needs.

Other instances could be cited, in India and other developing countries, of the effects of low priorities for agricultural development on food-production capabilities.

Conclusion

The following general conclusions appear valid. The developed countries cannot feed the world. On a short-term basis, food must be supplied to developing countries as needs exist. A long-continuing policy of supplying food grains, through donation or by sale, may be self-defeating if this practice tends to limit expansion of local food-production capabilities.

Tremendous possibilities exist for an expansion of food production within the developing countries. The extent to which this potential is realized will depend upon the scope of assistance programs undertaken, and upon the priorities assigned to agriculture by the developing nations. Even though capabilities are fully utilized, the result may still be inadequate if population growth remains unchecked.

Can We Prepare for Famine? 77

A Social Scientist's View

E. JAMES ARCHER

1. The Death Rate

Most people think that the population explosion is due to an *increased* birth rate, i.e., number of births per 1000 people. This is a gross oversimplification. As Robert Cook, the president of the Population Reference Bureau said, "We've been trying for years to get people interested in death rates, to get people to understand that the 'explosion' is due primarily to falling death rates and not to changing birth rates."

The relationship is quite simple: *Only* live people have babies and live people *do* have babies. The more people you save from death due to typhoid, cholera, diphtheria, smallpox, malaria, and bubonic plague, the more people will be around to have babies.

In many underdeveloped countries the death rate has been cut in half since World War II. The relationship between death rate and population explosion is nicely illustrated by the following observation, "If by 1975 the death rate in Guatemala fell somewhere near the 1950 United States level (9.6)—a not unlikely development—this alone would increase the number of women reaching the beginning of the child-bearing period by 36 percent and the number at the end of the child-bearing period by 85 percent."

2. The Younger Generation

Nearly one-half of all the people in the underdeveloped countries are under the age of 15. Young people marry and married people have babies. One statistical prediction presents the case: by 1975 there will be 60% more marriages formed in Latin America than in 1960. Sixty per cent more marriages formed in 1975 will mean 60% more babies in 1976. Again, it is not the birth rate, i.e., births per 1000 population, which accounts for the explosion, rather there are just more people in the child-bearing ages.

3. The Birthrate

For many years it was thought that a birthrate of 45 per thousand was the physiological maximum. This figure was based on the observation that of 1000 people 500 will be women. Of that number, 410 were either too old or too young or sterile. Of the remaining 90, we could find another 45 who were pregnant or who just had a child and had not had time to conceive and deliver another child. However, with a shift to a lower average age (Population Dynamic Number Two) we find a few instances of birth rates exceeding the "classical limit" of 45/1000. For example, in 1963, Costa Rica had a birthrate of 50.2/1000.

We also see an interaction of some of these Population Dynamics in that those techniques which lower the death rate generally also improve the health of the individual and people who are both young *and* healthy, are more fertile, have more frequent intercourse, and if a child is conceived, it is more likely to come to full term, i.e., there will be fewer miscarriages and still births.

4. Man's Reproductive System

"Man has been evolving and reproducing for a million years. Those who expect science to be able to find quickly a birth control method which can successfully circumvent this million years of such single-mindedness both overestimate modern science and underestimate the efficiency of the reproductive system which evolution has provided man."

Now the optimists will react with a list of things that will assure themselves that all is well. For example, they might cite the control of population in Japan, but that is a very special case and not applicable to other areas. Specifically, Japan has a literacy rate which is so high that they don't even bother with this measure in their census taking today. In 1948 Japan showed an illiteracy level of 1.1%. In contrast, Africa's is 84% and Latin America's is about 40%. Japan also had legalized abortions in 1948. The impact of this decision is best seen in the following statistics: In 1955 there were 1.2 million abortions performed. Even assuming the higher proportion of males at birth, because these 1.2 million conceptions did not come to full term, Japan will have approximately 0.5 million *fewer* women entering the child-bearing age next year than would have occurred in the absence of the abortions which took place in 1955.

Japan has a large medical profession as compared to the underdeveloped nations. If we look at the number of inhabitants per physician ratio, we see Japan's is 900:1, but Mexico's is twice that ratio. Pakistan has a ratio of 11,000:1 and Ethiopia has 96,000:1. If you think the intrauterine device (the IUD) is the answer, you have another problem. Who will insert it?

The IUD is another false hope of avoiding widespread famine due to the exploding population. Consider these data. The designer of the most widely used IUD claims it can be inserted in 6 minutes. One well trained team even managed to insert 75 IUD's in a 3-hour session—that is one IUD insertion every 2 minutes and 24 seconds. While this sounds good, it must be recognized that 850,000 women entered the child-bearing age in India alone last year and the number will increase in succeeding years. You cannot insert IUD's fast enough.

The hope of the Pill is equally discouraging. Its use requires daily attention plus motivation. Remember also when a woman goes off the Pill, or forgets to take it regularly, her fertility is actually increased. Furthermore, because of the undesirable side-effects, the Pill is not recommended for all women. Until a "morning after" or monthly pill is developed, the Pill as it is now known is only promising and not an answer.

Let me mention a few other hopes which the optimists cite but which also appear to be *false* hopes. We have frequently heard, and the PSAC report emphasizes this point, that what we need to do is to improve the agricultural production of the developing countries. One way to do this is to send them seeds, stock, and fertilizers; then they can raise more food to feed their exploding population and all will be well.

First, many strains of wheat and corn which do very well in the United States either perform poorly or even fail to come to seed in other climates and on other soils. You cannot export seed; you have to develop the appropriate strains and agricultural technology in the field where the grain is to grow. For example, it is estimated that corn production in Mexico has been increased about 200% by the work of the Rockefeller Foundation program. This sounds great and may seem to be the obvious solution, i.e., we export the know-how and all will be saved. There are a few hitches, however. First, half of the increased yield was due to double cropping (but getting in two growing seasons is not always possible). Second, the research program did *not* find just *the* right strain of corn to grow in Mexico. The soils, micro-climates, macro-climates, and irrigation conditions are so different in different areas that about a dozen different strains are needed —each appropriate to its growing conditions. Third, the program took 25 years. We just do not have 25 years.

Look at it this way—in the best of our agricultural research and training institutions, how long does it take you to train one plant pathologist? One geneticist? And remember, he comes from and lives in an environment that financially supports him, offers rewards for successful work, and has a supporting intellectual climate of chemists, biochemists, cell biologists, plant physiologists, biophysicists, and agricultural engineers. Finally, he has the elaborate infra-structure of an agricultural extension system to communicate his work to the point of meaningful effect—the farmer. Even if we had all of the personnel, equipment, and financial resources available, we do not have the time—no matter how many chickens sit on an egg, it still takes 21 days to hatch it. The same principle applies to successive plant breeding tests.

Some of the optimists will feel safe because man will solve his food problems by "harvesting" the sea. Paddock and Paddock point out the special relish with which the word "harvest" is used. Hoping to harvest the sea in time to avoid major famines is truly a false hope. How little we know of the sea is shown in another PSAC publication entitled "The Effective Use of the Sea," which appeared in 1966. We are a long way from ever understanding the processes of turbulence which contribute to the essential stirring of the sea. The sometimes cyclic churning action brings necessary organic material to intermediate depths to provide food for plankton, which becomes food for shrimp, which becomes food for man. We do not even have a satisfactory buoy network technology to enable us to study the microclimate of the seas. If you do not understand the climate on land, you will be a poor farmer and if you don't understand the "climate" in the ocean, you will be at least as poor a harvester of the sea. How

long will it take to train an oceanographer? The climate for such personnel
development is nowhere comparable to that which exists for training a plant
pathologist.

Even if I have not persuaded the optimists that there is cause for concern
about the population explosion, I hope I have brought the matter to their attention.

78   Paying The Piper

PAUL R. EHRLICH

The battle to feed humanity is over. Unlike battles of military forces, it is
possible to know the results of the population-food conflict while the armies are
still "in the field." Sometime between 1970 and 1985 the world will undergo vast
famines—hundreds of millions of people are going to starve to death. That is, they
will starve to death unless plague, thermo-nuclear war, or some other agent kills
them first. And we are not embarking upon any crash programme. These are the
harsh realities we face . . .

The trends in both population growth and food production are clear. Only
the U.S. will be in a position to donate food to starving countries, and a catastrophic gap will appear soon between her supply and demand. The United States
Department of Agriculture has predicted that the curve representing possible
exportable U.S. grain surpluses will intersect the curve representing the food aid
requirements of 66 developing countries in 1984. In an excellent book *Famine
1975* (Little, Brown; Boston, 1967), William and Paul Paddock argue cogently
that the 1984 prediction is optimistic, and that calamity awaits us in the middle
of the next decade. In either case it is too late to prevent the famines, and probably
too late to do much to decrease their magnitude. . . .

For a moment, let us take the simplistic view that a solution involves only
either increasing human food or limiting the human population. First let us look
at the problem of increasing food supplies, either from the land or the sea. We
rapidly can do away with what I have called the "Food from the sea myth." With
very minor exceptions, man hunts the sea, he does not farm it or herd its animals.
At the moment he cannot take advantage of its primary productivity, and so must
feed at levels in the food chain at which much of the sun's energy bound by
photosynthesis has been lost in the inefficient transfers from producer to primary
consumer to secondary consumer, and so forth. There already are disturbing signs
that our relatively meagre present yield from the sea will be threatened by
over-exploitation of fisheries, as the world's protein shortage gets more acute.
And what of farming the sea? The insignificant bit that we do now (much less
than one-tenth of one percent of the yield) is done along the shoreline and is best
viewed as an extension of terrestrial farming. No deep-sea farming is done now,
even experimentally—and we lack the technical knowledge even if we wished to
start. Some very optimistic people think that with colossal effort and strict inter-

national controls, we might conceivably almost double our yield from the sea in the next decade or so. But it should be obvious to all that such effort is not being made, and that such controls are not being developed. And our experience with attempting such controls in the international whaling industry gives us little hope that they would be effective if they were imposed. So from the point of view of the coming crisis, we can relegate the idea of saving mankind by tapping marine food supplies to the same fairyland as using hydroponics, synthesizing food from petroleum, and using desalination plants to make the deserts into vast granaries. None are practical in the short run—indeed, most would present serious difficulties even if we had a century instead of a decade in which to act. . . .

The United States, as the only world power with a prospect of food surpluses, should take immediate action in two areas. First, it must set an example for the world by establishing a crash programme to limit its own serious "population explosion." Then it must establish tough and realistic policies for dealing with the population crisis at the international level. We can hope that other Western countries will follow suit.

Some biologists feel that compulsory family regulation would be required to stabilize the population of the United States at a reasonable level—say 150 million people. Americans are unlikely to take kindly to the prospect, even though the alternative way of stopping their population growth may be thermonuclear war. I have proposed four less drastic steps which might get the job done, and which would at least make American intentions clear to the rest of the world. The steps are socially unpalatable and politically unrealistic, but, unfortunately, the time when sugar-coated solutions could be effective is now long gone.

The first step would be to establish a Federal Population Commission with a large budget for propaganda—propaganda which encourages reproductive responsibility. This Commission would be charged with making clear the connection between rising population and lowering quality of life. It would also be charged with the evaluation of environmental tinkering by other government agencies—with protecting the U.S. from projects such as the Federal Aviation Agency's supersonic transports.

The second step would be to change American tax laws so that they discourage rather than encourage reproduction. Those who impose the burden of children on society should, whenever they are able, be made to pay for the privilege. The income tax system should eliminate all deductions for children, and replace them with a graduated scale of increases. Luxury taxes should be placed on diapers, baby bottles and baby foods. It must be made clear to the American population that it is socially irresponsible to have large families. Creation of such a climate of opinion has played a large role in Japan's successful dealing with her population problem.

Third, the United States should pass federal laws which make instruction in birth control methods mandatory in all public schools. Federal legislation should also forbid state laws which limit the right of any woman to have an abortion which is approved by her physician.

Fourth, the pattern of federal support of biomedical research should be changed so that the majority of it goes into the broad areas of population regulation, environmental sciences, behavioral sciences and related areas, rather than into shortsighted programmes on death control. It is absurd to be preoccupied with the medical quality of life until and unless the problem of quantity of life is solved. Quantity is the first problem. If that one can be solved perhaps we will buy the time for scientists in fields such as biochemical genetics to solve some of the problems of quality. If the quantity problem is not solved, the quality problem will no longer bother us.

If the United States can attack the problem at home it will then be in a position to bring its prestige and power to bear on the world problem. Perhaps then the time of famines can be shortened. Even more important, perhaps the educational groundwork can be laid which will permit further cycles of outbreak and crash in the human population to be avoided. The United States should:

1. Announce that it will no longer ship food to countries such as India where dispassionate analysis indicates that the unbalance between food and population is hopeless. As suggested by the Paddocks, our insufficient aid should be reserved for those whom it may save.

2. Refuse all foreign aid to any country with an increasing population which we believe is not making a maximum effort to limit its population.

3. Make available to all countries extensive aid in the technology of population control.

4. Make available to all interested countries massive aid for increasing the yield on land already under cultivation. The United States' most important export in this area should not be fertilizers, but teachers who understand not only agronomy, but ecology and sociology as well. Centers should be established in each developing country for the training of technicians who can promote the increase of yield while minimizing environmental deterioration.

5. The United States should use its power and prestige to bring extreme diplomatic and/or economic pressure on any country or organization impeding a solution to the world's most pressing problem. The U.S. has gone against world opinion in other areas—why not in the most important area?

The Price We Pay for Agriculture

Many people of the underdeveloped world have looked at their "virgin territory" or mature ecosystems as having great potential for agriculture. Brazilians, for example, refer to their land as "the infinite country." But the price that is paid for agriculture is seldom calculated. Besides the fact that globally, agriculture has destroyed the land where it has been carried on for very long, there are other "short run" costs that have to be paid.

In the mature ecosystem, all the work costs have been paid by various species components. When the mature, complex system is reduced to immaturity, and therefore simplicity, for agricultural purposes, the costs for yielding energy must be paid by some other means. When a prairie is plowed or a woodland is cut, such systems as natural dispersion of seed, re-cycling of minerals, weed maintenance through shading, soil building, chemical (species) diversity, and evolution must be replaced respectively by mechanized and commercial preparation of seed and planting, increased use of fertilizer, chemical and power weeding, soil preparation, pesticides and fungicides, and plant breeding.

The "Principles of the Ecosystem" (next reading) are well understood, but not widely known. If our agricultural schemes for virgin territory fail, we should be prepared to accept that ecosystem redemption (movement toward stability and maturity) will be slow in coming. In some cases it may not come at all. (See reading 90.)

Principles of the Ecosystem 79

ROBERT LEO SMITH

1. The ecosystem is the major ecological unit. It has both structure and function.
2. The structure is related to species diversity. The more complex the structure, the greater is the diversity of species.
3. The function of the ecosystem is related to the flow of *energy* and the cycling of materials through the structural members of the ecosystem.
4. The relative amount of *energy* needed to maintain an ecosystem depends upon its structure. The more complex and mature it is, the less *energy* it needs to maintain one unit of that structure, or complexity (Margaler, 1963).
5. Ecosystems tend toward maturity; and in doing so they pass from a less complex to a more complex state. This directional change is called *succession*. Early stages are characterized by an excess of potential energy and a relatively high *energy* flow per unit of biomass. In mature ecosystems, there is less waste and less accumulation of *energy* because the energy flows through more diverse channels.
6. When an ecosystem is exploited and that exploitation is maintained, then the maturity of the ecosystem declines.
7. The major functions: unit of the ecosystem is the population. It occupies a certain functional niche, which is related to the population's rate in *energy* flow and cycling of nutrients.
8. Relationships among populations create new functional niches, so that the accumulation of species in an ecosystem, and the increase in maturity, are to some extent self-reinforcing processes.
9. However, a functional niche within a given ecosystem cannot be simultaneously and indefinitely occupied by a self-maintaining population of more than one species.
10. Both the environment and the amount of *energy* fixation in any given ecosystem are limited. When a population reaches the limits imposed by the ecosystem, its numbers must stabilize or, failing this, decline (often sharply) from disease, strife, starvation, low reproduction, and so on.
11. Changes and fluctuations in the environment (exploitation and competition, among others) represent selective pressures upon the population to which it

must adjust. Those organisms that cannot adjust disappear, perhaps decreasing for a time the maturity of the ecosystem.

12. The ecosystem has historical aspects. The present is related to the past, and the future is related to the present.

Some Effects of Starvation

80   Starvation Patterns

JEAN MAYER

As a nutritionist who has seen famines on three continents, one of them Asia, and as a historian of public health with an interest in famines, I can say flatly that there has never been a famine or a food shortage—whether created by lack of water (droughts, often followed by dust storms and loss of seeds, being the most frequent), by plant disease (such as fungous blights), by large-scale natural disturbances affecting both crops and farmers (such as floods and earthquakes), by disruption of farming operations due to wars and civil disorders, or by blockade or other war measures directly aimed at the food supply—which has not first and overwhelmingly affected the small children.

It is very clear that death from starvation occurs first of all in young children and in the elderly, with adults and adolescents surviving better (pregnant women often abort; lactating mothers cease to have milk and the babies die). Children under five, who in many parts of the world are often on the verge of kwashiorkor (a protein-deficiency syndrome which often hits children after weaning and until they are old enough to eat "adult" food) and of marasmus (a combination of deficiency of calories and of protein), are the most vulnerable. In addition, a general consequence of famine is a state of social disruption (including panic). People who are starving at home tend to leave, if they can, and march toward the area where it is rumored that food is available. This increases the prevailing chaos. Families are separated and children are lost—and in all likelihood die. Adolescents are particularly threatened by tuberculosis; however, finding themselves on their own, they often band together in foraging gangs, which avoid starvation but create additional disruption. The prolonged and successful practice of banditry makes it difficult to rehabilitate members of these gangs.

Malnutrition, Learning, and Behavior

81

PHILIP H. ABELSON

Children reared in poverty tend to do poorly on tests of intelligence. In part this is due to psychological and cultural factors. To an important extent it is a result of malnutrition early in childhood.

It seems likely that millions of young children in developing countries are experiencing some degree of retardation in learning because of inadequate nutrition, and that this phenomenon may also occur in the United States.

Because of complex social and psychological factors associated with malnutrition, it is not easy to assess the effects of dietary deficiencies in man. However, observations in underdeveloped countries, coupled with studies on animals, provide substantial evidence. In rats and pigs the brain reaches 80 percent of adult size by normal weaning time. At that stage, body weight is 20 percent of that at maturity. During the period of rapid growth the brain is vulnerable to nutritional damage. A relatively short period of undernutrition results in smaller brain size at maturity even if the animals are maintained on a good diet after weaning. Changes in brain size are accompanied by persistent anatomical and biochemical changes.

In humans, the brain of the infant attains 80 percent of adult weight by age 3, when the body weight is about 20 percent of that at maturity. Thus the animal experiments suggest that good nutrition during the first 3 years of life is particularly important.

When the Famines Come

What Will We Do?

82

JAMES BONNER

I stress again that all responsible investigators agree that the tragedy will occur. They differ only as to whether it will take place in ten years or less, or in ten years or a little more. The underdeveloped world is on a collision course with starvation. No technology short of nuclear warfare can be spread with sufficient speed to avert the catastrophe. The only remaining question for the United States and for the nations of the developed world is how to deal with the starving nations, when starvation comes.

83   # What Have We Done?

UNITED STATES SENATE CONCURRENT RESOLUTION

Whereas reliable reports indicate that there is a tragic loss of life in the Nigerian civil war, caused by starvation and disease in areas controlled by the Federal Government and under the control of the Biafran authorities; and

Whereas present relief operations are inhibited by poor roads, bad weather, inadequate transport, and the inaccessibility of certain areas to overland supplies; and

Whereas increased shipments of food and medical supplies are needed to reduce the tragic rate of starvation: Now, therefore, be it

Resolved by the Senate (the House of Representatives concurring), That (1) it is the sense of the Congress that the President should act to increase significantly the amount of surplus food stocks, relief moneys, noncombat aircraft, and such other vehicles of transportation as may be necessary for relief purposes; and this relief assistance should be made available to and at the request of the Organization of African Unity, UNICEF, the International Committee of the Red Cross, and such other suitable religious and charitable relief agencies now or hereafter operating in the area with the consent of the responsible authorities; and (2) the Government of the United States should solicit the cooperation of other nations in this humanitarian effort.

HOPES FOR DELAYING THE FOOD CRISIS

Viewing proliferating human numbers without alarm, optimists have pointed to a Christmas sack of hopes for averting the food crisis. Some have suggested, for instance, that water for irrigation projects might come from desalinization from dams, and from the importation of water for hundreds and thousands of miles.

While governments urge the development of tropical areas, biologists are not so enthusiastic. The tropics are vast and untapped, to be sure; but careful study reveals that we should not count on large regions of the tropics for substantial food production. Hope in the potential of our oceans remains high, all the while they are being polluted and over-hunted.

Other positive thinkers, unruffled by dwindling reserves of fossil fuel, suggest that there are vast amounts of potential energy yet untapped.

Finally, some see a ready solution if we simply change the religious customs and taboos of "backward people."

Some of these alternatives may help delay the inevitable crisis. Others will not.

IRRIGATION PROJECTS

Desalinization

Dry Lands and Desalted Water

GALE YOUNG

Men spread now, with the whole power of the race to aid them, into every available region of the earth. Their cities are no longer tethered to running water and the proximity of cultivation . . . they lie out in the former deserts, those long-wasted sun baths of the race, they tower amidst eternal snows. . . . One may live anywhere.
—H.G. Wells, *The World Set Free*
—*A Story of Mankind*(1).

Mounting population and pollution exert pressure on man to enlarge his living space. At present, the most rapidly growing part of the United States is the desert of the Southwest, into which the Colorado and Rio Grande rivers have been largely diverted. Water from the Feather River will shortly be added, crossing over a mountain range 2000 feet (600 meters) high, by way of conveyance facilities now under construction.

The building of the Colorado Aqueduct of the Metropolitan Water District of Southern California was undertaken 40 years ago. Since then, the assessed valuation of the region served by this water supply has increased by $20 billion, or by $5 for each 1000 gallons of water that has flowed through the pipes.

These remarks are not intended to impute some exaggerated value to water, but are made, rather, to point out that people seem to like desert climates (better than, say, rain forests or frozen tundras) and that they will move into them and build vigorous societies. Since the water is essential to the welfare of all, whether they be large direct users or not, the cost of the water in arid areas is often carried in part as overhead. For example, the Metropolitan Water District derives funds to meet about half of its costs from water revenues and levies taxes for the balance.

Water-supply projects tend to proceed by large steps. When they are first completed there is an excess of water, and this can be used for agriculture while population and land values build up (2). Later on, the suburban farmland and its water allotments are absorbed in urban growth. This process in now under way around the large cities in our dry Southwest.

A third of the world's land is dry and virtually unoccupied, while half of the world's people are jammed—impoverished and undernourished—into a tenth of the land area. A major part of the coming increase in population will occur in the less-developed countries and, as *Nature* expressed it (3), "this huge army of uneducated, untrained, underfed, underprivileged recruits to humanity is being bred at the very moment when science and technology are rapidly undermining the need for and the status of the unskilled. ... What stands out most emphatically is in fact the insufficiency of economic factors or motives if the challenge is to be met."

The past decade has seen a quickening of interest in the large-scale desalting of seawater as another means of opening up dry areas of the earth for human occupancy. Thus, Jacob Bronowski writes (4), "let me ask first what is going to be the single greatest technological change in the physical sciences over the next twenty or thirty years. My guess is that desalting of seawater is going to be the most important advance for overall world development. Without this the whole complex program of bringing under-developed countries to an acceptable level of economics, education and political maturity is insoluble." And Charles Lowe writes (5), "The desert is man's future land bank. Fortunately, it is a large one, offering eight million square miles of space for human occupation. It is also fortunate that it is a wondrously rich bank, which may turn green when man someday taps distilled seawater for irrigation. Bridging the gap from sea to desert will be greatly facilitated by the geographical nearness of most of the world's deserts to the oceans. When this occurs it will surely be one of the greatest transformations made by man in his persistent and successful role in changing the face of the planet." As an example, imagine what changes would follow if Baja California were to be opened up for settlement with the help of desalting and power stations. What might another thousand miles of southern California be worth in a few generations?

This process has already begun to take place on a small scale in certain locations. Thus, Kuwait on the Persian Gulf and Shevchenko on the barren eastern shore of the Caspian Sea, where the Russians are building the world's largest desalting unit, are two oil field communities which depend upon desalination for their water supply. As in other locations where desalination would be employed, no cheaper sources of fresh water are available.

In general, desalination will be able to meet the freshwater needs of municipalities and industries located along the ocean shore, or in some interior regions having salty lakes or groundwater. And anywhere that cities go, some agriculture, for fresh fruits and vegetables at least, tends to follow. For example, Kuwait, in one of the most devilishly hot and sandridden environments on earth, has recently ordered acres of enclosed greenhouses at a cost of many thousands of dollars per acre to supply garden produce which will be fresher and reportedly cheaper than imported produce. But it is less clear whether agriculture that depends on desalted water ("desalination agriculture") may someday expand to include substantial production of staple foods as well. Here opinions differ, and, as the saying goes, the less light sometimes generates the more heat.

Water Requirements for Crops

In enclosed agriculture, such as Kuwait will have, so little fresh water escapes that its cost is not important. The situation is quite different in open-field agriculture, since the amount of water lost to the atmosphere in evapotranspiration is generally (6) many times that actually involved in the plant's growth reactions, and the cost of supplying this total by desalination is of prime importance.

Some authors have stated that the cost of desalted water will be for many years "at least one whole order of magnitude greater than the value of the water to agriculture" (7). Other writers have been more optimistic. Thus, the value of distilled water for agriculture in Israel has been estimated by MacAvoy and Peterson (8) to be about 27 cents per 1000 gallons. A generalized study (9, p. 28) indicates that "arid tropical and semitropical regions with year-round growing climates appear potentially capable of growing food at costs in or near the world market import price range, using desalted water at prices like 20 cents per thousand gallons." Estimates have been made of the total (direct plus indirect) benefits of irrigation water in several U.S. locations. There is considerable variation, estimates of losses due to taking water away from crops being 25 to 36 cents per 1000 gallons for the Texas High Plains and 32 to 44 cents for the Imperial Valley (10).

As noted above, the growing of some high-value crops tends to follow the occupation of a dry area, and an economic enterprise would, of course, first seek to saturate the market for this produce. But one is not going to feed the teeming millions on orchids or avocados, so the inquiry turns inevitably to the bulk staple foods. Of the staples, the grains are the most important, and, of the grains, rice is the staple and preferred food of half the human race. Rice, because of this demand, has a value double that of wheat on the world market—but it is not usually talked about in connection with desalination agriculture. Let us, therefore, talk about it.

Rice is indigenous to southern and eastern Asia, where much of the world's starvation occurs. In the monsoon countries, where fields are flooded periodically, the rice plant has the great virtue of being able to conduct oxygen to its roots through a hollow stem, and to flourish where other crops suffocate. Cultivation under such conditions leads to heavy use of water. In Table 1, from a talk by the dean of agriculture of the University of Sydney (11), it may be seen that in Australia, the most favorable of the instances shown, a price for water of 20 cents per 1000 gallons would add 10.6 cents per pound to the cost of rice. This is more than the rice is worth and provides little basis for enthusiasm about desalination.

Table 2 gives data on yield and water use for several other crops which are widely used. The "Rice" row of Table 2 is left blank for the present. The water-use rates were estimated (and checked against measured rates for farms when these were available) for a coastal site in the southeastern Mediterranean area, an irrigation efficiency (the fraction of the applied water which is lost to the atmosphere in evapotranspiration) of 80 percent being assumed. The other 20 percent of the water is that part which evaporates before reaching the crop, or which is carried away by deep percolation below the root zone. With efficient sprinkler or soaker irrigation systems this efficiency can usually be bettered, even without allowing for partial recovery of the deep drainage water. The yields assumed are those obtained regularly today by efficient farmers in production areas specializing in the crops in question. Record yields are considerably higher—more than double in the case of wheat, potato, tomato, and maize and in the case of an assumed yield for rice, discussed below.

Table 1 shows that rice growers typically use several times as much water per pound of grain as is needed for the other grains of Table 2. While some people

TABLE 1: Amount of Water Used in Growing Rice in Various Countries.

Location	Pounds of water per pound of paddy rice	Gallons of water used per pound of milled rice
Thailand	10,000	1,800
India	10,000	1,800
Japan	4,900	900
California	3,300	610
Australia	2,900	530

TABLE 2: Relation of Yield to Water Use for Various Crops.

Crop	Yield $(10^3$ lb/acre)	Food Value $(10^2$ Cal/lb)	Water use Inches	Water use Gal/lb	Water use Gal/10^3 Cal
		Grain			
Wheat	6.0	14.8	20.0	91	61
Sorghum	8.0	15.1	27.6	94	62
Maize	9.0	15.8	27.6	83	53
Rice					
		Vegetable			
Potato	48	2.79	16.0	9.0	32
Tomato	60	0.95	19.0	8.6	91
		Citrus			
Orange	44	1.31	53.1	33	250

TABLE 3: Estimated Capital Investment.

Item	Dollars per acre
Irrigation and storage-well system	375
Land, land development, and roads	85
Drainage system	110
Water for initial leaching	130
Grain storage	85
Machinery	115
Farm buildings	25
Interest during construction	25
Total	950

TABLE 4: Estimated Overhead Costs.

Item	Dollars per acre per year
Maintenance	14
Pumping power	1
Water losses in storage and canal leakage	12
Experimental station	1
Management and miscellaneous	7
Total	35

TABLE 5: Estimated Direct Costs for Grain Production.[*]

Item	Dollars per acre per crop
Fertilizer	11
Pumping power	6
Seed	5
Labor	2
Machine operation	2
Storage and marketing	3
Other chemicals	3
Miscellaneous	8
Total	40

may have doubted that rice requires this much water, this is the way the picture has stood historically. Just recently, however, results have appeared which do not support the classical view of rice as a water hog. In an experiment with IR 8 rice at India's Central Rice Institute, in Cuttack, a good crop 6350 pounds, 2900 kilograms, per acre as paddy rice was obtained with consumption of only 16.7 inches (42 centimeters) of water, irrigation being applied only when the soil was completely crusted. This work was reviewed and reported by J. S. Kanwar, deputy director general of the Indian Council of Agricultural Research (12). Kanwar states, "The common notion that continuous submergence is essential for paddy is belied." In a corresponding experiment based on the classical practice of continuous submergence, six times as much water (100 inches) was used and the yield was 6 percent higher. Obviously, most of the 100 inches of water was forced into the subsoil by the head of standing water.

If confirmed in subsequent tests and field experience, this finding may turn out to be one of the landmarks in the war against hunger. We add that rice can be grown the year round in warm climates; for example, in the Philippines three crops per year have been grown, yielding a total of 1,800 pounds of rice per acre.

If the results of the Indian experiment are taken at face value, the missing numbers for rice, which can now be added to Table 2, are as follows: yield, 4.2 (10^3 pounds per acre); food value, 16.5 (10^2 Calories per pound); water use—16.7 inches, 108 gallons per pound, 65 gallons per 10^3 Calories. This puts rice right in among the other grains as a user of water. It may be seen that to supply a person a minimum adequate allowance of 2500 Calories per day (13) in this highly intensive and scientifically managed type of agriculture would require an average of 160 gallons of water per day in the case of grain, or half this in the case of potatoes.

Production Cost Estimates for Grain

For any selected price of water, Table 2 enables one to compute the cost of water per pound of product, as illustrated for rice in Table 1. However, water is only one component of the total cost. We have, therefore, made some illustrative estimates of the total production costs for grain for a large, intensively operated farm. These costs are not expected to vary greatly with farm size. The estimates were made for a farm of 300,000 acres (120,000 hectares) which uses about a billion gallons of water per day.

These estimates are summarized in Tables 3 to 5. Table 3 shows the capital investment per acre, while Table 4 gives annual out-of-pocket costs for items which cannot be allocated directly to specific crops in the year-round rotation. The costs which can be specifically assigned are shown in Table 5.

It should be noted that the water is priced at the farm inlet and that it is supplied to the farm at a rate that is constant throughout the year, except for the time when the desalting plant is shut down for maintenance or other reasons. Thus, because of seasonal variations in the requirement for irrigation water, it is necessary to resort to such measures as (i) making seasonal adjustments in the size of the irrigated area and (ii) storing water in underground aquifers at certain times of the year and pumping it back up at other times (10 percent of the stored water is assumed to be lost in this process). Allowance for such storage has been made in Tables 3 and 4 (14).

An interest rate of 10 percent on the investment shown in Table 3 amounts to $95 per acre per year, and allowance for depreciation and for working-capital needs adds about $10 more. With the overhead costs shown in Table 4, the total fixed charges are thus $140 per acre per year. In regions where a second major crop, of the same or some other product, can be grown in the same year on the same land and share fixed costs with the grain, the cost of an acre crop of grain would be ($140/2) + $40 + cost of water = $110 + cost of water. In some areas, such as parts of India, where it might be possible to grow three crops per year the corresponding cost would be $87 + cost of water.

The resulting costs for milled rice and for wheat are plotted in Fig. 1, along with some representative prices.

In effect, what is here being contemplated is that the high cost of water may be at least partially offset by the opportunity to conduct intensive year-round "food factory" agriculture in favorable growing climates with many conditions under unusually good control. For example, recent observations suggest that very frequent or drip irrigation can cause substantial increases in the crop yield (15). In these experiments the nitrogen fertilizer was applied in the water. There is also speculation that slow release of carbon dioxide beneath the plant canopy might enhance yields. Thus it is entirely possible that future yields may exceed those of Table 2.

Desalination

The newest United States desalting plant, at Key West, Florida, produces 2.5 million gallons of fresh water per day at a cost of about $1 per 1000 gallons. It is anticipated that the larger plants envisaged for future regional water supply will be able to attain lower costs through the economies of scale and the benefits of more advanced technology. A plant producing 8 million gallons per day (16), which will be built around a gas turbine, will have vapor-compressor heat pumps coupled to vertical-tube evaporators and will use the engine-rejected heat in flash evaporators, is expected to produce fresh water at a cost of about half that for the Key West plant (17).

Heat transfer enhancement is currently being introduced into evaporator designs. For example, doubly finned or doubly flutted vertical tubes give several times the heat transfer of plain smooth tubes, and their use can considerably reduce the size and cost of a plant (18). To some degree the heat transfer in the horizontal tubes of a flash evaporator can be similarly augmented. Such advances are now being tried in test units and pilot plants. The preferred large-plant design at present is a combined flash and vertical-tube evaporator with heat transfer enhancement (19).

Economies can be achieved through the design and construction of dual-purpose plants which produce both power and water, as compared to single-purpose plants that produce only water. In terms of 1967 dollars at 10 percent interest (20), the cost of water at a large (billion gallons per day) single-purpose plant, in which most of the steam bypasses the turbine without generating any power, was estimated (9, pp. 3, 4, 19, 20; 21, p. 39) to be 26 to 32 cents per 1000 gallons, while at a dual-purpose station the range for incremental cost of water was 16 to 24 cents. At an interest rate of 9 percent, another study (22) indicated 15 to 26 cents for the dual-purpose cost range. These large-plant studies were based on the use of reactor heat sources, with technology ranging from reactors of the type (light-water) and size being built in the United States today to advanced fast and thermal breeder reactors of the type that will be operational some two decades hence. Since these estimates were made there have been sharp increases in reactor prices, and it may turn out that the costs of water will have to be revised upward by 2 or 3 cents per 1000 gallons (23). On the other hand, advanced evaporator and agricultural technologies appear to be moving ahead more rapidly than had been expected.

The saving effected through dual-purpose operation works the other way as well. Once you have decided to build a single-purpose steam bypass water plant, the incremental cost of producing power also is very low—say, 1.5 mills per kilowatt-hour (21, p. 39) for reactor stations of the largest sizes being constructed today, such as Brown's Ferry (3000 electrical megawatts). This power may be transmitted to a network in some instances, or to adjacent industrial plants in a so-called agro-industrial complex, to help develop and build up the region. A number of industrial processes have been studied in this connection (9, 21, 24), as well as several possible locales (25) and some of the implementation problems (26). One of the large energy consumers is the production of ammonia for fertilizer by way of electrolytic hydrogen, with only air and water used as raw materials. Potassium fertilizer can be produced from the sea, as can other products, such as chlorine, magnesium, salt, and caustic. Hoyle writes (27):

. . . the older established industries of Europe and America . . . grew up around specialized mineral deposits—coal, oil, metallic ores. Without these deposits the older style of industrialization was completely impossible. On the political and economic fronts, the world became divided into "haves" and "have nots," depending whereabouts on the earth's surface these specialized deposits happen to be situated. . . . In the second phase of industrialism, . . . no specialized deposits are needed at all. The key to this second phase lies in the possession of an effectively unlimited source of energy. . . . Low-grade ores can be smelted—and there is an ample supply of such ores to be found everywhere. Carbon can be taken from inorganic compounds, nitrogen from the air, a whole vast range of chemicals from seawater. So . . . a phase in which nothing is needed but the commonest materials—water, air and fairly common rocks. This was a phase that can be practiced by anybody, by any nation. . . . This second phase was clearly enormously more effective and powerful than the first.

Summary

The fastest-growing region in our country is the desert of the Southwest. This suggests that the vast, warm, dry areas of the world may be attractive for human occupancy as earth's population soars, if the water and power needs can be met. It may also be that nuclear energy—not tied by any umbilical cord to fossil deposits—will have a significant role in opening up these arid areas and creating usable land for human living space.

Since much arid land lies relatively near the sea and the aggregate length of the coastal deserts nearly equals the circumference of the globe, desalination is a freshwater source of broad potential applicability when cheaper alternative sources are not available. Cities and industries can now spread widely along the ocean shore, bringing with them some agriculture for garden produce.

A more difficult question concerns the extent to which desalination agricul-

FIGURE 1. The costs of growing grain (sec. 30). [Oak Ridge National Laboratory]

ture will be used in newly occupied arid lands for the production of staple foods. Since we cannot predict with any accuracy either the population growth or the increase in food production by various means, let alone the difference between these two large quantities, our knowledge of future food shortages is very poor indeed. It therefore appears prudent to conduct research, development, and pilot planting projects to investigate such potential methods for augmenting food production. These activities should be conducted on a scale sufficient to permit practical evaluation, so that the option of invoking such methods will be open, should circumstances require it. To quote R. R. R. Brooks (28), "The key to (the) ... future of two-thirds of the human species is rising productivity in agriculture. All political dogmas, party slogans, planning strategies, and models of economic growth shrivel to irrelevance in the face of this fact."

A preliminary and generalized study was conducted at the Oak Ridge National Laboratory with the collaboration of outstanding agricultural and engineering people from other countries and from U.S. government agencies, universities, foundations, and industries. This study considered intensive year-round farming in warm coastal deserts, based on the use of distilled seawater, in association with clustering industries. As indicated in Fig. 1, production costs for rice and wheat appear (29) to fall, for water costs of around 35 and 20 cents per 1000 gallons, respectively, in the general area of recent grain prices. These water prices, in turn, fall (barely) within the estimated future cost range for desalinated water.

The significant conclusion, we believe, is that desalination agriculture is in the realm of practical possibility, rather than being far afield. To our mind this appears of sufficient importance, in view of the population expansion and the interest in opening up new lands and communities, to warrant the development of advanced desalting plants and intensive scientifically managed agriculture. We hope that desert research farms running on distilled water, and controlled-environment agricultural test chambers, may become as well known to you on your TV screen in a few years as starving Biafran babies are today.

REFERENCES AND NOTES

1. H. G. Wells, *The World Set Free—A Story of Mankind* (Dutton, New York, 1914), p. 241.
2. In Los Angeles some strawberry growers use land worth $10,000 per acre and pay city taxes on it.
3. *Nature* 199, 411 (1963).
4. J. Bronowski, *Saturday Rev.* 1969, 45 (5 July 1969).
5. C. H. Lowe, Jr., in A. S. Leopold, *The Desert* (Life Nature Library, New York, 1961), introduction.
6. There are xerophytic plants (such as pineapple) that carry on photosynthesis with closed stomata in the daytime, using stored carbon dioxide absorbed through open stomata at night. They thus transpire much less water per unit of plant matter produced than ordinary crops do.
7. M. Clawson, H. H. Landsberg, L. T. Alexander, *Science* 164, 1141 (1969).
8. P. W. MacAvoy and D. F. Peterson, Jr., *The Engineering Economics of Large-Scale Desalting in the 1970's* (Praeger, New York, in press).
9. "Nuclear Energy Centers; Industrial and Agro-Industrial Complexes: Summary Report," *Oak Ridge Nat. Lab. Rep.* ORNL-4291 (1968).
10. C. W. Howe, in *Arid Lands in Perspective,* W. G. McGinnies and B. J. Goldman, Eds. (AAAS, Washington, D.C., 1969), p. 379.
11. J. R. A. McMillan, "Water, Agricultural Production and World Population" (Farrer Oration) (1965).
12. J. S. Kanwar, "From protective to productive irrigation," *Econ. Polit. Weekly Rev. Agr.* (29 March 1969). Data, cited from M. S. Chaudhury and R. G. Pandrey, are given in more detail in an article in *Indian Farming,* in press.
13. R. Revelle, *Proc. Nat. Acad. Sci. U.S.* 56, 328 (1966).
14. If suitable aquifers are not present and an above-ground storage reservoir is constructed in the farming region, there is an increase in cost such that the value $140 in the next paragraph of the text changes to about $150 per acre per year, it being assumed that the reservoir is of a size adequate to supply a farm region with an intake of about 10^9 gallons of water per day.
15. D. Goldberg, B. Gornat, M. Shmueli, "Advances in irrigation in Israel's agriculture," paper presented at the 1st World Congress of Engineers and Architects, Israel (1967). See also D. Goldberg and M. Shmueli, "Drip irrigation—a method used under arid and desert conditions of high water and soil salinity," unpublished.
16. This plant is now in the preliminary planning stage.
17. "Design and Economic Study of a Gas Turbine Powered Vapor Compression Plant for Evaporation of Seawater," *Office Saline Water Res. Develop. Progr. Rep. No. 377* (1968).
18. Such tubes are to be used in the gas turbine unit discussed in the preceding paragraph.
19. "Conceptual Design Study of a 250-Million Gallon per Day Combined Vertical Tube-Flash Evaporator Desalination Plant," *Office Saline Water Res. Develop. Progr. Rep. No. 391* (1968).
20. The cost of desalted water is sensitive to changes in interest rates because, like conventional means of providing new water supplies such as dams and aqueducts, the process requires a large capital outlay.

21. *Oak Ridge Nat. Lab. Rep. No. ORNL-4290* (1968).
22. "Nuclear Power and Water Desalting Plants for Southwest United States and Northwest Mexico" (1968), pp. 113 and 136; this is a preliminary assessment made by a joint United States-Mexico International Atomic Energy Agency study team.
23. This expectation is based on the assumption that combined flash and vertical-tube evaporators are adopted; otherwise, the increase in water costs would be expected to be larger.
24. A. M. Squires, "Steel making in an agro-industrial complex," in *Oak Ridge Nat. Lab. Rep. No. ORNL-4294* (1968); W. E. Lobo, "Acetylene production from naphtha by electric arc and by partial combustion," in *ibid.*; H. E. Goeller, "Tables for computing manufacturing costs of industrial products in an agro-industrial complex," *Oak Ridge Nat. Lab. Rep. No. ORNL-4296* (1969).
25. T. Tamura and W. J. Young, "Data obtained on Several Possible Locales for the Agro—Industrial Complex," *Oak Ridge Nat. Lab. Rep. No. ORNL-4293* (1970).
26. J. A. Ritchey, "Problems in Implementation of an Agro—Industrial Complex," *Oak Ridge Nat. Rep. No. ORNL-4295* (1969); R. L. Meier, *Bull. At. Sci.* 1969, 16 (March 1969); R. D. Sharma, *ibid.* 1969, 31 (November 1969).
27. F. Hoyle, *Ossian's Ride* (Harper, New York, 1959), p. 146.
28. R. R. R. Brooks, *Saturday Rev.* 1969, 14 (9 August 1969).
29. The estimates are based on an interest rate of 10 percent.
30. Figure 1 is based on data and publications as follows. The average price paid the U.S. producer for wheat in the period 1956-65; the average price per pound of milled rice, at 0.65 paddy weight (0.65 pound of milled rice from each pound of paddy), paid the U.S. producer in the period 1950-65; the average price of Siam Patna No. 2 rice imported into the United Kingdom in the period 1955-65; the average wholesale price of wheat in India (the Punjab) in the period 1951-65 *(FAO (Food Agr. Organ. UN) Prod. Yearb. 20 (1966))*; the world average export value of wheat in the period 1961-67; the world average export value of rice in the period 1955-67 *(The State of Food and Agriculture: 1968 (Food and Agriculture Organization of the United Nations, Rome, 1968))*; the average U.S. export value of rice in the period 1960-65; the European Economic Community's wheat support price *(The World Food Problem* (President's Science Advisory Committee, Washington, D.C., 1967), vol. 2, pp. 145, 149)): recent world prices for wheat and rice delivered in Asia, as given by R. P. Hammond in a paper presented at the International Conference on Water for Peace, Washington, D.C., May 1967.
31. The research discussed here is sponsored by the U.S. Atomic Energy Commission under contract with the Union Carbide Corp.

Importation of Water

85　　　　　　　　**Water Importation into Arid Lands**

JAY M. BAGLEY

What is the philosophic basis for the regional water transfer and how does it differ (or does it differ?) from the philosophy of water resources development within a particular river basin? What are the legal and administrative problems involved in conveying large quantities of water across state boundaries wherever doctrines, principles, and regulations of water rights vary? How are these complicated when sovereign nations are involved? What are the large-scale and long-term physical implications on local water balances and the maintenance of water quality? Can regional growth patterns be regulated by regional water transfer and should they be? What are the ecological implications and can they be predicted? Can existing institutional patterns be adapted to the considerations of large-scale transfers? What institutional changes seem desirable? What are the intrastate, interstate, and international political realities? What are the economic impacts to regions that export and import? If a region has a surplus of water needed by neighboring regions, how can it be determined whether exported water will limit its own future economic growth? How does economic development stemming from regional water transfers compare to alternative investment plans not water-oriented? How can costs and benefits be evaluated and allocated where states and nations are involved? Are there alternatives to large-scale water imports? How can these be evaluated and compared? Will considerations of large-scale water transfer entail a painful reorientation of present philosophy on water resource development? Can this philosophy serve as an instrument for peace between neighboring countries?

The Use of Arid Lands 86

DAEL WOLFLE

The approximately 14 percent of the world's cropped lands that are under irrigation produce a fourth or more of the world's agricultural crops. As the food needs of a too rapidly growing population continue to increase, more and more of the arid and semiarid regions will be cultivated, for much of this land is capable of year-round use, and conditions are more favorable than in humid regions for the control of insects and disease and the advantageous timing of water application. One estimate is that by the year 2000 there will be twice the present 370 million acres under irrigation, even though the cost of new irrigation projects, which now averages almost $400 per acre, is substantially higher than the cost of bringing new land in humid regions under cultivation.

The investment required means that irrigation agriculture can be economically successful only when combined with sophisticated farm technology. Yet too often, over the world, expensive water storage and distribution facilities have been uneconomically coupled with moderately primitive methods of farm operation.

There are a few examples of long-enduring irrigation successes. But they are more than counterbalanced by reminders of how extensively man has unwittingly turned grassland and food-producing areas into wasteland and desert. The Sahara, for example, is still increasing by 40,000 acres a year.

The arid lands experts are uncertain whether the pressure to exploit more of the arid lands would, quite literally, in the long run make the deserts bloom or produce more Saharas.

Dams

---

87   Dam Building and the Four Criteria

WES JACKSON

A seemingly obvious way to capture water out of the water cycle is to build a dam. Simplistic thinking may cause a hungry or near-hungry nation to seek foreign aid and rally the citizens to action. The economy is stimulated, hope is rekindled, and the focus is diverted from their misery, at least until the project is finished. Then what?

Many problems, which on the surface seem to have simple solutions, must be abandoned when a very few interrelated criteria are established. Harvey Brooks and Raymond Bowers (February, 1970, *Scientific American*) suggested that before we go into an act, we cannot claim good intentions unless we consider effects in terms of: (a) how many people are going to be affected, (b) for how long, (c) at what level of culture, and (d) with what effect on freedom of future action. These must be treated as an interdependent set, as indeed they are. A project which would surely enhance one criterion is not immediately approved. It must deal seriously with balances and compensations among the whole set of criteria.

Consider, for example, a project to introduce a higher-yielding crop into a country that is short of food by building a dam and using some of the water for irrigation. Obviously, the increased yield will increase the size of the population that can be supported. Has anyone considered for how long? Will the new crop condemn many of the population to monotonous work, or place them in soul-starving isolation? After starting the project, is it possible to back out? What does one do with a dam that has silted in, that has increased the incidence of water borne diseases, that has disrupted the fisheries near the delta or has driven delta farmers into slums because the annual replacement of soil nutrients due to flooding has stopped?

Before we call for more dams to avert the food crisis, perhaps we should look at the history of dam projects of civilizations past and present. This history and the local conditions, including physical, social and economic, can then be considered in the background of the four criteria. A few projects which originally were of little appeal may, on the balance, have virtue. Others with high initial appeal may not fare so well.

The following, cheerfully presented tongue-in-cheek call for escalation of large dam building projects came at a time when conservationists were passionately attacking the proposed new dams at Bridge Canyon situated 80 miles below the famous Grand Canyon National Park, and at Marble Gorge about 12 miles above the park. Then Secretary of the Interior Stewart L. Udall, a conservationist himself, argued in favor of both dams by saying that the 91 miles of river within the park would remain undisturbed and that electric power could be sold to repay the federal investment.

Think Big   88

BRUCE STEWART

An Open Letter to the Secretary of the Interior

Dear Mr. Secretary:

The Bureau of Reclamation in your department is to be commended with faint praise for its recent accomplishments in the southwestern United States. True, it has completed the Glen Canyon Dam (authorized 1955) and 193 other dams without a failure, thus contributing to flood control, irrigation, and power development. Also it is agitating vigorously for dams at Marble Gorge and Bridge Canyon. But these are piddling enterprises. You must learn to think BIG if you hope to leave your mark indelibly written on the face of America. And what bigger project could you choose than to dam the Colorado River, right across Grand Canyon? Think of it. A waterfall one mile high! A lake one mile deep! A solid wall of concrete from the south rim to the north!

If such a dam were constructed, a few of its benefits can be dimly foreseen. First there would be the opportunities for power development. A Grand Canyon Dam would make the generating facilities at Hoover (1936) or Glen Canyon look like a lightning bug on a summer's evening. My rough calculations indicate that you could expect to produce enough electricity to light up not only Grand Canyon Lake area (hereafter called Lake Udall) but Bryce, Zion, the Petrified Forest, and Painted Desert, with enough left over to decorate 1,742,651 evergreens with Christmas lights.

The Grand Canyon Dam would also have great uses for irrigation and flood control. The Colorado River would be permanently tamed. Experts have assured me that with the waters from Lake Udall we could irrigate a maximum of 2,165,000 acres of dry land. Thus we could look forward to wheat fields in the Painted Desert, flower gardens around Sunset Crater, and the Petrified Forest no longer petrified but rather filled with thousands of living trees — orange, grapefruit, fig.

A third, fast-growing use of Grand Canyon waters would be for recreation. With the construction of a few fish hatcheries in southern Utah and northern Arizona, the lake could be kept stocked with fish, and a lake one mile deep and twenty miles wide would accommodate some monsters! Think of sturgeon, muskellunge, pike, ten- or twenty-pound trout. . . . Have you considered the fact that boating is the wave of the future? The steady increase in number of boats, in size, draft, and horsepower will soon make most small lakes obsolete. Putting the family boat of 1980 on one of these old lakes will be like trying to float the Queen Elizabeth in a teacup. Also the family submarine about the year 2000 will require depth beyond anything now present in the government lake system. Viewing the scenery of Grand Canyon underwater would be a thousand time more thrilling than seeing it from the distant north or south rim.

We come to the last but by no means the least of the great advantages of a mile-high Grand Canyon Dam—the magnitude of the economic enterprise. It would require at least twenty years and employ some 100,000 men, benefiting nearly a half-million people directly. Indirectly the economic benefits pyramid almost astronomically. The dam would contain at a conservative estimate some 17,659,873,151.85 cubic yards of steel, copper, rubber, generators, and all the thousands of items required by this great project.

There will of course be carping critics of a Grand Canyon Dam . . . do-gooders, conservationists, starry-eyed liberals and wild-lifers. They will wax lyrical about the beauties of nature, the awe-inspiring depths of great, lonely canyons, the history—white and Indian—to be buried by the waters of Lake Udall. Indeed they are already attacking those two small-time proposals, Marble and Bridge Canyon Dams, just because these will back up a little water into Grand Canyon National Park. Sooner or later, however, every foot of every big river in America must be backed up behind a retaining wall. This is our ultimate goal, and since it is, let up take a giant stride toward that goal by constructing a dam across the Grand Canyon—a marvel of engineering which will put to shame all the Pyramids, the Great Walls, bridges, and dams which have ever been built in the past.

"There is the mighty Colorado River flowing down to the sea. Dam it!"

THE TROPICS

89   The Myth of Fertility Dooms Development Plans

DARRYL G. COLE

Not long ago Adrian Alfaro came to our home to tell us that his wife had been in labor for a week and could not give birth to her baby. Adrian owns a small farm near our coffee plantation at Canas Gordas in southwestern Costa Rica. A young man, he had been married a little more than a year. Now he was haggard and distraught. His wife was dying, he said.

My wife and I went to Adrian's farm and found Mrs. Alfaro resting on a bed of boards in a hut with a dirt floor and walls fashioned of split saplings. A white flour sack had been spread on the floor by an elderly midwife to receive the baby. We carried Mrs. Alfaro on a stretcher to our pickup truck. Adrian, two brothers, and his father held the stretcher in the back of the truck to ease the jolting of travel, and we began the trip to the regional medical station at San Vito de Jaba. It was in the middle of the wet season, a light rain was falling, and Adrian covered Mrs. Alfaro with a large sheet of plastic. The road to San Vito, 13 miles distant, was in bad condition. With heavy chains on its tires, and with a front-mounted winch, our truck would get through the mud. But as the rain fell over the soggy land, and the truck churned on, I felt immeasurably depressed.

Great Expectations

My family and I had come to Canas Gordas 13 years earlier. It was a frontier settlement then, emergent in the highland rain forest. We proposed to establish a diversified farm, employing the latest techniques of modern agriculture. Over the years my parents and my wife and I devoted a considerable amount of money and effort to the project. But our venture has yielded only a small measure of the rewards we expected. The emergency involving Adrian Alfaro and his wife underscored for me how mistaken those early expectations were.

I am frequently dismayed by articles appearing in the Costa Rican press asserting that agriculture in this country must be diversified and that the rich bounty and natural fertility of new land must be harvested. Such assertions seem to be made with all of the best intentions and with an eagerness from their writers suggesting that with this or another government program, with a loan or technical assistance, with the right attitude on the part of farmers, the new lands would yield prodigiously. Well-being and even prosperity would follow. I would like to submit that such hopes have not been realized in the Canas Gordas-San Vito area, that they are not being realized in other areas of Costa Rica, and that, on the basis of our present knowledge of tropical agriculture, they will not be realized in similar new lands in underdeveloped nations.

The Myth Persists

The myth of the fertility of these virgin lands has been too long in dying. It has long been dead for the farmers like Adrian Alfaro, whose subservience to a meager soil leaves them few illusions about the "untapped riches" of virgin lands. But the myth persists, and even thrives, among sectors of government and the public where misinformation has been accepted as fact.

When we came to Canas Gordas we purchased a tract of rain forest in an area widely acclaimed at that time as a future center of farming progress and development. An Italian colony had been started two years earlier in San Vito de Jaba, a project eventually involving the investment of about $2,000,000. We looked at the rain forest on our land, at the moist, dark soil supporting it, and concluded that anything would grow in soil so apparently fertile.

Fertility Restricted to Forest

We felled the forest, cleared the land, and planted the first crops. They were a failure from the beginning. We weren't discouraged; we began experimenting —using fertilizers, lime, manure, insecticides, fungicides, varieties of seed, cover crops, various methods of tillage. We consulted agronomists, farm-research and extension agencies, and farmers' publications, and called upon the experience that had enabled us to farm successfully in the United States. We discovered that other settlers in our area were making similar efforts with equally unsatisfactory results.

Finally, we learned what we might have been told at the beginning, had we been less adamant about our ability to succeed where others had demonstrated no remarkable success. We learned that the fertility of these virgin lands is mostly in the forest and in the thin layer of humus carpeting the forest floor.

The soil nutrients needed to sustain plant life are circulated from the soil through plant tissues. Drawn from the humus and top soil by the roots of the forest vegetation, the nutrients return to the soil in falling leaves and dead branches. At any given time the forest itself is a storehouse of soil fertility.

Cut down, the forest ceases to hold nutrients in suspension; violent rains drive over the land, leaching nutrients below root levels; sunlight invades shade-loving retreats; and, unwittingly, the farmer, by tilling and exposing the soil to the sun and rain, outrages its microbiotic order. Fertility vanishes in a sudden, stunning conflagration.

Diversity Is No Solution

Much can be done, of course, to supplement soil fertility with fertilizers. However, where rain drives month after month through loose, permeable soil, where terrain is hilly and erosion carries soil away, where sunlight burns fiercely into the land, it requires an art beyond the ability of most farmers to grow crops well over sustained periods, even with fertilizers and modern techniques. What is more to the point, such methods applied to soils divested of their original forest cover are seldom profitable.

There is a good deal of discussion today in Costa Rica about agriculture diversification. Hardly a week goes by without a pronouncement by someone on the important subject. It is evident that the traditional mainstays of the Costa Rican economy—coffee, cacao, bananas, sugar, which are embroiled in market surpluses or in rising production costs—cannot be relied upon.

What to do? The solution, most frequently advanced, to diversify, is little better than a restatement of the problem. It too frequently ignores the harshness of the land.

Farmers whose livelihood is dependent upon a monoculture crippled by the woes of international overproduction do not continue to rely upon that monoculture by choice; their dependence on the economic loser is largely the product of conditions that at no time have offered any significant measure of flexibility. Planners and economists, serving up the latest potpourri of diversification, might well consider that, where agriculture has seized upon one or two successful crops over a period of years, diversification has probably been tried and been found to be competitively impractical.

The basis of our planning from the beginning of our work here in Canas Gordas has been to develop a diversified farm. Yet, after 13 years, we have been reduced to dependence upon a monoculture, the production of coffee. It is true that the soil here will produce other crops: pasture grass, vegetables, corn, beans, fruits. But given the conditions of climate, soil, and topography, they cannot be produced and marketed competitively.

Enthusiasm Fades

The enthusiasm and confidence that characterized the beginning steps in development in the Canas Gordas-San Vito area have languished. They have been replaced by a lean skepticism, more closely defined by a need to survive than by a will to succeed. Under the circumstances of these latter years success has become merely the ability to subsist. Yet, what is more disturbing are the repeated assertions made publicly purporting that the limitations of this area either do not exist or can be eliminated with relatively simple measures.

Such arguments abet a form of social irresponsibility. They suggest that solutions to basic problems hinge on but a few steps that, if taken, would lead shortly to sweeping remedies.

Too often the standard of living in more-developed nations is used as an example of what can be accomplished by pursuing this or that technique. This point of view ignores the basic differences between the ingredients of agriculture in the developed nation and those in the nation seeking development. It would be preferable in underdeveloped nations to work within the limits of the environment and recognize that the blessings of fertility and productivity are not everywhere evenly distributed.

Mrs. Alfaro returned to her home not long ago with a baby boy, Adrian Alberto. I would like to believe that when Adrian Alberto goes to school he will follow a road no longer beset with the quagmires that made his arrival in the world the subject of an emergency, that as a man with a family he would enjoy the benefits his father has been denied. I would like to believe this, but 13 years of work in Canas Gordas have left me doubtful.

Will the Amazon Basin Become a Desert? 90

WILLIAM E. MORAN, JR.

Few areas of the world have provoked greater agricultural fantasies than the Amazon Basin, which is itself larger than any other Latin American country. Various schemes have been advanced to turn this steaming jungle into a "breadbasket" for the continent. Few of these master-plans have adequately taken into account the fragile ecosystem of the tropical rain forest, which supports a profusion of plant and animal species but which erodes with stunning suddenness under the slash-and-burn cultivation that is now so tragically on the increase. While scientists have not yet defined the precise relationship between mycorrhizal fungi and tree roots which enables the jungle to thrive on very poor laterite soil, they do agree on one vital point: this incredibly lush jungle, where the rainfall averages over 80 inches a year, is ecologically only a few steps removed from a wasteland. If the forest vegetation were to be cleared, says Colombian geologist Carlos Eduardo Acosta, the Amazon Basin would become "a desert like the Sahara."

THE OCEANS

91   **Human Food from Ocean and Land**

K. O. EMERY
C. O'D. ISELIN

During recent years many claims have been made about the importance of the ocean to man's future well-being. Some of these claims appear to us to be reasonable, whereas others have an Alice-in-Wonderland quality.

The difference in the former productivity of the ocean and the land is so great as to suggest that an enormous effort will be required before the production of the ocean can be comparable with that of the land.

A sort of genetic classification of food resources was used to compare the present stages of technology in the ocean and on the land. For plants, the primitive stage is that of gathering wild plants (on land—berries, nuts, mushrooms, herbs); the next stage is farming (whereby seed are planted and the plants are tended and then harvested). For animals, the primitive stage is that of hunting wild animals for food (on land—deer, rabbits, quail); the next stage is herding (whereby selected breeding, culling of young, and controlled slaughter are practiced along with the nondestructive taking of by-products such as eggs, milk, and wool). This terminology, gathering and farming of plants, and hunting and herding of animals, is also applied to the ocean in a strict sense. For example, we consider that only algae or bacteria can be farmed, and that oysters, clams, and fish can be herded (not farmed) as an improvement over catching them in their wild state. Note that nonedible materials such as lumber, whale oil, shells, pearls, wool, hides, and fertilizer are not included in this study.

Since farming is far closer to the energy source on the complex and inefficient food pyramid than is herding, one should expect greater rewards from farming than from herding. However, farming of the ocean (for plants) has as its major obstacle the difficulty of harvesting. Most of the bulk of plants that live in the ocean are microscopic in size and they are distributed in three dimensions. The cost (energy) of harvesting them exceeds the value (energy) that is recovered by eating (or burning) the crop. Near shore in clear water larger attached algae can be grown, but most of them are not particularly tasty and few are used directly as food. We do not know of a single experimental project in the United States that is designed to farm the ocean! Many projects investigate laboratory aspects of photosynthesis, plant physiology, and biochemistry, but none appear to be making direct tests of planting and harvesting in the ocean. One answer is that "we must understand the processes before they can be utilized," but we may ask in return "how well did early man understand photosynthesis and biochemistry when he improved and adapted to farming the primitive corn and other wild plants that he had encountered in his gathering stage of economy?"

1. Photosynthetic production in the ocean is comparable to that on the land, although great regional variations in productivity exist in both environments. Since the area of the ocean is nearly three times that of the land, the potential harvest is proportionally large, even without equivalent agricultural practices.

2. The old concept of the freedom of the seas, which developed because the ocean was considered nearly worthless except for cheap transportation and defense, is diametrically opposed to wise utilization of the seas.

3. Fishermen prefer to sell fresh fish because the price is much higher than for the so-called "trash" fish, which are being increasingly processed into fish meal as an additive for chicken and cattle food. Fish flour, a more refined product that is fit for human consumption, is just coming onto the market; it is an efficient source of cheap protein for the human diet.

4. Fishermen are likely to remain hunters rather than herders or farmers unless responsibility is clearly defined for management of the biological resources available in the saltwater envelope that covers so much of the world. For some resources national agencies can be adequate, but for others some international agency is needed.

CHANGING RELIGION AND TABOOS

Hindus make up 70 to 80 percent of India's 547 million population. Hindu scriptures say, "All that kill cows rot in hell for as many years as there are hairs on the body of the cow they killed." Of India's 17 states, 10 ban the slaughter of cattle.

It has been estimated that there are more than 200 million cattle in India, or one-fourth of all the cattle in the world. Ten percent of this total are supposedly strays, and tens of thousands die of malnutrition and disease each year. Agriculture officials have estimated that a cow or steer will eat in grain in a day what seven people would eat.

It seems immediately obvious to the non-Hindu mind that the religion should be changed. Doesn't it seem logical that the Indian people, thousands of whom also die of malnutrition and starvation every year, should eat their sacred cattle?

The following reading questions the wisdom of people eating their tractors. Perhaps the Hindu religion is so wide-spread now because in the past other tribes that did not hold the cattle sacred became extinct during lean years. Perhaps all the problems with the cattle described above represent the built-in price tag for subsistence. One could argue that at least they could kill the strays, the malnourished and the disease-ridden.

However, such "mercy-killing" creates the same moral dilemma that "mercy-killing" of humans would in our own country. Where does it stop?

92   Religion and Energy Flow

HOWARD T. ODUM

An example of a primitive agricultural system of man and nature is provided by the system of rice and cattle in India and in other monsoon climates where the severity of the dry season essentially forces all systems of vegetation, whether controlled by man or not, to recommence each year. There is a flow of energy through rice and some grass, man, and the sacred cattle (work animals) with loopback circuits of work control. Harris[1] opposes those who state that the sacred animals on the intensified, nonsubsidized farms are superfluous. He mentions that they glean from a different plant base than man, serve as a source of critical protein, and especially facilitate mineral cycling and work on the plots necessary for a fast start on crop production when the wet monsoon begins. Those who advocate removal of the sacred cows needed under the present agricultural system refer to the simple principle of shortening the food chain to save energy. In this case, a little knowledge about one process without understanding the complete system may be producing recommendations that endanger millions by upsetting a self-supporting system. Harris cites Gandhi's comment that cows are sacred because they are necessary. The more general principle may be that religion is the program of energy control necessary for survival encoded in behavioral language.

1. Harris, Marvin. 1965. *The Myth of the Sacred Cow.* Pp 217-228. *In:* Leeds, Anthony and Andrew P. Vayda. *Man, Culture, and Animals.* Publ. No. 78 of the Amer. Assoc. Advancement of Sci., Washington, D. C. 304 pp.

THE FUTURE

93   The Human Enterprise

GEORGE WALD

We have come to a time of great decision not only for man but for much of life on the earth. We are in a period of great crisis, in fact, of many crises. John Platt has spoken of them as a "crisis of crises." They are all coming upon us at once, all coming to a head within the next fifteen to at most thirty years; and this, of course, faces us with multiple problems. We have very hard decisions to make.

The things we need to face and try to do are terrifying in their complexity and their difficulty. We need in fact a revolution. I use the word in its literal sense, a turn-about. We here in America, living in a democracy, still hope that we can *vote* ourselves that revolution; but vote it or not, that revolution must come if we are to survive.

Nor can it be done piecemeal. Most of our problems are closely interrelated, so that we have to deal with them together, each one dependent upon the others. That calls for a tremendous effort that involves not only the people of this country but to a great degree of the globe. That means that we will have somehow to learn to move and work together; and that in turn calls for some sort of common acceptance of the questions that men have always tried to answer throughout their history: Whence they come, what kind of thing they are, and out of these realizations at least some hint of what is to become of us.

Those are the age-old questions. Men have always tried to answer them, and all the traditional religions try to answer them. Fortunately for us at this time one can find a kind of answer in the world view of science, an answer that presents an astonishingly unified view of the universe, the place of life in it, and the place of man in life. In that unified view I think we can find new sanctions for our beliefs in the sanctity of life and in the dignity of man, more credible and more reliable than any that the older traditions offered us.

What is that unified view? We know now that we live in a historical universe, one in which not only living creatures but stars and galaxies are born, come to maturity, grow old and die. That universe is made of four kinds of elementary particles: protons, neutrons, electrons, and photons, which are particles of radiation. If not the whole universe then surely large parts of it began in a kind of gas, a plasma, of such elementary particles, filling large sections of space. Here and there, quite by accident, within that plasma an eddy formed, a little special concentration of material, and this, through the ordinary forces of gravitation, began to pull in the stuff around it, to pull in the particles out of the space around it. So it grew, and the more that there was, the harder it pulled. It swept the material out of larger and larger sections of space and grew and grew, a condensing mass of elementary particles. As that mass condensed, as all such masses in condensation do, it heated up. When the temperature in the deep interior reached about five million degrees, something new began to happen.

That new thing was that one of these particles, the protons—a proton is the nucleus of a hydrogen atom, so that one speaks of them as hydrogen—the protons began to join together, four protons condensing to make a nucleus of the atom helium, four protons, each approximately of mass 1, condensing to make a helium nucleus of mass approximately 4.

But in that transaction a little mass is lost; and that little bit of mass is converted into radiation, according to Einstein's famous formula, $E = mc^2$, in which E is the energy of that radiation, m is the little bit of mass, and c is a very big number, the speed of light, 186,000 miles a second, 3×10^{10} centimeters per second. Multiply even a little bit of mass by that big a number and you get an awful lot of energy. That energy beginning to be poured out in the deep interior of what had been a condensing mass of particles backs up the condensation, and this mass comes into an uneasy steady state, in which its further impulse to collapse through gravity is held back by the outpouring of energy inside. What I have just described, of course, is the birth of a star. Our own star, the sun, was born in that way about six billion years ago. It is just an ordinary run of the mill, middle-aged star. It has approximately another six billion years to run.

Stars live by this process. They live by the so-called "burning" of hydrogen to helium. Inevitably the time comes when every star begins to run out of hydrogen. With that, it begins to produce less energy; and with that it begins to collapse again. With that, it heats up again. When the temperature in the deep interior reaches about one hundred million degrees, something new begins to happen.

That is the "burning" of helium. Those helium nuclei of mass 4 begin to unite with one another. It's all simple arithmetic. Two helium nuclei condense: four and four make eight. That is beryllium 8, an atomic nucleus so unstable that it disintegrates within so small a fraction of a second that it has never been measured. Yet always at these enormous concentrations of matter and enormous temperatures there are a few beryllium atoms; and here and there a beryllium nucleus captures another helium nucleus. Eight and four make twelve, and what is twelve; *Carbon;* and that is where carbon comes from in our universe. And when you have got the carbon, that carbon 12 can capture another helium nucleus: twelve and four make sixteen, and what is sixteen? *Oxygen;* and that is where oxygen comes from. And when you have some carbon, that can do another thing. The carbon itself can begin to pick up protons, hydrogen nuclei. And carbon 12 plus two protons make fourteen, and what is fourteen? That is *Nitrogen.*

These processes produce a new enormous outpouring of energy in the deep interior of the star, enough energy not only to back up the further condensation but to puff it out to enormous size. It is now a red giant, a dying star, gigantic because it has been puffed up to enormous size, and red because it has cooled off somewhat in its outermost layers. A red giant, a dying star.

Those red giants are in a delicate condition. They are always distilling a lot of stuff off their surfaces into space. Every now and then a great streamer of material goes shooting off into space: a flare. Every now and then a whole star threatens to blow up: a nova. Every now and then it does blow up: a supernova. And in all these ways the stuff of which red giants are made is spewed out into space to become part of the huge masses of gases and dust that fill all space. It is sometimes estimated that as much as half the mass of our universe is in the form of gases and dust.

Then here and there in the gases and dust a new eddy forms, a new little knot of material, that once again by gravitation begins to pull in the stuff from all around it; and a new star is born.

But those later generation stars, unlike the first generation of stars made entirely of hydrogen and helium, contain the carbon and nitrogen and oxygen; and we know that our sun is such a later generation star, *because we are here*— because we, as all other living creatures we know, and I am sure, though that is another story, that must be true everywhere that life occurs in the universe, because 99 percent of our living substance is made of just those elements I have been naming: hydrogen, carbon, nitrogen, and oxygen. It is a moving realization that stars must die before organisms may live.

Stars are at too high temperatures for the atomic nuclei to gather the electrons about themselves in orderly ways. That can happen only in the cooler places of the universe, on the planets. There, where the electrons can be brought into orderly ways around the atomic nuclei, those electrons can begin to interact with one another, and so become the first molecules.

Molecules are a great new thing in the universe, for until there are molecules nothing has a shape or size. We are still in the world of Heisenberg's Indeterminancy Principle. So long as one is in the world of elementary particles, even atoms, there are no shapes or sizes of even definable positions and motions. All those things come into the universe with the first molecules.

So molecules are a great thing. As soon as the earth was formed, some four and a half billion years ago, the molecules began to form. In the primitive atmosphere of the earth there were such molecules as hydrogen, ammonia, water and methane; and in the upper layers of the atmosphere, sparked by sunlight and electric discharges, those and other molecules began to interact to form that which would eventually give rise to life, the so-called *organic* molecules, the molecules made of hydrogen, carbon, nitrogen and oxygen. Over the ages they were leached out of the atmosphere into the seas. About three billion years ago somewhere, sometime, or perhaps several times in several places, an aggregate of such molecules in the ocean reached a condition that a competent biologist, had he been present, would have been willing to concede to be alive.

Life, too, was a great new thing in our universe. I have heard life called disparagingly a disease of matter. No, it is no disease of matter. It is a *culmination* of matter. Give matter a chance, and give it that chance for long enough, and life appears inevitably. It is a culmination of matter, so far as we know the most complex state of organization that matter achieves in our universe.

And life, since it appeared on the earth, has transformed the whole environment. Even biologists still occasionally make the mistake of thinking that the environment is something given for life to fit itself into or perish; that it is the environment that plays the tune to which life must dance or die.

But it isn't that way at all. The early atmosphere of this planet in which those first organic molecules appeared that led to life, contained no oxygen gas, O_2, the stuff with which all animals and all higher plants respire. There was no oxygen gas in the early atmosphere of the planet. It was put into the atmosphere by living organisms, by plants in the process of photosynthesis; and it is now held in the atmosphere entirely by that process.

All the molecular oxygen gas in our atmosphere comes out of plants in the process of photosynthesis and goes into plants and animals in the process of cellular respiration, and so is completely renewed, about every two thousand years.

Two thousand years is just a moment in geological time. With carbon dioxide it is still more strange. All the carbon dioxide, not only in the atmosphere but dissolved in all the waters of the earth, goes into photosynthesis and comes out of respiration and so is completely renewed every three hundred years.

Life is a great thing on this planet. Two-thirds of the planet is covered with water; yet all the water on the earth goes in and out of living organisms and is completely renewed every two million years; and two million years is just a day in geological time. We have had men on the earth for that long.

The appearance of oxygen through the process of plant photosynthesis did another very strange thing for life on the earth. You see, the radiation from sunlight produced in the way I have described, by turning hydrogen into helium, contains short wavelength ultraviolet components that are incompatible with the existence of life, that no life or even such large molecules as proteins or nucleic acids can tolerate. So long as that radiation poured onto the surface of the earth, life could not exist on the surface. It had to stay under water.

But there in the ocean photosynthesis began. About four-fifths of all the photosynthesis on the earth still occurs in the upper layers of the ocean. The photosynthesis poured oxygen into the atmosphere; and in the uppermost layers of the atmosphere, sparked by sunlight, some of the oxygen formed a little *ozone*. (Oxygen gas is O_2, ozone is O_3.) That little ozone absorbed and still absorbs those ultraviolet radiations out of sunlight that are incompatible with life. It is only because of that little ozone in our upper atmosphere that animals and plants were able to come out from under water and populate the earth and the air.

How much ozone? The whole story represents a delicacy, a sensitivity of control almost beyond belief. The only thing that lets us survive outside of water on the surface of the earth is that ozone; yet all the ozone in the upper atmosphere, if brought to 1 atmosphere pressure—ordinary air pressure at the surface of the earth—and zero degrees centigrade, would form a layer only three millimeters thick, about one eighth of an inch.

And so, particularly after the oxygen and the ozone had arrived, life flourished on the earth and populated every corner of the earth with a most extraordinary ingenuity—every corner. Every place where a little energy can be obtained that makes life possible, you find life there, fitting itself into the most extraordinary conditions.

About two million years ago, man appeared. Man too is a great new thing, man and his like, a great new thing in the universe. You see, you have to wait a long time, all those things have had to happen, and then at last—and I think, given enough time, inevitably—a creature appears who begins to know; a science- and art-making animal, who begins to cast back on this whole history, and begins for the first time to understand it.

You may have heard it said that a hen is only an egg's way of making another egg. In just the same sense a man is the atom's way of knowing about atoms. If you wish, a man is the star's way of knowing about stars—a great new thing.

But in his knowing, man also begins inevitably, as part of that knowing, going hand in hand with that knowing, to breed a technology. The technology isn't artificial; it is part of nature, since it is part of human nature. The technology comes along with that kind of knowing on the part of any such creature, wherever he arose.

I have heard the silly question asked, "Why is the earth about five billion years old?"—and the silly answer—a silly question always deserves a silly answer: Because it took that long to find that out. That is the way it is. Now we are coming to ask another curious question: When you have come to the point of finding that out, can you go much further? Is such a development self-limiting?

I am sure that there is not only life in very many places in the universe, but there are also man-like creatures; not men, but similarly contemplative, technology-making creatures, in many other places in the universe. I see no reason offhand why many of them shouldn't be far ahead of us.

We are beginning to develop our technology very rapidly, and at an increasing pace. If that kind of thing is true for us, it might well be true for them. If they have had another thousand years—and a thousand years is nothing—why not a hundred thousand, a million years, why indeed not a billion years—where might they have reached by now?

Think of where we might reach in even another hundred years if we survive, if we manage well. One has to begin to ask, are there such highly superior technological civilizations elsewhere in the universe, or is there not only a time in which such a creature arrives, but a somewhat later time, perhaps not very much later, in which he departs? That problem now very much concerns us.

Because we have reached a point suddenly in which our very existence and continuance, not only as a civilization but as a species, is threatened by wholly new problems. One of the most important of those problems is overpopulation. It is entirely new. Darwin gave us the phrase, "the survival of the fittest"; and biologists, who like to measure all things, long ago began asking how we were to measure fitness. Long ago we decided that the measure of fitness would be reproductive success—that we would consider those lines of organism most fit that breed the largest number of offspring that themselves survive to sexual maturity and reproduce. I suppose that man is the first species on earth, animal or plant, to be threatened by his own reproductive success.

As everyone knows, by all present indications, unless we can bring something different to happen very quickly, the present world population of something over three and a half billion will have increased by the end of the century to perhaps double that number. Long before that we expect famine in many parts of the world on an unprecedented scale. Yet those famines aren't the heart of the problem. If they were, one could even feel slightly optimistic, because in the last decade the world production of food has increased a little faster than the world population; but that isn't the heart of the problem.

The heart of the problem, as of all human problems, is one of *meaning*. It would be altogether meaningless and bankrupt now to make of the human enterprise a simple exercise in production, an attempt to see how many people one could keep alive on the surface of the earth. Our problem isn't one of numbers, but of the *quality* of human lives. What we need to do is to produce that size of population in which human beings can most fulfill their potentialities.

From that point of view—some may disagree with me and quite properly—in my opinion we are already overpopulated, not just in such places as India, China, and Puerto Rico, but here and in Western Europe. With that overpopulation in our Western world there has been, I think, a signal deterioration in our culture all through the last century.

I think that though this period is kinder to the sciences than to the arts, the life of the individual scientist is nothing like it was. It has deteriorated enormously. I look back a century and envy those scientists who lived then—the way they lived, the way they made their science, the amount of science they succeeded in making, and its quality. All those things have gone badly downhill.

And then we have a closely related problem, also enormously threatening and important, and that is the way we are wasting all our remaining resources and polluting the surface of the earth—a terrible problem, and to an extraordinary degree an American problem.

We are the worst offenders—not *they, we.* We with six percent of the world's population are said to consume about forty percent of the world's irreplaceable resources, and to account for about fifty percent of the world's industrial pollution. It is we Americans who do those things not only to this country but to all the world.

And then there is a third gigantic problem. We have come into the nuclear age. I should like to say something about that, because what should have come to humankind as a promise of a new degree of freedom such as men on earth and life on earth had never experienced before, comes upon us instead as a threat, perhaps the most serious threat we now have to face.

Why do I say a promise? It is very simple. You see, there came a point for life on earth that was absolutely critical and revolutionary. (The big revolutions are the revolutions of nature. The big revolutions among men are the revolutions of science. Make no mistake about that. Darwin nursing his dyspepsia in a garden in Cambridge was a much greater revolutionary than Karl Marx. He changed our world.)

Life first arose on the earth out of that aggregation of organic molecules leached out of the atmosphere into the seas over ages of time. Having arisen, it lived on those molecules. That is a losing game, because just so many of those molecules had accumulated, and living organisms had begun to use and destroy them, just as we have almost finished by now using and destroying our accumulations of fossil fuels.

Eventually that process would have had to come to an end, and life would have come to an end. All of it would have had to begin again from the beginning. But before that happened something else took place: living organisms invented photosynthesis, by which using the energy of sunlight, they could begin to make their own organic molecules. That made them independent of their previous history, of the stores of organic molecules that had accumulated over previous ages on the earth.

Now with the coming of the nuclear age we have a similar opportunity, one of those things that happen only once in several billion years, if then. Because, you see, all life up until now has lived on sunlight, the plants directly, the animals by eating the plants.

Now we can begin to make our own sunlight. That process that the sun lives by, turning hydrogen into helium, is the same process that goes on in a hydrogen bomb. What a disgrace! Think of it! A nuclear reaction which could mean that we could shortly make our own sunlight, that we could make a new basis for life on the earth, that we could make our own energy—that reaction is turned mainly into a weapon that threatens our lives, that promises to become the biggest polluter of our environment, and that now threatens our existence and much of the rest of life on the earth.

It is a symptom of the illness of our society that people think of that as inevitable. Of course one makes a bomb as fast as one can. But there is nothing inevitable about it. That is just our present way of life. It is our western culture at work, our western culture with its beautiful Judeo-Christian ethic. It is our culture alone among the cultures of the earth that sees it that way, that has brought the technology of killing and destruction much further than any culture on the earth ever dreamed of doing before.

It was the Chinese who invented gunpowder. And what did they do with it? They used it for firecrackers. Poor people! All of us know, we are all being told, that the Chinese are crazy. They can't be trusted, they didn't know what to do with gunpowder as we did. But we have taught them.

And the space program: The next person who says to me that we can solve the population problem because we can now get to the moon, I think I will kick him. That is the wrong model, and if we follow it we will be in terrible trouble. That trip to the moon was an exercise in what you can do with lots of wealth and power. The scientific content was trivial and negligible. It was an exercise of power; and as for its technology, that is expected to be very useful in our future weaponry.

There is no inevitability about using all our technology for killing and destruction. We have just taken the wrong turn. So I should like to end with a parable—not a Biblical parable, a biological parable.

Some 200 million years ago we were in the Age of Reptiles. The dinosaurs were the lords of the earth. They looked very fine, those dinosaurs. They were big, the biggest land animals that have ever existed. They were well-armed: horns, teeth, claws. They were well protected: scales, armor plate. They looked awfully good, those dinosaurs.

And back in the shadows, hiding among the roots of the trees was a small, tender, defenseless group of animals. They were the first mammals. They had little to offer, but one thing. They had rather large brains for their size. The dinosaur had a very small brain for its size. The proportion of brains to brawn in a dinosaur was very low. The mammals were doing better in that regard.

And pretty soon there were no more dinosaurs. The Age of Reptiles had given way to the Age of Mammals.

And the mammals kept working on the beautiful brain. Two million years ago they gave rise to man.

Man, as I have been telling you, is a wonderful thing. A man, standing on his own two feet, with that wonderful brain—gentle, harming no one and nothing, altogether in control—a beautiful creature, something one could love. But put him in a car! Now he is making a roar and a stink through the streets. You hardly see the man. It's hard to love a man in a car. And the proportion of brains to brawn has again sunk very low. He has become a kind of medium sized dinosaur.

And dangerous. Cars kill more than 50,000 Americans per year. Please notice one says that cars kill those Americans, not men in cars; because we realize all too well that the man isn't altogether in control. While we weren't watching, we've become dinosaurs again. And cars are just the beginning of it. There are trucks and trains and planes and hydrogen bombs—the proportion of brains to brawn has sunk terribly low, and it is going down fast. And this time if we have an extinction it will be a do-it-yourself extinction. And this time there is no other creature to take over.

Mammals brought another thing into life on earth, infinitely precious. Mammals take care of their young. Dinosaurs laid their eggs and left them. That was the way it was with all the previous creatures: the fishes, the amphibia, the reptiles. Not mammals. Mammals carry their young inside them, and after they have given birth to them they nurse them for months more (that is where the word "mammal" comes from, the nursing); and after that they watch them play in the sun, and protect them, and feed them, and teach them the ways of life.

That is another of our problems. We are no longer taking good care of our young. We have introduced them into a world that offers them little that they want and threatens their very existence. We have become dinosaurs again, and that is our problem.

So what are we to do? Please realize where we are, because whatever we do now we have to try somehow to do as men and not as dinosaurs. The temptation is great to do those things as dinosaurs. That is true every way one turns now. There are traps besetting us now in everything we try to do.

Take the population problem, for example. We are being told from some quarters that the attempt to control population is an attempt to commit genocide, an attempt on the part of the well-to-do to limit the numbers of the poor, an attempt on the part of the well-to-do nations to limit the numbers in the underdeveloped nations. Yet the only hope of the poor and of the underdeveloped nations is to limit population.

So what is wrong? One has to couple that attempt to limit population with a genuine and effective taking care of all the people there are. To do the one without the other would be conscienceless. We need to limit population, but we need meanwhile to take care of people better than we do now, and most of all we need to take care of children, all children everywhere, very much better than we are doing.

So I have almost done, because it is that way with the pollution problem, too. That, too, is beset with such traps, two of them rather obvious. One trap is to try to make of pollution, of our new concern with the environment, an issue that will distract people, mainly young people, from all the other problems that now properly concern them. The second trap is to turn pollution into a new dinosaur, to turn pollution into the new multi-billion dollar business. The only way to deal with pollution that really would mean anything is to stop it at its source; but that is difficult, and very strongly opposed by some powerful forces. The temptation is great to let the pollution go right on, but to superimpose on it a new multi-billion dollar business of anti-pollution; and in these days of conglomerates it would be the same business: one division would pollute, the other division would clean up; and both would make a lot of money.

So here we are at the crossroads. We have to make hard choices. We have not only to try to do, but to succeed in doing those fantastically difficult things, so difficult that if there were any alternative we would be well advised to avoid them. But there is no alternative. Those are the things that *must* be done, for us, and much more for our children. For it is they who must inherit a good earth, a decent place in which they can live their lives—they and their children, and their children's children.

WHERE DO WE GO FROM HERE?

Nothing concentrates the mind like waiting to be hanged.

Samuel Johnson

What we are coming to realize is that solutions to the problems of the planet have no simple answers. There may have been simple causes here and there which collectively have generated new problems. Merely to dissect out those early causes and correct them is not enough, because the "new baby" born out of the synergisms is, in many cases, now a fully grown monster.

Grandiose schemes should be viewed with suspicion. "Technology got us into this mess; technology can get us out of this mess," is our religious conviction. Many of the young are not so sure, and it is this age group that will have to generate the solutions, if there are to be any.

Knowledge of human psychology and social dynamics is not yet sufficient to change attitudes or alter human behavior significantly, even though we recognize that a new land ethic and new patterns of consumption are necessary.

Some have despaired. Others have faint hope. What do we do? Are we like the American astronauts that experienced the accident on the way to the moon? "Survival now became a matter of initiative and ingenuity," said James Lovell. "There were moments when I didn't know whether we had enough consumables (oxygen, water and electricity) to get home. In a situation like that, there's only one thing to do. You just keep going."